The
Ultimate Edge

Professional Blackjack in the 1980s

Mark Billings

D1218400

ISBN: 1-4392-1592-8

ISBN-13: 9781439215920

DEDICATION

The Ultimate Edge is dedicated to all those players—past, present, and future—who have, are, and/or will beat the casinos at their own game. The casinos offer the game and set *all* of the terms: the rules, the number of decks, the depth of the deal, the limits—right down to the number of spots on the felt layout. The players accept the challenge, play on enemy turf, and win anyway. Continued power to them.

Additionally, The Ultimate Edge is dedicated to all of those cocktail waitresses, dealers, pit bosses and players who read the accounts herein and say to themselves, "So that's what those bastards were doing!"

INTRODUCTION

A number of years ago I met an individual introduced to me as a "professional gambler." As I had enjoyed the occasional good night at the blackjack tables (the memories of which were somehow clearer in my mind than the memories of my more frequent losses), I fancied myself a pretty good player. We spoke, this "professional" and I, and he outlined some of the common blackjack errors nonprofessionals make. Realizing I was guilty of more than one of these so-called "errors," I took umbrage. I told him that I disagreed, and why.

"You're wrong," he said.

"That's your opinion," I replied.

"It's not a matter of opinion," the player stated. "You're wrong."

I bristled. Who the hell—?

"Who was the first man to walk on the moon?" he asked.

"Neil Armstrong."

"Is that just your opinion?"

"Well…"

I've often thought about that exchange since then. I was talking to an individual who had played blackjack in casinos all over the world. It wasn't his hobby—it's what he did for a living. I played for fun, and usually lost. Yet, somehow I thought my opinion on the subject was just as valid as his.

When did this happen? When did opinion begin to encroach into the realm of fact? And when did all opinions become equally valid?

We have long lived in a world where people can and do believe just about anything.[1] However, due to a relatively recent confluence of events that includes twenty-four-hour cable television news, the Internet, and talk radio, one man's opinion is somehow just as legitimate as anybody else's. I believe one thing, you believe another; we'll just have to disagree. Loudly. End of discussion.

In today's world, it seems any meathead who can maneuver his mouth in front of a microphone and bellow is someone to whom people will listen. I see it on television, or read it on the Internet, or hear it on the radio. I repeat it. Others hear it, and before long, it just *is*. Even if it's not.

It may not be possible to pinpoint exactly when this began. However, I like to use the 1986 explosion of the Challenger space shuttle as a demarcation; the point at which the consequences of inserting matters of opinion into areas that should be reserved for matters of fact became startlingly clear. The Challenger disaster certainly wasn't the first time this had happened, but it was the clearest example of reality emphatically trumping opinion, and doing so in a situation in which the consequences were clear, and clearly caused.

The engineers *knew* what happened to the consistency of the O-rings when they froze. They knew the freezing temperatures that January morning greatly increased the risk of a disaster, and advised that the launch be postponed.

However, the civilians in charge of NASA knew something else. They *knew* they had a schedule to keep. They *knew* they wanted that shuttle orbiting the planet when the president made his State of the Union address several days hence. So, they argued that the freezing temperatures would not increase the risks faced by the shuttle and its crew.

The stunning part is that they actually believed their risk calculations were just as valid as the risk calculations made by the engineers, even though they were political hacks with knowledge of neither engineering nor probability.

---

1 For most of human history people believed that the earth was flat, that the earth stood still at the center of the universe, and that dozens of vengeful, jealous gods flung plagues, diseases, crop failures and more our way, lest they were placated. Very few of us would now argue that the truth or falsity of the above beliefs is simply a matter of opinion.

These hacks, who inhabited a sequestered political world where objective reality need never intrude on their thought process, actually believed their own bullshit.

> "For a successful technology, reality must take precedence over public relations, for nature cannot be fooled."
> ~*Richard Feynman*

But herein lies the nub (to coin a phrase): risk is what it is. If you calculate it incorrectly, the actual underlying risk *does not change*. The actual risk stays the same, and it is not simply a matter of opinion, as the Challenger so emphatically showed seventy-three seconds into its final flight. It is frankly a shame that the consequences of the incorrect belief weren't borne more directly by those holding those beliefs.

We should have learned much from the Challenger disaster; much about matters of opinion, calculating risk, and consequences. However, it is abundantly clear that we have not.

The professional players about whom I write taught me quite a bit about the nature of the world. Although it is impossible to say which led to which, it should become apparent that these players view the world objectively. What they believe—at minimum, what they believe in terms of the game of blackjack—is not a matter of opinion. And a large part of this has to do with clear consequences. In professional blackjack, belief systems not rooted in the fundamental realities of the game rapidly become extinct, along with their adherents (or, at the very least, their adherents' bankrolls).

If you think you should stand with a fifteen against the dealer's ten up-card, go ahead. See what happens. You will be right occasionally, but you will be wrong more often. The direct consequence of your incorrect opinion is that it will cost you money. Either your opinion will change, or you will never become a professional blackjack player.

Would that that were the case with all unsound belief systems.

What follows is the kind of adventure that can ensue when a belief system does in fact accurately map an underlying reality. Only players like these could have traveled the world the way they did, winning so much that the sheer bulk of foreign currencies became one of the issues they were forced to deal with. Only players like these could have examined the game and developed entirely new ways of obtaining significant mathematical advantages over the house.

There is simply no room in their repertoire for belief systems not rooted in the mathematical realities underlying the game of blackjack. And, knowing these players as I now do, I can say that their ability to see though the everyday haze to certain underlying realities below is not limited to the game of blackjack. They all have the ability to look at a broad spectrum of life, from the mundane to the arcane, and see glimpses of what really makes the world tick. It is a skill that makes for consistent and meaningful world views, if nothing else.

And we could all use more of that.

—Mark Billings
Vancouver, B.C.
2008

CHAPTER 1
TAHOE RULES

God does not play dice.
~*Albert Einstein*

But if He did, would He ever crap out?
~*Alexander Taylor*

Alexander Taylor opened his eyes, remembered where he was, and completed a sentence he had begun the night before. Although a verbatim account is not extant, the phrase "goddamn cheating bastards" played a major structural role.

When Taylor began gambling professionally, he knew his career wouldn't last forever. He had begun largely by accident—a fluctuation that until now could have appeared in Webster's under "fortuitous." In seven years, Taylor had been to more than three hundred casinos in twenty-four different countries on four continents, and had won in excess of one and a half million dollars. He had beaten casinos by methods that were traditional and by those that were not. Several of the latter had resulted in some new statutes, and changes in dealing techniques in casinos from *Aspinalls* in London to *Foxy's Firehouse* in Las Vegas. Alexander Taylor was an impact player. He had made his mark.

And now it was over. His wrists were swollen to twice their normal size, his face was busted and sore, and he had been pissing blood all night. Alexander Taylor, thirty years old and arguably one of the best blackjack players in the world, was lying on a concrete floor beneath flickering fluorescent lights in the holding tank of the Douglass County Jail on the south shore of Lake Tahoe.

And the irony was, the bastards beat up the wrong guy.

A drunk was snoring in the corner of the tank, his mouth wide open. He had long ago lost the war on tooth decay. When the cops dragged Taylor in the night before, the drunk had stared, wide-eyed, and asked what had happened.

"Handcuffs," Taylor had replied, rubbing his swollen wrists.

"No, man," the drunk said. "I'm talkin' about your face."

Taylor stared at the ceiling. He thought about the stories he had heard about jail. Wormy food. Electric cattle prods. Hairy brutes with "Bruce" tattooed on their forearms. As a professional gambler Taylor had learned to live with bad fluctuations, but this was off the chart. He had to get out.

The door clanged open. "Taylor," the cop called.

The Nevada Gaming Control Board was established in 1955, ostensibly to exercise some measure of control over the thugs and gangsters that were running not only the casino industry in Nevada, but the entire state as well. To the surprise of only the extremely naïve, the Gaming Control Board quickly fell under the control of those same pillars of the community the Kefauver Commission warned us about. And now, two balding Gaming Control agents had arrived at the Douglass County Jail to protect Nevada from Alexander Taylor.

They wanted to know what he was doing. With whom. Where. How much. How often. And how.

Taylor thought carefully. Then he spoke.

"Listen," he said, "if you guys pooled your efforts, maybe you could grow one legitimate head of hair."

They locked the door and threw away the key.

Taylor resumed his perusal of the ceiling. He was no stranger to heat. A large number of Nevada casinos refused to let him play. He had been detained by customs officials the world over. There was hardly a casino left in Europe he was allowed to set foot in. And he was *persona non grata* in several Caribbean nations.

This was different. For the first time in his career, he felt exposed. Naked. Vulnerable. The journey from invincibility was complete, and the last step hurt. More than Taylor's existence as a professional gambler had been compromised—his vision of himself was at stake. And that wasn't all. The bastards who had failed to break his ribs had succeeded in ruining Lake Tahoe for him. From this day forward, Taylor would associate the beautiful lake with aching kidneys and broken teeth.

Lake Tahoe is an aquamarine gem mounted in the belt buckle where California bends at the waist. The California-Nevada border punctures Tahoe at its southeastern shore, runs northwest to the middle of the lake, and then abruptly heads due north, giving California bragging rights to two-thirds of what is easily the most spectacular piece of alpine real estate this side of Switzerland.

The violence that conspired to produce the geology which would eventually support the Douglass County Jail began twenty-five million years ago, when an earthquake that may have measured fifteen on the pre-Richter scale opened a trough several times the width of the Grand Canyon in the midst of the Sierra Nevada mountain range. Twenty million years later, enormous volcanoes belched up a broad river of lava and ash that flowed into the trough and dammed up the southern half. Nine or ten thousand years ago—yesterday, in earth years—an anonymous glacier pushed its way north into the trough. Then, instead of joining its brethren for the regularly scheduled interglacial retreat, the glacier sat, forlorn, until its liquefied remains were discovered by the Washoe Indians.

What the Washoes found was a beautiful alpine lake nestled comfortably in the Sierra Nevadas six thousand feet above sea level, and ringed with magnificent snow-capped mountains that rose another four thousand feet above the gleaming surface. Profoundly deep and bitterly cold, the lake is seventy-one miles in circumference and contains about a half billion gallons of crystal clear, absolutely pure water. The Washoes named the lake "Tahoe," meaning "big water in high place."

The first white men to see the lake were Captain John Charles Fremont and the members of the Fremont Party. In search of a pass leading from the Carson Valley to the Valley of the Sacramento, they came upon the lake in 1844. Fremont renamed it, probably pissed in it, and moved on.

Other white men followed. In 1861, Mark Twain visited one of several logging camps on the lakeshore and wrote gushingly about the beauty of the Tahoe Basin for the *Nevada Territorial Enterprise*, a daily paper published in nearby Virginia City. Later, Twain showed his respect for the area by accidentally burning most of the north shore of the lake to the ground.

By far the most famous of the lake's denizens remains a family of cowboys who rode into American living rooms every Friday night from 1959 to 1974. Every episode of *Bonanza* was filmed on location in the Tahoe Basin. The Ponderosa still exists. And the introductory sequence—where the four Cartwrights ride toward the camera to the tune of possibly the most famous theme song in the history of television—was filmed not two miles from the Douglass County Jail.

Recently another eruption shook the region, this time man-made. Unlike the volcanoes of five million years ago, however, the results didn't serve to trap a glacier or any remnant thereof. The towers that now rise above the ponderosa pines to dominate the south Tahoe shoreline trap money. Lots of money. Ivan Boesky may have uttered it, but it was the casinos that lived, breathed, *exuded* the credo of the eighties: Greed is Good.

Alexander Taylor had traveled to Lake Tahoe for some therapy. He would swim in the frigid waters and visit some friends. Of course, the trip would include a little blackjack. Of course. Brian Manning—a computer programmer and Taylor's blackjack partner for nearly seven years—had arrived that morning. Taylor picked him up at the tiny Lake Tahoe Airport and drove across the state line to Nevada.

By 1987, the blackjack games on which Taylor and Brian had supported themselves for the better part of the decade had deteriorated almost beyond recognition, and the poor playing conditions they found in three of the major south shore casinos reflected this grim reality. Then, in Harrah's, they located what looked to be a beatable situation. A dealer was exposing her hole card. Taylor sat down to play.

The situation evaporated when Taylor pulled out his bankroll. This wasn't unusual—just an encroachment of Heisenberg into the world of the large. Dealer behavior often changed when real money was on the line.

Having a keen eye for futility, Brian signaled "end of session" after only a couple of rounds and left the casino. Taylor played a few more hands and got up to leave. The dealer thanked him profusely. Alexander Taylor was a generous tipper. He considered it an investment in his future.

While waiting in line to cash his chips, someone who looked like a pit boss approached Taylor and introduced himself as Frank Grant. And for once, Alexander Taylor missed something.

"I'd like to talk to you when you've finished cashing out," Frank Grant said.

"Sure," said Taylor, and the end had begun.

There were two possibilities, Taylor had thought. Either Grant was going to comp him to dinner, or he was going to throw him out. Because he hadn't played enough to warrant getting barred, Taylor figured the odds at about 70–30 in favor of the comp.

The odds swung dramatically when six security guards surrounded him at the cage. The smart money was now squarely on the guards.

"Over here," Grant said when Taylor had finished cashing out. Taylor took a couple of steps away from the cage, and the security guards closed in. Taylor turned, and they grabbed him.

He was dragged into a small room just off the main casino floor. Once Taylor's hands were securely handcuffed behind his back, the guards proceeded to beat the shit out of him. It was quite a goddamn party, and Alexander Taylor was the piñata.

Taylor's initial reaction was more astonishment than anger. Something wasn't quite right. After all, he had played only ten hands.

"What the hell—" Taylor began, after he had been thrown into a plastic folding chair in the corner of the room.

"Shut the fuck up," one of the guards said, punctuating his limited vocabulary with a right hand that connected just below Taylor's left eye. A quick study, Taylor concluded that further efforts to communicate would likely prove fruitless, and decided to keep quiet.

Frank Grant was now standing in front of him. "What's your name, boy?" he asked.

"Alexander Taylor. What the hell—?"

"Cut the bullshit, Sandler. We know who you are."

It hit Taylor harder than the guard's right hand.

"You stupid bastards!" he said. The guard stepped forward to teach Taylor some more respect, but Grant held up his hand.

"What are you saying, boy?"

"My wallet's in my right back pocket. You should have checked first."

Frank Grant looked uncomfortable. He motioned subtly with his head, and four of the guards quietly left the room.

"Check his ID, Howard," Grant said to one of the remaining guards.

When Grant discovered his error, he cleared his throat. "Well," he said, "if you're not Rick Sandler, why did you attack these guards?"

Under Grant's direction, the two remaining guards filled out complaint forms. Alexander Taylor was hauled off to the Douglass County Jail, charged with two counts each of assault and battery. The security guards at Harrah's never discovered that the man they thought was Rick Sandler just happened to be another professional blackjack player. When they discovered they had beaten up the wrong guy, they decided to deal with the problem quickly with the phony assault charges. In their haste to get Taylor out of the casino, the guards never found the device strapped to his right calf. But the cops who booked Taylor did.

An hour after Taylor failed to arrive at their prearranged meeting spot, Brian Manning was on the phone. Brian—computer programmer *extraordinaire*, blackjack player, 1966 graduate of the University of Baltimore with a degree in American History ("Those who fail history are condemned to repeat it, man")—was a unique individual. He knew everything. Today he knew the following:

1. Something was seriously wrong.

2. Taylor had probably been arrested.

    3.   Someone was going to have to bail him out.

Brian knew one other thing:

    4.   It wasn't going to be *his* ass strolling into the Douglass County Jail carrying the bail money.

Brian was no coward, but he wasn't stupid either. He needed to find a warm body. Fast.

Brian had already moved out of his motel room and out of the state. He knew Taylor wouldn't provide any information voluntarily, but casino security guards have a well-deserved reputation for their persuasive abilities. A player detained at the Sahara was told that if he didn't talk, he would be given a free helicopter ride over the desert; more precisely, a half a ride: the player wouldn't actually enjoy the assistance of the helicopter to maintain altitude on the way back. A couple of players who were caught peeking at the dealer's hole card at the Horseshoe had left two spleens, a pancreas, and part of a lung in the hospital to which they were sent when the Horseshoe security guards had finished their recreational activity for the evening. Another player back-roomed at the Imperial Palace in Vegas had had burning cigarettes held up to his eyes until he talked. The player had opted for vision, and told the security guards where the rest of the team was staying. His teammates were subsequently arrested and charged with a variety of interesting crimes they hadn't committed. And the beat goes on.

Taylor hadn't talked. Because the security guards missed the device strapped to his right calf, and because they realized they had gratuitously kicked the shit out of the wrong person, they saw no reason to harass Taylor further. Harrah's simply covered its ass with the phony assault charges, and hoped never to see Alexander Taylor again.

The Gaming Control agents did not resort to physical abuse. They had other methods.

Five hours after the abortive conversation with Gaming Control's finest, a cop came into the holding tank to inform Taylor that bail had been set. He was laughing. "I hope you like the food here," he said.

The bail was set at twenty-six thousand dollars. The grinning cop informed Taylor that it would be several days before a judge would be available for a bail reduction hearing. Apparently, the gaming agents thought this might loosen Taylor's tongue a bit—and perhaps give his injuries a chance to heal before anyone could witness the damage.

Taylor was fingerprinted, photographed from three sides while holding a numbered card, and taken to Cell Block B, where he played poker with four of Lake Tahoe's sorriest denizens. Two were in for attempting to hold up a liquor store. They had been in jail two days—unable to make their $700 bail. The drunk Taylor met in the holding tank was in for disorderly conduct. He had entered a convenience store and removed his pants. What he had been attempting wasn't clear, but he did manage to scare the girl behind the counter and get himself arrested. Bail—fifty bucks. Last and least, a misbegotten soul named Ray had been hauled in for driving drunk after guiding his 1972 Olds Cutlass through a red light and plowing into a woman driving a Nissan Sentra. The woman was taken to the hospital and Ray was sent to jail, where he argued the relative merits of suicide versus telling his wife. It sounded to Taylor like suicide would be the less painful option. Ray had been arguing with himself for a day and a half. He couldn't scrounge up the $900 bail.

When Taylor told his cellmates what his bail was, they wanted to know how many people he had killed. When he told them why he was there, they dealt him out of the poker game. And when Brian's emissary came through with the twenty-six grand—in cash—just two hours later, they all but genuflected. Taylor was the king of Cell Block B.

"Exactly what did they find on your leg?" Taylor's attorney asked. "What were you guys up to?"

Lawrence Semenza, of Semenza and Associates of Reno, Nevada, had handled a couple of blackjack cases in the past. Both clients had been guilty. Protestations to the contrary were cheap.

"It was legal. Look up *Einbinder and Dalton* versus *Sheriff.*"

"Never mind that. Talk to me."

Semenza studied his client as he spoke. Taylor was not your prototypical riverboat gambler. There was no swagger in his step, no gleam in his eye, no gold in his smile. He looked nothing like James Garner. Taylor was of average height and weight and, save the recently acquired bruises courtesy of Harrah's, had no distinguishing features. He looked to be between twenty-five and thirty years of age. He wore a tweed sports jacket the color of Semenza's carpet, an ordinary brown tie, and a plain white shirt. Gone from his wrist was the gold Rolex—Taylor now wore a quartz Seiko. It kept better time.

Taylor gestured infrequently. When recounting the incident at Harrah's, a certain urgency in his voice belied his outward calm; otherwise, he displayed little emotion. Although Semenza didn't realize it, he was looking at a version of Taylor no casino had ever seen: a straightforward, articulate individual with no flash and no bullshit. A professional.

Taylor spoke for an hour and a half. In that time, he told his attorney more about the game of blackjack than most players learn in a lifetime. Semenza learned about counting, spooking, front-loading, and tells. He learned about tracking. He learned about warps. He learned about computers. And, according to Taylor, none of what he and his teammates did was illegal.

Semenza gave him a look. "Cheating, conspiracy to cheat, possession of a cheating device, burglary, and two counts of assault and battery. Three felonies and three misdemeanors. This is serious."

"I know it's serious. That's why I'm here. By the way, twenty-six thousand dollars bail? One of the guys in the can told me bail for attempted murder is usually between five and ten grand."

Semenza shrugged. "The idea was to keep you in jail until your face healed, and maybe soften you up a bit. The Gaming Commission was very eager to talk to you."

"How did they get a judge to go along?"

The attorney shrugged again. "This is Nevada."

Taylor stopped talking. For seven years he had played on their turf by their rules. Due to some misguided sense of fair play, he never used any of the methods that would boost his edge into the upper reaches of the stratosphere. He had never cheated. Lodged somewhere in the deep recesses of his psyche—perhaps coded for in DNA inherited from ancestors long dead—resided the unarticulated and somewhat embarrassingly naïve notion that somehow the universe was fair. For some incomprehensible reason, he had believed that if he played by the rules, the casinos would as well.

But Harrah's had provided an education in real-world values. Certainly by the age of thirty he should have known better, and perhaps he owed the establishment a debt of gratitude for the lesson. In the depths of his fury an idea, inchoate and gray, began to form. This was going to get ugly.

"They made a mistake," Taylor said, the edge returning to his voice. "The gloves are off. The next time they see me, I'll be beating those bastards out of twenty-six thousand a *day*."

Semenza sighed, and slid a standard legal contract across his desk for Taylor to sign. It would be costly.

Taylor's eyes glided down the contract, stopping at the five-figure bottom line. "I no care," he muttered. "Only fitty dollah."

"Excuse me?" Semenza asked.

"Nothing," Taylor said, signing the contract. "Inside joke."

CHAPTER 2
BIRTH OF AN IDEA

Serendipity favors the prepared mind.
~Blaise Pascal

If there was any early indication that Alexander Taylor would spend a significant fraction of his adult life traveling around the world with a computer on his leg and buttons in his shoes, it would be apparent only with a very selective brand of hindsight. For Taylor's youth was not simply average—it was actively unspectacular.

Alexander Taylor was born to first-generation Americans in the Flatbush section of Brooklyn, in the midst of the Eisenhower stupor. His paternal and maternal grandparents had fled poverty and pogroms, respectively, and arrived in the land of opportunity to find conditions not terribly unlike those they had left. But they persevered, and instilled in their children the notion that hard work and honesty would someday be rewarded. Taylor forgives them their ignorance.

Before Taylor was old enough to begin grade school, his father packed up the family and left Brooklyn for upstate New York. He claimed he did it for his kids. Later, he would complain that the trouble with kids today was that they had it too easy.

Until Taylor was about eight, his world was dairy farms, apple orchards, and fields of corn separating scattered housing developments. Then IBM invaded the area with a vengeance. Tractors and overalls disappeared with the arrival of thousands of suits, and thousands of people tailored to fit them. The suburbs had arrived, and with them a unique combination of ennui and awareness that would cause the offspring of perfectly sane middle-class parents to grow long hair, shun showers, and ingest a broad spectrum of illicit substances.

Still innocent, Taylor was convinced he had found his calling when his father bought him a book about dinosaurs and took him to the American Museum of Natural History. Staring open-mouthed at the bones of these enormous creatures that lived a hundred million or more years ago imbued him with a feeling of awe and reverence that would remain for many years. "It was my first love affair," says Taylor, and the ancillary knowledge he gained as a result of this fascination—among other things, he read his father's entire twenty-volume Time-Life Science and Nature set—resulted in the complete rejection of the religious indoctrination his mother was attempting to foist upon him. "After reading about herds of sauropods marching through swamps and titanic battles between triceratops and Tyrannosaurus rex," Taylor says, "the stuff in the Bible read like a bunch of fairy tales." He was in fourth grade.

As Taylor grew older, his interests traveled the well-worn boyhood path from dinosaurs to football to magic tricks. When he was twelve, a television commercial enticed him to send away $3.95 for something called "TV Magic Cards," a trick that relied on a cleverly rigged deck and—to his surprise—didn't fool anyone until he developed a long, sordid line of bullshit to prop it up. He applied the principle to other magic tricks, and soon discovered that the effectiveness of a trick depended only slightly on the particular gimmick involved. The key, he learned, was to use subtle misdirection to lead his subjects to conclusions they thought they arrived at themselves. It was a theme he would return to later.

Throughout grade school Taylor enjoyed learning, and worked hard at it. He displayed those occasional flickers of brilliance that all kids are capable of and ultimately learn to suppress. His teachers liked him and his classmates copied from him.

When he entered high school the rules changed. Any display of cerebral candlepower beyond a flicker was suspect. Testosterone had begun its aggressive rampage through the bodies of rapidly growing zit-faced boys, and anyone showing intellectual abilities beyond those of a half-eaten grapefruit was branded a nerd and shunned. What was admired was physical prowess, and the ability to ingest vast quantities of illegal substances and remain in an arguably vertical position. Taylor realized that some major personality changes would be necessary if he were to remain sane.

Taylor made a conscious effort to become an average high school student. He stopped studying, displayed the proper amount of disrespect for authority, and "experimented" with drugs. (Despite Taylor's boyhood interest in science, these experiments were neither single nor double-blinded, and nothing was controlled for.)

By Taylor's senior year his grades had buried him in the center of his class. Good enough. He had survived untraumatized; he wasn't the starting quarterback, nor was he a nerd ridiculed for attempting to understand the world in which he was soon expected to become a cog. Taylor had learned an important lesson about survival and—at least as important—had learned not to take himself too seriously.

Taylor's closest friend in high school was Bob Graham, a classic underachiever who possessed an incisive criminal mind and a baby face—a lethal combination that augured well for the future. It was Graham's idea to begin the weekly poker games in the unused garage that adjoined Taylor's parents' home. Taylor commandeered the damp concrete bunker at the age of sixteen, and Graham saw great potential. They began running the game every Friday night, providing snacks, cigars, and scratchy, poorly lit 8 mm stag movies projected onto the backs of four black light posters held together with masking tape.

It was no accident that Taylor and Graham were consistent winners. None of the other players seemed to know that folding was one of the options in the game of poker; they simply held each hand until the end to find out who won. Inevitably, some of the other players began to catch on to this novel folding idea, but by then Taylor and Graham had improved their playing strategy in other areas of the game. They had begun a couple of steps ahead of their competition, and remained there. It was yet another theme to which Taylor would later return.

Given the overwhelming advantage biographers have—they know the end before they begin—a careless one could point to this poker game as a foreshadowing of the lifestyle Taylor was to choose. But it would be incumbent upon the scrupulous chronicler of events to explain how Taylor's baby-faced friend managed to escape the insidious attraction of that very same game. Graham now owns a small accounting firm on Long Island and lives in a 3,200-square-foot split-level house on a rehabilitated potato farm with his wife and three girls. He has added a few extra chins—augmenting the babyish appearance—and happily lives his version of the American Dream. If the poker game is to be singled out as the source of the path Taylor was to follow, it rightfully should be forced to provide an explanation for Graham's more traditional success as well. By any fair measure, it's a wash.

By the time Taylor finished high school in 1974, the picture of his nation as the planet's last bastion of morality and righteousness had frayed considerably about the edges. Television provided a vision of reality to which no previous generation in history had been privy, and it was not a pretty sight. Napalmed Asian children vied with burning American cities for the top news story of the day, and the felons responsible for curtailing this hateful parade of gore were too busy bugging their enemies and themselves to notice. To argue that Nixon's particular bunch of bastards was more venal than any previous bunch is to miss the point. Taylor's generation was the first to come of age with a close-up view of the machinery—grease and all—in living color on NBC. He wasn't impressed.

After graduation, Taylor watched as his classmates collectively collapsed into a neatly organized Gaussian distribution. A few busted out and found themselves occupying the thin left tail, several others made it big and ended up on the equally slim right tail, but most shelved the revolution and lumped around the bulging middle of the bell-shaped curve as they struggled to become their parents. They found spouses, mortgages, and miracle fertilizers, and began to lose their ideals, dreams, and hair. Life revolved around a job at IBM that permitted a lifestyle requiring a substantial monthly nut; a nut that necessitated the job at IBM. The subtlety and completeness of the trap wasn't lost on Alexander Taylor. "I'd rather have my teeth drilled," he said, and headed off in pursuit of higher education.

His college education was largely uneventful. Once again, the clues are apparent only in retrospect. Taylor was an above-average poker player in the regular dorm games. By definition, so were half of those with whom he played. He was above average in math ability. So was everyone admitted to his university. He wasn't particularly impressed with his options for the future, but neither was anyone he knew.

College did provide Taylor the opportunity to remove the intellectual straitjacket with which he had bound himself since high school. His ability to think originally was appreciated, and he quickly rose to the top of his class.

After four years he had received a legitimate education and a degree in political science. Due to his field of expertise and a facility for languages, he was recruited by the CIA. Taylor listened carefully. When the CIA man finished, Taylor said, "I'd rather stick an ice pick up my nose," and headed west for graduate school in the fall of 1980.

When Taylor aimed his 1973 Ford Maverick toward the Pacific and put the car in gear, he was continuing a long, illustrious heritage that began soon after the Mayflower scraped bottom on the left side of the Atlantic. Most of the pioneers who left Europe were searching for the "from" brand of freedom: freedom from religious persecution, hunger, and poverty. Others, however, were looking for the "to" brand of the same product: the freedom to go where they wanted and do what they wished. They had been infected by that insidious genetic rash; an itch that grew more acute the longer they remained in one place.

For most of U.S. history, the Great American West served as a dusty Calamine lotion, temporarily soothing the itch and allowing the dreams to continue. Although robber barons and industrial tycoons closed the American frontier long ago, the gene pool remains infected.

The image of the lone cowboy standing on a hilltop with a Stetson on his head and a lariat in his hand, sun blazing orange behind him, has long tugged at something deep within the American psyche. This is not at all surprising, since most of us descended not from those who stayed and suffered but from those who got up off the floor to find something better, and we carry the legacy of those genes in our blood and our guts and the marrow of our bones.

By the time Taylor headed west, the cowboy with the Stetson was hawking Marlboros, and the big-rig truck driver had replaced him as the embodiment of the American Dream: freedom from screaming kids and dictatorial time clocks; freedom to roll as many miles as aching kidneys and amphetamines would allow. The divorce from nine-to-five tedium even manifested itself in a unique lexicon: "Ten-four, Big Beaver, there's a bear on your tail and fleas in your hair." That this was the ideal to which many young Americans aspired in the late '70s indicates the degree of deterioration the dream suffered. At least Joe DiMaggio spoke plain English.

Because Taylor arrived in Southern California completely broke, fulfilling the six-month residency requirement before he could attend graduate school at UCLA meant finding a job. Since his truck driving skills were nonexistent, he was forced to wheedle himself into a position at Hal Gruber's Valet Service—a lucrative operation that performed same-day dry cleaning and laundry service for the wealthy guests of seven of the finest hotels in Los Angeles.

After two weeks in L. A., Taylor was thinking nostalgically about having his teeth drilled.

Steve Wallace was a major casualty of the television age. He loved baseball. By the time he was old enough to play the game, he had watched thousands of baseball players dance across the several black and white television sets that lived and died in the Wallace household over the course of his youth. Steve had made up his mind by the age of ten. He would become a professional baseball player.

Steve starred in Little League, Senior League, and high school ball. He was a natural shortstop. His scouting report read: Great range, good arm, average power. The California Angels signed him to a minor league contract.

Two months later in Class A ball, Steve called upon some of the speed that made the great range possible and stretched a single into a double. A spike caught during the slide, and his left knee protested loudly. The center fielder heard the pop.

The doctor who reconstructed the knee told Steve he would probably walk without a limp. His baseball career, however, was over. The doctor was right on both counts.

"What the hell," Steve's father had said between beers. "If God intended for you to play baseball, he would have given you four balls." Steve's father was a real comedian.

Four balls or two, Steve had prepared for nothing beyond a career in professional baseball. He found himself driving a van for Hal Gruber's Valet Service, picking up and delivering underwear in Los Angeles, California, in the fall of 1980.

In 1963, a meteorologist named Edward Lorenz was performing weather simulations using an analog computer and accidentally discovered that long-term weather forecasting is impossible. Technically, the culprit is referred to as *Sensitive Dependence on Initial Conditions*, but Lorenz coined a more elegant term. He called it "The Butterfly Effect."

What Lorenz discovered was that excruciatingly small, random disturbances in any complex system can have dramatic long-term effects. Lorenz likened this to the flap of a butterfly's wings in Brazil causing a tornado in Texas a month later.

When Lorenz wrote of the Butterfly Effect, he was referring to minuscule fluctuations in systems such as weather and strange water wheels. But he could have been referring to something else.

On October 3, 1980, the city of Los Angeles was in the throes of a Stage 2 smog alert, the result of a textbook temperature inversion. A layer of hot air blanketed the city for ten days, trapping a foul mix of stagnant air and pollutants below it. The smog grew thicker by the day, and the temperature soared.

Somewhere across the Pacific a butterfly didn't flap its wings. Perhaps it was on vacation.

Steve Wallace's last laundry pickup on this sweltering Friday morning was the Hyatt Regency hotel in downtown Los Angeles. Steve loaded two enormous canvas sacks into the back of his van and hesitated. It was over a hundred degrees outside, and the forty-minute drive back to the cleaning plant would be miserable. He decided to get something cold to drink before leaving.

Steve pumped a couple of quarters into the Coke machine stationed in the employee break room. A bellman was seated at a table playing a form of solitaire Steve had never seen. There was a book spread face down on the table in front of the bellman.

After watching for a moment, Steve asked him what he was doing. The bellman pointed to the book. It was *Playing Blackjack as a Business*, by someone named Lawrence Revere. The bellman wasn't playing an exotic form of solitaire. He was practicing something called card counting.

"Is it hard?" Steve asked.

"Not if you're good at math."

Steve wasn't. He shrugged his shoulders and left.

When Steve arrived back at the cleaning plant, he and Taylor hauled the load of bulging canvas sacks to the back of the plant. Within the hour, several hundred pink laundry tickets appeared on Taylor's desk. Taylor's job was to add them up. He was unusually adept at this.

Taylor sat down to add the stack of laundry tickets. And for some reason, Steve decided to watch.

Homo sapiens is a unique species indeed. We don't have great speed to escape predators, sharp fangs to down prey, or horns or armor to protect ourselves. All we have to recommend our species to a lifestyle suitable to the blue planet on which we find ourselves is an unremarkable three-pound blob of gray matter. And all this gray blob lays claim to is the facility to escape the hardwired behavior that enslaved all of our animal ancestors. The blob is capable of thinking thoughts never before thought.

A billion years of evolution didn't fail him. Steve watched Taylor rapidly adding the laundry tickets, thought of the bellman, and uttered the phrase that would send Taylor around the world and ultimately into the holding tank at the Douglass County Jail.

"You oughta be a card counter," said Steve.

Taylor grunted and reached for another laundry ticket. Priorities.

If the course of human lives resembled the stately, predictable procession of the planets, Alexander Taylor might have continued to labor under the assumption that laundry tickets somehow represented a priority in his life. He likely would have obtained his Ph.D. from UCLA, and today might be teaching at an obscure liberal arts college, teeth intact, wearing a sweater, brown loafers, and corduroy pants.

But human lives more resemble the motion of pinballs than planets. We careen from decision to decision and place to place with maddening uncertainty, and any predictions about consequences beyond the first few rebounds perform no better than chance. Quantum mechanics has quantified this experience, and the new science of Chaos has provided the exclamation point: there is a fundamental random element underlying nature, and we are just as subject to that randomness as the protons and neutrons and electrons of which we are made.

At the quantum level, only the laws of probability can be relied upon to predict the behavior of particles. Classical Newtonian physics that can accurately predict that the relative positions of the sun, moon, and earth on Wednesday, October 30, 2069, at 1:45 a.m. Greenwich Mean Time will produce an eclipse cannot deal with the motion of subatomic particles. And the laws of probability that can reliably predict the motion of large aggregations of subatomic particles allow for the possibility of some pretty unlikely events. Within the constraints of the theory, one renegade electron in a hundred billion may get away with performing a double back somersault in the pike position while whistling "Dixie." And another may dramatically change direction in midstream.

In some respects, Taylor can be viewed simply as a victim of contingency. In November 1980, while Taylor's 1960s-infected brain was attempting to absorb the shock of Ronald Reagan's election victory, the universe was conspiring to cough up two completely unrelated fluctuations that would crystallize in a mind primed by Steve and the country's lurch to the right to reject any chance of living an average life.

And although Taylor now argues that he simply took advantage of an option offered up by random fluctuations, those fluctuations cannot be entirely separated from the receptive audience on whose personal stage they were played out. Very few people would view playing blackjack professionally as a legitimate alternative to wearing a suit and tie, and if Taylor had been aware of the ride in store for him, he might have chosen differently.

"Like hell," says Alexander Taylor.

In the early morning hours of November 21, 1980, while 3,400 registered guests slept and a few diehard gamblers tried to get their money back, an electrical short occurred in some ungrounded copper wires located behind a dessert display in a restaurant next to the vast casino in the original MGM Grand in Las Vegas, Nevada. For perhaps a half hour the wires smoldered and burned, doing little more than melting insulation and scorching the junction box in which they resided. Patiently, the heat worked on the plywood facade of the dessert case, maintaining its integrity long enough to ignite the wood. Once the fire started, it was fed by a rich supply of oxygen arriving from the spacious casino and exploded into a wall of flame—a fireball accelerated by a backdraft created by holes punched in the ceiling of the casino to make room for equipment used by the "eye in the sky." In minutes the entire casino was fully involved. The MGM Grand fire was under way.

Taylor read about the scandalous fire with more than morbid interest. Amid all the death and destruction, with nonexistent sprinkler systems and fire alarms that remained silent, with elevator shafts and seismic folds that provided perfect conduits for the deadly smoke that traveled to the top of the twenty-three-story structure, one fact leaped out at Taylor—glaring and brilliant and ugly as hell. Eighty-five people lost their lives and 600 others were injured as a result of the fire on that day, but not a dollar of the MGM's cash burned in the blaze. Of all the emergency systems designed to deal with a major fire, only one worked—the one designed to save the money. Taylor cut the article out of the *Los Angeles Times* and taped it to his refrigerator door.

Two weeks after the fire, Steve invited Taylor to watch a videotape he had borrowed from the Hyatt Regency's card-counting bellman. It was a *60 Minutes* segment featuring an individual named Ken Uston. Accompanied by Harry Reasoner and filmed by a hidden camera, Uston entered the Flamingo Hilton in Las Vegas, Nevada, and attempted to play blackjack. After Uston had played a few hands, a pit boss approached the table and asked him to leave the casino.

The Flamingo Hilton is located only several hundred yards from the original MGM Grand on the Las Vegas Strip. The Flamingo likely had stacks of cash in the cashier's cage that were almost as high as the stacks of cash that didn't burn in the MGM fire. Yet, for some reason, the Flamingo management didn't want Ken Uston to play blackjack in their casino. For some reason, they viewed the short, unassuming Uston as a legitimate threat to their stacks of cash.

"Why won't you let this man play?" Reasoner asked, appearing genuinely perplexed. "What has he done?"

The pit boss refused to give Reasoner an explanation. But befuddled Harry Reasoner, playing the Columbo role to the hilt, already knew.

The Flamingo, owners of huge stacks of unburned cash, wouldn't let Ken Uston play blackjack because Ken Uston was a card counter.

The light went on. Taylor turned to Steve.

"What did you say the name of that book was?" Taylor asked.

CHAPTER 3

HISTORY 101

The gambling known as business looks
with austere disfavor upon the business
known as gambling.
~*Ambrose Bierce,* The Devil's Dictionary

The race is not always to the swift, nor the battle to the
strong, but that's the way to bet.
~*Grantland Rice* in More Than Somewhat
by Damon Runyon

The origin of the most popular casino game in North America is still a matter of some dispute. The French games *Vingt-Un* and *Trente et Quarente,* the Spanish *Uno y Trenta,* and the Italian games *Baccara* and *Seven and a Half* all resemble modern casino blackjack in that the winning hand is one that has come closest to a certain total. Of the five, the Italian *Seven and a Half* was most like casino blackjack because any player attaining too high a total *busted,* and automatically lost.

As a private game, blackjack was second to craps in popularity among American servicemen during World War I. In this early version the deal rotated around the table, similar to the way in which the deal changes in home poker. The banking version—in which the players play against a "bank" (a dealer who works for the house)—didn't make its debut in the U.S. until 1910 or so, and was dwarfed in popularity by such casino games as faro and roulette throughout the '20s and '30s. Then Adolph ("Let's win one for the Fuhrer") Hitler struck up a familiar tune, prompting a great deal of overseas travel for yet another generation of young Americans. Hundreds of thousands of GIs learned to love the banking version of the game during the Second World War, and shortly after the war's end blackjack was second only to craps as the most popular casino game in the United States.

In the States the game of blackjack was originally called "Twenty-One," a direct translation of the French "Vingt-Un." (The English bastardized the word and called the game "Van John"; in Australia, their French was worse—they called the game "Pontoon.") Then, in an Evansville, Indiana, horse room in 1912, a new rule was invented to help lure the punters to the twenty-one tables between horse races. Players whose first two cards totaled twenty-one were paid three to two instead of even money, and two-card twenty-ones that consisted of the ace of spades and either the jack of spades or the jack of clubs were paid a bonus of ten to one. Because this bonus hand had to contain a black-suited jack, players began calling the hand a "Black Jack," to distinguish it from an ordinary twenty-one. Before long, players began referring to the game itself as "blackjack."

During the 1920s, the rules of the game varied widely from year to year and from card room to card room. Then, in 1931, the game was introduced to the newly legalized casinos of Nevada. Gamblers visiting Nevada from all over the country returned home to their local games and informed their buddies in no uncertain terms how the game was played in real casinos. By the time American GIs headed across the Atlantic to engage the Aryan Ideal for the second time, the rules had been reasonably standardized nationwide.

The banking game of blackjack is dealt by a dealer who works for the house. Unlike the dealer in the private version of the game, the house dealer makes no playing decisions. Dealers function as automatons, rigidly following the rules stipulated by the casinos in which they work.

The game is played as follows: The dealer receives one card face up and one card face down, and the players each receive two cards; both either face up or face down (the days when the players received one card up and one card down are long gone; an anachronism from the private game in which the dealer made playing decisions based on what he thought his opponents had). Each card is worth the value on its face; tens and face cards are collectively referred to as "tens," and all contribute a value of ten to the hand. Aces can count as either one or eleven. Players can choose to stay with the total dealt them (stand), add to that total by asking for an additional card or cards (hit), double their original bet and receive exactly one more card (double down), or double their original bet and play a pair as two separate hands (split). It is the availability of these options—the ability to control one's destiny—that makes the game so attractive.

Unlike their poker-playing counterparts, blackjack players do not play against each other. Each player's hand competes independently with the dealer's hand.

Once the players have completed their hands, the dealer flips up her *hole card* (her face down card). If the dealer's hand totals less than seventeen, she must take another card until she has at least seventeen. If the dealer has a total of seventeen or greater she must stand. No other options are available to her.[2]

If the dealer has a higher total than the player, the dealer wins. If the player has a higher total than the dealer, the player wins. If their totals are the same, they tie (push). If the dealer's total exceeds twenty-one, all players who have not already busted (gone over twenty-one) win. If a player busts and the dealer subsequently busts, the player does not get his money back; once a player busts, the hand is over for him. It is this "double bust" phenomenon that gives the house its built-in advantage over most of the players in the game of blackjack.[3]

Most casual blackjack players are repositories of more misinformation than your typical political campaign, and the problems usually begin with the very first line. "The object of the game," announce players who routinely lose their asses at the green felt tables, "is to get a hand totaling as close to twenty-one as possible without going over twenty-one."

Believing this to be the object of the game of blackjack is about as accurate as the belief that the object of the game of poker is to get a royal flush.

---

2 It is because the dealer does not make decisions based upon what she believes her opponents have that the game of blackjack is not amenable to game theory.

3 This is something that many quite intelligent people do not understand. "How can the casino offer the players all those advantages—time and a half for blackjack, doubling, splitting, standing short, and insurance," these people ask, "and still have an edge?" If the rules for players and dealers were identical, the double bust win for the house would give the house a whopping edge of 8.8 percent. The options available to the players simply whittle that down to a manageable level.

The object of the game of blackjack is not to get as close to twenty-one as possible. The object of the game of blackjack is to win. If that can be accomplished by totaling twenty-one, fine. If that can be accomplished by totaling twelve, well, that's fine, too.

Although the game of blackjack had become quite popular in Nevada by the early 1960s, the casinos offering the game did not know precisely what their overall advantage was. They did know a few things, however.

1) They knew that the "double bust" house win meant that the dealer was guaranteed to win the majority of hands played.

2) They knew that the *hold* (the percentage of every dollar with which a player buys in the casino expects to keep) for blackjack compared favorably to that for craps—hovering somewhere around 25 percent.

3) They knew that, although certain playing decisions seemed to be "better" than others—and therefore the house edge wasn't fixed, as it is in roulette and craps—they didn't have to worry about their exact advantage. There is no indication that casino management anywhere in the world suspected that the game of blackjack was qualitatively different from any other game offered by the casinos.

But as early as the 1950s, there were a few gamblers who had recognized a curious reality about the game of blackjack. Although the dealer was guaranteed to win the majority of hands played, that did not necessarily mean she would win most of the money wagered. If the player bet more money on the few hands he won than on the majority of hands he lost, he could come out ahead in the long run.

Blackjack is enjoyed for a variety of reasons across a broad spectrum of the gambling population. Different authors have likened the game to war, judo, and Eastern mysticism. Taylor once equated the first card out of a single deck with the broken symmetry that occurred a tiny fraction of a second after the Big Bang. Whatever one's idiosyncratic mental construct, the game is unique. And it is blackjack's uniqueness among casino games that enabled Taylor and players like him to extract tens of millions of dollars from casinos all over the world.

Any player who places a bet on the inside of a single-zero roulette layout anywhere in the world is playing with a disadvantage of 2.7 percent. It doesn't matter if he's James Bond, Jimmy the Greek, or Jimmy the Blowhard. It doesn't matter if today's his birthday, today's his lucky day, or today is the first day of the rest of his life. Betting systems such as Martingales, Reverse Labouchères, and betting your wife's birthday all work equally poorly. Roulette is a great equalizer. Grade-school dropouts can belly up to the green felt next to doctors and lawyers and hold their heads high, for all are equal in the eyes of probability.

Any player who places a bet on the pass line at a craps table anywhere in the world does so bucking a house advantage of 1.414 percent. It doesn't matter if the last ten rolls were losers, or the last twenty rolls were winners. It doesn't matter if the player is a mathematician, a statistician, or a damned fool. Every roll of the dice is a new universe, and that's as immutable as the law of gravity.

The technical term for this phenomenon is the *Law of Independent Trials*, which simply means that roulette balls and dice have no memories. A roulette ball doesn't know that the last ten numbers to come up have been black, so it's time for a red. Roulette balls are made of plastic or ivory or nylon, and have no thoughts to speak of. Roulette balls do not struggle with Boolean logic, non-Euclidean curved space, or issues of mind-body duality. Roulette balls contain no awareness, no ideas, no consciousness at all. Probability is the only force governing the outcome of the game of roulette, and it does so *one spin at a time*. The universe is renewed each time the croupier launches the ball.

A pair of dice doesn't know that the shooter hasn't crapped out in half an hour, so it's time to end the pit boss's misery by totaling seven. A pair of dice doesn't know that the shooter's baby desperately needs new shoes. Dice have no eyes to survey the bets on the layout, no ears to hear the shooter's fervent plea, no memory at all. The overall house edge in craps never changes. If the earth left its orbit tomorrow and began gallivanting around the solar system like a runaway truck, two dice would still offer six ways out of thirty-six possible combinations to roll a seven and only five ways to roll an eight.

Blackjack is different. There is no fixed house edge. Theoretically a player could play with a 100 percent disadvantage. (To test this particular system, simply go to any blackjack table and continue to hit every hand until you bust. Then enjoy the free meal the casino will undoubtedly offer you.) Bad players generally play with disadvantages ranging from 3–5 percent. Good players can whittle that down to less than 1 percent. And really good players can play with an edge.

Before 1962, the fact that good players could play the game of blackjack with an advantage over the casino was completely unknown to all but a few players. And those bastards had it made.

Characters known to blackjack historians as Greasy John (so named because he ate buckets of fried chicken at the table while he played), System Smitty, the Little Dark-haired Guy from California, and a handful of others played entirely unmolested for years. Nobody knows for how long. What is certain, however, is that it all started when somebody noticed the unremarkable fact that when the ace of spades is dealt out of a single deck on the first round, there is no way in hell anyone will get the ace of spades on the second round.

What could be simpler?

By all accounts these pioneers, whose actual systems remain as mysterious as their identities, played for years, winning with impunity. And they learned a few things.

1. They learned that if they bet a lot when big cards were coming and a little when small cards were coming, they could win money at virtually any blackjack table in the world.

2. They learned that the casinos had no idea what they were doing.

3. They learned that their blackjack system was better than having a job.

4. They learned that their blackjack system was better than robbing a bank.

And, most important of all:

5. They learned to keep their goddamn mouths shut.

These players traveled throughout Nevada and the world with their eyes open and their mouths shut, winning piles of dollars, pounds, francs, lire—whatever currency was popular in the country in which they found themselves. And the casinos did nothing to stop them. As far as the casinos were concerned, blackjack was every bit as unbeatable as craps and roulette, and in the long run these curious systems players would lose just like everyone else.

In the 1950s, Greasy John, System Smitty, and a few other characters with adjectives for first names had the world by the gonads. The testes. The absolute balls. And they knew it.

Then the shit hit the fan.

In 1962, a professor of mathematics at MIT named Edward Thorp published a book titled *Beat the Dealer*. In it, Thorp explained to anyone willing to shell out $1.95 how a player who keeps track of the cards can beat the game of blackjack. The book contained a card-counting system that could be mastered by a diligent student in just a few days.

To most of the professional blackjack players in the world today, Edward Thorp is a full-blown hero. His name is uttered with a reverence usually reserved for the likes of Joe DiMaggio and Willie Mays. If it weren't for Edward Thorp, the majority of today's professional blackjack players would be hard at work in the food service industry wearing paper hats.

But to Greasy John and his contemporaries, whose grip on the world's testicles was loosened forever, Edward Thorp was only the first in a long line of bastards who Spilled The Beans. Their world had changed forever.

Casinos offer games of chance. Individuals sometimes win, but usually lose. Now, thanks in no small part to Thorp's book, the situation had changed. A small number of players were capable of doing to the casinos what the casinos were doing to everybody else.

Question: How did the casinos of Nevada respond to gamblers who learned a skill and then won money playing within the established rules?

Answer: The casinos responded by showing the world what kind of gamblers they really are.

They changed the goddamn rules.

On April 1, 1964, two years after *Beat the Dealer* was published, the Las Vegas Resort Hotel Association announced that Nevada casinos were actually changing the rules of the game of blackjack. They restricted doubling down to totals of eleven, and didn't allow players to split aces. That's what kind of gamblers *they* are.

When the casinos instituted these rule changes to thwart the card counters, they hoped that ordinary players wouldn't notice. They wanted the attention of skilled players only who, presumably, would now find the game of blackjack about as attractive as the bubonic plague. Order would return to the sequestered world of the casinos.

Unfortunately for the casinos, ordinary players did notice the rule changes. Blackjack participation decreased so dramatically among players of all skill levels that, a couple of weeks after the new rule changes were instituted, the casino owners closed their eyes, held their collective breath, and reinstated the old rules.

The disaster they were sure awaited them never came. On the contrary— more people than ever before flocked to the game. Blackjack surged ahead of craps to become the most popular and the most profitable of all casino games—and today continues to grow faster in popularity than craps, roulette, and baccarat *combined.*

How can the game have become even more profitable for the casinos if the increased popularity was due to the game's inherent vulnerability? Simple. Players who fancied themselves winning players—but who, in reality, would sooner sprout wings—poured their money into gambling establishments the world over. Beating blackjack isn't easy. It only looks that way.

Over the course of the next decade more books followed, including one titled *Playing Blackjack as a Business.* Many more beans were spilled. The newer books contained card-counting systems that were easier to learn than the one revealed in *Beat the Dealer.* However, they were all based on the following fundamental principle:

> The players have a statistical advantage over the dealer when there are a lot of big cards (tens and aces) remaining to be dealt. The dealer has a statistical advantage over the players when there are a lot of small cards remaining to be dealt.

For fun and profit, design your own card-counting system by following these three easy steps:

1. Assign positive numbers to small cards and negative numbers to big cards. Keep track of the count as various cards emerge from the deck.

2. Bet more when the count is positive and less when the count is negative.

3. Add to this a strategy that tells you what to do with any given hand versus any particular dealer up-card. Call this Basic Strategy.

That's it. You may now go out and beat the casinos at their own game. *Rain Man* notwithstanding, counting cards is as simple as that. Getting away with it, though, is something else entirely.

Until 1976, no major bombs were dropped by either side in the blackjack wars. As in any war of attrition there were minor skirmishes, but no great battles were fought. Casinos began taking countermeasures by increasing the number of decks used in the game, and counters responded by teaming up to maintain their overall edge of between 1 and 2 percent. Because of the 1964 rule-changing fiasco, and because of the perception on the part of the average American that the Mafia ran the casinos in Nevada (and, by extension, the state itself), the casino industry was reluctant to do anything dramatic. It was finally becoming conscious of its image.

For more than a decade after the blackjack rules reverted back to the way the blackjack gods intended, the casinos in Nevada were content simply to escort suspected counters quietly to the street and send them on their way with a warning never to return. Then, in 1976, something reached critical mass and exploded. Casino management could no longer accept the idea that a few players were legitimately winning money in their casino.

Since the rule changes of 1964 had failed, something different had to be tried. "Goddamn it!" some pinstriped executive must have bellowed, banging a manicured fist upon a hand-tooled conference table, "Dere oughta be a law!"

There was, in fact. Nevada Revised Statute 465.015 to be exact, known colloquially as the "Bunco Steering Statute." According to the statute,

"Cheat" means to alter the selection of criteria which determine:
    (a) The result of a game; or
    (b) The amount or frequency of payment in a game.

In September 1976, a card counter was arrested in Las Vegas, Nevada, and charged with violating N.R.S. 465.015; to wit: he had willfully, knowingly, and with malice aforethought altered the selection of criteria which determine the natural odds of the game of blackjack. Specifically, he had the unmitigated gall to remember which cards were gone from the deck, and then play accordingly. In other words, his crime, according to the prosecuting attorneys representing the State of Nevada, was thinking at a blackjack table. The prosecution's plan, apparently, was to force the poor bastard to sit in the witness chair and state, "Judge, I swear on this here stack of Bibles that my mind was a complete blank when I stood with that sixteen against a ten."

In retrospect, Taylor thought it a shame that the case was thrown out of court so quickly. If playing blackjack properly alters the natural odds of the game, then playing badly does so as well. Had the counter been convicted, we could have looked forward to the day when casinos were forced to arrest players who split fives and stood with sixteen against the dealer's seven.

In fact, the court rejected the casinos' bid to make legal history and criminalize thinking, an offense the casinos themselves clearly had no intention of committing. It seemed that the casinos would simply have to lick their wounds, swallow hard, and put up with that one player in ten thousand who could play by the rules and beat the game.

That is not what happened.

In a classic case of one side losing a battle but winning the war, the casinos managed to convince a majority of people in and out of the industry that counting cards is cheating. For accomplishing this seemingly impossible feat, they deserve some sort of award.

Imagine the task involved in attempting a parallel assault on common sense—convincing your poker-playing pals that thinking while playing poker is somehow against the rules of the game. You are at your friend Ray's house on a Friday night, the beer and pretzels are circulating, and the game is seven-card stud. You have four spades. You look across the table at Ray's hand. He has three kings. A bunch of other cards are face up on the table, eight of which are spades. You think to yourself, "There is only one spade left in the whole deck, and even if I'm lucky enough to get it, Ray still might beat me with a full house or four of a kind." So you fold your hand.

Imagine your surprise if at this point Ray stands up and accuses you of cheating. You tell him you noticed that a lot of spades were out, so you figured your chances of winning were slim. He responds by telling you that noticing such things is cheating, and then throws you out of his house. How much luck would Ray have convincing his friends that you were indeed cheating?

This is precisely the belief casinos have managed to propagate with regard to card counters. For reasons too complex for this author to fathom, most people believe that if a blackjack player notices which cards have already been dealt and then plays accordingly, that player is cheating. This, argue the casinos, "changes the natural odds of the game."

Several times a year over the course of his career, Taylor participated in some variation of the following conversation with relatives and friends he hasn't seen for a while:

"So, Taylor, what are you doing for a living these days?"

"I play blackjack."

"Really? Where do you deal?"

"I don't deal. I play."

Pause.

"Yeah, but what do you *do*?"

"I play blackjack for a living. I'm a card counter."

"And you win?"

"Yes."

Longer pause.

"But isn't that cheating?"

"No."

"It must be cheating. The casino always wins."

"It's not cheating. It's just thinking."

"So they just let you walk in and win money?"

"They don't exactly let me. If they figure out what I'm doing, they throw me out."

A knowing nod of the head. "Then it *must* be cheating."

So, the court decision notwithstanding, casinos would and have continued their successful public identification of counters as cheaters. And it isn't only the public that is snowed. To this day, casino personnel are taught that card counters illegally subvert the inalienable right of casinos to maintain a mathematical advantage over the players, and in large measure this nonsense has been accepted as gospel. Dealers relish turning in suspected counters.

However, since counting cards is in fact perfectly legal, the casinos cannot actually have players arrested for it. So they have come up with a clever solution to their little problem.

Businesses in the state of Nevada have the right to refuse service to anyone for any reason. Further, since the casinos are private property, they are permitted to demand that a counter leave the premises, threatening arrest if he refuses. If the counter ever returns, the unfortunate waif could then be arrested—not for counting, but for *trespassing*.

This is how Nevada's casinos deal with card counters to this day. Casinos force good players to leave for reasons that are never specified (in seven years, the closest Taylor ever came to an explanation was "You know why."). The players are threatened with formal arrest if they return.

It is simple, elegant, and keeps the casinos safe for tourists, systems players, and degenerate gamblers. Sometimes.

Since the first lungfish crawled out of the primordial slime 400 million years ago, environmental change has been the single most important force driving evolution, and the game of blackjack would prove to be no exception. On a sunny day in July 1978, in Atlantic City, New Jersey, along a battered wooden boardwalk that had been rotting for more than a half century, Resorts International opened the first legal casino in the United States outside the state of Nevada. Within months, the uneasy truce that existed between casinos and card counters exploded into a full-blown arms race. Counters would develop methods that enabled them to get bigger and bigger edges, and the casinos would respond with increasingly draconian methods to thwart them.

This explosion was fueled in large part by the unique circumstances surrounding the early months of legalized casino gambling in Atlantic City. For the first six months of its existence, Resorts International was the embodiment of every casino owner's dream. It was the only game in town. Resorts was the only legal casino within a thousand miles, and players were literally lining up to play slot machines. Blackjack tables were three and four players deep. Spots at the tables were at such a premium that players were actually selling their seats to others desperate to gamble.

The only possible dark cloud threatening Resorts' idyllic heaven on earth was the fact that it was operating on a temporary gaming license. The New Jersey Casino Control Commission hadn't yet granted a permanent license and, with players fighting each other for the privilege of losing their money, the rumor was that Resorts would not dare bar skilled players from the game of blackjack and thus provide a reason not to receive a permanent license. No card counters would be barred at Resorts for the foreseeable future.

The underground communications network connecting professional gamblers is one of remarkable efficiency. Word spread rapidly, and within weeks Atlantic City was deluged by blackjack players of every skill level from all over the country. It was to become a card-counter convention.

Like some beady-eyed nocturnal beast that ventures out during the day, counters ultimately would learn to show themselves in the harsh glare of the casino's gaze only at their peril. But for a short time, before casino management allowed its greed to overcome its sensibility, the games were some of the best the professional blackjack world had ever seen. Not incidentally, Resorts was also the most profitable casino on the planet.

It was not to last. Resorts began barring skilled players in January 1979, six months after opening and mere weeks before the casino was to receive its coveted permanent gaming license. Resorts' top brass had worked itself into that unspeakable mental frenzy that convinces an otherwise rational human being that blackjack players should be forbidden from thinking at the table. In all likelihood, Resorts had received assurances from a compliant Casino Control Commission that barring skilled players would not jeopardize its license; otherwise, it surely wouldn't have taken the risk. So much for a fair and open gaming environment in New Jersey.

In fairness, there *were* players—in particular a group referred to as "the Czechs"[4]—who bear some responsibility for the destruction of the game in Atlantic City. Instead of playing like everybody else, raising and lowering bets along with the count, these players would stand behind tables and count, letting other players slog through dozens of negative expectation hands. When the count went positive, they would swoop in with huge bets. A number of other pros tried to convince these slimebags that it was in everyone's long-term interest to back off, but it was not to be. Atlantic City would become a modern-day Tragedy of the Commons. In part because some players weren't happy with their fair share of the lush grazing, everyone ultimately lost.

---

4 The Czech team consisted of eight players, only two of whom were from Czechoslovakia, but the moniker stuck.

By the time Taylor and Steve found *Playing Blackjack as a Business* at Crown Books in Marina del Rey on a chokingly smoggy day in late November 1980, card counting as a profession was slowly dying a horrible death, drowning in a sea of information. Books entitled *Professional Blackjack, The World's Greatest Blackjack Book, Blackjack Your Way to Riches* and others that outlined increasingly powerful blackjack systems were widely available at quality bookstores near you. If Taylor could learn the intricacies of a modern card-counting system simply by wandering into a local bookstore and plopping down five or six bucks, so could any curious casino manager or pit boss.

For those casino employees whose appetite for reading was somewhat lower on the scale than their enthusiasm for rectal exams, another source of information sprang up, demonstrating another immutable evolutionary law to which we are not immune. If there is an available niche in the environment, some mutant creature will emerge to exploit it.

The Griffin Detective Agency came into existence to provide a service to casinos. Since the 1976 court decision that card counting was not a criminal activity, the Nevada Gaming Commission did not include card counters among the photographs of mobsters, card cheats, and other assorted crossroaders in its infamous Black Book of Casino Undesirables. What the casinos now wanted was a way to positively identify suspected card counters.

Lumbering in to fill the information void was a thug named Bob Griffin. About the size of a corn-fed steer and possessing the intellect of three bags of hammers, the card counter's underground rumor mill had it that Griffin had tried and failed to learn how to count cards and play a winning game of blackjack. In what may have been a fit of pique, Griffin began his detective agency, which sold its services to any casino willing to pay the monthly subscription fee. In return, the casino received a copy of something called the Griffin Book—a book the agency published featuring photographs of a scattered assortment of real cheats among the several hundred pictures of card counters. In addition, Griffin and his crew of agents were available to subscribers to view from the "sky" individuals suspected of attempting to play with an edge. Those players determined to be playing a winning game would be dragged into a "back room" by the casino's security guards and photographed for the next edition of the Griffin Book. The player would then be escorted to the street with an admonition never to return.

If the information available in bookstores and in the Griffin Book wasn't enough, Ken Uston's appearance on *60 Minutes* had shown anyone who might be at all interested exactly how to spot a card counter. And if *that* wasn't enough, Uston initiated high-profile lawsuits in Atlantic City and Nevada, and continued his greedy quest for personal aggrandizement by making himself available for numerous talk shows and newspaper interviews, including an interview published in *The New York Times Magazine*. Caught up in the landslide of information, some counters began offering seminars to teach prospective players how to count cards, and others "crossed over" to teach the casinos how to spot card counters and how to take more effective countermeasures against them.

By November 1980, virtually every casino in Nevada employed individuals who knew how to spot card counters and how to thwart their efforts. The days when hardworking, dedicated card counters plundered helpless casinos were long gone. Casinos had armed themselves with an impressive array of countermeasures that made much of the strategy outlined in *Playing Blackjack as a Business* as obsolete as peace signs, well-built American cars, and truth in advertising.

The author of *Playing Blackjack as a Business* can't be held responsible for failing to inform excited young card counters about the pitfalls awaiting them, for the odd little guy with the bad grammar died in 1977, before much of the major shit hit the fan. He can, however, be blamed for failing to explain mathematical fluctuations. These financial swings—as fundamental to card counting as card values and Basic Strategy—have caused the demise of more capable card counters than all of the casino countermeasures and all of the Griffin agents arrayed against them. For some reason—perhaps because *Playing Blackjack as a Business* was meant to inspire rather than discourage—Lawrence Revere was entirely unforthcoming about blackjack ruin rates. His readers never really learned how close to the edge of financial disaster they were skating every time they went out to play.

However, there is no way that Alexander Taylor, sitting in his one-room studio apartment off Santa Monica Boulevard, reading Revere's book and getting more excited by the page, possibly could have known that.

CHAPTER 4

JUST DO IT

In Nevada, for a time, the lawyer, the editor, the banker,
the thief, the desperado, the chief gambler, and the
saloonkeeper occupied the same level in society,
and it was the highest.
~*Mark Twain*, Roughing It

Some things never change.
~*Alexander Taylor*

"Sixteen against a nine," said Steve, looking at the chart in his lap.

"Plus seven or higher, stand; otherwise, hit," Taylor answered immediately.

Taylor and Steve were crawling along Interstate 10 just east of El Monte, part of a massive traffic jam caused by rubberneckers eyeballing a truck fire on the other side of the freeway. Taylor had hoped to begin the maiden voyage early to beat L. A.'s traditional Friday traffic jam, but an unusually large load of dirty underwear had slowed things at the cleaning plant. He hoped it wasn't a portent of things to come.

History records that a spot in the middle of the Mojave Desert that was to become Las Vegas, Nevada, was first settled by Mormon missionaries in 1857, drawn there by the presence of a small underground spring that provided water in an otherwise bleak desert environment.

History is like that. When missionaries show up to play "My God is better than your God," they generally intend to participate *with* somebody. In this case, "somebody" was the remnants of a band of Aboriginal Americans, who had been living in the area since the ancestors of most of us were writing their names in the dirt with a stick. However, to the victor go the spoils, and that includes the telling of the tale.

Statehood began auspiciously enough. Although the Nevada Territory lacked the requisite population, Lincoln granted statehood because he needed the votes for his antislavery legislation. A lofty beginning to a state that would ultimately become the birthplace of "Sin City."

The city that was to become Las Vegas began as the point in the middle of the Mojave Desert where the Los Angeles & Salt Lake Railroad—running north and south—and the San Pedro—running roughly east to west—crossed. A group of bright prospectors quickly realized that a saloon, bank, or other business located where two railroads cross will generate approximately twice the revenue as the same saloon, bank, or other business located where only one railroad passes through. Nuclear physics it wasn't, but there is nothing wrong with a healthy measure of common sense.

This common sense was taken leave of when, in 1878, the city was incorporated with the name Las Vegas—Spanish for "The Meadows." The speck of green nourished by the small stream resembled a meadow roughly to the extent that Queen Victoria resembled your average Playmate of the Month. However, there were precious few language mavens among the desperadoes and horse thieves seated on the council of the Nevada Territory in the latter part of the nineteenth century, so the spot—the intersection until then shown on a map as merely an X—now officially had a name.

The railroads that crossed in the desert weren't there simply to transport people through the vast wasteland that constitutes the Mojave Desert. Vast stores of silver had been discovered in the northern part of the Nevada Territory around the time of the California Gold Rush, and thousands had gotten rich locating, mining, transporting, and refining the precious mineral. The Los Angeles & Salt Lake Railroad had been built largely to facilitate the movement of the rich ore from the mines in the northern part of the Territory to the refineries in California. The silver boom lasted for better than fifty years, and the inhospitable Territory was quickly peppered by towns whose inhabitants regularly went from rags to riches and back to rags again—often all in a matter of weeks. It was the Wild West at its finest, with gunslingers, horse thieves, and plenty of gambling. The Nevada Territory was surely wilder than any subsequent screen portrayals, and, unlike the film versions glorifying such aberrant behavior, the bad guys usually won.

Like all good things, this too came to an end. As the silver became scarcer and the money flow slowed to a trickle, hundreds of the towns that had sprung up like desert wildflowers after a rainstorm vanished, along with the dreams of thousands who had come to the area to find their fortune. The population, artificially inflated by the prospectors who had flocked to the Territory, plunged. Those who remained watched their world shrivel up and die in the relentless desert sun.

By the time unfettered capitalism's traveling smoke-and-mirrors show folded the Big Top and left the not-so Great Depression in its wake, Nevada had already been suffering greatly. The end of the silver boom had plunged the state into abject poverty, and the looming depression promised still deeper trauma. So, in 1931, the desperate Nevada State Legislature, showing more guts than any deliberative body we are likely to see in our lifetime, granted Nevada's counties the right to legalize gambling.

In fact, this decision simply applied the state's imprimatur to an activity that had been rampant throughout the area since Nevada was a territory. Games of poker and faro could be found in virtually every saloon. One-armed bandits stood ready and waiting in corner drugstores and coffee shops. The major change the new legislation brought was that the newly legalized casinos would be taxed—a consideration not entirely incidental to the decision made by the legislature.

Prior to World War II, Las Vegas played second fiddle to Reno in the state. "The Biggest Little City in the World" boasted plush dude ranches and high-class whorehouses. Harold's Club was a local landmark, offering classy surroundings and plenty of action to thousands of soon-to-be divorcées who had to do something while fulfilling Nevada's six-week residency requirement.

In contrast, Las Vegas was a bunch of dilapidated wooden shacks festooned with steer skulls and wagon wheels. There was no thick carpeting covering the creaking wooden floors in the joints along Fremont Street. Sawdust was a far more effective absorber of the tobacco juice dribbling from the mouths of the ranchers and grizzled prospectors who made up the bulk of the gambling clientele in those early days. In 1945, the population of the city was about 10,000, and although there were visitors, at least as many strangers came to town for the prostitution as for the gambling. The faro, craps, and blackjack games were strictly small-time.

Then Bugsy Siegel had a dream.

A charter member of the pantheon of red, white, and royal blue American psychopaths, Benjamin Siegel was born in 1906 and left home without finishing grammar school. He traveled to the Lower East Side of Manhattan and prepared for immortality by rolling drunks, burglarizing apartments, and learning how to use guns and knives. In the days immortalized by that monumental blunder referred to as the Eighteenth Amendment, these skills would prove indispensable to the young man. There was no limit to the amount of money an enterprising youth could make in the days of Prohibition, and Bennie Siegel—nicknamed "Bugs" or "Bugsy" because he was hotheaded—had the single most important characteristic necessary for success in that environment. He was completely crazy.

While still in his teens, Siegel and a boyhood friend named Meyer Lansky started what they called the Bug-Meyer Mob. This grew into what would become Murder, Inc. By the time Siegel was eighteen, his resume read like the feature article in *Who's Who in Thuggery*. He had been involved in loan-sharking, bootlegging, mayhem, white slavery, and murder.

In the early 1930s, Siegel began traveling to Los Angeles to strong-arm his way into the lucrative race wire service provided to bookies by the Chicago mob. During the Second World War, Siegel—no doubt via moral suasion—convinced hundreds of reluctant L. A. bookies to sign up for his wire service as well.

If it had ended that way, Siegel would have been nothing more than an insignificant historical footnote. But it didn't, and the rest, as they say, is history.

Bugsy periodically traveled to Las Vegas to terrorize the subscribers to his wire service and to check on his small gambling operations in the city. During one trip back to Los Angeles in the summer of 1945, he stopped on the side of Highway 91 to take a leak and, as legend has it, had an epiphany. Perhaps it was heatstroke. Whatever it was, Siegel fell to his knees and reached his arms heavenward, thanking the Good Lord above for the vision that would one day make him great. For Bugsy dreamed of an oasis in the desert—a gambler's paradise unparalleled in the world. The cactus, sagebrush, and caliche surrounding him would surrender to a self-contained world of its own; a jewel emerging from the wasteland that was the Mojave Desert. Siegel's resort would feature gourmet restaurants, exclusive shops, and world-class entertainment. Rich gamblers from around the globe would be transported to the resort, and have no need to leave until they had gambled away all their money. The select would leave broke but happy, singing the praises of their fantastic host and his inspired monument to taste.

As usual, reality doesn't live up to the legend. Maybe Siegel really had his epiphany in the desert. Who knows? In fact, what was to become Siegel's Fabulous Flamingo Hotel was already partially built when Siegel and his partners bought it from the financially troubled owners. The idea to build a casino far from the toilets on Fremont Street didn't originate with Siegel. By all accounts, however, the idea to build a plush resort that would stand in stark contrast to the downtown dives was Siegel's alone.

Ground-breaking for the Fabulous Flamingo began in December 1945. Within months, the project was so far in debt that Siegel was forced to approach Meyer Lansky and other mobsters, hat in hand, for more money. This would be repeated several times during the course of construction. The money was forthcoming, but at a price.

The partially built casino held its Grand Opening on Christmas Eve 1946, in a driving rainstorm. Siegel could not have chosen a worse day to open—almost none of the invited Hollywood luminaries showed. After the disastrous opening and a poor initial month, Siegel announced that the casino would close until construction of the hotel was completed, and scheduled a second Grand Opening for two months hence.

Although the second opening fared better than the first, Siegel didn't live to see the fulfillment of his dream. On June 21, 1947, a critical amount of his blood leaked out of a number of holes in his body that weren't part of the original design. Among those in Siegel's line of work, this was known as "dying of natural causes."

If Bugsy were alive today to see what his dream has wrought, he would probably drop dead. The barren desert around the Fabulous Flamingo has yielded a tourist Mecca unparalleled in the world. Although many forms of gambling are indulged in by rich and poor alike; although tens of thousands of otherwise law-abiding citizens engage in weekly poker games, and hundreds of thousands bet on their favorite sports teams, real gamblers ultimately end up in Vegas. And it was to Vegas that Alexander Taylor and Steve Wallace were headed.

That Alexander Taylor had lived for twenty-five years without having wagered a penny in a casino was due largely to the considerable dose of rationality introduced to his view of the world when he was a child. Why would any rational person choose to gamble in a casino? In the long run, he knew, the players had to lose.

Although Taylor would learn why so many people gamble, he himself would never experience that urge. He could not suspend himself in that cloud of disbelief that allows gamblers to hope that a $100 chip on the pass line will magically transform itself into $200. To Taylor, constitutionally incapable of thinking about a bet without automatically calculating the odds, a $100 chip on the pass line meant he just gave the casino $1.41. Where the hell's the pleasure in that?

When Taylor read Revere's *Playing Blackjack as a Business*, he experienced what one might call a paradigm shift. With little fanfare and less bullshit, the author quickly convinced him that the game of casino blackjack was entirely beatable.

The card-counting system outlined in the book was completely straightforward. The bellman's intimations notwithstanding, the only "math" involved was simple arithmetic. And, although it helped, it wasn't necessary to be particularly good at it. It just required practice. As the name suggests, card counting is, indeed, *counting*.

But what immediately sold Taylor on the efficacy of Revere's blackjack system was that it made intuitive sense. He didn't have to spend years poring over the details to realize that when an abundance of aces and tens are left in the deck, the player has an advantage over the dealer. When that abundance of aces and tens is dealt out in the form of hands, both the players and the dealer will get more blackjacks than normal. The difference is, the dealer only wins "even money" when she gets a blackjack (she simply wins the player's bet). The players, however, are paid "time and a half" for their blackjacks. It doesn't take a mathematical genius to realize that it is in the players' interest to raise their bets when the cards of which blackjacks consist—aces and tens—are due to be dealt out.

It also doesn't take a genius to figure out that tens have a nasty habit of busting bad hands. Since the player has the option to stand with bad hands—an option not available to the hamstrung dealer—it is obviously in the player's favor if a bunch of tens remain in the particular subset of cards remaining to be dealt.

Similarly, tens are good for splitting and doubling down—again, options available to the player but not the dealer. So, all the player has to do is raise his bet when the subset of cards remaining to be dealt favor him, lower it otherwise, and the casino is at his mercy. It almost seems unfair.

> "Lots of queens left."
> "Wait a minute, wait a minute. Lots of queens?"
> "Lots and lots of queens."
> —*Dustin Hoffman and Tom Cruise in* Rain Man

Taylor and Steve finally broke through the L. A. smog when they started up the hill west of Victorville. From that point on, they could see an unbroken line of traffic for the duration of the drive. The seemingly endless string of red taillights continued for over two hundred miles, finally dispersing among the various exits leading to the Las Vegas Strip.

Both sides of Interstate 15 were littered with beer cans, paper plates, grapefruit rinds, and other assorted trash. A weekend in Vegas was always a party, and it often started in the car. Hunter Thompson may have immortalized the insanity of the drive in *Fear and Loathing in Las Vegas*, but he didn't invent it.

Cresting the last hill outside the Vegas Valley, the pair could see the lights of Las Vegas expanding outward and upward as more and more of the city came into view. The lights glistened brightly in the clear desert air. Since both had grown accustomed to viewing the city lights of Los Angeles through a whitish-gray layer of smog, this view of the town that Bugsy built looked artificially brilliant. From a distance, the glitter—standing in stark contrast to the ink-black sky—was almost beautiful.

Adrenaline pumped as they drove past exits for famous casinos along the Las Vegas Strip. The Tropicana, the Dunes, and Caesars sailed past. The MGM Grand loomed large, visible between the Dunes and the aquamarine blueness of Caesars Palace. Unlike eighty-five people, the MGM was still standing—standing at once as a monument to greed and to Sensitive Dependence on Initial Conditions. Had it not been for the fire—and the abject lack of humanity the MGM displayed in its response to it—Taylor might never have learned to play blackjack. Taylor thought of the article that had appeared in the *Los Angeles Times* just a few months ago. Still taped to his refrigerator door, the brittle, yellowed article read, in part, like brutal poetry.

> The sprinklers did not sprinkle, the alarms did not blare, the fire doors did not work. But one emergency system worked smoothly during the early minutes of Friday's deadly fire at the MGM Grand Hotel and Casino—the one designed to save the money.

Taylor would have to thank the MGM one day.

They exited at Sahara Boulevard. Two rights brought them in front of the Silverbird Casino. The sign out front advertised single-deck blackjack and the place looked a little less intimidating than the larger hotels, so Taylor and Steve decided to begin their careers there.

Taylor felt an adrenal rush as he entered the casino. He had been in a casino only once before in his life, and that was to take a leak. The money, the flashing lights, and the noise had been a little daunting. Not this time. Taylor was under the impression he knew what he was doing.

Circling the pit, he found an empty table with a single deck spread face up in front of the dealer. Surprised to find that his hands were shaking, he fished a twenty out of his wallet and tried to hand it to the dealer. With a look of disgust, the dealer indicated that Taylor had to put the cash on the table before she could touch it.

He placed the twenty on the felt. "Changing twenty!" the dealer called over her shoulder. The nearest pit boss nodded without looking up from his clipboard.

"Do you want some silver with that?" the dealer asked.

Taylor stared, mute.

"Do you want some silver?" she repeated.

Taylor's mind raced. Plus two, minus four, split if minus one or higher... silver? He looked in the dealer's chip rack. Got it! "Yes," he answered. "Give me dollars."

Taylor received his chips and placed two of the metal ones in the circle in front of him. The dealer shuffled the cards, he cut them, and she began to deal. She flung two cards at him and he lifted them, one in each hand.

"No, no, no," she chastised. "Use only one hand to touch the cards."

The count is plus four, and a six against a seven is a hit... "What?"

"You are not allowed to pick up your cards with two hands like that. Use only one hand."

Taylor placed both cards in his right hand and stared at them, a two and a four. He cleared his throat. "Hit me," he said.

"What?" said the dealer.

"Hit me," said Taylor, louder.

The dealer rolled her eyes. "Scratch."

"Pardon me?"

"Scratch the felt with your cards if you want a hit."

Taylor scratched. The dealer hit him with a deuce.

Plus five, and an eight against a seven is a hit, Taylor thought, and scratched again. The dealer hit him with an ace. Ace-eight, Taylor thought. Plus three. Stand. Taylor placed his cards on top of his chips.

The dealer sighed. "You've never played before, have you?" she asked.

Plus three, Taylor thought desperately. "No," he answered. Plus three, plus three.

"When you want to stand, put your cards under your bet. Like this." She shoved Taylor's original two cards under the two chips in his betting circle. "Okay?"

Plus three. Plus three. "Okay." Plus three.

Using her up-card as a spatula, the dealer flipped her hole card face up and hit her hand twice. "Seventeen," she announced, and reached for Taylor's cards. Quickly she paid him, scooped up the rest of the cards, and shoved them in the discard rack. She then stood, waiting.

Taylor lost it. When the dealer used her up-card to flip her hole card, he lost track of which card was which, and so did not know which card he had already counted. He tried to back up, starting with "plus three," but could not reconstruct the hand. He froze.

His bladder saved him. He stood awkwardly and cleared his throat.

"Uh, where's the men's room?"

When Taylor finally located the bathroom he found Steve standing at a sink, talking to himself.

"How'd you do?" Taylor asked him.

Steve looked at him, wild-eyed. "I think they're on to me," he whispered. "I think they know."

"Come on. We just got here."

"I'm telling you, they keep doing things. They know."

"What are they doing?"

"Things to confuse me. Talking and stuff. I can barely figure out what I have in my hand without the dealer bothering me about some stupid rule."

"Don't worry," said Taylor, relieved. "I had the same problem. We'll get used to it. Let's try again."

They tried again. They learned to shove their cards beneath their bet when they wanted to stand on a hand. When Taylor grabbed his bet and placed it on top of his cards, the dealer nearly levitated. Apparently, a cheating player could palm a few chips and add more to a bet that way. Once a bet has been placed in the betting circle, the dealer informed Taylor, he may not touch it again until the hand is over.

They learned to place their double-down bets alongside their original bets. In practice, Taylor and Steve had been plopping their double-down bets on top of their original bets. No good. Again, someone could add more to a bet that way.

About twenty minutes into his session, Taylor rudely discovered that Revere's book—The Gospel According to Lawrence—was not exactly the Word of the Lord. The dealer had a three up, and Taylor had been dealt an ace and a three. "Hit," said his brain. He scratched, and received a four. Plus six, plus six, said his brain, ace-seven against a three, double. So he put out more money to double down.

"What are you doing?" asked the dealer. By now, nothing Taylor attempted could surprise her.

Plus six, plus six. "I want to double down." Plus six.

"You can only double on your first two cards."

Plus six. Now what? Plus six. Hit or stand? The goddamn book had neglected to mention this little trifle, plus six. Revere never said anything about how to play a three-card ace-seven. Taylor decided to hit it.

He scratched, and got a ten.

Plus four. The dealer had a five beneath her three and busted with an eight and a seven. Boom! Plus seven. Plus seven.

"Cocktails?" asked a waitress whose nipples indicated that it was cold in the casino. "Cocktails here?"

Plus seven. "Yes," said Taylor. Plus seven.

"What can I get you?" she asked, readying her pen.

Plus seven. "A plus seven, please."

"What?!"

Jesus. "A seven. Seven. You know, a Seven-Up."

She left.

The dealer looked at him. "You like her, eh?"

Taylor doubled his bet. "Why do you say that?"

"Because your face is all red."

Taylor stared at the table. This certainly didn't feel like a business.

During the next shuffle, Taylor leaned back in his seat and noticed some sort of commotion at Steve's table across the pit. The other players were laughing and congratulating him. He had stood with a total of eleven, and it had caused the dealer to bust. Steve didn't look too happy.

After forty minutes Taylor gathered his chips and left the table. He had been doing better, but Revere had said playing sessions were to be limited to no more than forty-five minutes. Now that he was able to play more than a couple hands in succession without being reprimanded by the dealer, Taylor wanted to play a little longer. However, he and Steve had agreed to play exactly by the book, and the book said it was time to stop.

Steve had already cashed out. He had lost five bucks.

Taylor pulled the chips from his pocket and counted them. He had been concentrating so hard on the count and the rules and the cards in his hand that he had no idea if he had won or lost. Now he discovered he had won $22.50. Taylor pushed his chips toward the cashier and told Steve not to worry about standing with the eleven.

"I had an eighteen, and I hit it. We'll be all right. We just need more casino experience. Come on, let's try another place. Did you see those waitresses?"

Two days later Taylor left Las Vegas with $216 more than he had arrived with, and he was eighty feet tall. The dollar amount wasn't important. He had proven to himself he could walk into real Las Vegas casinos and leave with more money than he had come in with. To say that he was excited is to understate the case considerably. The world would never be the same.

The world, however, would remain the same for Steve. He had lost, and Taylor was too excited about card counting and his own immediate success to think carefully about what had happened to his friend, and why.

Over the course of the next six weeks Taylor won a total of $1,860. As he returned to Vegas each weekend, he discovered that playing blackjack was getting progressively easier. He experienced no heat, largely because he wasn't betting enough to attract attention, but also because he adopted the disguise that had served him so well during high school. Taylor had perfected the ability to convince people he wasn't too bright, and he once again put this skill to good use.

As the weekends grew progressively hotter in the desert, he found himself conversing with the dealers and the waitresses while a separate part of his brain counted the cards automatically. Either the dealers were dealing more slowly, or he was getting better. Taylor suspected the latter, and his confidence grew.

Unfortunately, Steve continued to lose.

Steve remained uncomfortable in casinos, and it was to this that Taylor attributed his losses. Exactly how a player's discomfort could lead to losing hands Taylor never adequately explained—especially to himself. Maybe Steve's anxiety was causing him to make mistakes. Who knew? Taylor was winning regularly, and any serious thought about what was happening to his friend might have caused him to reconsider—or at least delay—the decision he now made.

For the second time in less than a year, Taylor stuffed all his worldly possessions into his Ford Maverick and drove his life off in another direction. This time he was a high-risk investment, for Revere's book, while great in terms of motivation, was less than forthcoming when it came to explaining mathematical ruin. Heading north on Interstate 15 with a playing bankroll of just over $2,000, Taylor remained blissfully unaware of the fact that he was no more than a minor negative fluctuation from busting out completely.

If you want to become a professional gambler, the first thing you'd better grasp is how dramatic mathematical fluctuations can be. Playing with an edge is no guarantee of fame, fortune, or anything of the sort. All that an edge will gain you is victory in the long run. There are two problems with this:

1) Before you get to the long run, you will experience monstrous financial swings completely out of proportion with the amount you expect to win; and

2) In the long run, you'll be dead.

Blackjack authors define the long run as the amount of time it should take for you to get on your expectation curve. In other words, if you have been playing blackjack for fifteen years and are below expectations, by definition you are not yet in the long run. The definition is a tautology—it's like defining an elephant as a beast with elephantine characteristics.

What is it that causes these wild fluctuations? After all, a skilled card counter playing a good game can play with an edge that rivals the house edge in the game of craps. What's the problem?

Say you place a $100 bet with a 1 percent edge—the average overall edge with which a card counter can expect to play. Your expectation—the amount of money you expect to win on that hand—is 1 percent of your bet, or $1. Now, ask yourself: under what circumstances can a player place a $100 bet and win $1?

Under no circumstances may a player place a $100 bet and win $1. And therein lies the reason for the dramatic fluctuations all professional blackjack players must learn to live with. They expect to earn a dollar or two per hand, but actually win or lose those hands in $100 increments. In other words, a professional blackjack player must place bets that are 100 times as great as his expectation. Add to this the theory of runs—dictating that wins or losses will tend to clump somewhat—and you can see that a player who places five $100 bets with an expectation of winning approximately enough money for a cup of coffee and a donut could easily lose $500.

The good news is that fluctuations, like Foucault's pendulum, swing both ways. It has nothing at all to do with skill. Had one card been displaced in the deck, that same player who lost $500 in his misguided attempt to win five bucks could just as easily have won $500. As you can imagine, his view of the game would differ considerably from that of the poor bastard who happened to be riding the underside of that same curve.

For the first three months of his newfound career, Taylor—largely unaware of the nature of the roller coaster he had boarded—rode the upside of the fluctuation curve. His win rate was a little over a hundred dollars an hour, with bets ranging from five dollars to fifty. He averaged six hours of play a day, seven days a week. Taylor could enter any casino and win at will. He was a monster. A card-counting machine. He could walk through brick walls.

In part to escape the relentless summer heat of Vegas, Taylor took a side trip to Lake Tahoe. Aspen Airlines' small turboprop plane banked sharply over the lake on its descent to the tiny Lake Tahoe Airport, and Taylor fell in love. One look at the crisp blue water and the snow-capped mountains, and he knew he would retire there. At the rate he was winning, he figured conservatively, that would be in about six months with a bankroll in the high six figures.

Taylor took another step toward that goal by winning three grand in four days of play at the Sahara Tahoe, Harvey's, and Harrah's. The blackjack rules weren't as good as those found on the Las Vegas Strip, but the casinos in Tahoe used single decks exclusively and dealt out almost all of the cards. Taylor lacked the mathematical tools necessary to determine if the depth of the deal neutralized the bad rules, but so what? He kicked their collective asses anyway. He was unstoppable. He returned to Vegas with a fattened bankroll and the confidence of the consummate professional. Just get out of the way.

Then Reality stepped forward, sporting a shit-eating grin and carrying a sledgehammer roughly the size and shape of the underside of the positive fluctuation Taylor had been riding. Taylor began to lose.

It started slowly. A few sessions began brightly, with all the promise and hope of a new day. Then, before Taylor had made his daily quota the cards began to turn, and his hands were never quite good enough. Nineteens lost to twenties, and twenties lost to twenty-ones.

Then the real ugliness set in. For three days he looked at nothing but fourteens, fifteens, and sixteens. Those he hit he busted, and those he stood with were beaten. When he bet five dollars he won, and when he shoved fifty out he lost. And there was nothing he could do about it. He doggedly stuck to Revere's strategy, and watched helplessly as his bankroll dwindled.

After three weeks of watching dealers pull incredible hands, the only thought with which Taylor could console himself was that it just couldn't get worse. And then, of course, it did.

He played a four-deck shoe at the Sands that should have been a monster. The count shot up to plus twenty after only a deck was dealt out, and Taylor started to raise his bet. As the count increased to plus thirty-five, he spread up to two hands of $100—the biggest bets he had made in his life.

The goddamn count never came down. It hovered around plus thirty until the yellow plastic stop card came out, which meant that a rich packet of aces and tens had been stuck in the back of the shoe, never to see the light of day.

Edge my ass, Taylor thought, as he drove his decrepit Ford Maverick down Paradise Road, visions of retirement shattered like so many beer bottles on the side of the road. A high count doesn't give the player an edge. There is no edge until the count begins to come down. Since the aces and tens never came out, trapped as they were behind the stop card, he was playing with no edge at all. In fact, he realized, because his playing strategy had changed as the count rose—a high count means more tens and aces than normal should come out, and the way he played his hands had reflected that expectation—he had actually played with a big disadvantage. Taylor had lost more than $1,400 in that one damn shoe.

When the dealer reached the stop card and pulled all of those unused aces and tens from the shoe, Taylor had stared wistfully. What a beautiful clump of cards! If there were only some way to play it. Had the dealer consented to deal that clump, Taylor's theoretical edge would have been 7 percent. Seven percent! Alas, she had shuffled the magic clump into the rest of the pack, and it was gone forever.

Or was it? Taylor pulled off the road and waited for the idea to crystallize. Maybe he could have followed the clump through the shuffle to see where it went, and then played it. Unfortunately, he didn't know anything about the cards with which it was going to be shuffled. If the clump of aces and tens was shuffled with a bunch of small cards, then its magical qualities would be diluted away.

If, on the other hand, the magic clump had been shuffled with a mildly favorable clump, or even a neutral clump, he could have played the next shoe with a huge edge.

Taylor sat on the side of the road, oblivious to the perspiration streaming down his face and the traffic rolling past him. He knew two things. First, fleshing out this idea required a very specific brand of expertise; and second, he didn't have it.

"I wish I knew a computer programmer," he said out loud.

CHAPTER 5
THE ROAD TAKEN

A man said to the universe:
"Sir, I exist!"
"However," replied the universe,
"The fact has not created in me
A sense of obligation."
~*Stephen Crane*

The journey Brian Manning took to the semi-lighted border between America's bland mainstream and its dark criminal underbelly exhibited as many random bounces, caroms, and fluctuations as the path Alexander Taylor traveled to that same nebulous region. If anything, Brian was an even less likely candidate for blackjack immortality.

Brian was born into an upper-middle-class Virginia household in early 1946, the unintended but not unpredictable result of a week-long V-E Day celebration. An attorney in the Department of Justice, Brian's father had two younger brothers in the European Theater, and for the first time in three years Wayne Manning knew he would see them alive again. The cathartic celebration was a release on many levels, and started the process by which Brian's father would settle down and become role model and mentor to an eldest son who would someday complete the path his father never would—election to high political office.

Brian completed six years of grade school in four. At the age of eight he was already asking questions his teachers couldn't answer, so they responded by passing him along to the next available grade. He had a remarkable mind; he retained almost everything he heard or read, and was able to incorporate new information almost effortlessly. Brian had developed a self-consistent worldview by the time he was twelve; one that—much to the consternation of his authoritarian father—allowed precious little room for "Because I said so" authority. If he had chosen to get into trouble, there was very little his father could have done about it. Fortunately, his worldview was logical as well as self-consistent, and so didn't allow for gratuitous troublemaking.

Brian's name appeared on every high honor roll from the moment he entered junior high school. He excelled at science and math, and his teachers knew they had something special.

And he didn't have to bear the social stigma of the intellectually gifted. He played varsity football in his senior year—when he was only sixteen—and was a member of the swim team for three years. Although he was two years younger than his classmates, Brian was extremely popular. In an unusual case for one so bright, his emotional development was as accelerated as the development of his intellect.

Admitted to the University of Baltimore on a full academic scholarship at the age of sixteen, his wheels were firmly on the path that would lead to graduate school, a law degree, a short stint as a highly visible prosecutor, and a run for the state legislature. From there his horizons were limitless. His dad had it all mapped out.

The strategy was a good one. Brian was articulate, thoughtful, and had an uncanny ability to make friends. He had been discussing complex political and social issues with his father's peers from the time he was wearing short pants, and was completely comfortable with those who were years older than himself. His self-confidence was abundant and growing.

Then the universe threw him a curve.

In the spring of Brian's junior year at the University of Baltimore, his father played a round of golf with some associates at the Burning Tree Golf and Country Club. He had a heart attack on the sixteenth fairway, and died two weeks later in the intensive care unit at Bethesda Naval Hospital with a tube up his nose.

Wayne Manning was to retire in two years. He had spoken longingly about enjoying the rest of his life watching the rat race from the sidelines and coaching his son. In his office were numerous glossy brochures from Boston Whaler and Bayliner, all exhibiting a variety of sleek sailboats from which he would one day choose his dream vessel. Now it was over. The elder Manning had spent his entire life preparing for his old age; now, it seemed to Brian, he had been robbed of all he had labored for. Suddenly, the universe didn't make as much sense as it had the day before. His life no longer made sense. Nothing did. In desperation, Brian traded *Foreign Affairs* and *Business Week* for Camus and Sartre, and found that they agreed with him.

Brian drifted through the rest of his undergraduate career in a daze. He started playing poker in the dorms, and discovered he had a talent for the game. More an excuse for drinking than serious gambling, the game was easy, and it also provided Brian with the opportunity to learn to hold his liquor. When he failed to qualify for a degree in political science, he switched to American History—a degree for which he had already earned enough credits. After graduating, he got a job loading trucks.

So what? Nothing mattered.

When an office manager learned that Brian had a natural aptitude for math, he began to teach him Pascal—the language in which the company computer was programmed. After only a couple of months, Brian was a better programmer than his teacher. He was moved into an office, handed a tie, and given a raise.

Brian moved aimlessly from job to job for the next seven years. His programming skills improved and he began to make a considerable amount of money. Throughout this time (to which Brian now wryly refers as his "Gray Period"), he continued to play poker at least once a week with several of the guys with whom he worked. Today, decades later, this is one of the few things he remembers clearly about that time. The game was the only strictly logical nail on which he could hang a view of the world. It was only during these games that he felt alive, because it was only when facing down an opponent or figuring the pot odds on a six-way hand that he felt a measure of control over his life. Otherwise, he was an insignificant particle buffeted by forces inconceivably larger than himself. Outside of those poker games, no amount of money and no degree of status would serve to penetrate the thick existential fog in which he felt himself enveloped.

It was while carelessly negotiating this fog one morning on the way to work in 1978 that he forgot he was driving and steered his 1973 Plymouth Duster into a guardrail. The car flipped and he was pinned inside. He passed out from the pain before the ambulance arrived.

When he woke up, he found himself flat on his back in a hospital bed, with three stainless steel pins keeping the two pieces of his left tibia together. None of his injuries was life-threatening, but the time alone staring at his elevated foot would force him to think seriously about himself for the first time in almost ten years. It wasn't a pleasant experience.

When word of the accident reached Brian's poker-playing pals, they decided to get him a book to help him pass the time while hospitalized. A cheerful fellow named Ralph volunteered to make the trip to the bookstore.

The B. Dalton's in the West Side Mall in South Philadelphia had an extensive Games section, including perhaps a dozen books on poker. Ralph reached for one and hesitated. Was a broken leg a legitimate reason to help Brian become an even better poker player than he already was? Ralph was a nice guy, but he wasn't an idiot.

Ralph's eyes wandered upward. Somewhere a butterfly flapped its wings. A gnat wrinkled its eyebrows. And an ant made a left instead of a right.

Nestled between a book on backgammon and several on bridge was an unassuming black paperback called *Playing Blackjack as a Business*. Ralph reached for it. That would do.

Ralph had chosen well. Brian smiles at the memory. "My hospital room was a complete mess. There were playing cards and cheap plastic chips all over the place. Nurses and orderlies were dealing to me during their breaks. My sister drew a huge strategy chart and taped it to the ceiling over my bed. The doctors must have thought they somehow damaged my brain while they were repairing my leg."

Revere's book was a godsend. The system itself appealed to Brian's fundamental rationality, and the lifestyle it offered struck a responsive chord in someone who had twice been taught not to postpone gratification.

Several months prior to the accident, the first casino had opened in New Jersey. When Brian was finally released from the hospital he wasn't ready to return to work, so he took a bus to Atlantic City. Unfortunately, he found nothing but four-deck shoes, and he had been practicing with only one deck. Brian went home, practiced for a week with four decks, and returned.

At that time, Resorts was the only casino open in Atlantic City. They were still operating on their temporary gaming license and had not yet begun to bar card counters.

The no-barring policy wasn't the only thing the first Atlantic City casino had to recommend itself to professional players. Resorts also offered something called *early surrender*. Early surrender offers the player the option to give up his hand and lose half his bet. The beauty of the rule is the "early" part: the player can surrender his hand before the dealer has determined whether or not she has a blackjack. Early surrender actually gives Basic Strategy players an edge off the top, and it cuts down mathematical fluctuations significantly; so much so that it was almost impossible for a good card counter to lose for any length of time.

When Brian arrived, armed with honed four-deck skills and his poker bankroll of $10,000, he began spreading his bets from fifteen to seventy-five dollars a hand. After six months of part-time play he was up over $35,000, and had lost on only one trip.

By this time Caesars and Bally's had opened, and the former quickly became Brian's favorite place to play. The waitresses wore low-cut, white toga-like outfits with short skirts, complete with hair extensions popping out of the top of a wreath-like contraption wrapped around their temples. Although the revealing outfits made it difficult to concentrate on the count, Brian accepted it as part of the cost of doing business. What a way to make a living. The fog lifted completely. Brian had found his niche.

When the game began to deteriorate early in 1980, Brian knew he had a major decision to make. Atlantic City was going to go into the toilet, and he either had to go back to work or move to Las Vegas.

"In retrospect, it doesn't seem like much of a choice," says Brian. "I could either wake up at five thirty in the morning and go to work five days a week for forty-eight weeks a year wearing a noose disguised as a tie, or play blackjack in casinos all over the world, working whenever I wanted for as long as I wanted. But the decision wasn't that simple, because the games in Nevada were a lot tougher than those in A. C., and of course I had heard all those stories about the mob."

Those stories included one about Ken Uston—the same publicity-seeking counter who appeared with Harry Reasoner on the *60 Minutes* episode, and who had done so much to destroy the game in Atlantic City—who at the time was having reconstructive surgery done on his face after he came in second in a one-round non-title bout with the security guards at the Mapes Casino in Reno. It was something to think about, and it made his mother hysterical, but Brian decided that, as a member of the fifty United States, enforcement of the law in Nevada couldn't be that different from that in the rest of the country. So he flew out for a two-week exploratory trip, liked what he saw, and moved.

To his surprise, the heat in Vegas wasn't as great as Brian had imagined it would be. Mob or not, Las Vegas had legal competition for the first time in its history, and the casinos there were carefully cultivating action players. They could no longer afford to throw a player out unless they were sure he was playing with an edge.

Playing quietly and leaving with the onset of any attention whatsoever, Brian averaged $5,000 per month playing green ($25) chips exclusively and spreading from $25 up to two hands of $100. Because early surrender wasn't offered in any Las Vegas casinos, his financial swings were greater than they had been in Atlantic City, but Brian was a professional. Using a concept known as the Kelly Betting Criterion, the size of his big bets went up and down commensurate with the size of his bankroll—reducing his risk of busting out to almost zero—and he didn't let the inevitable bad fluctuations affect his play or his demeanor.

He visited the Gamblers Book Store every two weeks, and in two months read everything it stocked on the game of blackjack. There was still a lot he didn't know about the game and, as he would discover, quite a bit that nobody knew. Not surprisingly, it was the unknown aspects of the game that most intrigued Brian.

In Atlantic City, the game of blackjack was strictly regulated by the New Jersey Casino Control Commission. The rules, number of decks used, the way in which the game was dealt—even the depth to which the dealers had to deal before shuffling—were all dictated by the Commission. When Caesars in Atlantic City decided to deal a double-deck game for a short time in early 1978, they were allowed to do so—provided they dealt the game from a shoe.

There was a reason for the regulations with which the Atlantic City casinos were saddled. The proponents of legalized gambling in Atlantic City had gone to great lengths to convince the voters in New Jersey that they could have the best of both worlds—the enormous tax revenue that legal casinos would provide without the corruption, fraud, and slime that existed in the state of Nevada. When the citizens finally approved casino gambling in 1976, the nascent Atlantic City Casino Control Commission focused its attention on combating one area of slime in particular—collusion between dealer and player—and did its best to eliminate the possibility.

First, no employee of any Atlantic City casino was permitted to gamble in any other Atlantic City casino. This was meant to keep friends from "helping" each other at the tables. Second, the Commission forbade handheld blackjack games. The Commission knew that in order to deal an effective "second"—the second card from the top of the deck instead of the top card—and perform a variety of other cheating moves, the cheating dealer had to hold the deck in her hand.

Lastly, the Commission forbade "peeking"—the practice by which the dealer looks beneath her ten or ace up-card to see if she has a blackjack. Since all of the players lose when the dealer has a blackjack, it is in the casinos' interest to ascertain this state of affairs right away. Peek under the ten, see the ace, flip it over, scoop everyone's bet, and get on with the next hand. It speeds up the game, and more hands per hour translates into a healthier bottom line for the casino.

However, the Commission was aware that for every thirteen tens the dealer peeks under, she will *not* have an ace beneath twelve of them. That means that twelve out of thirteen times the players will have to play their hands after the dealer has peeked beneath her ten. Since the dealer now knows what danger lurks beneath that ten—after all, to determine that the card wasn't an ace she had to look at it—it would be a simple matter to relay that information to a confederate at the table. In the long run, that hole-card information would give the recipient an edge of 2.3 percent. By eliminating peeking, Atlantic City went a long way toward eliminating collusion between dealer and player.

Unlike the game in Atlantic City—and disavowal by the Nevada Gaming Commission notwithstanding—there were virtually no controls over the game of blackjack in the state of Nevada. There were handheld games and there were shoe games. There were games in which the dealers peeked underneath their tens and there were games in which they didn't. There were single-deck games and there were multiple-deck games. In a joint called the Eldorado—located just south of Las Vegas in Henderson—one could find a four-deck shoe with rules so poor that a player playing perfect Basic Strategy would do so bucking a house advantage of 0.68 percent. Only twenty minutes from the Eldo stood Caesars Palace, where a Basic Strategy player playing the single-deck game enjoyed an advantage of 0.25 percent. And one could find everything in between. Different rules, different numbers of decks, different depths—all this forced professional players to know more about the game of blackjack than simply how to count.

Perhaps more important than the differences in rules was the fact that in many Nevada casinos the game was dealt by dealers who held a single or double deck in their hands. As Atlantic City's Casino Control Commission knew, this allowed skillful dealers to cheat—either in their favor or in favor of a partner playing at the table. What they probably didn't know was that handheld games also opened a world of opportunities to players skillful at taking advantage of what some professional players refer to as *dealer weaknesses*. To the player who knows how to exploit them, dealer weaknesses are beautiful to behold.

Effective exploitation of certain of those weaknesses, though, required more than one player. Brian had maintained his Lone Ranger status for a full year, but now felt that these handheld opportunities—sporting such idiosyncratic names as *spooking* and *front-loading*—deserved further study.

He bought a Tandy TRS-80—a ridiculous personal computer by today's standards, but a real powerhouse in 1981. With no hard disk, no speed, almost no memory, and a price tag of almost two thousand dollars, today the thing looks more like an expensive abacus than an actual computer.

But to Brian, his "Trash-80," as everyone called it, represented the Keys to the Kingdom.

To ordinary gamblers, the game of blackjack is a lark; an entertaining diversion that can transport mind and body away from the petty inconveniences that constitute everyday life. But to Brian, and to other professional gamblers like him, playing blackjack is a struggle for information. And nothing processes information like a computer. In the Silicon Age, it was inevitable that professional gamblers, looking for more information and better ways to process it, would turn to the magic of semiconductors.

That professional gamblers would turn to computers to perform ever more complex and tedious calculations was predictable. The ricocheting pinball path that resulted was not.

Appropriately, Brian began his computer study by focusing on fluctuations. Questions like How big? How often? How long? were not adequately addressed in the literature. Brian began by running million-hand simulations that took a week to run (sounds like Stone Age technology, but this was state-of-the-art for PCs in 1981), and the results both scared the hell out of him and inspired him. Simulated silicon players playing perfectly often lost for months—one poor imaginary bastard was actually down after 100,000 hands, the equivalent of half a year of full-time play. And these ephemeral silicon pioneers never got tired, never got frustrated, and never made mistakes. Imagine the effect a six-month negative fluctuation would have on a carbon-based player relying on faulty, wet neurons.

There was, however, good news among the carnage. The computer runs showed that increasing the player's edge not only increased his hourly expectation—it dramatically reduced fluctuations as well. Brian had read of several ways to increase his overall edge, and recognized that effectively employing these odd-sounding methods required more than one player. It was time to form a team.

Brian had been living and playing in Vegas for just over a year when, one day in August 1981, he was standing in line at the Golden Nugget coffee shop, waiting for a seat at the counter. There were a couple of scraggly looking guys standing alongside him, waiting in the restaurant line. Brian overheard one of them say something about "a true count of seven," so he suggested that perhaps they should be standing in the "counter" line with him. Introductions immediately followed, and the players began to talk. Their names were Guppy and Reed, they were from Southern California, they had been playing for about a month, and, as Brian soon discovered, they were pretty good.

"I had written a practice counting program for the Tandy, and they tested out fine," Brian said. "They were counting unnecessarily complex counts, but they were counting them well." Without the tools to judge one count against another, Guppy and Reed simply bought Revere's most expensive card-counting system, memorized it, and began to play.

Brian had verified all of the theories about the power of a joint bankroll— one player with $5,000 must play as if he has $5,000, but three players with $5,000 each can pool their money and play as if they *each* have $15,000— and he explained the concept to the two young players, along with methods by which they could increase their edge over the casinos. The three players agreed to form a team.

Before they could think about implementing the more esoteric techniques, though, Brian's new teammates had a lot to learn. The Californians had been playing too long in the same casinos, and had been barred in several. They would have to tailor the length of their playing sessions to the amount of attention they were getting. Usually, heat is some function of the amount of money bet and the amount won, so Brian made a schedule and laid down the law. Sessions were to be limited not only in terms of dollars won or lost, but also in terms of time. No more marathon sessions would be tolerated.

One cardinal sin Reed had committed early on in his career was to run out of money in the middle of a monster shoe. Thinking a grand would be enough for any contingency, he had begun a shoe and proceeded to lose every hand. The count reached plus forty-six as Reed shoved out his last quarter chip, and the dealer got a blackjack. Reed had to leave the casino with a shoe just begging to be had, an unforgivable sin when playing with an edge.

"By the time Brian got through with him, Reed wouldn't have left a positive shoe for anything," Guppy says. "A herd of elephants could have marched through the pit led by a parade of naked women, and Reed would have said, 'Deal the cards.'"

Brian taught his teammates about fluctuations, standard deviations, and cheating. He showed them the results of his computer runs that indicated the financial swings they could expect to experience. In two weeks, Reed and Guppy learned more about the mathematical underpinnings of the game of blackjack than most professional players learn in a career. Although it is the case that the game can be beaten by players blissfully unaware of some of the uglier aspects of the mathematics, it was Brian's esteemed opinion that there was nothing wrong with knowing too much.

One Friday in September, after Brian, Reed, and Guppy had been playing together for about a month, Reed and Guppy left their apartment to play the good double-deck games at the Aladdin, the Dunes, the Silverbird, and the Flamingo Hilton, in that order. They would choose their dealers carefully, spread from one unit to six, play for thirty minutes, and go to the next casino on the list. Brian would stay home and work on a program he was writing. It had something to do with tracking clumps of high cards through the shuffle.

On that same Friday, Alexander Taylor found himself in the Silverbird, bleary-eyed. Except for a few breaks for meals and a couple of fitful naps, he had been playing straight through since Wednesday. He looked bad, felt worse, and smelled terrible. The negative fluctuation seemed to have bottomed out, but he still wasn't winning. He had broken even for the last three days.

Why wasn't he winning? After getting pounded for almost a month, Taylor finally faced head-on the unthinkable possibility that had been tickling the edge of his consciousness for the last several days. Maybe—just maybe—it was him.

He decided to stand behind a table and count without playing, to see if his count would distribute itself somewhat equally around zero. By counting without playing, he could concentrate on the count without the added pressure of having to play his hand while talking to dealers and waitresses. Taylor wandered through the pit until he spotted a table with only one player, and then watched from behind.

The single player was seated in the middle of the table, wearing a threadbare denim jacket, a Caesars Palace T-shirt, and faded jeans. Stringy brown hair stuck out from beneath a blue Los Angeles Dodgers baseball cap. This guy, for whom shopping at Goodwill would have been a step up, pulled a tattered wallet from his jacket and bought in with four hundred-dollar bills. He bet fifty dollars on the first hand out of the deck, and Taylor began to count.

After three rounds the count had risen to seven, indicating an edge for the player of more than 0.5 percent. I would double my bet now, Taylor thought to himself. The player at the table doubled his bet. Taylor hardly noticed.

Another two rounds were dealt, and the player lost both hands as the count soared to plus eleven. Taylor's count indicated a huge edge—he should bet his maximum bet. The player bet two hundred dollars, the table maximum. This time, Taylor noticed.

Son of a bitch! Taylor thought. This guy's counting!

The dealer continued to deal, and the player continued to bet with the count and vary his strategy perfectly. However, Taylor's negative fluctuation seemed to be contagious. The player was getting his ass kicked.

When he was down about a thousand dollars, the player ordered a cocktail. "A double Chivas on the rocks," he told the waitress, in a voice loud enough to be heard throughout the pit.

Taylor bit his lip to keep from smiling. He knew the guy would not drink the cocktail, because most counters cannot drink and continue to play properly. He could hardly contain himself as he waited to see what the guy would do with the Chivas.

By the time the cocktail arrived, the player had lost a couple thousand dollars. The count had dropped to zero, and the player rose to his feet. "Where's the bathroom?" he asked, and left the table with his drink.

Taylor followed the player into the men's room and stood at the sink while the player banged around noisily in a stall. Thirty seconds later he emerged, still carrying his drink.

The player returned to the table, sat, waited for a pit boss to come near the table, and downed the drink in one huge gulp. He gasped, wiped his mouth with the back of his hand, and ordered another.

When the waitress arrived with the second cocktail, the player got to his feet, announced that he had had enough, and walked to the cage to cash out. Taylor watched from behind a bank of slot machines.

After the player finished cashing out, Taylor emerged from behind the slot machines, walked up to him, and said, "I know what you're doing."

The player blanched.

"How long have you been doing this?" Taylor asked.

The player swallowed, his eyes darting furtively around the casino. "Uh, doing what?"

"You know. *This.*"

"I...I...um, I don't know what you're talking about."

Taylor laughed at the player's discomfort. "Don't worry. I do it too."

The player looked a little relieved. "Listen," he said quietly, "I have a partner in here. Let me signal him, and we'll talk outside."

When they met outside, the player introduced himself as Robert Richards. "But everybody calls me Reed," he said, and introduced his quiet partner as Guppy.

Garrulous and open as hell, Reed told Taylor about the count he and Guppy were using, how they had gotten started, where they had been playing, and how they were doing. When Reed asked how Taylor had known what he was doing, Taylor explained what had happened. Reed almost fell over backward when he learned he'd been followed into the men's room, and then produced the small bottle of apple juice with which he had refilled his glass after dumping the Chivas down the toilet.

"Looks just like scotch," said Reed. "Let's go. I want you to meet our partner. The guy knows everything. And he's a computer programmer."

It was Taylor's turn to fall over backward.

When Robert "Reed" Richards graduated high school in 1976, armed with a blue tassel and the free education provided by the Los Angeles Unified

School District, there were few options available to him other than yard work and McDonald's. Reed chose well, and landed a lucrative position waiting tables in Henry's Hamburger Hamlet.

Reed had never planned to become a waiter—who did?—but he also had never expected much better. He had been educated in a school system woefully unprepared for the huge bulge of individuals whose numbers constituted the baby boom. Consequently, he and his classmates had been herded through classes and out the door as quickly and painlessly as possible. Students were more or less on their own, and Reed had gotten out of school exactly what he had put in.

High school had been a nightmare. Reed was not a jock, had the musical ability of a lawn chair, and was far too neurotic to resort to drugs. He did not fit in with any of the available cliques, and his "mod" outfits, hairstyles, and other attempts to conform were met with ridicule. Ultimately, he found himself running with a crowd that consisted largely of himself. Reed resigned himself to his dreams, and his plans for revenge. Someday, he knew, he would show them.

After four years of serving hamburgers, the circumference of his planned vengeance had expanded to include his boss, a dozen or so fellow employees, and hundreds of goddamned customers who treated him like crap. He was, however, still a waiter.

And then it happened. The clouds under which he had been living parted briefly, allowing a brilliant beam of light to shine upon his head. Robert Richards, whose only claim to fame was that not once in the twenty-three years of his existence had he made a favorable impression on anyone, was to be given a chance.

Reed had a cousin who regularly baby-sat for some neighbors while they went out to play poker in Gardena. During a family get-together, Reed's cousin told him about their five-bedroom house with the citrus trees in back and a magnificent view of the ocean. She told him about their great stereo system, their outsized television, and their three cars. And she told him more.

Before Linda and Tom Henke began playing poker, they had enjoyed enormously successful careers as professional blackjack players. They quit not because they wanted to but because after half a decade of play they had been barred from virtually every casino in the state of Nevada. Several of the players with whom they had teamed up continued their careers overseas, but both Linda and Tom wanted to start a family, and neither relished the thought of traveling the world with screaming kids in tow. They had retired from blackjack to play the quiet, mathematically friendly games of lowball in the legal California card rooms. Their screaming kids stayed home with Reed's cousin.

Reed's mind lurched out of neutral. Visions of Mercedes automobiles and exotic foreign locales flooded his stimulus-starved brain. He figured that if the casinos actually resorted to barring certain "professionals"—whatever that meant—those players must have been doing something that really worked. Reed accompanied his cousin to the five-bedroom house the next day, introduced himself to Linda, genuflected, and asked how he could learn to play blackjack. With the solemnity such an occasion deserved—and with an admonition about how tough the games were these days—Linda presented Reed with *Playing Blackjack as a Business.*

He was smitten. Reed carried the book everywhere for three months, devouring every page. He made hundreds of flash cards, and placed decks of naked-lady playing cards strategically in his car, at work, and all over his apartment.

He got no support. His parents told him the mob would kill him, and his friends told him that if the system really worked, the casinos would never have allowed the book to be published. Everyone else just laughed at him.

When Reed returned the book, Linda told him about a place called the "Ungambling Casino" in Placentia, a suburb just south of L. A. It was a dealing school, and the owners had dreamed up a unique way to provide live players to whom the trainees could deal. Players purchased a thousand dollars' worth of phony chips for a buck and played to their hearts' content. The casino would even keep a running account for regular players. Worthless chips weren't much good to degenerate gamblers who got their fix from risking the rent money, but they were perfect for systems players and aspiring card counters.

Reed began driving to Placentia five days a week. No one could have invented a better place for counters to practice blackjack—the game was dealt professionally, the pace was that of the casino version, and the dealers even agreed to spread the remaining cards before they shuffled so that Reed could see if his count was right at the end of the shoe. More often than not, it was.

Against the advice of his mentor, Reed sent a $200 money order to the Lawrence Revere School of Blackjack in Las Vegas for a more advanced card-counting system. Linda said that any additional edge a more complicated count could give him would be marginal at best, and would be eliminated by an increased error rate and slower play due to the increased complexity of the count. Reed figured that a simple count might have worked when Linda was playing, but the increasingly difficult conditions she had warned him about necessitated a more powerful count. In theory, he had a legitimate argument. In practice, he couldn't have been more wrong.

Revere's Advanced Point Count was a bear to learn—it used four different values for small cards and three for big cards—and it was almost a month before Reed could keep up with the dealers at the Ungambling Casino. He lost back most of what he had won previously before he felt comfortable with the count, and then broke even for a few weeks. When Reed attributed his losing streak to his unfamiliarity with the count, Linda launched into an exegesis on mathematical fluctuations. There were horror stories about professional players who had experienced six-month losing streaks, busted bankrolls, and ruined lives.

Reed was having none of it. He was convinced that his more powerful count—more powerful than any count Linda or her husband had ever used—would protect him from the horrible losses she described.

"When I said that, she just shook her head," Reed says now. "There is no way you can appreciate fluctuations until you've experienced them yourself. And there's no way to predict how you're going to react to them, either."

After he had been playing in Placentia for a month, Reed noticed that a quiet guy playing third base at his table was spreading his bets up and down with the count, and playing his hands properly as well. When Reed introduced himself and asked what count he counted, the player looked at him and said, "Are you lookin' at me? Are you lookin' at me?"

"I thought the guy was completely out of his mind," Reed remembers. "I just sat down and stared at him. Then the guy said, 'What's the matter, don't you recognize that? It's from *Taxi Driver*.' It turns out that the guy has a mental storehouse of movie lines, and he just blurts them out when an appropriate situation arises. It's pretty strange, I know, but the guy was a damn good card counter." That guy was Guppy.

Reed and Guppy started talking—or, more accurately, Reed talked while Guppy tried to figure out if there was an end somewhere to this guy's barrage of bullshit. Reed was a master of what his mother euphemistically called "embellishment," which is like saying teenage boys have a mild interest in sex. In Reed's hands incidents were inflated, twisted, and stretched so dramatically that those about whom the stories were being told often failed to recognize themselves. And, not surprisingly, Reed usually emerged from his fanciful accounts with the money, the girl, and well-deserved recognition for his heroics.

There was nothing malicious about Reed's imaginative tales; in fact, it seemed to Guppy that Reed's intention was to see how far he could go before someone stopped him. It was just a game, and he would simply smile and go off on an unrelated tangent as soon as Guppy said, "That's a load of crap." They got along famously.

Bullshit aside, Guppy could see that Reed was a very capable card counter, and they decided to team up. They started to fly to Vegas on "mini-junkets" offered by the Four Queens. Players who put up $300 in front money, drew markers, and played at least eight hours of blackjack with bets of at least five dollars had their airfare paid for and were given a room for the weekend. After two months of mini-junkets, they had broken even and were completely sick of listening to Mo Schepley and the Car Toons, appearing on the stage beyond the far end of the blackjack pit. Then they met Brian, standing in the counter line at the Golden Nugget, and soon learned how little they really knew about the game of blackjack.

When Reed brought Taylor to Brian's apartment less than an hour after they met, Brian reacted predictably. The team had been together for less than a month, and the players still had a lot to learn about each other. Brian had explained such esoterica as spooking and front-loading—two of the techniques about which Brian had read that convinced him to join forces with other players—and the players had attempted an abortive foray into the Sundance. They had made a couple of mistakes, not the least of which was deciding to use Reed as the man betting the big money, and the results were unpleasant. Reed had been barred, and it would be a long time before the security guards at the Sundance would forget the foul-mouthed lunatic they had hauled out to the street. Now Reed had been caught *in flagrante delicto* at the Silverbird by an unknown quantity, and his response was to bring the guy home to meet the family.

"Bullshit," said Brian, after he had reamed out Reed for bringing a player to his apartment without knowing who he was or who he knew, and Reed had responded with a story. When Reed uncharacteristically refused to back down, Brian came out to see for himself.

Although it was the case that Reed didn't know much about Taylor, he did know one thing. Alexander Taylor was the fastest card counter he had ever seen.

When our close cousin the male baboon happens upon a stranger, he grins and displays his genitalia; a curious and—to baboons—decidedly competitive gesture. Civilization and superegos have largely cured us of waving our johnsons at each other, but we have found a variety of interesting substitutes. Businessmen sport dark suits and heavy gold watches, teenagers drive muscle cars with faulty exhaust systems, and card counters count down decks.

All professional-level card-counting systems use what are called balanced counts, which means that all of the card values on the positive side of the ledger neatly cancel out those on the negative side so that every complete deck—or combination of decks—counted properly will result in a count of zero.[5] All good counters have counted down hundreds of decks—pros count down thousands—and a universal method by which counters test themselves and each other is to remove a card from the deck without looking at it and count the remaining cards. Since the count must equal

---

5 There are also "unbalanced counts" which result in counts other than zero. According to Reed, the technical term for such a count is "a piece of shit."

zero at the end of the deck, the count after fifty-one cards tells the counter the count value of the one remaining unseen card. It may look like magic, but it isn't; there's no trickery involved. It's just a basic skill.

When Taylor climbed into Guppy's car in the parking lot behind the Silverbird, Reed fished a dog-eared deck of Horseshoe cards out of the glove box, shuffled them, removed a card, and solemnly handed the remainder of the deck to Taylor. No words were needed. Guppy looked at his watch, waited for the second hand to sweep past the twelve, and said, "Go."

This was something Taylor had done a couple thousand times in the recent past. He had a talent few outside a very small fraternity could appreciate, and he took full advantage of the opportunity. He smoked the deck. When he flipped the fifty-first card and said, "Stop. It's a ten," Guppy stared at his watch.

"That can't be right," Reed said, looking at Guppy's watch, and turned up the king of spades.

"About thirteen seconds?" Taylor asked.

"Twelve," said Guppy.

Reed wanted to see it again. His best time was eighteen seconds, and he had done that only once.

Taylor did it again, this time in just under twelve seconds. "Two or a seven," he said when he finished. (Both twos and sevens are assigned a value of plus one in the count Taylor used, and his fifty-one-card deck had ended with a count of minus one. Either card would make the deck total zero.) Reed was holding a seven.

It was to Reed's account of Taylor's prowess that Brian was referring when he expressed the aforementioned "Bullshit!" When Brian came out to see for himself, Taylor repeated the performance in eleven seconds, and Reed asked Brian not to ask to see it again. "The bastard's just getting faster," he said.

The vote was unanimous. Taylor became a member of their team.

CHAPTER 6
SPOOKING

It is the dealer's responsibility to hide her card. It is not
the responsibility of the player to look the other way.
~*Nevada Supreme Court*, Einbinder and
Dalton v. Sheriff

They had known each other two days when Brian—his face illuminated like a bad kaleidoscope by the lights of Fremont Street—handed Taylor a roll of hundreds as thick as his wrist and said, "Here's five grand. Good luck." Before Taylor could say anything, Brian said, "I know. You're not going anywhere, and don't ask me how I know."

Given the rules by which ordinary businessmen conduct themselves, Brian's behavior might seem inordinately risky. But the rules by which professional gamblers operate must allow for the possibility of some major negative fluctuations in a department that would be labeled "petty theft" in a more traditional business atmosphere. Team members often play alone, and when they report back to their teammates at the end of the day they leave no tangible audit trail to be checked. If a player reports a thousand-dollar loss when in fact he spent the afternoon guzzling beers at the Crazy Horse Saloon, there is no way his teammates are going to know the difference in the short run. In the long run, his overall win rate *vis-à-vis* his expectation curve may show an unacceptable gap, but by then, that player could easily have retired and taken to guzzling beers in Hawaii.

Although it happens, professional blackjack players rarely steal from each other. There are several reasons for this. First, it doesn't make financial sense. Anybody intelligent enough to learn a professional-level card-counting system is bright enough to know that, in the long run, far more money can be made playing with one's teammates than stealing from them. And, in a subculture where a reputation for dishonesty cannot be explained away or overcome, one incident is enough to send a player off alone, forever.

As easy as it would be to steal, the fact is that those few blackjack players who do so are usually caught. In their dealings with pit bosses and other casino personnel, all successful pros develop a keen antenna tuned to such things as body language and emblematic leaks, and this sense serves them well when dealing with teammates.

Beyond that, there is a bond between players engaged in a higher quest. They have more than a little in common—they've given society's traditional values the high hard one, and they share the desire to beat the evil, greedy casinos at their own game.

So when Brian handed Taylor the wad of fifty greenbacks sporting the leering Francophile who flew kites and spewed aphorisms with equal facility, he had already assigned a probability of near zero to Taylor's fleeing with the money. His mind, busy as always, had moved on to the business at hand—the upcoming play. Guppy had located a dealer with a particular weakness at the Mint, and Taylor's first chore as a member of a blackjack team was going to be the front man for a three-man enterprise referred to in the business as *spooking*.

As is the case with any enterprise faced with complexity, card counters have developed a rich lexicon all their own—a jargon needed to describe the particular circumstances of their unique trade. Some of this vocabulary is shared with the rest of society. "I got home late and my wife gave me *massive heat*," or "After calling in sick, George ran into his boss on the golf course yesterday; *bad fluctuation*," are phrases intelligible to someone who has never heard those terms used in that context.

There are other terms, however, that relate only to the specific arena for which they were originally coined. Activities like front-loading and first-basing will never be engaged in by more than an inconceivably small percentage of society, so the terms—rightfully—will remain the purview of those who play blackjack for a living.

Spooking falls into this latter category. Almost certainly borrowed from the CIA's argot for "spy," counters use "spook" as both a noun and a verb, and—strangely—they use it to describe both ends of the transaction. A spook is both a dealer who can be spooked and the individual perpetrating the spooking. Spooking is one of the "other things" that had prompted Brian's fateful decision to form a team.

In all Nevada casinos in 1981, dealers peeked beneath their tens and aces to see if they had a blackjack. If the dealer had an ace beneath a ten or a ten beneath an ace, the hole card was flipped up, the players' money was scooped, and the hand was over. If she did not, however, the players continued to play their hands. On average, a dealer with a ten up-card will have an ace beneath it only one hand in thirteen, so in twelve of thirteen hands the dealer would hoist her ten into the air, peek beneath it, and then turn to the players to ask how they wanted to play their hands.

In order to peek beneath that ten or that ace, the dealer must lift the hole card high enough to see it. In doing so, about one dealer in fifty lifted the card high enough so that somebody with relatively good eyesight standing somewhat behind her could also see the card. The individual lurking behind the dealer—usually somewhere across the pit, since most blackjack pits are arranged in roughly elliptical configurations—is spying from behind. Hence the term "spooking." That the dealer is also called a "spook" simply highlights the fact that blackjack players involved in this nefarious activity are less interested in lexicography than in the edge this activity provides.

When Taylor slapped four hundred-dollar bills onto the unique red felt with which the blackjack tables in Del Webb's Mint were covered and said—per Brian's instructions—"Give me some green ones," he was the only member of his team the casino was meant to notice. He was going to have a lot of help and, if everything went according to plan, there still would be only three people in the world who knew what had transpired. Playing blackjack on this level was performing a high-wire act for an audience that would know there had been a show only if one of the performers fell.

Her name was Ruth. "Thirty-five, short, big tits, name tag says she's from Idaho," Guppy had reported. Almost certainly a nice enough person, but her most endearing characteristic was pointedly absent from Guppy's description. Ruth had a horrible weakness.

It first happened about twelve hands into the session. Ruth was dealing out of a four-deck shoe, and Taylor was flat-betting one hundred dollars per hand. A thick-necked pit boss—who had been sufficiently interested in Taylor's buy-in to write it down in a small, spiral-bound notebook—was rapidly losing interest in the game. No one can beat a four-deck game flat-betting.

Ruth dealt Taylor a pair of nines, and dealt herself a ten up-card. She peeked beneath it, and waited for Taylor to play his hand.

Taylor split his nines.

When the first computers became available for nonmilitary applications in the middle of the 1950s, several groups of mathematicians indulged themselves in a Bayesian study of the game of blackjack; that is, they directed the computer to figure out what a player should do with any given hand versus any given up-card. Although it turned out that there are a number of plays existing on a hair-thin line between one decision and an alternative, a pair of nines against a ten was not one of them. Under no circumstances, said the computer, should a player *ever* split a pair of nines against the dealer's ten.

Taylor split his nines.

He hit his first nine with a ten, stood with his total of nineteen, and hit his second nine with a five. Fourteen.

Not surprisingly, the computer had an opinion on this hand as well. It wasn't as categorical as it had been in the case of the nines against a ten, but it was close. Only under very unusual circumstances that arise at the bottom of the pack every thirty shoes or so will a player stand with a fourteen against the dealer's ten. Taylor was halfway through his first shoe.

Taylor stood with his fourteen against the dealer's ten. The pit boss smiled.

Ruth flipped up her hole card. There was a four of spades lurking beneath her ten, and she hit with the jack of diamonds. Boom.

> "Oh my god, the quarterback is *toast*."
> –Theo (*Clarence Gilyard*) in Die Hard

"I'll never forget the first time," Taylor says. "When I saw her flip up that big, fat four of spades, I felt like the assistant in a magic trick."

Or maybe the guy in the top hat and tux. Guppy, the assistant hiding in the crowd and without whose visual acuity this trick would have been impossible, was seated across the pit quietly playing two dollars a hand, invisible to Taylor behind Ruth. Brian manned third base at Taylor's table. Unlike Taylor—and not incidentally—Brian could see Guppy just fine.

Brian's logbook shows that over the course of the next four hours, Ruth had a ten up seventy-eight times. Each time she showed a ten, Brian rested his chin on his left hand. Each time he did so, Guppy glanced across the pit and beneath Ruth's right arm just as she was hoisting that ten into the air to check for the ace that would give her a blackjack. Four times she found it. The other seventy-four times Guppy sent a signal.

If Ruth had a *pat* hand—that is, a seven, eight, nine, or ten beneath her ten—Guppy touched the right side of his face. If she was *stiff*—a two, three, four, five, or six in the hole—he touched the left side. On those peeks where he wasn't able to see Ruth's hole card, he didn't signal at all.

Rather ingenious, except that Taylor couldn't see Guppy. Certain parts of Ruth's ample anatomy were in the way. Guppy's signals, however, weren't meant for Taylor. Not yet.

When Brian received Guppy's signals he translated them for Taylor. Mouth open meant pat, closed meant stiff, left hand remaining on his chin meant no signal.

To those who know how the trick is done, these signals look about as subtle as semaphore, and Taylor did his best not to watch the show. He simply glanced at Brian on those hands for which the additional information could help, and studiously ignored him the rest of the time.

After the first few calls went smoothly and the pit bosses weren't on the phone, the security guards weren't breathing down his neck, and the guys in the sky hadn't fallen through the ceiling, Taylor began to relax. His bets began to spread a bit with the count. He told Ruth a few clean jokes, and she pretended to enjoy them. He ordered a beer and nursed it. Brian's signals were impossible to miss. Taylor had agreed to avoid such hair-raising plays as splitting tens and doubling down with totals of four and five—correct plays when the dealer is stiff, but too obvious. "We'll have to give a little to get a lot," Brian said, and during Taylor's initiation into the world of spooking they did both.

By the time the first couple of shoes were dealt out, all of the tension in the pit had dissipated. The pit boss was convinced Taylor was a poor player, so he wasn't draped over the table making Ruth nervous. The more relaxed she got, the higher she hoisted that ten to check beneath it. And the higher she hoisted it, the better Guppy liked it.

The rhythm would have been beautiful to behold—had there been anyone to behold it. Out came the cards, face up in front of the players. If Ruth had anything other than a ten up, Taylor just played Basic Strategy. If she had a ten up and he had a pat hand, he didn't bother looking at Brian—he simply waved Ruth off and continued talking to the bearded mailman sitting next to him. Only when Ruth had a ten up and Taylor had a hand for which he had a decision to make would he reach for his drink and stall momentarily so the signals could traverse the pit from Brian to Guppy and back, and then register on Brian's face.

Every forty-five minutes Ruth was replaced while she took her fifteen-minute break, and Taylor escaped to the men's room for a few minutes. Because the Mint was a "return joint"—a casino in which the dealers return to the same table for the duration of their shift—Taylor stayed in the same seat all evening. Although just as many spookable dealers could be found in "rubber-band joints"—so called because the dealers returning from their breaks are sent to different tables by a pit boss who consults a clipboard and rolls a rubber band, cinching its width along the names of the dealers—they were more difficult to play because the entire operation had to get up and follow the dealer every hour. It looked every bit as ridiculous as it sounds, and it was in part this chasing behavior that had caused Reed's downfall in the Sundance several weeks earlier.

Only once during the session did Guppy make a mistake. Ruth lifted her ten a bit shallower than usual, and Guppy caught a glimpse of white in the middle of the hole card. He signaled "stiff," indicating Ruth had a total between twelve and sixteen, which meant Taylor was to stand with any total greater than eleven. Taylor had a ten and a fifteen, so he doubled the ten and stood with his fifteen.

When Ruth flipped up her hole card, there was a rude surprise. She had a seven lurking beneath her ten, giving her a total of seventeen. Taylor lost his bet with his fifteen, but got lucky and won on his double down. Guppy attempted to crawl under his table.

As Brian explained later, the spook only rarely sees the index—the value printed in the upper right-hand corner of the cards. He usually sees the pattern of the pips. Upside-down sevens look exactly like sixes, and there is nothing anybody can do about it. Upside-down sevens are part of the overhead in the spook business.

After four hours Brian decided to end the session. The Mint had seen quite a bit of the show, and quitting too soon was infinitely preferable to quitting too late. He asked the relief dealer for the time, and then pointedly tipped her five bucks.

Taylor stood up, stretched, and said, "I think I'm going to call it a night." As he began gathering the piles of green and black chips that had accumulated during the play, a pit boss came over and handed him a wooden rack. As Taylor filled the rack with his chips, the pit boss offered his business card and his hand.

"Name's Eddie Carozza," he said.

"Larry. Larry Mercer," Taylor replied, shaking hands.

"Can I get you anything, Larry? Something to eat? The coffee shop's still open."

"No, thanks. I have to get some sleep."

"Well, come back and see us again, Mr. Mercer. Thanks for gambling at the Mint."

They met back at Sassy Sally's about thirty minutes later, and Brian knew he had found what the players called the *Big Player*, or BP—the guy who shoves the money out. Taylor didn't know it, but he had been preparing for this role since "TV Magic Cards" and high school. When Taylor left the table to cash out, Brian had remained behind. The pit boss counted down the rack, figured Taylor had won about $3,600, grunted, and said, "Asshole."

Taylor had left the right impression, and had shown his teammates that he possessed the two most important attributes of the professional gambler—*cojones*.

Some might argue that with this play Taylor crossed an unspoken moral boundary, if not a legal one. Keeping track of which cards have been dealt and then playing accordingly is one thing. Employing someone to peek at the dealer's hole card from behind and send surreptitious signals across the pit is a different bucket of smelt. Even a five-year-old knows it is cheating when you look at another player's cards.

Taylor would run headlong into the legal issue later in his career. The short answer is that spooking is completely legal. As far as morality is concerned, as Reed says, "This ain't Go Fish."

This first foray into the world of high-stakes professional blackjack changed Taylor's view of his new career dramatically. Until this session, Taylor had focused almost all of his energy on the skills he learned from Revere's book. His job had been to count perfectly, and then bet and play according to that count. With the spook play his job description had changed. From this day forward, Taylor's counting skills would remain necessary, but would take a backseat to what professional players call "the act."

For the most part, players who bet nickels ($5 chips) can sit in a casino for hours, methodically raising and lowering their bets as the count rises and falls. If a casino notices this behavior the counter will be barred—a casino will not knowingly deal to *anyone* playing with an edge—but it is a simple matter for the small-stakes player to blend in with the rest of the great unwashed. However, once a counter begins betting quarters or blacks—especially blacks—he will no longer blend in. He will be the focus of attention of everyone from dealers to pit bosses to the guys in the "eye in the sky."

According to Revere and most other system sellers, the ideal strategy for the professional player is to slink into a casino, play with an edge, and slink out again without being noticed. This is surely a noble sentiment, but not a terribly practical one. When you shove a stack of black chips out onto the layout, you *will* be noticed. It's that simple. At that point, you had better figure out some way to convince all those curious onlookers that you are just an ordinary gambler with too much money for your own good. If you don't, you soon will find yourself with a one-way escort to the front door.

In the spooking session, Guppy was necessary to obtain an edge. Without his visual acuity, coupled with his strategic position across the pit, there would have been no edge to be had. Brian, however, wasn't strictly needed to obtain an edge. He was there for one reason—misdirection. Cover. He was part of the act.

Over the course of the next several months, Taylor would learn a lot more about acting than he ever thought he cared to know. And his most profound lessons would come from a pair of unlikely sources.

At this level, card counting in and of itself is like treading water. It is a *sine qua non* without which you cannot gain that all-important edge over the house. But to carry what was until recently the casino's money past the security guards and out the front door with all of your body parts intact requires more than the ability to add several numbers rapidly and do a little division in your head. You need an act. Taylor figured he had a choice of one or several of the following:

1) Rich
2) Stupid
3) Horny
4) Drunk
5) Happy
6) Sleepy
7) Any of the remaining Seven Dwarfs except Doc

Here's how he couldn't act:

1) Smart

> The most difficult character in comedy is that of the fool,
> and he must be no simpleton that plays that part.
> ~*Miguel de Cervantes*, Don Quixote

But there was more to the session than the act. The spook play was the first time Taylor applied a second-tier version of misdirection against a casino. There is a bit of recursion here (and not for the last time), so hang on.

By the time Taylor started playing blackjack in 1981, most casino personnel knew how to detect card counters. Look for someone who bets low, waits for a number of small cards to come out, and then bets big. That's your man.

This is what the casinos knew. Importantly, Taylor and his teammates knew that the casinos knew this. And, they knew that the casinos didn't know—or, at least didn't *act* as if they knew—that the players knew this. So, if the players could play without raising and lowering their bets, they would turn the casino's expertise on its head. Taylor clearly wasn't counting at the Mint (because the bosses knew what counting looked like, and that wasn't it), so they let him play. Ironically, had the bosses known nothing about counting, they likely would have had a better shot at pulling up the spook play, because they wouldn't have dismissed Taylor as a non-counter!

Brian's excitement with Taylor's success at the Mint was directly related to this. The act, coupled with turning the casino's knowledge against itself, proved to be as powerful as he had hoped. The spook play had been a success in its own right. However, it was an indicator of much bigger things to come. Spooking was possible against only a small fraction of casino dealers. When the computer program that Brian was writing was finally loaded into a piece of hardware and carried into a casino for the first time, it would provide much greater cover than the spook play had, while being possible against virtually every dealer in the world. And that was the real beauty of what was to become known as *shuffle tracking*.

But that was several months and many dollars into the future, and it wasn't going to be easy. In the meantime, there was money to be made.

In an attempt to stem the tide of card counters flooding into Las Vegas as a result of the publication in 1969 of Lawrence Revere's *Playing Blackjack as a Business*, the casinos slowly began the introduction of multiple-deck games. Replacing single decks with multiple decks indeed adversely affects card counters, but not in the way most people think. Four or even six decks are not significantly more difficult to count than single decks, *Rain*

Man notwithstanding. They are, however, significantly more difficult to beat.

The reason that the game of blackjack is beatable by skilled players is something called the *effects of removal* of the various cards in the deck. It is because the effect of removing an ace from a deck or decks differs from the effect of removing a five that the game can be beaten. What multiple decks do is dilute these effects of removal, and that is what makes games played with multiple decks so much more difficult to beat.

When you play perfect Basic Strategy against a single deck on the Las Vegas Strip, you are for all intents and purposes playing an even game.[6] If you remove one ace from that deck (let's say it was the burn card), you are now faced with a disadvantage of 0.61 percent. That is because the effect of removing one ace from a single deck is to increase the casino's advantage by 0.61 percent.

If, however, the dealer burns a five instead of an ace, your advantage shoots up to 0.69 percent. That is because the effect of removing one five from a single deck is to increase the player's advantage by 0.69 percent.

In terms of its effect of removal, each card has a unique contribution to make. What follows are the effects of removal for betting[7] for each card, given Vegas Strip rules[8]:

A	**2**	**3**	**4**	**5**	**6**	**7**	**8**	**9**	**T**
−0.61	0.38	0.44	0.55	0.69	0.46	0.28	−0.00	−0.18	−0.51

---

6 Actually, the "perfect" Basic Strategy player—using all possible multiple-card decisions—plays with an advantage of 0.02 percent. The typical Basic Strategy player plays with a disadvantage of 0.00015 percent, meaning that for every $10,000 in action shoved out on the table, this player's expectation is to lose fifteen cents. Close enough to even for our purposes.

7 The effects differ slightly for playing strategy, due largely to the schizophrenic nature of the ace. When playing the hand, aces act for the most part like small cards. See appendix 3 for a more complete explanation.

8 Because rules differ, the effects of removal of certain of the cards differ as well. For instance, in Northern Nevada, where soft doubling is forbidden, the removal of an ace is not quite as devastating to the player.

These are the effects of removing individual cards from a single deck. When casinos began foisting multiple decks on the multitudes in the early '70s, the direction of the effects of removal didn't change. The removal of aces, tens, and, to a lesser extent, nines still favor the casino, and the removal of small cards still favor the player. What multiple decks do is greatly dilute these effects.

First, because of the additional cards, the player playing perfect Basic Strategy on the Las Vegas Strip is no longer playing an even game. Against four decks the off-the-top disadvantage is 0.48 percent. Half a percent might not sound like much, but after eight or ten hours of play at twenty bucks a hand, it is the difference between staying another night and taking that long bus ride home.

How does the addition of a few decks increase the Basic Strategy player's off-the-top disadvantage? It does so by diluting the effects of removal.

Here's an example: When playing a single deck, Basic Strategy dictates that you double down against the dealer's five or six if you have a hand totaling eight that consists of a 5-3 or a 4-4. However, you do not double with an eight consisting of 6-2. Why not? Because the hands containing the 5-3 and the 4-4 consist of cards that are very helpful to the dealer when she has a five or a six up. The fact that they are in your hand means they are unavailable to her—unavailable as hit cards or as hole cards—and therefore doubling down is the correct play. However, the hand containing the 6-2 consists of cards that are not quite as valuable, so doubling down is no longer correct.

When a few decks are added, however, Basic Strategy dictates that you *never* double down with a total of eight against the dealer's five or six, no matter what your eight consists of. That is because the removal of that 5-3 or that 4-4 is no longer so dramatic. It is diluted by all the other threes, fours, and fives that are still left to be dealt.

Increasing the off-the-top disadvantage the player faces is not the most significant consequence of the addition of those extra decks. Still more detrimental to the professional is that far more cards must be removed from multiple decks before the information gleaned from the removal of those cards becomes significant. In a six-deck shoe, *thirty-three* cards must be seen before the player gains the same information available from glimpsing just one card from a single deck.

This dilution of the effects of removal of various cards does not make multiple-deck games invulnerable to the skilled player. What it does is make the skilled player more obvious to the pit and to the guys in the sky. Whereas a counter can beat a single deck by spreading his bets from one to two, and kill it to the tune of a 1.5 percent edge by spreading from one to four, that same counter must spread on average from one to ten to obtain the same edge in a four-deck game. In terms of attempting to remain inconspicuous, a bet spread of one to ten is about as effective as firing a bottle rocket into the pit.

Because of a need both to increase their bet spread and hide the fact that they were doing just that, blackjack teams began employing what was to become known as the *BP-Spotter Routine*. Pioneered by an individual named Frank Sandler, this strategy successfully disguised the large bet spreads necessary to obtain a substantial edge in the new multiple-deck games. Later, and entirely unwittingly, Frank Sandler would play a tangential role in what was to become The Ultimate Edge. Now, however, his influence on Taylor and his teammates was more direct.

In 1974, Ken Uston was introduced to Frank Sandler. Sandler taught Uston the intricacies of the BP-Spotter Routine, and Uston reciprocated a few years later by publishing the details for all the world to see. Two members of the world's population at that time were Brian Manning and Alexander Taylor.

Another author writing in the mid-seventies was an individual who called himself Stanford Wong. In *Professional Blackjack*—a book that would become a classic—Wong said that if it is indeed the large bet spread that was giving counters away, then the large bet spread had to go. Flat bet, said Wong, and all your dreams will come true.

Unfortunately, though, and as Wong well knew, multiple-deck games cannot be beaten by flat-betting from start to finish. So Wong suggested that players stand behind the table and count. If the count goes down, sayeth Wong, simply move on to another table. If, however, the count goes up, the *back counter* could jump into the game with his maximum bet and play either until the count comes down or the shoe runs out. Employing this strategy, the counter would play only hands for which he had an edge, and effectively have a minimum bet of zero when the casino had an edge.

This method quickly became known as *Wonging*, and almost as quickly was burned out by the great number of players circling pits like vultures and swooping down on tables at which small cards had come out. But Brian had other ideas.

In July 1981, eight months after the disastrous fire that helped launch Taylor's career, the MGM Grand reopened. Two months later, and with the respect such an occasion deserved, Brian introduced Taylor to his Wonging version of the BP-Spotter Routine.

During the three weeks following the successful spooking assault on the Mint Brian had stayed home, working on what at this stage was simply referred to as The Project, while Taylor, Reed, and Guppy played the good single-deck games at the Holiday, the Silver Slipper, the Castaways, the Frontier, and Caesars Palace. Overall they experienced a positive fluctuation—Guppy won more than seven grand in one session at Caesars—so by the time the players were ready to hit the MGM, they were one good win away from breaking the bank.

Taylor was the only member of the team to enter the MGM through the main entrance. He wore a rented suit and a name tag pinned to his left breast pocket—courtesy of a friend of Brian's who owned a print shop. The name tag indicated that Taylor was an agent with Sands Realty named Bert Schummann.

Taylor's teammates were already scattered around the main pit. They had filtered in through three of the MGM's various entrances. Now they were hanging around, dressed neither well nor poorly. Under no circumstances were they to attract attention.

Dealt at the tables were five-deck shoes. Realtors—real realtors with real name tags—had filled the hotel for a convention and the casino was jammed. It was not difficult for Taylor's teammates to blend in with the mass of humanity slowly circulating throughout the pit.

Finding a crowded craps table with a good view of the rest of the pit, Taylor feigned interest in the game while he watched his teammates, who were busy standing behind different tables in the main pit.

Moments later, Taylor saw Brian put his right hand in his back pocket, but he removed it two rounds later. False alarm. Then Guppy did the same thing. Taylor relaxed and listened to a guy at the craps table begging the dice to cooperate. Glancing around the pit Taylor spotted Reed, and never found out if the dice had heard the shooter's plea.

Both of Reed's hands were jammed into his back pockets. Taylor walked straight toward Reed, his finger on his nose. Reed turned, arms crossed, with three fingers of his left hand extended on his right bicep. Then he walked away.

Running count of twenty-eight, Taylor thought, taking a spot at the table. He bought in for five hundred, saying, "Let me have some of those green ones." The dealer smiled and counted out his chips. As she did so, Taylor looked at the discard rack. It contained about two decks. Two decks gone, three decks left. He did the arithmetic automatically. Twenty-eight divided by three—a true count of a little over nine. Almost a 2 percent edge. He bet two hands of $150 each.

After four rounds had been dealt the count dropped to plus three. The edge was gone. Taylor pocketed his chips and walked. No one had said a word to him.

Ordinarily, a player betting "a buck and a half" a hand would have attracted some attention, but not tonight. Taylor's bets had been the smallest action at his table. The real estate business was good.

Another shoe heated up, and Taylor started toward Brian. Brian's arms were crossed, with one finger on his left forearm. Thirty-one, thought Taylor, digging chips from his pockets and eyeballing the discard rack. Divide by two and a half. Big edge. Over 2 percent. He bet two hands of $200. No one noticed.

For the next four hours Taylor wandered around the casino, seemingly choosing tables at random and playing a few hands. Between hot shoes he would count his chips and mutter, but the act really wasn't necessary. The huge crowd eliminated the need for an actual act.

The only real work involved was the betting. Most professional card counters use a version of something called the Kelly Betting Criterion to dictate how much to bet on a given hand, and Taylor's team was no different. Kelly dictates are simple in principle: figure out your edge and bet that percentage of your bankroll. Due to rounding, estimation errors, and because players have to bet when the house has an edge, Brian opted for caution. His teammates figured out their edge and then bet half that percentage of their bankroll. It wasn't absolutely optimal betting, but it avoided overbetting—the downfall of many aspiring professional gamblers.

Technically the session was perfect. The signaling was smooth, and the back counters were completely hidden by the huge crowds. Taylor won eight hundred bucks—slightly under expectation for the action he had shoved across the table—but the realtors would be in town through the weekend. Taylor needed to win just over two grand to double the $20,000 bankroll the team had started only four weeks earlier.

But it was not to be. By the end of the weekend, Taylor was down a few hundred dollars. There was nothing wrong with the team's performance; Taylor just didn't win. It wasn't a return of the monster negative fluctuation he had been suffering when he met Reed, but it was annoying. He was getting ground down like any other degenerate gambler playing without an edge. Taylor knew in his head that it was only a minor negative fluctuation, but he couldn't help but feel some responsibility for the loss.

Although Brian repeatedly told Taylor not to worry about short-term results, Taylor sensed some restlessness. Brian was very anxious to win the remaining three grand, break the bank, and travel to Lake Tahoe for a gambling conference.

Brian had read abstracts of a few of the papers that were going to be presented at "The Fifth Annual Conference on Gambling and Risk-Taking," and it sounded like the kind of thing he adored. Pure theory. Blackjack in a Petri dish, studied in a pristine, purified environment by theoreticians who write formulae in thick notebooks and run long computer simulations. None of the worldly contaminants that befoul the game as played with real money in real casinos, wreaking havoc with their calculations. Most of the papers submitted to the conference explored blackjack as if it were played in a laboratory.

The team could have continued the bank in Tahoe during the conference, but Brian was opposed to that. Breaking the bank involved a party—it was mandatory—and Brian didn't want to interrupt the conference for a drunken binge. They would do their best to break the bank in Vegas before the conference began.

Reed and Guppy were eager to break the bank as well. A bank break is more than just a payday. It gives everyone a chance to relax, and provides underfinanced players the opportunity to take a larger fraction of the next bank. And, because of the way blackjack banks are split up, it is in the players' interest to break a bank and begin playing on a new one as often as possible.

When the BP-Spotter Routine crapped out at the MGM, Reed reminded Brian of an agreement they had made prior to the play. It was now Reed's turn to be the Big Player. Not everybody experiences the self-satisfaction that accrues from performing well as a spotter. Reed wanted to shove some money out, starring in something called the "Gorilla BP Routine" at the Golden Nugget. Brian disagreed, arguing that the team should try to put the bank over the top playing the single-deck game at Caesars Palace.

Most gamblers think that blackjack is the same wherever it is played. Well, blackjack is not blackjack is not blackjack, a lyrical player might wax poetic. Rules, number of decks, and depth of the deal all must be considered to figure out how much a given game is worth. Just because the game being dealt is blackjack doesn't necessarily mean that it can be beaten by professional players, or beaten to the tune of, say, 2 percent.

Theoretically, Caesars single-deck blackjack game was the best game offered in Nevada, and one of the best games in the world. Caesars dealt a single deck, with Vegas Strip rules, double-after splits, and late surrender. Whether they knew it or not, Basic Strategy players actually played with an edge without counting.

For the first time, Taylor sided with Reed. Caesars single deck nicely demonstrated the difference between a theoretical edge and a practical one. Although Caesars provided a theoretical edge that was the highest in all of Nevada (0.25 percent edge off the top), the actual dollar value of the game was not that great. Standing behind one of the two single-deck tables at Caesars and counting the number of hands the players were dealt per hour, Taylor figured that the players were averaging only fifty hands per hour, largely due to the fact that the tables were always full.

Playing alone, Taylor and his teammates could play over two hundred hands per hour, thus earning four times as much playing a different game simply because of the increase in the number of hands played. Those are the kinds of practical considerations that are often overlooked in the Petri dish studies of which Brian was so fond.

Another consideration that would not fit neatly into that Petri dish was Reed's Gorilla BP Routine, which entailed getting drunk and acting obnoxious at the table. He was able to play properly because he received signals from a team member sitting at the table with him. A Gorilla BP play was great fun for the Big Player—all he had to do was remember a few signals and act like a Neanderthal—but it was a lot of work for the small player.

Reluctantly, Brian agreed to the Gorilla BP play. He possessed information Taylor didn't—Brian had seen Reed play the Gorilla before, and it made him nervous. Usually, blackjack players avoid getting barred by attracting as little attention to themselves as possible. Avoiding attention was not part of Reed's repertoire.

Taylor found a double-deck game at the Golden Nugget in downtown Las Vegas and began playing, betting the table minimum. Reed—ever the conscientious professional—was in the men's bathroom gargling with scotch.

After ten minutes of killing every germ within five yards of his mouth, Reed staggered over to the table. He was wearing an orange and brown plaid jacket, green pants, and a wide purple tie.

"Look!" he exclaimed, pointing at one of the players at the table. "Ladies and gentlemen, Humphrey Bogart!" The man Reed referred to only remotely resembled Humphrey Bogart. Taylor covered his face with his hands.

"How you doin'?" Reed asked the dealer, breathing heavily enough to give her the full benefit of the scotch. "I better win some goddamn money, or my girlfriend's gonna castrate me." He pantomimed the assault on his manhood in case she had missed the allusion, then threw four hundred-dollar bills on the table and ordered a drink.

"Changing four hundred!" the dealer called out over her shoulder. A pit boss arrived at the table and conspicuously scribbled in a small notebook.

"Look, everybody!" Reed announced, pointing at the pit boss. "Jack Klugman!" Jack Klugman frowned and stepped back several paces.

Reed began playing, raising and lowering his bets according to the position of the chip in Taylor's betting circle. If Taylor's bet was at the bottom of the circle, Reed bet his minimum bet: between $25 and $50. If it was in the middle of the circle, Reed would bet a middle bet: around $100. If Taylor's bet was near the top of the circle, Reed bet a top bet: between $200 and $300, or two hands of from $150 to $200. Most card counters raise and lower their bets mechanically as the count rises and falls. It was hoped that a measure of flexibility in his betting scheme would disguise the fact that Reed was indeed betting with the count.

Whenever Reed looked at his cards, he lifted them at an angle so Taylor could see them. If Taylor wanted Reed to hit his hand, he played with his chips. If he wanted Reed to stand, he put his right hand on the felt. Two hands on the felt meant Reed should put more money—double down or split, whichever was appropriate for the hand he held.

A leggy waitress appeared with Reed's drink. He took it right off her tray and downed it. "Thanks, baby," he said. "I'll have another of those. And here," he added, flipping her a five-dollar chip, "put that in your bra."

Reed glanced at Taylor's signal, took a hit, and turned to Humphrey Bogart. "You here for the golf tournament?" he asked.

"Yeah."

"Me too," Reed belched, taking a swing with an imaginary club. "Played sixteen holes this morning."

"Sixteen?" Humphrey Bogart asked. "What happened?"

"What happened? I played damn well, that's what happened."

"I mean, why didn't you finish?"

"Huh? Oh, I—well—look! Lucille Ball!"

The woman to whom Reed referred looked about as much like Lucille Ball as Ernest Borgnine. She did, however, have red hair.

"Hey, baby," Reed said to the dealer, "lemme ask you something."

"Sir, please," said the dealer, turning away. "If you don't mind, please don't breathe on me."

"Lemme ask you," Reed repeated, leaning toward her, "are you married?"

"Sir, please just play your hand."

A pit boss hawking the game stepped up to the table and asked the dealer if everything was all right. Before she could respond, Reed blasted him with a blend of scotch he wouldn't soon forget.

"Sure!" he exhaled. "Everything's great. How are you tonight?"

"Fine," he answered curtly. He stepped back a few paces, crossed his arms, and watched Reed play.

Reed turned to Humphrey Bogart conspiratorially, speaking loudly enough for the dealer to hear. "Didja hear about the new pit boss doll? You fill it with water, and it sweats for eight hours!" The dealer failed to suppress a smile.

Reed looked at his cards, an eight and a nine, and dropped them face up on the table. "Split 'em," he said, putting another hundred dollars out on the table.

"Sir, you can't split those," the dealer said impatiently. "You don't have a pair." Smirking, the pit boss turned away from the table.

Reed stared at his cards. "Oh, I'm sorry. Gee, I thought I had two sixes. I changed my mind. I want to stand." He tucked his cards, looked around the pit, and banged his fist on the table hard enough to make the chips in the dealer's rack jump. "Jesus Christ, what's a guy gotta do to get a drink around here?"

"You just ordered, sir," the dealer snapped.

Reed leaned on the table and gazed at her. "Listen, baby," he said, gesturing for her to come closer. "What's the difference between a blackjack dealer and a Mercedes?"

Trying to ignore him, the dealer said nothing.

"Not everybody has had a Mercedes!" Reed bellowed, and laughed uproariously.

The dealer glared at him, dealt herself a ten up, and peeked underneath it. Taylor saw the muscles in her jaw tighten after she peeked.

Reed had a fourteen, and Taylor signaled a hit. Reed busted. Too bad. The dealer had a five under her ten, and would have busted.

Two hands later the dealer had another ten up, and again peeked. This time her jaw muscles did not tighten. Reed played his hand, and now the dealer had a ten under her ten—a total of twenty.

Taylor was surprised. The dealer wanted so badly to beat Reed, her hand actually showed on her face. When she knew he had a bad hand, she clenched her teeth. When she had a good hand, she relaxed.

In the next twenty minutes, she had a ten up four times, and Taylor was able to read her face three of those times. These inadvertent physiological responses—called "tells"—had been described in detail in *Winning Without Counting*, another book written by Stanford Wong. Although tells are an indispensable part of a winning poker player's strategy, they were relatively rare in blackjack.

After forty minutes Guppy replaced Taylor at the table. Guppy would signal for forty minutes and, unless Reed was ahead $3,000 by then, Brian would then relieve him.

Brian never made it to the table. Slurring and slobbering, Reed won a couple of big double downs. After only ten minutes with Guppy, Reed had a big stack of black chips. By now he was far too drunk to count his chips, so Guppy eyeballed the stack. He estimated that Reed had about $3,500 in front of him. Close enough, Guppy decided. It was time to party. He signaled Reed to leave by asking the dealer for the time. Reed stood, knocked over his stool, and staggered to the cage. What an exit. What an act.

CHAPTER 7

TAHOE: EPISODE 1

My advice to the unborn is, don't be born with a
gambling instinct unless you have a good
sense of probabilities.
~Jack Dreyfus

"The Fifth Annual Conference on Gambling and Risk-Taking" was held at Caesars Tahoe in October 1981. Sponsored by the University of Nevada and held not quite yearly starting in 1976, the first four such conferences were attended almost exclusively by gaming executives and the like. However, due perhaps to some inexplicable morphic resonance, the 1981 version would be all but hijacked by blackjack theoreticians. And this just months after three of the four members of Taylor's team began their professional careers.

Scouting the four major casinos located on the south shore of Lake Tahoe, the players found single-deck games almost exclusively, and noticed that the dealers were dealing deep into the deck. In blackjack parlance, this is known somewhat seductively as "good penetration."

In the early eighties, the casinos in Northern Nevada thought they could afford to deal deep because the rules were so poor. Doubling down was restricted to totals of ten or eleven only, and the dealers hit soft seventeen. Compared to what the players were used to in Vegas, these rules cut almost half a percent off the player's edge. Brian said he would have to run a program to see if the deeper penetration made up for that.

Because the conference itself was being held at Caesars, many counters were avoiding that casino and swarming to the three other major Tahoe properties. It quickly became apparent that this was not a good idea. In each of the three casinos, Taylor and his teammates saw at least one player get thrown out. During a brief walk through Harrah's they watched an entire table get barred, including an extremely pissed off old man who merely happened to be sitting there. The players met for dinner at Carlos Murphy's on the California side of the line and decided not to play at the Lake during the conference. There was just too much heat.

The decision not to play as a team during the conference turned the trip into a vacation. Since the bank had been broken in Vegas before they left town, the players were all flush—both with cash and confidence.

A blackjack bank is an investment portfolio in some ways and a limited partnership in others. A group of individuals pool their money, and make arrangements to divide it up at some later date given certain occurrences. The bank of which Taylor was a part originally totaled $20,000. The agreement was that the bank would be "broken"—that is, divided up—when the players had doubled it. It was Reed's play at the Golden Nugget that had put the bank over the $40,000 target.

Because playing blackjack professionally is a business proposition—with all that that entails—the breaking of the bank is a serious financial transaction. In general, though, it isn't carried out with the solemnity of, say, the reading of a will.

"Reed!"

"Yo!"

Brian looked over the computer monitor on which the financial transactions of the past several weeks were displayed in glowing amber. "You were in for two. Your investor's share is a grand. Your player's share comes to twenty-eight hundred. Here." Brian threw a rubber-banded wad of hundreds in Reed's general direction.

"Guppy!"

"Yessuh!"

"You were in for four thousand. Your investor's share is two grand. Your player's share comes to twenty-four hundred. Count it." Brian tossed a thick wad of bills at Guppy, and then began pelting him with a half dozen or so black chips he retrieved from the pile of cash and chips that covered the kitchen table.

"Thank you, sir! May I have another!"

"You watch too many movies. Taylor!"

"What?"

"You invested two thousand. Investors split half the win. That gets you a grand profit, plus your original two. Half the player's share is split evenly among the players; the other half is divided up according to hours played. Your player's share is the same as Reed's: twenty-eight hundred. Count it." Brian casually tossed fifty-eight hundred dollars in cold, hard cash into Taylor's lap.

Until this point, the wins and losses had been simple notations on tattered scraps of paper. Now they took on meaning. Taylor had earned more in a month than he would have in six months at the dry cleaners. And he had done so doing something most people would be happy to do for free.

> Money won is twice as sweet as money earned.
> ~*Paul Newman in* The Color of Money

The rest of the money belonged to Brian. Since $12,000 of the original bankroll had been his, his investor's share alone totaled six grand. He scooped the remaining cash and chips from the tabletop—an even twenty thousand dollars—counted to make sure it jibed with the total on his computer screen, and said, "Anybody hungry?"

The celebration took place at Battista's Hole in the Wall—an Italian restaurant where the portions were generous and bottomless carafes of wine were an integral part of the meal. This latter feature was not incidental to the choice of restaurant. In preparation for the feast, the players took a cab. There was to be no "designated driver" this night.

As per the plan, they ate huge plates of spaghetti and drank enormous quantities of wine. Reed—several yards ahead of the others in alcohol consumption—began strolling around the restaurant with the Italian accordion player, serenading couples who wanted to be left alone. Guppy fell asleep at the table, and Brian's face got redder and redder as he smoked, and drank, and thought. What a job. What a team.

"Luck," Taylor blurted out, verbally completing a wholly internal train of thought. "Pure luck."

"What?"

"The odds of my being here," Taylor replied. "If that bellman hadn't been learning to count. If Steve hadn't watched me add the laundry tickets. If I hadn't counted down that deck behind Reed. If any of that hadn't happened, we never would have met."

"Short-term fluctuation," said Brian. "Not luck. It's Chaos, man."

"Semantics."

"No. If Reed had been some random gambler, maybe you would have gone on to Caesars and met players with a million-dollar bankroll. Maybe you'd be making a couple of grand an hour with them right now, instead of grinding it out with us."

"Yeah, and maybe I would have been barred. Or worse."

"Exactly. So it wasn't luck—good or bad. It was a fluctuation. Everybody's life is a series of fluctuations. Seemingly insignificant fluctuations, leading to dramatically different lives. That's all."

When Reed was finally thrown out for disturbing the other patrons, he and Taylor staggered down the Strip to the Castaways, a relaxed "locals' joint," where the dealers and the pit bosses wore cowboy shirts and jeans. Taylor managed to negotiate the slot machines and find a seat at a blackjack table, and discovered that although he could barely focus on his cards, another part of his mind was still counting. His bets spread up and down with the count, and he played his blurry hands properly. To his utter surprise, he and Reed were barred after only ten minutes.

"Are you kidding?" Taylor asked, staring at the pit boss through a thick alcoholic haze. By this time his tongue was so heavy he could barely talk.

"Take your fucking act somewhere else," said the pit boss, and four security guards led the staggering counters toward the door.

The conference was well-attended, the talks covering a range of topics from how accurate certain counts made insurance decisions to using Bayesian analysis to conquer the financial markets. Edward Thorp—he of *Beat the Dealer* fame—presented a paper entitled "How I Made $48 Million in the Financial Markets." When he rose to deliver his talk, he began with an apology. "The title is incorrect," Professor Thorp stated. "The preprint went out three months ago. As of today, the title should read 'How I Made *$56 Million* in the Financial Markets.'" A real comedian.

Also presenting papers were Stanford Wong (author of *Professional Blackjack*), mathematician Peter Griffin (*Theory of Blackjack*), and an until then unknown author who called himself Arnold Snyder. The air was thick with information.

The experts representing truth and justice weren't the only individuals in attendance. There were quite a few pit bosses there as well, no doubt hoping to pick up a few pointers about the game it was their job to oversee. To the detriment of card counters throughout the state, they would do just that.

Due to the presence of these bosses, Brian and Taylor attended the talks in disguise—false beards, sunglasses, and hats. Curiously, there were quite a few bearded, bespectacled, and behatted individuals in attendance at Caesars Tahoe that weekend.

During a break in the presentations, Brian and Taylor wandered around the casino at Caesars Tahoe. Since Reed's BP play at the Golden Nugget, Taylor was spending as much time as he could simply observing regular gamblers in action. There is a wide range of subtle and not-so-subtle habits that distinguish gamblers and losing systems players from true professionals who play with an edge, and Taylor—who didn't need a course in psychology to tell him how important this was—intended to incorporate as many small clues as he could into his BP act.

He and Brian stopped behind a $100 minimum single-deck table and watched an Asian gambler in action. He wore a thick gold nugget watch on his wrist and a gaudy diamond ring on his right hand. Around his neck hung a gold Mercedes-Benz emblem encrusted with diamonds. His shirt was open down to his stomach, exposing his hairless chest.

Whenever he was dealt a hand he played with his two cards, passing one card over the other a half dozen times or so. He then lifted the two cards as one and peeked at the exposed card. Then, ever so slowly, he began to squeeze the cards until the index of the second card became visible. Only after completing this ritual would the guy play his hand.

At another table sat a beefy cowboy-type who was wearing a big hat, boots, and a silver belt buckle the size of a Frisbee. Whenever he won a hand, he hit the table with his big hat and let out a whoop. Each time he whooped, his face grew redder and his voice grew hoarser. Apparently, he had been at the table for quite some time, because his face was rather red indeed, and his whoop had been reduced to a croak.

His system was to double his bet every time he lost a hand. That way, he would have to lose nine hands in a row before bumping up against the table maximum of $2,000.

This double-up system of betting is called a Martingale, and its adherents don't realize that the system is just as flawed as any other money-management system. The cowboy would win far more sessions than he lost, but when he ultimately did lose, he would lose big. That one big loss would more than eliminate all of his small wins.

Taylor and Brian moved to another table, and there sat The King.

They didn't recognize him at first. Kings are like that sometimes. This one looked a lot like a clean-cut gambler in his early thirties. He was wearing a white silk suit, a burgundy shirt, and a white silk tie. On his wrist he wore a gold Rolex. He was smoking a thick, foul-smelling cigar and drinking Courvoisier from a large brandy snifter. Between sips he cradled the snifter in his hand and gently swirled the cognac around the bottom of the glass. Then he would bring the glass to his lips, inhale deeply, and sip. The cognac was followed by a sip of Perrier water and a puff on the cigar. Then the ritualistic swirling would begin again.

Whenever a pit boss drifted within earshot of the table, The King established eye contact and engaged him in idle conversation. What time is the late show? asked the King. Which restaurant would you recommend? How late is the spa open?

Taylor and Brian watched the guy through a thick haze of blue cigar smoke. He was playing poorly, making a lot of mistakes, but he was winning. Fluctuations—the bane of the professional gambler's existence—are an absolute necessity if casinos are to survive. How many gamblers would remain if every time someone rolled the dice the house simply took $1.41 of every hundred dollars wagered? If it is the devastating negative fluctuation that has caused the demise of countless aspiring professional gamblers, it is the occasional positive fluctuation that keeps the long-term losers coming back for more.

But this was no ordinary loser. This was The King. When the relief dealer came to the table, the guy stopped playing like a schmuck and immediately started playing perfect Basic Strategy.

Taylor nudged Brian, and Brian nodded. Players who know Basic Strategy play it. Learning it makes little sense otherwise. They decided to watch a bit longer, interested to see how he played once the regular dealer returned from her break.

When the regular dealer returned, The King welcomed her back, bemoaned his bad luck at the hands of her replacement, commented on her hair, and started playing poorly again. There didn't seem to be any pattern to his mistakes. Sometimes he would hit a fourteen against the dealer's ten, and other times he would stand. Occasionally he hit a stiff against a small card. Regular gamblers often exhibit this type of erratic behavior, because most of them play hunches. For the ordinary gambler, each hand is a new struggle; a new attempt to outguess the cards.

Whatever it was this guy was doing, he wasn't gambling. Since he knew Basic Strategy, he knew how to play properly, which meant he was making "mistakes" on purpose. What the hell was going on?

Taylor noticed the signals before Brian did. The King had a partner seated at third base. If the guy at third played with his stack of chips at the end of a round, The King would bet big. If the guy at third did not play with his chips, The King would put a small bet out. Taylor elbowed Brian and quietly pointed out the signals.

Brian watched for a few hands, and noticed that the third baseman was playing even more erratically than the King.

When the relief dealer again returned, both The King and the third baseman reverted to Basic Strategy.

Taylor decided to wander around and watch some other players. Brian remained rooted to his spot. The King and his partner were up to something, and he intended to figure out what it was.

Taylor strolled around the pit for about an hour, observing other gamblers in action. A couple of card counters exhibiting some pretty big *cojones* were trying to put a play down. The challenge was too much for them to resist, Taylor supposed. Apparently, they wanted to try their act in the midst of the most intense heat possible. Because the conference was taking place right at Caesars, the pit bosses were prepared for the onslaught of hundreds of professional players. These counters were really playing an edge—an edge with which Taylor was as yet unfamiliar.

It was a Gorilla BP play, and their act was mild compared to Reed's version. This guy just talked a lot and made a show of not looking at anyone else's cards, but he didn't become obnoxious or unruly. He and his partner were barred rather quickly. So much for that edge.

After watching the barring, Taylor began to rethink his position on Reed's Gorilla act. Originally he thought it attracted too much attention. There was no way the bosses at the Golden Nugget would soon forget Reed.

According to *Playing Blackjack as a Business*, this was a cardinal sin. Professional blackjack players were supposed to remain as inconspicuous as possible, playing short sessions and leaving with any pit attention at all. Revere never mentioned exactly how a player was to avoid all that attention while betting $500 per hand.

The players who had just been barred had been inconspicuous, playing comparatively quietly. They had attracted attention not because of the way they were acting, but because of the size of their bets.

No matter how invisible professional players try to be, they simply will not blend in if they are betting hundreds of dollars per hand. Taylor realized that Reed's Gorilla BP act had succeeded in part because it had given the bosses something other than his big bets to focus on. It seemed that the esteemed Mr. Revere didn't know everything, or perhaps wasn't telling all that he knew.

Taylor found Brian, still parked behind The King's table. After standing there for half an hour, Brian had figured out what the players were doing, but couldn't figure out why it was working. After another half hour, he thought he knew why they were doing what they were doing, but was convinced that it didn't work.

Brian insisted that they wait for the players to leave. Usually he didn't like to talk to other players, but he was too intrigued to pass this up.

When The King finally left the table Taylor wanted to follow him, but Brian shook his head. It was better to follow the small player—the guy at third base. The small player would lead them to the King soon enough.

A few minutes later the small player got up to leave, and Taylor and Brian followed him outside. He walked across the street and met The King in front of the Sahara Tahoe.

Brian walked up and introduced himself. The small player ignored him. The King was friendlier, introducing himself as Tony Ricco, and the small player as Harry. Brian introduced Taylor and, timing his shot, said, "I know what you were doing in there."

Harry looked past Brian to Taylor as if to say, "Do you know this clown?"

"You were playing as if each small card would be followed by a big card, and vice versa," Brian said, and paused to relish the look of astonishment that registered on Harry's face.

"Now that I have your attention…if the last card of a round was a small card, you would signal Tony to bet big, because you would be expecting a big card. Otherwise, he bet small. Also, you were playing third base, hitting until a small one came out, so the dealer would more likely hit her hand with a big card. How am I doing so far?"

Harry just stared.

"I only have one question. What makes you think the cards are in that high-low order?"

"Uh, are you in any way affiliated with the casino?" Harry managed to ask.

Relieved to discover that Brian was not a member of the opposition, Harry said he was scheduled to give a talk on the phenomenon he and his partner had just exploited. His presentation would be given the following day, and he hoped that Brian would attend. He would make a good witness for the defense.

"No," Brian said. "It took me an hour to figure out what you guys were up to. What I don't understand is: Why does it work?"

Tony Ricco nudged Harry, and Harry sighed. "Well," he began, "some dealers are taught to alternate the big cards and the small cards when they scoop them from the table. I call that a 'high-low stack.'"

"And how does that stack last through the shuffle?" Brian asked.

Harry shook his head. "I really don't know. It just does."

"And that's good enough for you?"

Harry shrugged his shoulders.

"Fuckin' worked," Tony said, patting the conspicuous wad of bills in his pants pocket.

"Yes," Brian nodded. "It worked." He thought for a moment. "Good luck at the conference."

"Here," Tony said, handing Brian a business card. "In case we don't see each other, here's my number in Chicago."

Brian looked at the business card deposited in his hand. The card said that Tony Ricco was a writer.

Back at the hotel, Brian and Taylor found their teammates stoked. Guppy had found what he called a "third-baser." The dealer was exposing her hole card as she tucked it under her up-card.

"That's a front-loader," Brian told him.

Whatever the terminology, the dealer's hole card is a valuable chunk of information. Guppy had won a hundred bucks in about half an hour, just betting ten dollars a hand. Then he and Reed decided to look around for more front-loaders, and found three others.

A good front-loader was a gold mine—worth about four times as much as a good spook. And those Reed and Guppy had found were good. However, because of the heat generated by the conference, they would have to wait to play them.

Brian had lasted as long as he had without confronting Gaming Commission agents or any of Bob Griffin's thugs because he never openly challenged them. He had become a successful blackjack player by exploiting cracks and seams in the casino's zone defense, quietly playing where the agents were not. He didn't intend to begin butting heads with them now.

The players donned their disguises, attended a few talks the following day, and then headed back to Vegas. The plan was to play Vegas for a couple of months, and then make a trip back to Reno and Tahoe after all the excitement had died down.

Back home they were in for a rude surprise. What was at least in part a response to information presented at the conference, the games in Vegas had deteriorated dramatically. Most of the papers presented at the conference focused on the single-deck game and its specific vulnerabilities—things like the effects of removal of certain cards or combination of cards and efficiencies of counts for insurance. These vulnerabilities are drastically reduced as the number of decks increases.

The casinos had responded to this information by replacing a large number of the single-deck games with multiple-deck shoes, and the shuffle points of those single decks that remained worsened. Preferential shuffling—shuffling early when the count goes up, but continuing to deal if it goes down—became more prevalent. And a few casinos instituted draconian shuffle policies—often shuffling the deck after only one round had been dealt. Since counters depend on subsequent rounds for favorable situations, a "one round and shuffle" policy defeats them. This ultimately costs the casinos far more than they save on those few counters in the world capable of playing a winning game—casinos make money from no one while their dealers are shuffling—but this was of a piece with their historical policy of costing themselves thousands of dollars an hour to prevent a handful of talented players from winning a few hundred bucks a week.

This wasn't the first time the casinos had overreacted, and it wouldn't be the last. In the meantime, though, the players had to play. The Project—still months from completion—was sorely needed, now more than ever.

Until The Project was ready for prime time the players would play, but in a fashion least likely to get them barred. Once The Project was ready and the players strapped computers to their legs, they would be extremely valuable commodities, and they now had to play with an eye toward the long term. Getting barred with a counting expectation of $100 an hour didn't make a lot of sense when, in a few months, they would be able to stride into any Vegas casino and play with an expectation of $500 an hour or more, doing something that would make them look like ordinary degenerate gamblers.

Whence the paper route.

Taylor dragged himself out of bed at seven thirty in the morning and drove to the Tropicana. He opened a dead game and started playing a shoe, betting nickels. Playing alone, the game was extremely fast.

For the first three shoes, the count never went above plus two. Taylor drank orange juice, talked to the dealer about UNLV's Runnin' Rebels, and randomly bet from one to four nickels per hand.

Then, midway through the fourth shoe, the count shot up dramatically. Taylor stood up, looked at his watch, and said, "Is this right? Is it eight thirty already?" The dealer looked at his watch and nodded.

"Damn. I'm supposed to meet someone in the coffee shop in five minutes." Taylor then pulled a few hundred dollars from his wallet and began making large bets. He continued to bet big, looking nervously at his watch between hands. When the cut card came out, he scooped his chips and left for his nonexistent appointment.

He then drove down the Strip to Caesars, the Sands, and the Hilton, repeating the performance for one hot shoe in each. After the shoe at the Hilton, he drove home and crawled back in bed. Graveyard shift was over.

Guppy and Reed would do the same thing later in the morning. When the shifts changed, they started over. Nine hot shoes a day, seven days a week. The rest of their time was devoted to The Project.

Before devoting all of his waking hours to The Project, Brian had booted up his computer and tested some of the theories that had been presented at the conference. He also wanted to see if the deep deck penetration they had witnessed in Tahoe compensated for the poor rules.

The first program he wrote tested Harry's high-low stack theory. The program quickly indicated that in all likelihood Tony and Harry had not won because of a high-low stack that magically managed to maintain its integrity through the shuffle. No. They had won as a result of another magical force known as luck. A simple positive fluctuation. Better to be lucky than good, someone once said.

On to penetration. To Brian's surprise, one extra round toward the bottom of the deck easily made up for the poor rules offered by the casinos in the northern part of the state. Two extra rounds—which was common in the Tahoe casinos—made the game far better than the best single-deck games offered in Vegas. They would have to return to the lake.

The paper route occupied the better part of the next six months, and Taylor learned the meaning of the term "grind." As difficult as it may be for a nonprofessional to imagine, playing in this fashion is a lot like a regular job, with all the boredom and tedium that accompanies it.

To break some of the tedium, Reed introduced Taylor to a bar in which he had recently run into another professional player. "Good player, but was losing his ass," Reed said. He and Taylor had a few drinks, took a run at a couple of waitresses, and then Reed recognized someone. "Look!" he said. "A Czech!"

Reed had spotted a member of the infamous Czech team that had been instrumental in burning the game in Atlantic City. Reed sidled up to the guy, put his elbows on the bar, turned, and said, "How you doin'?"

The guy grunted.

"One of the Czechs from A. C., am I right?"

The guy grunted again.

"We're players, too," said Reed, waving his beer bottle in Taylor's general direction.

The Czech looked at him as he might a bug. "Yeh?"

"That's right," said Reed. "Pros."

"Bullshit."

"Bullshit yourself."

"All right," said the Czech. "Vot count you double ten against ten?"

Reed froze. "A ten…?"

"Dat's vot I t'ought," said the Czech, and walked away.

"Stupid, stupid, stupid," Reed grumbled on the way home. "What a stupid fucking question."

"You're right," Taylor agreed. "The guy's an idiot."

"Yeah, but he thinks I'm the idiot. He thinks I'm just some schmuck."

"Who gives a shit? It's stupid. 'Ten against a ten.' Depends on the count you count."

"What's your number?" Reed demanded.

"Four."

"Mine's seven," said Reed. "For Brian, it's two." Reed looked out the window, burning. "Asshole."

"Yeah," said Taylor, thinking. "What he should have asked was, 'At what percent advantage do you double a ten against a ten?' That way, it wouldn't matter what count you counted."

"Yeah," said Reed, distracted. Then: "What?"

"My count of four gives me a two percent edge. Your count of seven—two percent edge. Brian's count of two—two percent edge. See? It doesn't matter what count you count. You double a ten against a ten when you have a two percent…Jesus!"

Reed looked at Taylor. He didn't have to say it.

Reed had introduced himself to a presenter at the Gambling Conference who called himself Arnold Snyder. Snyder had developed an interesting analytical formula for calculating a count edge. You plugged in the number of decks, the depth of the deal, the rules, and your bet spread, and out popped your advantage. It was a big improvement over running a million-hand simulation to get the answer.

The development of "The Blackjack Formula" had launched Snyder's career as a blackjack savant. He followed it up with a small publication for professional players called *The Blackjack Forum*. In it players could find rules, number of decks, and playing conditions for many Nevada casinos. Reed and Taylor had sent along conditions for a number of the games in town, and Snyder had published them.[9]

Now Snyder was working on a book about blackjack. It was to be a how-to book called *Blackbelt in Blackjack*, and he wanted to provide his readers with a count of his own. So he developed a count, and hired a well-known blackjack theoretician named Peter Griffin to run millions of simulated hands to determine the various counts at which the player should vary Basic Strategy.[10] Snyder had sent the count and a few of his newly minted "index numbers" to Reed. Griffin's program was spitting out an index number every couple of days or so.

When Taylor and Reed returned to Reed's apartment after the fiasco with the Czech, they managed to locate a calculator beneath the monumental mound of shit piled on Reed's desk and went to work. First, they converted Reed's index numbers into their respective percent advantages. Then they converted those numbers back to index numbers, based on the percent advantage per count offered by Snyder's new count. They matched the numbers Snyder already had, calculated about fifteen new ones, and gave Snyder a call, leaving the new index numbers on his answering machine.

About a week later Snyder called. "How'd you get these?" he demanded. Peter Griffin's program had provided a few more index numbers by this time, and they matched the numbers Taylor and Reed had sent. It was a sweet moment—almost sweet enough to make Reed forget his embarrassment at the hands of the Czech. Almost.

---

9 To Taylor's everlasting embarrassment, in one of these missives he had described the game at the Sahara Tahoe as having "orgasmic penetration."
10 See appendix 3 for a discussion of how and why card counters vary Basic Strategy.

It was about this time that The Project hit a wall. Brian had already spent $5,000 on a dead end: several Sharp programmable calculators with extended memory. The code ran, but too slowly—it often took as long as forty-five seconds to compute a key decision. Almost as devastating was the need for four separate buttons to provide inputs—one in each shoe, one on the stomach, and one positioned under the arm. At the end of each round the player was forced to depress that button by pressing his right arm close to his body, prompting the nickname "the flapper."

It was doomed, but the money had been spent. It was becoming clear that it would be necessary to build a dedicated machine—a miniature computer built expressly for the task of running the program Brian had written. Unfortunately, it was going to be quite expensive.

They were stuck. They could raise their bet levels—perhaps do more spooking—but that meant increasing the risk of getting themselves barred. The whole idea of the paper route was to tread water financially and avoid heat until The Project came on line. As unsatisfactory as the Sharp calculators turned out to be, they had given the players a glimpse of what they could expect. Shuffle tracking would be nothing short of incredible.

Brian refused to give up. Unlike someone setting off for buried treasure that may or may not exist, Brian knew for certain that what he dreamed of doing could in fact be done. Another blackjack pioneer had already blazed a trail.

The idea of carrying a tiny computer into a casino did not originate with Brian. In 1976—before the two dope-addled founders of Apple introduced what ultimately would change the world—a resident of Sunnyvale, California, named Keith Taft wired together a miniature computer, named it David, glued some buttons in the toes of a pair of boots, and strode into a large number of the Nevada casinos to play a little blackjack. This David—so named because Taft viewed the competition between himself and the casinos as a David versus Goliath kind of thing—proved to be the best blackjack player the world had ever seen.

Alas, Taft's secret was not to last. A team consisting of Keith, his two sons, Ken Uston (yes, him again—the Forrest Gump of the blackjack world), and several others were "pulled up" at Harrah's in Lake Tahoe. Although it was ultimately determined that the computers were not cheating devices—after all, the devices only did in silicon what regular players did in their heads—the damage was done. The casinos now knew that it was possible to build a small computer, conceal it on the body, and carry it into a casino.

Feeling that there no longer was a secret to protect, Keith agreed to an interview with a journalist. From the June 1978 issue of *Sports Illustrated* a large number of subscribers learned about David. Brian was one of those subscribers.

One of the things Brian learned from the article was what was possible. A tiny dedicated computer could be carried into a casino and used surreptitiously under the very noses of casino bosses. He wouldn't waste years of time and effort attempting something that might ultimately prove to be impossible. It had been done once. It could be done again.

As we will see, Brian would learn from some of the assumptions and mistakes Keith had made. When it comes to blazing a trail, it is in some respects better to go second than to lead the way.

Because Brian was unwilling to shell out his own money indefinitely, and adamantly refused to give up on The Project, he and his teammates were going to have to open their minds and their team to an investor. And one guy came to mind.

CHAPTER 8
TONY RICCO

Half a loaf is better than a rotten apple.
~Tony Ricco

When Tony received Brian's call, he immediately agreed to fly to Las Vegas for a demonstration of Brian's shuffle-tracking program, to finance The Project if it worked the way Brian said it did, and to undergo whatever scrutiny his new teammates thought necessary to determine the ways in which he could best contribute to the team.

It is an understatement to say that neither side was immediately impressed with the other. Because he lost the show-and-tell coin flip, Brian had to go first.

Brian's original plan was to use off-the-shelf hardware for the shuffle-tracking machine. As mentioned, he had spent five grand on a number of Sharp programmable calculators—calculators with standard keyboards into which a basic program could be punched. Very flexible machines. They could run any program, provided:

1. It was written in Basic; and
2. It could fit into 8K of memory.

No, not eight gigabytes. Or even eight megabytes. Eight K. As in kilobytes. Eight. And the only reason it had even 8K was that Brian had sprung for the version of the calculator that had "extended memory."

For the sake of comparison, a Microsoft Word document containing nothing more than the title of this book occupies 24K of hard disk space.

The program had been written in Basic on Brian's Trash-80. Once he was reasonably convinced that it worked, he transferred it to the Sharp calculator. Using the eraser end of a pencil, Brian punched his shuffle-tracking program into the calculator, one letter at a time. Then Taylor began to deal, as Brian keyed in the cards with the end of the same pencil. He poked the letter A for tens and aces, S for small cards, Z to insert a series of cards into the discard rack, and Q to start the shuffle.

Highly controlled conditions aside, it was clear that shuffle tracking was going to be a kick-ass monster. Obviously, however, the casinos wouldn't show much patience for a player punching values into a calculator as the cards were dealt. The hardware would have to go under the knife for a serious makeover.

Using a couple of screwdrivers, Brian removed the plastic outer case. Bad move. All of the keys fell out, along with a bunch of springs and the small rubber diaphragms covering each of the little plastic stubs emerging from the body of the calculator. One down.

Brian cursed, successfully opened a second calculator, and soldered two wires to each of the four keys closest to the left side of the calculator. Next, Brian touched the ends of the wires together that were soldered to the letter A.

The LCD screen went blank, never again to display so much as a decimal point.

Brian cursed anew and, undaunted, reached for another Sharp. He managed to get the A and the Q to work before this one went to wherever electronic devices go when their innards are fried.

Brian managed to get all four letters working with the fourth device. He hooked the A to a button he glued to a left-foot flip-flop, the S to a button glued to the flip-flop's right-foot mate, the Z to a button he affixed under his right arm with an Ace bandage and some adhesive tape, and the Q to a button located just above his belly button.

Now that the players could communicate with the calculator more or less surreptitiously (more surreptitiously than poking letters with a pencil eraser; less surreptitiously than was necessary for casino play), they needed a way for the calculator to talk back. Currently, the calculator sent its decisions to a small LCD screen. This would have to change.

A number of suggestions surfaced and were quickly rejected. Put the readout on a watch. Put it behind dark sunglasses. Put it in a shirt pocket and put an angled mirror in the bottom half of the left lens of a pair of glasses.

It is a testament to their desperation that they actually tried the mirror idea. The LCD was difficult enough to see in the best of circumstances. It was almost impossible to see wedged into a shirt pocket, and completely impossible to see using a mirror.

And then Reed came through, and in a way that put his unique imprimatur on the whole project.

By this time, Brian had figured out a way to store the program on a cassette tape. It would load in just under fifteen minutes, which was far better than typing it in each time he made a change. Until the cassette breakthrough, Brian had opted to keep the calculator on at all times, using a dozen nine-volt batteries held together with electrical tape and wired in parallel. This meant that once a calculator was turned on, it was not turned off.

One morning after he had made some changes to the program, Brian turned the calculator on and prepared to hook up the cassette recorder. The calculator went through whatever internal processing it went through before displaying "SHARP" on its display screen, and then it beeped.

"What was that?" asked Reed.

"Boot-up," replied Brian. This was long before an operating system would announce its existence with "chimes" or "ta-da!" or anything resembling a short musical ditty. When the calculator or the Trash-80 was ready to roll, it beeped. It was the equivalent of a caveman's grunt. Brian didn't even notice it anymore.

But Reed did.

Brian destroyed only one calculator removing the little speaker responsible for the beeps and rewiring it. After a few days, he figured out how to cause the calculator to output beeps based upon the program. He then developed a simplified Morse code. A short beep for one, a slightly longer beep for three, and an even longer beep for zero. Add some pauses, and they were able to output any number from zero to ninety-nine.

This worked beautifully, except that beeps loud enough for the players to hear could be heard by other players—and, of course, by dealers and pit bosses. Unless they could find an extremely small speaker that could fit in the ear, and somehow disguise the wires leading to it, they would have to start over.

And that's when Reed stepped up to the plate. He suggested they send the output to some kind of device that would vibrate instead of making a sound.

"What kind of device?" asked Brian, and less than an hour later, Reed had returned with a vibrator. And it wasn't the kind you use on your back.

Brian took one look. "I don't even want to know where that's been."

"Give me a break," Reed said as he tore the vibrator apart, exposing the insides of the contraption. The guts consisted of a simple electric motor with a lopsided, elliptical weight fastened to the shaft. The offset weight caused the motor—and therefore the whole unit—to vibrate when the motor spun.

"And there you have it," said Reed.

They didn't have it quite yet. They needed a way to convert the sine wave that drove the speaker to a more powerful square wave to run the motor. Fortunately, Taylor's brother fiddled with electronics as a hobby, and was able to build a small circuit board which translated the "beep" into a direct current that started the motor.

By the time Tony arrived for the show-and-tell, the Sharp detected inputs from the four buttons, ran Brian's program, and output vibrating dots and dashes. What it now needed was a name. Because the shuffle tracker was, indeed, a "tracker," they wanted something that would in some way connote that. "Mohawk," "Hiawatha," "Daniel Boone," and other such names had been suggested and discarded. Then Guppy, the movie expert, had suggested "Butch."

In *Butch Cassidy and the Sundance Kid,* the two main characters had been tracked for days by a posse over impossible terrain. Time and time again, the leader of the posse—an individual wearing a white hat—would stare at the ground and finally head the posse off in the correct direction. This prompted several exasperated "Who *are* those guys?" from Butch and Sundance, watching their relentless pursuers from high in the hills.

Although technically speaking, Butch was not the tracker but the tracked, the team agreed that "Butch" was a better name than "The Guy with the White Hat."[11]

As Brian prepared Butch for the demo, Taylor explained the gory details of shuffle tracking to Tony Ricco.

"It's based on counting fundamentals," Taylor began, using a four-deck stack to demonstrate. "Big cards good, small cards bad…"

Shuffle tracking was just that—tracking cards through the shuffle. Butch wouldn't track individual cards—he would not know that an eight would be followed by an ace, which would in turn be followed by a three. He would track clumps—clumps of big cards, and clumps of small cards. Just as in card counting, the players would bet more when expecting big cards, and less when expecting small cards.

In casino blackjack, cards that have been played are scooped up and thrust into a translucent red plastic contraption called a *discard rack*. When it's time to shuffle, the cards are removed from this discard rack, split into two stacks, and then packets of cards from one stack are shuffled with packets of cards from the other stack.

Butch would keep track of which packet went with which, and what the overall count of each clump had become.

"And then Butch outputs a cut point. We cut, moving the clump with the most tens and aces to the front. So, instead of sitting there, waiting for a bunch of small cards to come out before betting big, we can bet big off the top. Perfect cover. And," Taylor finished, "we get to play each clump to the bottom. No more juicy packets of tens and aces stuck behind the cut card."

---

11 In reality, the guys tracking Butch and the Kid were actually Pinkerton Detectives; however, the name "Pinkerton" would have quickly devolved into "Pinky," and was therefore never seriously considered.

By now wired from armpit to ankle, Brian told Taylor to deal while Tony watched.

The left side of the Sharp's keyboard got quite a workout. Small cards—twos, threes, fours, fives, sixes, sevens, and red eights—were entered by depressing the button beneath the right big toe. Internally, Butch saw the letter A. The left big toe input black eights, nines, tens, and aces, and these were represented by the letter S. The end of each round was signaled by entering a Z—the button under Brian's arm. And the program was informed that the shuffle was commencing by entering a Q—the button affixed to Brian's stomach.

Tony was less than impressed with this arrangement. "Red eights?" he said. "What the fuck?"

Brian explained his problem. The calculator could only handle one letter at a time, and he wanted to use a balanced count. Further, the players only had two feet. That put a drastic limit on the inputs available. Right now, he could reduce the inputs necessary to run the program to no fewer than four.

"So what you're tellin' me is that when a bunch of nines and black eights are left, this fuckin' thing is gonna tell us to bet?"

Brian attempted to explain that this was the first step in a process, that the eights situation wouldn't matter in the long run, and that the next version would be better.

"I sure as shit hope so," said Tony. "The first time I shove five hundred out and get a pair of black eights against a ten, I'd goddamn better win."

Things didn't improve much as the demo began. As Taylor dealt, Brian entered the cards quickly with his toes. However, when Taylor scooped the cards and jammed them into the discard rack, Brian raised and lowered his right arm to depress the button attached to his torso.

"You're kidding," said Tony.

"Afraid not," said Taylor, dealing.

"How often do you have to flap that thing?"

"Every time they stick cards in the discard rack."

"Jesus, why don't you join the friggin' circus and get it over with."

Brian burned. He understood the limitations of his calculator, but had convinced himself that it really wasn't that bad. Apparently, it was.

However, Tony's attitude changed as he saw the calculator begin to predict the cards that emerged from the shoe from which Taylor was dealing. Black eights or no, Butch was impressive. Round after round, the calculator would indicate a large bet, and Taylor would paint the table with tens and aces. Along with nines and the occasional black eight. And hands following small bets consisted largely of small cards. After the fourth shoe, Tony had stopped complaining. Then:

"How much you figure you'll need?" he asked.

Brian wanted a custom computer, built from the ground up. He wanted more than 8K of memory. Most important, he wanted the players to enter a great number of commands with just two buttons: one located in the toe of each shoe. No more flapping.

"I'll need an interrupt mask that checks gates every millisecond or so," said Brian. "It'll know when a button was depressed, which button was depressed, and when it was released. With overlapping button presses, we could easily have ten or fifteen commands."

"You got it," said Tony. "I'll talk to this guy I know. Kevin Mitchell. Mitch. Engineer. Owes me big. Meantime, we oughta go out and make some money."

Initially, it appeared that the players had traded in one collection of problems for another. Although Tony could count, his best time for a single deck was twenty-two seconds. And his strategy decisions were weak. He made several errors on a number of marginal plays when playing against Brian's test program on the Trash-80.

"The King, you said," Reed complained. "What the hell made you guys think he was the King?"

"Because he didn't have shit all over him," said Guppy immediately.

"*The Holy Grail!*" Taylor said proudly, finally getting one of Guppy's allusions.

The team agreed to bring Tony aboard, but with restrictions.

"Half a loaf is better than a rotten apple," Tony said, agreeing to limit his activities to the Big Player end of the table. While Mitch—Tony's engineer friend—began designing the custom computers, the team, now five members strong, traveled to Reno.

Writers naturally rely upon imagery to help describe physical locations. Lake Tahoe reminds one of gemstones; the gleaming sapphire-blue water, or the aptly named Emerald Bay. Vegas at night is a million shimmering diamonds strewn on a carpet of deepest velvet.

Reno, however, evokes a different category of imagery. Certain body parts are often referenced; usually those covered with hair. Armpits and crotches immediately come to mind.

The players paired off and began looking around "The Biggest Little City in the World" as soon as they arrived. The armpit comments were quickly dispensed with. Compared to the dried-up, burned-out blackjack games in Las Vegas, the games in Reno were lush. There were front-loaders, first-basers, spooks, and tells. And many of the dealers were dealing almost to the bottom of the deck. Because of the relatively poor rules—players were restricted to doubling totals of ten or eleven only, and the dealers hit soft seventeen—the pit bosses apparently thought that it would take a large bet spread to beat the game. As Brian's program had showed, they were simply wrong. Add a little front-loading to the mix, and no bet spread at all was necessary.

The first play was at the Sands, where Guppy had found a front-loader. Guppy and Taylor separated and walked toward the pit, while the rest of the team sat at the bar to watch. Since no one on the team had ever bet big against a front-loader before, the rest of the team would play the role of critic, checking for leaks that would be corrected later.

Guppy found Jerry, the dealer he had noticed earlier. When Jerry put his hole card underneath his up-card, he inadvertently tilted it toward the player at third base, exposing it slightly.

There was an older blue-haired woman already seated at the third base position, so Guppy sat in the seat to her right. He played a few rounds, watching for the hole card, and stuck his finger in his ear. The signal meant that Guppy couldn't see the card from his seat, so Taylor continued to pump quarters into the slot machine he occupied. They would have to wait for blue-hair to leave.

After maybe ten minutes, the blue-haired woman experienced some bad luck, losing about six hands in a row. She got up and left the table, muttering.

Guppy immediately threw a chip on her vacated playing circle and scooted over. Two rounds later, he began scratching his stomach with his right hand.

That was Taylor's signal. He came over to the table, nodded solemnly to the dealer, and bought in with a hundred-dollar bill.

"Changing one hundred!" Jerry called. The pit boss nodded and wrote something in a small notebook. Jerry changed the bill, counting out a tall stack of nickels, along with some silver. "No, no," Taylor said. "I want some of those green ones."

First mistake. No one in the pit was betting more than $2 per hand. Jerry lifted four green $25 chips from the tray and called to the pit boss. "Green out."

Lesson number 1: Never begin your session by out-betting the entire pit. Green action went largely unnoticed in the larger casinos in Las Vegas. Here in Reno, in early 1982, quarters were strictly high-roller territory. A pit boss was at the table instantly, scribbling in a small notebook and introducing himself. Taylor, not ready to begin acting before playing his first hand, accepted the boss's business card and introduced himself as "Bert." The pit boss looked at him expectantly. "Uh, Bert…Smurrmer," said Taylor, unsuccessfully attempting to dredge up the rest of the fake name he had used at the MGM Grand.

Lesson number 2: Have your fake name ready before you sit down to play.

"Could you spell that, Bert?"

Actually, I can't, Taylor thought. What he said was, "S-M-U-R-R-M-E-R." The pit boss wrote the name in his small notebook.

"Where ya hail from, Bert?" the boss asked.

"Uh, Southern California," said Taylor, and shoved a single green chip toward the middle of his betting circle. "Green action!" yelled Jerry, announcing the obvious, and began to deal.

"No, I mean the family," said the pit boss. "Unusual name."

Taylor grimaced as the hole he had begun to dig for himself grew deeper. "Uh, my father's family's from Ireland."

"I gotta tell ya," said the pit boss. "You don't look Irish. And Smurrmer?"

The mustached tourist to Taylor's right smirked. With absolutely no thought in his head at all, Taylor decided to study the cards Jerry had dealt him. He had a fourteen, and Jerry had a five up-card. Taylor somehow had the presence of mind to glance at Guppy. Managing to keep a straight face, Guppy was holding his two cards in his left hand, parallel to the table.

Small pat, Taylor thought to himself. That meant Jerry had a two, three, four, or five underneath his five. Taylor hit his fourteen and busted with a ten. Jerry smiled slightly as he scooped Taylor's chip into the rack. Hitting a fourteen against a five is a very bad play. Taylor hoped the pit boss knew enough about the game to realize that.

Unfortunately for Taylor, his tormentor seemed to be more interested in Taylor's genealogy than in his blackjack ability, or lack thereof. He waited patiently for Taylor's answer.

Taylor placed another chip in his betting circle and dug another shovelful of earth from the hole he was digging for himself. "I look like my mother's side of the family. And my grandfather changed his name when he came over."

"From what?"

Christ. Taylor looked at his hand. He had an eleven, and Jerry had a ten up-card. Guppy's cards were crossed, which meant he hadn't been able to see the hole card. Taylor reverted to Basic Strategy and doubled down. He got a three, and the dealer flipped over a nine in the hole. Another loser.

Taylor's losing was having no apparent effect on the pit boss, who appeared to have nothing whatever better to do than to wait for this player to explain his name and his clear lack of Irishness.

Taylor bought in again, and bet $50. The pit boss recorded the buy-in and stood there, making no indication that he was ready to let Taylor off the hook.

"Uh, MacSmurrmer."

"That a Mac or an M-C?"

"Mac. Listen—"

"Reason I'm askin' is, we usually don't get this kind of action around here, especially from young guys. However, since your name seems to be such a problem for ya, how 'bout you show me some ID?"

"Very impressive," Tony said when they arrived back at the hotel. "Maybe next time you can burn Guppy, too."

"When you learn how to play you can criticize us, not before," said Brian.

"I may not be able to count as well as you, but I sure as shit can play," said Tony. "And you'd better learn the goddamn difference before you burn this town down without making a dime."

Taylor started to argue, but stopped. Tony was right. Taylor wasn't in character when he began to play, and that was why he had gotten heat. It was his fault.

Things improved greatly over the next few weeks. They started playing nickels, and only raised their bets as they either won or lost. (Real gamblers do both: "pressing" when they win, and "steaming" when they lose.) It turned out that the bosses and dealers in Reno were genuinely friendlier than their counterparts in the southern part of the state. As long as the players started each session betting small and kept their wins in the thousand-dollar range, heat was minimal.

Interestingly, the locals proved more difficult to handle than the bosses. Free liquor is not conducive to safe, tranquil surroundings in a city where the vehicle of choice is a four-wheel drive pickup truck with a shotgun slung across the front seat. One dealer told Taylor about a neighbor who got drunk on free booze, drove his truck to the wrong house, rammed the car that was parked in "his" driveway, and shot the lock off the front door when his key failed to work.

For the most part, Reno was easier for the small players than for the BPs. A small player wearing jeans and work boots fit right in with most any crowd. The BP, on the other hand, had to walk a fine line. He had to dress well, to convince casino personnel that he had plenty of money to lose. However, as Tony soon discovered to his chagrin, he couldn't dress the way he had in Vegas. He had worn his fancy silk and linen suit to the Eldorado Casino, and a group of rowdy locals had nearly destroyed the threads with a bombardment of spitballs, ice cubes, and beer-soaked coasters.

Tony was forced to be a BP because of his inadequate counting abilities. Since Taylor had relatively poor eyesight and was too tall to read most front-loaders, he alternated between betting and spotting duty—counting decks and signaling Tony when he wandered away from the prime target.

Reed desperately wanted to be a BP. He liked the attention. Tony argued against it, saying Reed just wasn't a legitimate big bettor.

Reed bristled, and described his drunk act. "It fools them every goddamn time."

Tony explained. High rollers who are drunk do not stagger around, drool, and fall down. They act like a drunk person attempting to act as if he is not drunk.

"Great act," said Reed sarcastically. "'Look at me. I'm not drunk.'"

"They do small things that give it away. It's the difference between slapping them in the face with it, and letting them figure it out for themselves."

They went to Harold's Club for the demo. Tony played while the others watched from the second-floor balcony.

Tony bought in, and carefully counted his chips. His movements slowed down. He placed his chips carefully, and momentarily, ever so slightly, lost and then regained his balance. He gathered his thoughts before speaking. He didn't slur his words, but his voice took on a nasal quality. He almost knocked over a stool, but caught it in time and very deliberately put it back in its place.

Tony taught the team the difference between playing and, well, "playing."

It was analogous to the misdirection a good magician uses. A good magician doesn't wave his left hand in the air like a flag while his right hand reaches into his pocket. He uses his left hand naturally, gently leading his victim's eyes to the hand. Tony was right. Reed's act got attention, and to some extent worked, but Tony's act was far better. Why would someone who was acting drunk try to act as if he wasn't drunk?[12]

Tony quickly became the most popular BP on the team. He always managed to get comped to the best restaurants, and knew how to make the most of it. Tony really knew his wine, so dinner with him frequently was the last activity of the evening. No one was in any condition to work after a dinner with Tony.

Unfortunately, the small player running the show when Tony got the comp could not enjoy it. Since the BP and his small player were not supposed to know each other, it would look rather suspicious if suddenly the two of them were seen having dinner together.

To make matters worse, Tony's small players had trouble with him at the table. Since he had never spooked or front-loaded before, he had difficulty improvising in the middle of a session. If Tony and a small player went into a casino to front-load, for instance, and a first-baser came to the table, Tony required a trip to the bathroom for a new set of instructions. To add to the small player's frustration, Tony often spent more energy seducing the waitresses than playing blackjack. And, to top it off, Tony did have a tendency to drink at the table. After two weeks in Reno, Taylor was the only player who hadn't walked out on him in the middle of a session.

Shortly before a session at Harrah's one afternoon, Taylor went to Tony's room and found him reading Hunter Thompson's *Fear and Loathing in Las Vegas*.

---

12 This may explain why Taylor and Reed were tossed out of the Castaways on the night of the bank break party. The players were "obviously" drunk, and yet they were spreading their bets with the count. Therefore, the bosses probably figured their behavior was an act.

"Pretty good book, huh?" Taylor mentioned.

"Jesus, this is great!" Tony said enthusiastically. "I love this guy's style. I wish I could write like this."

"Why would you want to write like that?" asked Taylor. "That's his style. Wouldn't you want to develop your own style?"

"I've tried to come up with my own style, but I always end up beating a dead horse till the cows come home," Tony answered. "Whenever I write anything, it comes out sounding like whatever I just read. I don't know what it is."

"You mean you plagiarize?"

"No, no. I write my own stories. It's just the style that I imitate. Unconsciously."

"What are you going to do?"

"I don't know. My old man says all great writers have to live through a war or a great tragedy or some shit like that. Maybe I'll move to the Middle East."

"What have you written?" Taylor asked curiously, remembering that the card Tony had handed Brian when they first met indicated that he was a writer.

"Nothing. Where are we playing today?"

"We're supposed to be playing Harrah's day shift right now," Taylor replied, glancing at his watch. "Let's get out of here."

"All right. I'll be ready in a couple of minutes. I'm a little hung over."

Tony got up and tossed Hunter Thompson's book at Taylor. "Why don't you read some of this while I wash up," he said, and walked into the bathroom.

Taylor noticed that certain of the passages had been underlined. "What are you doing, studying this, or what?" Taylor called. Tony didn't seem to hear him, so he set the book aside and forgot about it.

Toward the end of their first Reno adventure, Taylor, Guppy, and Tony visited a joint with the unfortunate name of Boomtown. Located on Interstate 80 close to the California border and frequented by truckers and locals, it was a fairly typical locals' dive in the early eighties—no big-name entertainment, an almost edible buffet, and air colored by layer upon layer of blue cigarette smoke. Because Boomtown was a rubber-band joint, the front-loader Guppy had found wouldn't return after each break. Instead of leaping up and moving the Guppy-Tony front-loading operation to a new table when their dealer returned from her break, Tony instead would wander over to the craps table for a few rolls, and then over to Taylor's table (when the count was up). Only then would he find his way back to the front-loader's table, where Guppy had reestablished himself at third base.

Early in his career, Taylor began punctuating his blackjacks with a little verbal exclamation point. He would slam the ace-ten combo face up on the table and yell, "Boom!" He had borrowed this from a gambler with whom he had shared a table at the Frontier only weeks after he moved to Vegas. Something that eluded most card counters was that real gamblers actually get excited when they win. In contrast, many card counters responded to winning by attempting to crawl under the table.

In honor of his host, Taylor had tagged "town" to the end of his "Boom." "Boomtown!" he would yell with each $5 blackjack. There was something about the repetition of that word that made the name of the joint sound even more juvenile than it already did. A number of other gamblers picked up on it, and before long, "Boomtown!" rang out throughout the pit every couple of minutes or so. (For some reason, the pit bosses didn't share the players' enthusiasm for this. Working in Boomtown will do that to you.)

One of the methods for flushing out card counters taught in The Nevada School for Sweaty Pit Bosses is to hang around a suspect's table, alternately whispering, glaring, and talking on the phone. Regular gamblers don't even notice this behavior. Many counters do, however, and often give themselves away.

Being the player he was, Tony knew enough not to react when a couple of bosses established themselves in the pit behind Tony's dealer and started their heat routine. On this occasion, however, Tony wasn't ignoring the pit bosses based upon his vast experience as a card counter. He didn't even notice the heat from the pit. Tony's attention was focused with laser-like intensity on a bombshell of a waitress who was strutting around the pit, driving him crazy. Tony would manage to redirect his attention just long enough to follow Guppy's signal, play his hand, and then once again zero in on the waitress.

It was when the relief dealer showed up and Tony headed for the bar and a rendezvous with said waitress that Taylor—stationed across the pit—realized something was wrong. The sweating and the heat from the pit didn't abate. Bosses usually take a break when the object of their concern heads for, well, the object of his concern. Whoever the bosses were sweating was still at the table, and that could only mean only one thing: Guppy.

Taylor caught Guppy's eye and started pounding on his chest and coughing—the team's signal for intense heat. Guppy quietly gathered his chips and hit the road. To Taylor's surprise, the bosses didn't react when Guppy left. Either they were displaying a coyness Taylor had never seen before, or something else was going on.

Seated in the middle of the table was a player who was having what can only be described as a monumentally bad hair day. His hair was scraggly, yellow-brown, and looked like road kill. Mr. Hair had a number of red ($5) chips in front of him, and was obviously uncomfortable. Taylor couldn't believe the pit bosses could get that worked up over a nickel bettor, but then this was, after all, "Boomtown!"

And then Tony, his mind clearly on something other than the game, returned to the table and sat down. Taylor did everything but shout to get Tony's attention. No luck. Tony didn't even seem to realize that Guppy was no longer there. Testosterone had addled his mind completely.

A few blue-shirted security guards gathered behind Tony's table. Oblivious, Tony continued to ogle the waitress.

Then Mr. Hair lost a hand, pounded the table with his fist, and his stringy, yellow-brown mat fell forward over his face. But it didn't spill forward. It kind of slid forward.

Taylor watched, unable to take his gaze off the train wreck taking place right before his eyes. The guards moved in, grabbing Tony and Mr. Hair. The hair continued its slide, listed dangerously to the left, and finally fell to the floor as the players were dragged off to the back room.

Six hours later, Tony sauntered into Brian's room at the Reno Days Inn without a care in the world and with the Boomtown waitress at his side. "What's up, guys?"

"What's up?" Brian repeated hollowly, and hung up the phone. He had called the police, the Gaming Commission, and the hospital, and presently was on hold with the morgue. "You tell us. What the hell happened?"

"What happened? I'm in love, that's what happened. This is Julie. Julie, guys."

Tony had spent about an hour in Boomtown's back room, and then actually had the balls to hang around in the parking lot across the street and wait for Julie to get off work.

"It's no big deal," Tony said. "They thought I was with the asshole with the wig, but they couldn't put us together because we weren't together. So they read us the riot act, and we left."

"Like they'll give a damn," Reed said. "They grabbed someone at the same table with that dickless wonder with the wig, who was obviously up to something. That's good enough for them."

Tony explained that they asked for ID and took photos. He and Mr. Hair—whose name was Jim something-or-other—denied knowing each other.

"Photos," Brian murmured. "Not good."

"They thought Jim was signaling me or something, but he was spreading his bets with the count and I wasn't," Tony said. "How stupid can they be?"

The players would learn the answer to that. Now, Tony had to stay out of sight until they figured out how much damage the Boomtown fiasco had done.

"Meantime, I think Julie oughta be on the team," Tony said.

"Tony—"

"We're gonna need some more players once The Project kicks in. Look, it can't hurt."

"All right," Brian said, trying hard not to look at Julie's legs. "Can she count?"

"No."

"Spook?"

"No."

"Play Basic Strategy?"

"No."

Brian looked at Tony like he wanted to kill him. "So, what can she do?"

Tony grinned broadly. "Nothing!"

He glanced at Julie. She smiled, turned toward Brian, and began unbuttoning her shirt. The entire team stood, mouths open, as if struck by lightning.

"Misdirection," Tony said, as Julie stopped her impromptu striptease. "We'll talk about this tomorrow." And he turned and led Julie out the door.

During a front-loading play a couple of weeks earlier at John Escargot's Nugget[13] in Sparks, Nevada ("Where there's smoke, there's Sparks"), a trucker started talking to Guppy and, despite his best efforts, Guppy couldn't get the guy to stop. So he signaled end-of-session, sending Tony off into the night, and began drinking with the trucker and flirting with the dealer.

The trucker, headed west to the Bay Area with a trailer full of furniture, had stopped at a number of joints located on Interstate 80, which spans the top of the state of Nevada before diving south through Reno and, ultimately, to San Francisco. Guppy was only half listening until the trucker complained when the dealer shuffled with about fifteen cards left in the single deck she was dealing.

"What the hell!" the trucker bleated. "Deal the goddamn cards."

---

13 The players also referred to John Ascuaga's Nugget as Snails 'R' Us.

When Guppy prodded, the trucker told him that in a lot of the joints he had visited across the state, they dealt to the bottom of the deck. Why weren't these pussies doing the same?

A day after the Boomtown bust, the team packed up and hit the road. They headed east, hitting Winnemucca, Elko, and Wells. They ran out of Nevada real estate at Wendover, fastened to the left side of Utah like a leech, and then headed north to Jackpot, stuck to the bottom of Idaho like—a drain plug. On their road trip they found relatively low limits and not much action, but the games! Single decks everywhere, no heat, and dealers who dealt close to the bottom of every deck. In Wendover, the dealers routinely went to the last card, and had to shuffle the discards to complete a hand. The players, used to dropping their mental counts toward the bottom of the deck, had to remember to maintain the count no matter what. And they learned a few things about playing extremely depleted decks. It was like traveling back in time. Imagine, those card counters who started it all in the 1950s played games like this everywhere.

Six weeks after traveling to the casinos of Northern Nevada, Tony received word from Mitch that he had something to show the team. When the players returned to Vegas, Mitch had a prototype shuffle tracker ready for testing. A number of semiconductor chips were stuffed into a "breadboard" with a rat's nest of wires holding it all together. It didn't look like much, but after tweaking some wires and changing out some resistors, the thing actually began to communicate with an oscilloscope. Butch may have been Stone Age technology by today's standards, but it was the beginning of the team's trip down Silicon Way. And it would rock their world.

CHAPTER 9
AN UNFORTUNATE DIGRESSION

Suckers have no business with money anyway.
~*Canada Bill Jones*

Gamble only when you're sure you're not.
~*Alexander Taylor*

As painful and as unintended as this may be, it is now time to breach the unspoken yet sacrosanct barrier between author and reader. This author should have known better; however, it appears the players about whom I have been writing are far better at this gambling business than I.

A number of years ago, after meeting someone who had been introduced as a "professional gambler," I had opined that the phrase was an oxymoron—an internally inconsistent statement on par with "pretty ugly" and "jumbo shrimp." How could one gamble professionally? I had asked dismissively. This resulted in another introduction, and now I had accompanied members of Alexander Taylor's team on several forays into enemy territory. I quickly learned that these characters did indeed gamble, and were in fact professionals. However, the degree to which they played with an edge had unfortunately not fully saturated my consciousness, as I was about to learn.

It was shortly after an enormous comped meal at the Chinese restaurant at Harold's Club. The team minus Guppy was present—Guppy was the small player when Tony obtained the comp, so this night he was enjoying the fine cuisine at Burger King—and collectively we had put a significant dent in the supply of Harold's fried rice. Tony signed the check, unbuttoned his pants, and moaned. "I'll never eat again," he declared.

Somehow, the conversation drifted toward physical prowess. Tony—or perhaps it was one of the other players—mentioned Tony's raw physical strength. I looked at him, stomach flowing freely over his gaping slacks, and smiled.

"Seriously," Tony said. "I used to be able to do a couple of thousand push-ups."

In retrospect, I should have known better. Perhaps the MSG had clouded my judgment. Maybe I was just tired. Whatever the case, I had no idea that the hook was being set, and that I was participating in my own demise.

"Yeah. You could do two thousand push-ups. And I could do cartwheels from here to San Francisco."

"I'm not kidding. Hell, right now I could do between five and six hundred."

"In how long? A week?

Tony looked at his watch. "Ten minutes."

"That's like, what? One push-up a second? For ten minutes? Come on."

"Seriously."

"Real push-ups."

"You be the judge."

"Right now?"

"Right now."

"How much?"

Tony threw some bills on the table. "A grand."

I ogled the cash, which, as far as I was concerned, was as good as mine. "I don't have that much on me. But—"

"Tell you what. If I win, I get to write a chapter in that book you've been mumbling about into that recorder of yours."

"You guys hear this?"

148

Reed nodded, not meeting my gaze. But I was too busy counting my money to pay attention.

I looked at Brian, then Taylor. "Ten minutes, I judge each one—"

"—and I do between five and six hundred push-ups," Tony interrupted.

"We're witnesses," said Reed.

I told Tony we were on.

To my everlasting embarrassment, and to the great amusement of the waitresses, Tony proceeded to do exactly what he said he would. He dropped to the floor of the restaurant and belted out between five and six hundred marine-quality push-ups.

To be precise, he managed seven. (Seven is indeed "between five and six hundred.")

Without further ado, and with my sincerest apologies...

BEER AND (FRONT-) LOADING IN RENO

There was some tremendous ugliness in Reno over the holiday weekend. I could feel it in my spleen. The rednecks were out in force, and I began to wish I had brought my pet wolverines after all. I hadn't, because traveling with wolverines is like dealing with a mother-in-law who has steel teeth and a voracious appetite for human flesh. Instead, I settled for cleaning my gun and preparing the drug dosages for the blackjack play we had planned for later that afternoon.

Playing blackjack alone while wasted on heavy drugs is virtually impossible. There are too many goddamn things to remember. Counting, truing, index numbers—who the hell needs it? With a small player, though, there was a chance to pull it off. The small player does all the counting and the signaling, while I eat the drugs and raise hell at the table. Of course, the small player wouldn't be able to participate in the hallucinations, but I figured the drugs should work wonders for cover.

Our trip had stunk like a week-dead carcass until now. Even the small players were getting heat, largely because they stood out among the Reno rednecks like Richard Pryor at a KKK rally. The rednecks, atavistic assholes whose progenitors rode cattle and women with equal aplomb, thought manhood was measured by the size of the chaw of tobacco a fellow could fit in his cheek. To blend in with this scum, we decided the small players should wear work boots, checkered shirts, and those dopey red hunting caps with ear flaps. Naturally the small players had balked, but what the hell.

We had to do something to keep the wretched bastards off-balance, and also inject a little fun into our tired old game plan. Until now, we had been playing like a bunch of old women at a sewing bee.

Just yesterday we played Harrah's. I had a pretty serious hangover, so I wasn't my usual ebullient self. Taylor was counting, and I was betting the money and following his signals.

Well, the bastard called end-of-session after only twenty minutes or so. I left, and when we met in front of the Hilton, I asked him what was wrong.

"I'm counting for you so you can put on your act. Well, act! Do something. You haven't said a word. You're sitting there like my grandmother, and she's dead."

"I'm a little under the weather today. What the hell do you want me to say to these vultures?"

"For crying out loud, tell some jokes; sing songs. Anything. I don't care. Just do something to take some heat off me."

We went next door to Fitzgerald's, and Taylor sat down to play a dealer who had a couple of Band-Aids on her face. I sat down and smiled at her.

"What happened to you, baby? You get beat up or something?"

The dealer glared, and said, "I was in a car accident, and my kid's still in the hospital, if you really want to know."

That's exactly what I mean about these people. They lure you in by playing on your natural human sympathy, and then attack like frenzied sharks.

Well, today would be different. I downed two tabs of blotter acid while Taylor was waiting outside. Since it was my first experience with this batch, I didn't want to risk eating more than two tabs. I packed a few essentials, pulled our rented Ford Escort around front, and Taylor climbed in.

The goddamn car was riding even worse than usual because of a large flat spot on one of the rear tires. Earlier, I had barely missed killing myself as a dumbshit tourist attempted to negotiate a crosswalk in front of me. I locked up the brakes, and the loud squeals and acrid smell of burning rubber caused the misguided toad to leap back to the sidewalk. Since then, the car had ridden like a bowling ball rolling over the thumbhole.

I steered the Escort into the Comstock parking garage. The fucking car had no power to speak of, and the suspension felt like day-old Jell-O. My eyes labored vainly to adjust to the reduced light in the garage. Too late.

The front bumper scraped against a thick cement pylon, leaving a white powdery scar.

I parked the wounded vehicle in the nether regions of the parking garage, and managed to extricate myself from the so-called passive restraint system. "As your attorney, I advise you to leave the rest of the drugs in the car," Taylor suggested, but I knew the Valium and the speed would be necessary for fine-tuning once the acid really kicked in. I pretended to put the vials in the glove box, but pocketed the stuff instead.

"Remember," Taylor said, "we don't know each other." He looked at me carefully. "Are you all right?"

"Of course I'm all right. I could do this in my sleep. Just worry about the counting, and I'll take care of the rest."

We swaggered into the Comstock. I was sweating profusely, and could feel the acid taking hold. "Not yet," my brain implored, but the damn drug had other ideas. The acid had already pinned my frontal lobes to the mat, and was now beating my limbic system into submission.

My bloodshot eyes focused on the fuzzy green blackjack table Taylor had chosen. I felt my teeth begin to grow, and the hair on the back of my neck stood on end. Good sign. My glands were still working. I knew I would need all of the adrenaline my body could produce when the really heavy shit came down.

The dealer was a short, arrogant battle-ax with a harelip. The right side of her face was contorting grotesquely right before my eyes, and the ribbon in her hair was changing colors like a hologram. Who the hell is she trying to kid? I thought. Clearly, someone needed to teach this treacherous bitch the meaning of the word "respect."

Taylor put a bet out. The miscreant playing next to him glared murderously. He shifted slightly in his seat, and I barely caught a glimpse of the hunting knife cleverly concealed up his sleeve. Apparently, Taylor hadn't yet noticed this weapon poised to cut through muscle and sinew the minute he screwed up at first base. One ill-advised hit and Taylor's guts would spill out all over the table like so much sausage. I knew I had to divert this wretched dirtbag's attention if we were to get out of the place alive.

I tripped on a stool and fell heavily against the table. "Get me a goddamned drink!" I bellowed, and wiped the snot from my nose with the back of my hand. The dirtbag was staring at me, feigning curiosity. I knew he wanted to put me off guard; to get me out of there so he could slice Taylor to ribbons and make a clean escape. I had seen it all before.

I knew the dealer knew of his plans; I could see her eyes gleam when the light caught them just right. Now the bitch looked petrified. She knew I knew.

"Deal!" I screamed, sitting at third, where I could watch the game and keep my eyes on the murderous fiend with the knife. This was proving to be rather difficult, as the acid was now eating away at my optic nerves, and my brain was beginning to overheat trying to decipher sensory input that lacked coherence. The dealer babbled something incomprehensible, and I barely controlled the urge to throttle her right there.

"You don't have a bet out," she whispered, trying to take my mind off the knife-wielding maniac to my right. "Minimum is five dollars."

I tried to look at her and at the same time hold the bloodthirsty cur in my restricted field of view. My bulging eyeballs started to jitter in their sockets, and to stop the shaking I smacked myself on the side of my head like a recalcitrant television set.

I saw Taylor looking at me, concerned. Good, I thought. He is finally getting the message that something is wrong. Jesus, the guy can be slow sometimes.

Meanwhile, the acid was continuing its attack, ferociously pounding away at my brainstem with the force of a sledgehammer. My temples were throbbing, and I held my head in my hands. I knew I needed a Valium to slow the insurgent acid, but I couldn't bring myself to leave. Taylor would not stand a chance at the table alone. The minute I left, the cunning, ruthless bag of scum would attack like a frenzied shark, snarling and tearing at anything fleshy in his path. I was Taylor's only hope.

I pulled a crumpled bill out of my pocket and tossed it at the dealer. She handed me a stack of chips, and again waited for me to place a bet. Unfortunately, my eyes had unilaterally locked onto a cigarette burn in the green felt blackjack layout while my mind took a brief hiatus. I knew if I didn't eat the Valium soon I could no longer be held responsible for my actions, so I pocketed my chips and headed for the bathroom.

I barely suppressed a scream when I saw myself in the mirror. A stream of spittle had hardened on my chin, and my hair was standing almost straight up in the air.

Before I had a chance to clean up I heard someone coming into the bathroom, so I attempted to steer myself into one of the stalls. Neglecting to get out of the way first, I opened the door to the stall and nearly broke my nose. My eyes started to water, and through the blurry wetness I saw a figure advancing toward me.

"No, no!" I screamed, crossing my arms in front of me in case my tormentor turned out to be a vampire. "Back, you bloodthirsty cur! I'm armed!"

"Jesus, Tony, calm down, will you?" It was Taylor. "For crying out loud, are we going to play or not?"

"Yeah, yeah," I said, composing myself. "I just need a few of these to take the edge off." I reached for the vial and extracted four Valium tablets. "Down the hatch," I mumbled, and swallowed the pills.

The trek back to the table was brutal. Someone had covered the floor of the casino with warm molasses while we were in the bathroom, and I hadn't worn my cleats. I had to fight for my life with every step.

When I got back to the table, the murderous fiend and the dealer stopped whispering and looked at me. The knife-wielding maniac was about five feet tall, balding, and had a tag on his lapel indicating that he was an Amway salesman. The dealer was a forty-year-old mother of three whose husband had run off with a cocktail waitress, leaving her to raise the kids alone. I wanted to help her; I wanted to help her kids. I wanted to make the world a better place for humanity.

Instead, I looked across the table to Taylor's bet. It was toward the bottom of his playing circle, so I put a minimum bet out. I received my two cards, and played Basic Strategy.

Our Big Player-Small Player routine was working beautifully. The dealer, careful to avoid reigniting a bout of my initial behavior, was politely dealing a very good game. I was following Taylor's signals and spreading like a madman, and there was no heat from the pit. No one was worried about my play. The pit bosses were more concerned with the possibility that I might puke all over their blackjack table. Whenever a boss got close enough to the table to see the action, I retched and drooled on my sleeve. They quickly learned to stand clear.

After about twenty minutes the relief dealer came to the table, and Taylor began to scratch his stomach furiously. The Valium had softened what few remaining neurons the acid had missed, so it took me a few minutes to realize the stomach-scratching was a signal. "Aha!" I said to myself. "A front-loader!"

I began to play flawless front-loading strategy. Whenever Taylor's mouth was open, it meant the dealer was stiff. If his mouth was closed, it meant the dealer was pat.

"Damn, what a play!" I congratulated myself as I stood with a thirteen against the dealer's eight up-card. Taylor looked on in horror as the dealer flipped up her ten in the hole and took my money. Taylor then grabbed his crotch, signaling me to meet him in the bathroom, and stalked off.

"What's the matter?" I asked when I got to the men's room and occupied the stall adjacent to Taylor's. "It's working great! Mouth open is stiff, closed is pat. I'm getting all the signals perfectly! We have them completely fooled!"

"You asshole!" Taylor hissed from his stall. "I was scratching with my left hand! That means she's a first-baser, not a front-loader. For crying out loud, I only know her hole card when she has a ten up! We're getting killed!"

"Oh."

"How the hell do you expect me to front-load from first base anyway? Huh?"

"I don't know."

"You got it straight now?"

"Yeah, yeah." I paused, trying to gather my thoughts. "But if you were only getting hole cards beneath tens, why were you signaling me on every hand?"

"What the hell is wrong with you? Those weren't signals! My mouth has to be either open or closed. I swear, this is the last time we make a play when you are on drugs."

"Relax, will you? Just stop signaling me if you don't mean it, and I'll stop obeying your signals."

"Goddamn it!" Taylor's voice rose about two octaves. "What the hell do you want me to do, put my mouth in my back pocket? Listen. Just look for a signal if she has a ten up, and forget about it the rest of the time. You got that?"

"Yeah, all right. Don't make a federal case out of it." I pulled the vial containing the speed from my pocket and snorted some to clear my head.

"What was that?" Taylor asked from his stall.

"Nothing."

"I swear, this is the last time. No more drugs after this. You got that?"

"Yeah, right. Sure."

Taylor banged out of his stall. Since it would look suspicious if we arrived back at the table at the same time, I waited for a minute in my stall. While I was waiting, I absentmindedly scratched Taylor's name and phone number into the brown paint on the door with the key to the rented Escort. Proud of my handiwork, I returned to do battle at the blackjack table.

The regular dealer had returned. The speed was beginning to make me sweat, so I pulled my handkerchief out of my back pocket and wiped my forehead. My nose was running a bit, but I thought I might need the handkerchief if I continued to perspire. When I finally decided to risk blowing my nose, the buzzing in my ears stopped, and my hearing became incredibly acute. For the first time that evening, I heard the music playing in the casino. It sounded wonderful. Too few people appreciate the twang of authentic country music.

I was also able to catch bits of conversation floating over from the roulette table. A couple of the dealers were discussing a football game that the Reno

Wolf Pack had won earlier that day, and it sounded exciting. If I do say so myself, I am quite a football handicapper, yes sir, yes sir.

"Sir!" the dealer called. "Are you going to play, or not?"

"Certainly," I answered magnanimously. I bet, and the dealer dealt. She had an ace showing, and asked if anyone wanted insurance. When she asked, she placed her right hand on the felt.

I looked at Taylor, who signaled "no" by sticking his finger in his ear. The dealer peeked under her ace, flipped her hole card—the queen of clubs—face up, and took everybody's money.

"Son of a bitch!" I thought. "She has a tell!"

I could hardly wait to use this new information. This would certainly show Taylor that I'm a better player than he thinks.

Several hands later, the dealer dealt herself another ace up, and again placed her right hand on the felt when she offered insurance. Again, Taylor stuck his finger in his ear, signaling "no." I smiled and said, "Yes, I think I'll take a little insurance." Taylor buried his finger so deeply in his ear that I expected it to come out the other side of his head, but I paid no attention. I knew what I was doing.

The dealer peeked. She had a blackjack, and I nearly burst with pride. What a play! I beamed at Taylor, but he simply glowered back.

Unfortunately, I got the next insurance call wrong. Again, Taylor grabbed his crotch and headed toward the men's room.

"What's up?" I asked confidently, entering my stall.

"What the hell do you think?" Taylor asked.

"The insurance plays."

"That's right. The insurance plays. What do you think you're doing?"

"Well," I said proudly, "maybe I noticed a little something that you didn't. Maybe I noticed a little tell."

"Oh yeah? What is it?"

"I'm surprised you didn't notice."

"What is the tell?" Taylor asked deliberately.

"She puts her right hand on the table when she has a ten in the hole."

"Is that right?"

"Yeah."

"And you noticed that all by yourself?"

"Yes, that's right. Pretty good, huh?"

"Yeah, that's great. Listen, Mr. Tell, tell me this. Answer just one question."

"You don't have to be an asshole just because I found the tell and you didn't."

"How can she give you a tell before she looks underneath her ace?"

Shit.

"She can't give you a tell until after she has looked and knows what she has in the hole," Taylor said in a voice that was too calm. "Do you understand that?"

"I guess—"

"DO YOU UNDERSTAND?"

"Yeah. For chrissakes, don't treat me like an idiot."

"Give me one reason why I shouldn't."

I thought for a minute. As I did, Taylor left the casino.

CHAPTER 10
WIRED TO WIN

Q: How many computer programmers does it take to
change a light bulb?
A: None. That's a hardware problem.

After dozens of phone calls to suppliers throughout the Southwest, stacks of components had arrived at Brian's apartment. ROMs, RAMs, Z80 processors, IO chips, and chip selects neatly filled long, antistatic plastic tubes. Crystals, voltage regulators, zero insertion-force sockets, transistors, dozens of ceramic and tantalum capacitors, and hundreds of resistors were waiting in small ziplock storage bags. The custom circuit boards sat in a translucent green stack. It was time for the boys to build their new toys.

The players surrounded Brian's kitchen table. Mitch had positioned the various components around the table on antistatic mats. A circuit board would be passed around the table, and each person would insert a few components. Twenty-eight-leg Z80 microprocessor chips, eight-leg chip selects, IO chips, ROM sockets, and five flat-pack RAM chips—2K each— were carefully pressed into position. When each board reached Mitch, he flipped it over and quickly soldered dozens of legs into place. The partially completed boards would then circumnavigate the table twice more, collecting more electronics—spindly legged resistors, capacitors, diodes, and more.

The completed computers were slightly larger than the circuit boards themselves: two inches by five inches, and less that half an inch thick.

Once each board was filled, Mitch's soldering prowess was put to the test. He stacked two more RAM chips on top of each of the RAM chips already soldered in place. These chips, the most expensive single components (about twenty bucks each), would have to be stacked three high in order to cram all 30K of memory onto the circuit board. A dribbled thread of solder linked legs to legs.

Once the computers were completed, Mitch burned a rudimentary assembly program into a ROM chip, plugged it into its socket, and one by one hooked each computer to his oscilloscope. To the amazement of everyone but Mitch, ten of the sixteen computers worked.[14] Mitch crossed two pads on the end of the circuit board with a screwdriver, and the sine wave dancing across the oscilloscope's green porthole changed.

Because the team had decided to go with low-energy RAM memory—which only held bits and bytes as long as the power was on—the program would have to be pumped in from another source. Mitch built a few relatively simple "loaders," which had zero insertion-force sockets fastened to the top. A ROM chip with the program "burned in" would be plunked into the socket, a lever depressed (pinching the legs of the ROM into place), and the two computers hooked together and powered up. The ROM would pump data into Butch's RAM memory, and the program would continue to run through Butch's circuitry for as long as battery power supplied him with life.

Once the computers were built, they needed an external skin for protection. Taylor found a guy in town who made air-conditioning ducts—a process that involved bending metal. Taylor handed him a blank circuit board and asked for a metal box with a tight-fitting lid that could accommodate the board.

The guy quoted two bucks a box, and built a test version out of steel. It felt like it weighed five pounds.

"Don't you have a lighter material?" Taylor asked, feeling the heft of the box.

The guy rubbed his chin. "I could make them out of aluminum, but it'll cost ya."

---

14 Static electricity, bad chips, bad circuit boards, and/or bad solder joints were likely responsible for the six failures. However, given all the things that could go wrong, Mitch was extremely pleased with ten working pieces of hardware.

"How much?"

The guy shook his head. "They're gonna run ya six bucks a box."

Taylor didn't have it in him to tell the guy they had already spent thirty thousand dollars on The Project. With a straight face, Taylor told the guy he'd spring for the sixty bucks.

After the computers had been built, Mitch burned a short loading program into a ROM chip and plugged it into its socket on the circuit board. He then set up his portable Kaypro computer and downloaded Brian's shuffle-tracking program. After a week of tweaking, compiling, burning, and testing, the program loaded. And then the fun began.

The program was far from perfect. And there were minor problems with the hardware. Unfortunately for the players, they found themselves caught between two eternal nemeses: hardware guys and software guys. The discussion regarding every perceived anomaly ran the same course.

Taylor: "Brian, the output is alternating between a high and low count no matter what I do."

Brian: "Sounds like a hardware problem to me."

Taylor: "Mitch, the output is alternating between a high and low count no matter what I do."

Mitch: "Sounds like a software problem to me."

This persisted through the first three weeks of practice, until Mitch and Brian finally came to an arrangement they both could live with. There would be no more hardware problems or software problems. From that point forward, there were only *operator errors*.

The reality was, the hardware was remarkably robust. Initially there were some issues with static electricity, but once the computers were sealed inside their six-dollar aluminum boxes, connected to the outside world through well-grounded static-proof plugs, virtually all of the issues turned out to be software bugs.

If debugging is the process of removing bugs, then
programming must be the process of putting them in.
~Dykstra's Observation

While Brian was tracking and squashing bugs, the players practiced. As mentioned in chapter 7, Brian and his teammates would learn a lot from Keith Taft and his experience with David, the playing computer Keith had built several years before. David required a lot of power: two three-volt lithium D cells that would last only three or four hours. Because the team planned a lot of travel, they didn't want to lug special batteries around. Brian insisted that Butch run on batteries found at any corner drugstore, and would last for at least one complete eight-hour shift. Mitch complied; Butch would run for eight to ten hours on one nine-volt battery. That was one of the reasons to run the program in RAM (David's program resided in a burned ROM).

The main benefit from following Keith's trail, however, was the following: in Butch's design, ease of use would trump everything. Keith's David had four buttons—two in each shoe—and required ten distinct toe inputs—one for each card. Right toe up for a two, right toe up then down for a three, left toe up for a four, and so on. Entering a single seven meant left toe down, right toe up and then down, all within half a second. Running David was exhausting, and error-prone.[15]

Butch would be a model of simplicity. The team applied the lesson all pros eventually learn—use the simplest count that will do the job. Instead of ten multi-toe card inputs there would be a grand total of three: left down for a ten/ace, right down for a small card, and both down for a neutral card. Simpler meant two things: more speed and fewer mistakes. In the case of tracking, there would be an additional benefit: endurance. These decisions, made long before the players had tracked their first shoe, would pay huge dividends for years.

Another array of decisions involved logistics. What commands would do what? Left toe for big cards and right toe for small cards had already been established when developing and testing the flapper. Both down would be a

---

15 In fact, the "legendary" Ken Uston never did learn to run David with his toes. Keith had to build a special four-button keypad for Uston to use with his hand.

neutral card. (Tony took the team out for dinner when he learned the black eights issue was no more.)

The arm flap itself, referred to as the *Z-out* (so named because the command to enter cards at the end of a round was originally hooked to the letter Z on the Sharp calculator keyboard) became an LRR; that is, depress and hold the left button, press the right button twice, and then release. The mirror opposite—RLL—became the command to erase.

Brian was aware of the momentous nature of the decisions he was making. Once the players learned these commands, they were stuck with them. Hence, these decisions weren't made capriciously. What resulted was a computer with a command structure that actually made sense.

Practice would require hundreds of relatively new decks of cards. If the players were to estimate the number of cards in a packet at a glance, they wanted to do so using cards as similar as possible to those they would encounter in casinos. The dog-eared decks the players used for count practice wouldn't do.

Reed found a cigarette machine at the Horseshoe, selling used Horseshoe decks for twenty-five cents each. He emptied it out weekly.

The cards were perfect. Usually, when casinos sell their used cards they chop a corner off, or drill a hole, or otherwise mutilate the deck. That way, the cards can easily be identified as used cards if someone attempts to cheat with them—you know, like show up at the table with a ready-made blackjack. This would be considerably tougher to get away with if the cards constituting your blackjack had holes drilled through them.[16]

Unfortunately, apart from changing the look of the deck, the burs left from the drilling or cutting can make a deck look like a deck and an eighth, or more. For players learning to accurately eyeball packets of cards, this has obvious drawbacks.

16 Although anything is possible. Taylor heard a rumor that someone managed to drop a homemade blackjack on a table at one of the downtown joints. The cheater was paid, and immediately hit the road. It was only later that the bosses found a red-backed ten and ace in a blue-backed deck!

However, the Horseshoe, known for its brutalization of suspected card counters and other undesirables, appeared to be challenging anyone to bring extra cards into play. "Here they are, boys," they seemed to be saying, "a nice, clean deck of cards. Take your best shot."

This was the first time Taylor had handled a fresh deck actually used in casino play. Taylor immediately began opening boxes. After examining about ten decks, he found what he was looking for and called his teammates over to the kitchen table.

Taylor squared the deck, placed it on the table, and said, "I'll bet you I can cut to a ten four times out of five."

Since Taylor had already shown each of them a number of card tricks, no one was willing to take the bet. So he did it anyway.

Gently, he lifted about half the deck and turned his hand over. Boom. King of diamonds. He completed the cut, shuffled the cards, squared them, and cut again. Boom. Jack of spades. He did it twice more, and cut to tens both times.

"How the hell are you doing that?" Brian demanded. "These can't be trick cards. They just came from a casino."

Taylor had read about something called "warps," and thought these might be possible. When dealers peek beneath tens to check for a blackjack, they bend the ten up. Since the up-card and the hole card are back-to-back, the hole card gets bent the other way. After a while, the tens tend to be bowed away from their faces, and the non-tens are bowed toward their faces. So, when Taylor cut gently, the deck tended to break at a card that was bowed away from its face.

Brian grabbed the deck and squared it on the table. He cut the deck gently and looked at the half deck in his hand. He had cut to the king of diamonds.

"Well, I'll be a son of a bitch," he said quietly. "You know, that ten ends up on the bottom of the deck after the cut and never gets dealt. That lowers our edge."

"We can avoid cutting more tens than normal out of play simply by cutting hard," Taylor said. "If you squeeze the deck when you cut, the cut will be more random."

"What do you know," Brian murmured. "You learn something new every day."

"And you can't teach an old dog to see the forest for the trees," Tony added philosophically.

The motor Reed had extracted from the vibrator was proving to be a problem. In a word: it was cheap. It sometimes failed to start when powered up—occasionally it just hummed without spinning. There would be enough at stake that the players didn't want to depend on these thirty-five-cent motors.

A little research resulted in the purchase of Shimani electric train motors, $29.95 retail. They were perfect—small, high-quality cylindrical motors that started tens of thousands of times without fail. Mitch affixed a blob of solder off-center on the shaft, jammed the motor into a short section of small-diameter rubber hose to muffle the noise caused by its vibration, and thus was born a silent, reliable signaling device.

Finding proper computer shoes proved to be a bit more difficult. Brian bought a pair of cheap shoes at K-Mart, sawed the bottoms off with a Dremel Moto-Tool, stuck a pair of Mitch's homemade buttons to the soles, and glued the shoes back together. This initial effort was not an overwhelming success. The saw Brian used had chewed up the soles so badly that the tops and bottoms no longer matched up properly. The glue Brian first bought wasn't strong enough. And, because of the position of the buttons, Brian had to hold his toes up to keep from accidentally depressing a button. This resulted in cramps and, worse, the toes of the shoes started curling up like elfin footwear.

After purchasing several pairs of shoes and chopping them to pieces, the team began to discover the necessary characteristics of a proper computer shoe. The shoe needed a firm sole so that the toe wouldn't begin to curl up, and the sole had to be relatively thick. Some of the sole would be carved away, and a button would be glued in the resultant depression. In order for the button to fit in the toe, the shoe had to be a size or so too big, and the toe area needed to be unusually roomy.

Frequently, the players were able to find combat boots that met their admittedly stringent requirements, but shoes with big toes and thick soles that still looked like ordinary shoes were not packing the shelves.

Once a likely candidate was located, the battle would begin. The salesman was approached and grilled mercilessly about the construction of the shoe. The toe had to be bulbous, and the sole had to be firm, but not too firm. If the sole was too firm, the Dremel's saw would start smoking and burning as they attempted to cut through it.

At some point, the salesman would insist upon measuring a pair of feet. At first the owner of the feet resisted, attempting to explain that he didn't want to buy shoes that actually fit. This tactic didn't work well at all, due to some misguided sense of professionalism among shoe salesmen. It appeared shoe salesmen were somewhat uncomfortable selling shoes that clearly didn't fit.

Eventually the players acquiesced, allowing the salesmen to measure their feet, and only then explained that the shoes were for someone else whose feet were exactly one size larger than their own. Under those circumstances, the salesmen were usually willing to sell a pair of shoes that made the wearer looks as if he were employed as a circus clown.

Attaching the computer, batteries, and vibrator to their bodies was another problem. Initially, Taylor had strapped the entire contraption to his calf using a five-foot-long Ace bandage. The consequent bulge looked like a huge tumor.

When Tony saw that, he immediately headed home and returned with something he called a "dealer's sock."

Dealers in Las Vegas must wear pants that have no pockets. The casino management was worried that crooked dealers might slip a few chips into their pockets during each shift. Pocketless pants solved a problem for the casinos but created one for male dealers: where would they put their wallets and keys while working?

A stretchy, tubular spandex product called a "Comfort Carrier" came to the rescue. It fit tightly over the wearer's calf, and had two separate pockets: a large pocket for a wallet, and a smaller pocket for a ring of keys. It solved the dealer's pocketless pants problem, and it solved the team's problem as well. The computer and its battery fit into the larger pocket, and the vibrator fit snugly into the smaller one.

One seemingly innocuous issue involved socks. What the players had was a pair of shoes with a button in each toe. A foot-long wire extended out from each button. This wire had to travel from that button to a computer that was underneath their pants. The button was outside their socks. For obvious reasons, the players wanted the wire inside their socks. Somehow, the wire would have to cross the fabric barrier between foot and shoe. It was a topological necessity. In short, their socks needed holes.

The first incision was made in a black cotton sock using an ordinary pair of scissors. No good. This hole grew exponentially as time went on, eventually consuming most of the toe area of the sock. The next tool brought to bear on the issue was a soldering iron. This made a nice, neat hole, and because the iron cauterized the threads it initially prevented the sock from beginning to unravel, but eventually the same problem emerged—along with the wearer's big toe.

Ultimately, the solution was to stitch around the edge of a freshly burned hole. This neatly prevented the growth of the hole. What is unfortunate is that there is no visual record of this group of consummate professionals threading needles and repeatedly stabbing themselves as they sat around Brian's living room sewing holes *into* dozens of pairs of socks. All that was missing were the rocking chairs.

> We may have all come into existence five minutes ago...
> with holes in our socks and hair that needed cutting.
> ~*Bertrand Russell,* Religion and Science

As soon as the shoes were completed, and Mitch had managed to make Brian's program run in the miniature computers, the players threw themselves into their practice sessions. Appendix 4 explains shuffle tracking in some detail. The short version of what the players were about to do goes something like this:

1. Starting at the beginning of a shoe, they would enter cards in the order in which the cards were entered into the discard rack. That means when the shoe came to an end, Butch would know the count value of each card stacked in the rack. (Tens were not tens for Butch—they were –1, as were aces. Small cards were +1, and sevens, eights, and nines were 0.)

2. As the dealer shuffled, the players would enter where the dealer's grabs were coming from, and how many cards the dealer was grabbing with each grab.

3. Given this information, Butch would rearrange his internal representation of the cards in the discard rack. For example, based on the data input by the players, Butch might take cards 75–110 (for which it knew the count—let's say it totaled –5), and marry them to cards 180–208 (for which it also knew the count—let's say it was –3). The resultant clump of sixty-three cards would have an absolute count of –8; that is, the clump would have a net of eight more tens and/or aces than a balanced clump would have. This clump would be played with an edge of almost 3 percent.[17]

Sounded great. Now all they had to do was figure out how the hell to do all of that without looking like they were doing what they were doing. The various skills they would have to master were as follows:

1. They had to learn the variety of toe commands that told Butch all that was happening at the blackjack table. These commands had to be completely automatic. When the dealer began to shuffle, the players had to concentrate on what the dealer was doing, not on which toes they were depressing. There were commands during the deal, a separate set of commands during the shuffle, and yet

_____

17 The "true" count, or count-per-deck, of this clump would be 6.6, or an edge of 3.3 percent. Remove the off-the-top house edge, and you get a 2.8 percent advantage for that clump.

another area of the program for housekeeping (number of decks, shuffle type, off-the-top disadvantage, etc.). All this had to be done not with a keyboard for input, but with just two buttons—one beneath each big toe. Nor was there a nice color monitor for output—all Butch could muster were vibrating dots and dashes tickling the players' calves.

2. The players had to get the cards entered quickly and accurately, in the order in which the dealer shoved the cards into the discard rack.

3. The players had to train their eyes so that they could determine the size of clumps of cards, both relatively and absolutely. When the dealer split the four decks into two piles of roughly two decks each, they had to estimate which side had more cards, and by how many. When the dealer grabbed cards from each of these packets, they had to estimate these grabs to within five cards. Since the average time between a dealer's grab and the onset of the first riffle was less than one second, the players had to be extremely fast as well as accurate.

Learning this took quite a bit of time. Brian wrote a manual, and the players spent days sitting around, depressing buttons and learning what feedback to expect when they entered an LRR, an RLL, an LRRL, an RLLR, and a dozen other commands. (It was during this time that a number of Taylor's friends asked, "Wouldn't it be easier just to get a job?" To which he replied, "Yeah, but it wouldn't be as much fun.")

Learning to enter the cards themselves didn't take long. Each player flipped through decks, just as they had when counting down decks. Instead of counting, however, they allowed their toes to input each card—left toe for ten-value cards and aces, right toe for two through six, and both toes down simultaneously for seven, eight, or nine. After around a thousand decks, the players no longer had to think about card entry. Their eyeballs saw a ten, and their left toe went down. Out popped an eight, both toes went down. Their brains had been bypassed.[18]

---

18 They learned this so completely that, to this day, if you ask Taylor how to enter a small card, he first feels which toe goes down, and only then tells you "right." His toes know; "he" doesn't.

Once card entry itself was automatic, they had to learn to enter the cards in the order in which they were shoved in the discard rack. This would take a lot of practice. And there would be no shortcuts; they were simply going to have to deal hundreds of shoes and enter cards until their toes cramped.

There was a shortcut for packet estimation. Tony made card packets of twenty to sixty cards each and laminated them, writing the size of each on the side of the packet with a Magic Marker. (Why laminate and not simply use rubber bands to hold the packets together, you ask? Because rubber bands would compress the thirty-five cards down a bit, so they looked like thirty-two cards or so.) The "dealer" (one of the players) would hold a piece of cardboard vertically on the table, grab two packets from a shoebox, and position them on the felt approximately where a dealer would. The dealer then lifted the cardboard, and quickly slammed it down like a guillotine. After glimpsing the packets for half a second or so, the players—seated on the other side of the cardboard—would make their estimates, and then check to see how they did. After a month of practice, they got remarkably good at this.

To maximize training efficiency, one player would deal to the other four. After about an hour and a half, the players rotated. This rotation continued smoothly until it was Tony's turn to deal.

"Damn, this is boring," Tony complained, after dealing for about twenty minutes. "All work and no play spoils the child." After a few more rounds he took off, telling everyone he would be right back.

An hour later, Tony returned with a new video recorder (the latest in 1982 technology—a top loader with a remote control connected to the recorder by a fifteen-foot wire) and several movies he had rented. He hooked up the recorder to Brian's television, turned the kitchen table so that the person dealing could see the television screen, and took his place behind the table.

"That's more like it," Tony said, starting to deal a new shoe. He could now watch a movie while dealing, and the players could go on with their practice session with their backs to the set.

A beautiful scheme, with only one small flaw. Tony persisted in choosing pornographic movies to watch while dealing, and the moaning, groaning, and assorted other sounds emanating from behind the players was proving to be difficult to ignore.

"Damn it, Tony," Brian complained, after a particularly loud moan traveled through the apartment. "Are you aware you can actually rent regular movies?"

"He who laughs last is the mother of invention," Tony grinned, his eyes glued to the action on the tube. "You should thank me. If you guys can concentrate with this going on right behind you, concentrating in a casino should be a piece of pie."

"Don't act like you're doing this for our benefit," Brian said, attempting to input the round Tony had just dealt.

"Not exactly. But—oh my God, would you look at that!"

Four heads turned at once, and Tony quickly scooped the cards and thrust them into the discard rack.

"Gotcha!" Tony exclaimed, as four sullen faces turned back to the table. They had all turned to look at nothing more arousing than the shot of a traffic jam.

Despite the terrible working conditions, practice continued. The players' shuffle-tracking skills improved rapidly, and after a month they felt ready to go into a casino with Butch.

Largely due to his extraordinary eyesight, Guppy was the undisputed expert at estimating the size of dealer grabs. No matter how fast his teammates grabbed the cards during the shuffle, his estimates were accurate.

Taylor and Brian were not as good at assessing the size of the grabs, but were the best at operating Butch. They very rarely got lost traversing the program. Reed was reasonably good at estimating grabs and operating the computer, and Tony was—well, Tony was Tony.

"Tony gave a whole new meaning to the phrase 'getting lost in the shuffle,'" says Brian.

The team cut a deck of cards to see who would be the first to attempt a Butch-aided playing session in a casino, and Taylor lost.

A little nervously, Taylor slid the spandex dealer's sock up over his left calf. Brian handed him a computer and a battery, which he slid into the larger of the two pockets. He plugged the Shimani vibrator into its proper connection and inserted it into the small pocket. The vibrator fit snugly against the top of his calf, which was particularly sensitive.

A long wire—dubbed the "groin wire"—plugged into the computer and ran up his left leg, over the crotch of his pants, and down his right leg. Taylor poked the wire emerging from the button in his right shoe through the neatly embroidered hole in his right sock. He then carefully pulled the shoe on, and plugged the connector into the south end of the groin wire. Another short wire ran from the computer to the wire emerging from the button located in the toe of his right shoe.

Once everything was hooked up and his pant leg was smoothed over the slight bulge in his left calf, Taylor took Butch out of hold by depressing and holding his left toe down and then depressing his right toe five times. The vibrator responded by giving him two long buzzes. Taylor practiced some toe inputs, and walked Butch through a couple of his sub-routines. The vibrator responded to each input with a specific series of dots and dashes. Taylor again pressed LRRRRR, putting Butch back in hold, and looked at his teammates.

He was ready to go.

CHAPTER 11
BUTCH

He said, You must be joking son
Where did you get those shoes?
~*Steely Dan*, "Pretzel Logic"

Stepping carefully to avoid putting too much pressure on the buttons in the bulbous toes of his shoes, Taylor wobbled to Brian's Ford LTD and pulled himself into the passenger seat. Even though it was a clear, cool December afternoon, he was perspiring. No one talked during the drive up Flamingo Road and across Paradise to the monstrous Las Vegas Hilton. Taylor shuddered slightly as Brian pulled into the fifteen-minute hotel check-in parking area to drop Taylor off.

"Have fun," Brian said cryptically. "We'll be watching from the bar."

"You're sure this is legal?" Taylor asked, his normally formidable balls shriveling rapidly.

"For the fortieth time, Uston's team was caught with computers in Lake Tahoe, and it isn't illegal. Nobody's going to jail."

Taylor carefully lowered himself out of the car and glanced up at the Hilton towering above him. Keith Taft had named his playing computer David, after the Biblical character who had slain the giant Goliath. Eyeing the enormous building, which appeared to sway gently above him, Taylor thought Taft's choice of name had been particularly apt.

Walking gingerly, Taylor entered the casino and veered off to the right toward the blackjack pit. In hold since leaving Brian's apartment, Butch ignored any inadvertent inputs as Taylor hobbled through the casino.

After walking past several tables Taylor found Stan, a dealer he had scouted months before. Stan was the neatest shuffler Taylor had ever seen. Nervously, Taylor pulled out a stool and sat down. There were four other players at the table, but Taylor kept his mouth shut. He was a long way from being comfortable enough to talk and play at the same time, so he didn't want to initiate any conversation. He slid forward to the edge of the stool and lowered his legs so that his feet were flat on the floor. (Taylor was tall enough to manage this—Guppy and Brian would have to learn to play with their feet balanced on one of the stool's horizontal metal bars.)

He started playing nickels, waiting for the beginning of a fresh shoe. After a few hands, Taylor realized that he knew the count. Even though there was no reason to, his brain was on automatic pilot, counting all by itself.

When Stan finished dealing the shoe, Taylor took Butch out of hold and went into the setup sub-routine. By using a variety of toe combinations, Taylor told the computer that they were playing a four-deck game with an off-the-top disadvantage of 0.5 percent. The shuffle was type two, and the unused cards were placed either on the top or the bottom of the discards at the end of each shoe. When all the setup info had been entered, Taylor pressed RLLR to go to the main body of the program. Butch informed Taylor that everything was ready by giving him a long vibrating dash.

Stan began to deal from the freshly shuffled pack of cards. As with most multiple-deck games, the cards were being dealt face up. The woman on first base was dealt a thirteen, and promptly busted. Stan took her money, scooped up her cards, flipped them over, and shoved them into the discard rack. Taylor pressed his left toe, then his right toe, then his left toe, and then LRR. That told Butch that a −1 card, a +1 card, and a −1 card had been inserted in the discard rack. The vibrator acknowledged receipt of the information by giving Taylor a vibrating dot.

The woman seated between Taylor and first base stood with her sixteen. Taylor was next, and hit his fourteen with a four. The man to Taylor's immediate left stood with a twenty. The woman at third base had a blackjack. Stan paid her and put the ace and ten in the discard rack. Taylor informed Butch by pressing his left toe twice, and then LRR. Dot, said the vibrator.

Stan busted his hand, and began paying the other players. Taylor entered the cards that remained on the table, and finished with an LRR, which told

Butch that the cards that had been entered since the last LRR were being flipped over and placed in the discard rack.

Taylor continued to play, entering cards in the order in which they were inserted into the discard rack. Butch was storing the precise order of the stack of used cards in his internal electronic array. Taylor's toes worked effortlessly as Stan dealt the game. The hours of practice had made this part automatic. And without the distraction of Tony's feature films, the casino version was actually quite a bit easier than the home game.

After three of the four decks had been dealt out, Stan came to the plastic stop card. The cards would be shuffled when this round was completed.

Taylor gripped the rail with his hands, readying himself. Stan finished the round. Taylor entered the cards, pressed LRR, and then pressed LRL, telling Butch that the shuffle would now commence. A short vibration told Taylor that Butch was ready.

Stan removed the undealt cards from the shoe and placed them on top of the cards that were in the discard rack. Taylor pressed his right toe, telling the computer that the undealt cards were on top. A dot tickled Taylor's calf.

Stan removed the four decks from the discard rack and placed them on the felt in front of him. As Taylor watched intently, Stan broke the four decks into two almost equal piles, and separated them.

Taylor depressed his left toe, telling Butch that Stan had moved the top half of the pack to the left. Then he depressed his right toe, indicating that the pile to the right was five cards higher than the pile to the left, and then depressed both toes to enter the information. Butch responded with a short vibration.

Stan grabbed some cards from the right pile and some from the left, and shuffled them together. Taylor estimated that Stan had grabbed thirty-five cards from the left side and thirty from the right, and entered this information with his toes. The small electric train motor vibrated against Taylor's calf as each input registered.

Twice more Stan grabbed cards, and twice more Taylor entered his estimates of the grabs. After the last grab Taylor pressed RLR, telling Butch the shuffle was completed.

In printed form, the program that was now running in the computer strapped to Taylor's calf was 110 pages long. Electrons streaming from chip to chip were traveling hundreds of yards along the circuit board's maze of traces. Mitch estimated that the computer performed a quarter-million floating-point operations in order to come up with a cut point.

An eighth of a second after Taylor's toes requested it, Butch buzzed out a cut point.

Dash-dot-dash, dot-dash-dash. Six-three. That meant that the bottom packet was the one rich in tens and aces. If Taylor placed the cut card at six-three—that is, three decks less fifteen cards from the front of the pack—more tens and aces than normal should start coming out right off the top of the shoe.

Stan placed the four-deck pack on the felt and offered the cut. Taylor leaned forward, took the plastic stop card, and cut the cards.

In practice, cutting to cut point six-three was something Taylor had learned to do with considerable accuracy. His estimate was almost always within five cards. Here, however, he didn't have to estimate at all. Since Stan hadn't entirely smoothed the pack of cards before offering the cut, Taylor could still see the seam where the second packet ended and the third one began. Taylor inserted the cut card at the seam and his toes pressed right, left, right; then left, right, right. That told the computer that the cut card was indeed placed at cut point six-three.

Butch responded by vibrating out a long dash. That meant Taylor should bet a maximum bet, because the packet he had just cut to the front of the shoe had such a preponderance of tens and aces that he would be playing with at least a 2 percent edge.

Taylor bet two hands of fifty dollars. Stan raised his eyebrows, and called out, "Green action." A pit boss came over to the table, glanced at the empty discard rack, and shrugged. Not one card had yet been dealt. What was there to worry about?

Taylor continued to enter cards as before. Now Butch was keeping track of the order of the cards going into the discard rack (in order to track the next shoe), and simultaneously keeping track of the cards coming out of the current shoe (in order to inform Taylor if and when the current ten-rich packet was depleted of its supply of tens and aces).

Butch didn't know the exact order of the cards in each of the sub-packets. It only knew which packets were rich in tens and aces, and signaled bets accordingly.

As Stan worked his way through the four-deck shoe, Taylor spread his bets according to the vibrations he received on the back of his calf. A long dash meant a maximum bet—two hands of fifty dollars. A short dash meant a medium bet—one hand of a quarter. One, two, or three dots meant that the clump had a preponderance of small cards, and Taylor was to bet only a nickel.

When Stan reached the end of the shoe and shuffled, Taylor input information as before. When he completed the entries, he pressed RLR, and Butch responded by vibrating dash, dot-dot.

Three-two, Taylor said to himself. That meant the cut card should be inserted sixty cards from the front of the pack. Taylor reached for the cut card, but this time Stan offered it to the woman seated to Taylor's right.

Unconcernedly, she lopped about half a deck off the front of the pack. Taylor eyed the cut carefully. He estimated that the cut was about thirty cards from the front. Thirty cards is a cut point of one-six, so Taylor entered the cut point by pressing left-left-right, then right-right-left. Butch responded by giving him two dots.

Two dots meant that the clump the woman cut to the front of the shoe was poor; it contained a lot of small cards. That bitch. Taylor bet only a nickel.

After one round had been dealt, Taylor went into one of Butch's sub-routines. How many cards remain in this clump? Taylor asked with his toes. Butch responded with dot, dash dot dot. Fifteen cards. And what is the count of the upcoming clump? Dash dot dot, said Butch. True of plus five. Maximum bet.

Taylor looked at the unplayed cards waiting patiently in the shoe and smiled. The computer strapped to his calf was the next best thing to carrying an X-ray machine to the table.

A pit boss wandered over to the table and idly watched the game. Since there was no convention at the Hilton that week, there was very little action in the casino.

Taylor wondered what he looked like to the pit boss. Just some guy erratically spreading his bets from five dollars up to two hands of fifty. Sometimes he bet big off the top, and sometimes he didn't. Typical random tourist. He might hang in there for a while, but eventually the house edge would get him. After all, real players don't bet big off the top of a shoe.

After watching Taylor's table for a couple of shoes, the pit boss wandered off to find a more interesting game.

About two hours later, Taylor got up and left the table. His toes were beginning to cramp a little, and the adrenal rush that had accompanied him into the casino had worn off. Taylor put Butch in hold by pressing LRRRR and carefully walked to the cage to cash out.

Although he had lost a little over $200, he felt great. He had operated the computer for over two hours without getting lost in the program, he felt that he had played with an edge, and he had gotten no heat whatsoever. Betting off the top of a shoe was perfect cover; the pit boss responsible for Taylor's table had written him a dinner comp when he left.

Taylor's teammates were seated at the bar to the left of the main cashier's cage, giving the "question" signal by scratching their heads furiously. They had been watching Taylor play, and wanted to know what happened.

Taylor ignored them while he cashed out. Seated at the bar scratching their heads in unison, they looked like a tribe of monkeys that had just contracted fleas.

"I think you'd better practice walking with those shoes," Reed commented, when they all met back at Brian's apartment. "You look terrible."

"Yeah, well, so do you," Taylor responded. He was in a damn good mood.

"Seriously, you look like you have to go to the bathroom or something."

Taylor explained he was walking that way because he was afraid he would crush the buttons if he put too much weight on his toes.

"How was it?" Tony asked anxiously. "Did you win?"

"How did it feel?" Reed asked.

"Did you play with an edge?" Brian wanted to know.

"I lost, it felt good, and I think I had an edge," Taylor replied. "The count seemed to drop when I bet big, but that could have been wishful thinking. Could you add something to the program that keeps track of the cards that come out when we bet big?"

"That shouldn't be too difficult," Brian answered.

"Did you have any trouble keeping up with the dealers?" Tony asked.

Taylor shook his head. "When we practice, we do everything faster than they do."

"Did you get any heat?" asked Reed. Taylor again shook his head, and showed them the dinner comp.

"All right, Mr. Balls!" Reed exclaimed. "Everybody get out of the way!"

"How did you fit them under the table?" Guppy said.

"If those things get any bigger we're going to have to find you an apartment with a wider front door," Reed added.

"When can we go out and bet some real money?" Tony wanted to know.

"Not until we're sure everybody is playing with an edge," Brian said.

"Good idea," Tony agreed. "Slow and steady makes you healthy, wealthy, and wise."

Before anyone else went out with Butch, Brian wrote a short sub-routine that stored a recap of what actually happened at the table. At the end of each playing session, the player simply pressed a specific button sequence, and Butch dutifully buzzed out the recap; the edge the player had based upon the cards that actually came out during maximum, medium, and minimum bets.

One by one, the players strapped Butch to their calves and went out to play in a casino. After the initial nervousness had worn off, each player settled down and played just as he had played in practice.

Unfortunately for Tony, playing just as he had played in practice meant that he was unable to complete a shoe without getting lost somewhere. It was decided that Tony would be a Big Player until he became a better operator.

During a practice session at the Aladdin, Taylor perfected "the lean." Shuffle tracking offered two huge advantages over counting: cover (because they could bet off the top), and the fact that when they played a packet, they played it to the bottom. There would be no more situations like the one at the Sands that had started it all for Taylor: a huge count that never comes down because the tens and aces are stuck behind the cut card, never to see the light of day.

However, only the players knew where to cut optimally to ensure that the rich packet actually emerged. During his first practice session Taylor had reached for the cut card, but the dealer tended to move past him and offer the cut to another player. Reaching for the cut card was too obvious. However, by simply *leaning* toward the dealer, the subtle body language was enough to get the cut about every other deck.[19] Taylor taught the other players the lean. Later, when the big money was on the line, they would develop a set of signals so the operator could let a BP know where to cut.

The recap showed that Butch was providing an average edge of about 1.5 percent. Coupled with the automatic cover afforded by betting big off the top of a multiple-deck shoe, that edge looked mighty attractive.

Although an edge of 1.5 percent was only a little higher than a typical count edge, the real money came from the number of big bets they were able to shove out onto the felt. One of Brian's test programs indicated that approximately one hand in three would be played with an edge. Therefore, although the team would play with an edge that was only 0.5 percent or so higher than their average count edge, their financial expectation would be

---

19 When they started playing for real money, they would get the cut more often than that. Dealers tend to offer the cut to the big money at the table. That way, the big bettor can't blame his losses on another player's lousy cut. (He'd have to blame the guy at third base, like everybody else.)

about six times their count expectation, because they would get so many more bets out.

Everyone agreed that the most effective way to deploy the computer was to use the Big Player-Small Player routine. If the computer operators were to make large bets themselves, they might attract attention. Players betting five hundred bucks a hand who watched carefully as the cards are dealt out and also concentrated on the shuffle might give the play away. A BP would siphon off heat by drinking and talking and carrying on, while the operators performed in peace.

A few days before Christmas, someone with a Chinese accent and identifying himself as the personal valet of Mr. Edward Austin telephoned Jack Gordon, a junketeer who ran junkets from Chicago to the MGM Grand. The valet told Gordon that Mr. Austin would like very much to spend the holidays in Las Vegas, and had decided to stay at the MGM. Mr. Austin usually stayed at Caesars, the valet explained, but had vowed never again to play there.

Gordon ran through his litany of questions, attempting to discern the approximate size of the flounder he had on the end of the line. What games did Mr. Austin play? What accommodations was he used to? How long would he typically stay?

What Gordon was trying to determine without simply blurting it out was: how much can we expect this guy to lose? But the valet wasn't helping much. "He play brackjack and craps," "Suite…big suite," and "Couple days, three-four days" were the cryptic answers. Finally, the exasperated Gordon came out with it. "What kind of action can we expect from Mr. Austin?" he asked. "You know, what kind of player is he?"

"Oh, Mr. Austin velly good prayer," replied the valet. "Always ruse."

Mr. Austin's personal valet now had the junketeer's undivided attention. Of course Mr. Austin would be treated well, Gordon assured the valet. The MGM was accustomed to catering to dignitaries and other important guests. Mr. Austin had certainly made the right choice. The junketeer thanked the valet a little too unctuously, and hung up the phone.

Mr. Austin certainly had made the right choice, Reed thought, hanging up the phone. The game was good, the shuffle was one they could track, and the MGM could handle big action. Mr. Austin would be wined, dined, and treated like royalty while the rest of the team exercised their talented toes.

Through Milt—an ex-pit boss friend of Tony's—the team learned that a photograph of Tony had appeared in the latest edition of the Griffin Book as a result of the wig fiasco in Boomtown. Because the MGM was one of Griffin's subscribers, Tony would have to change his appearance before playing there.

First, he visited a hair salon, where for three hours a variety of chemicals stripped his hair of its natural color. Then, with his scalp still burning, his hair was dyed. When Tony entered the salon, he had had wavy black hair. He now strolled out of the salon a strawberry blond. His eyebrows, however, were still big and black.

Tony stopped at a supermarket for Nature-Dye, a product developed to bleach a woman's facial hair in order to make it less noticeable. Nature-Dye came with one tube of goop, a container of powder, a little plastic dish, and a little plastic spatula. Following the instructions carefully, Tony squeezed some of the goop onto the little plastic dish, added some of the powder, and mixed the two together with the little plastic spatula. He then painted his eyebrows with the resulting mixture. Fifteen minutes later, he used a washcloth to remove the stuff and—voilà! Tony had blond eyebrows.

Tony took four pictures of his new face in a do-it-yourself photo booth. He then delivered the photos and four hundred dollars to someone he knew in town. The following morning, Tony returned to collect an executive identification badge, a credit card, and an Illinois driver's license bearing Tony's very blond countenance and the name Edward Austin.

Brian dropped Tony off at McCarran International Airport a half hour before American flight number 122 was due in from Chicago. All precautions had been taken. Brian had called the airline to be sure the flight was on time. Tony was carrying a warm overcoat. He even had a pink ticket carbon for the very flight he was theoretically taking, courtesy of a female travel agent he had impressed one evening. Now Tony waited in the gift shop near Gate B16, the gate at which the flight was scheduled to arrive.

Fifteen minutes before the scheduled arrival time, a guy wearing a chauffeur's uniform and a bored expression showed up with a sign reading "Mr. Austin." He sat in one of the molded plastic chairs and lit a cigarette.

When the arrival of the flight was announced, the chauffeur ground out his cigarette, straightened his uniform, and held the sign in front of him. Passengers emerging from the Jetway streamed past him. Tony waited a few minutes, and then stepped up to the chauffeur from behind and tapped him on the shoulder.

"I'm Mr. Austin," Tony said, extending his hand. "I guess I walked right past you the first time. Sorry."

"No problem, sir. Luggage?"

Tony shook his head. "Just this," he answered, indicating the large suit-carrier draped over his shoulder. The team had decided that causing Mr. Austin's luggage to arrive on the baggage carousel was more trouble than it was worth, so Mr. Austin of necessity became a very light traveler.

Lamentably, the limo ride was very short. Tony hardly had time to introduce himself to the girl he found in the backseat before they were pulling up in front of the MGM Grand.

"See you again?" Tony asked hopefully. The girl straightened her clothes and smiled.

Tony met the junketeer at the registration desk and handed him an envelope containing $30,000 in cash. As he played, he would draw markers against this "front money." At the end of the trip, any outstanding markers would be paid off with the money he had just handed over. It was Gordon's fervent hope that Mr. Austin's outstanding markers would amount to at least thirty grand.

Tony's suite was nice, but not quite what he had expected. Wait until they see my action, he thought. They'll give me the biggest room they've got. Money makes their heads go round.

Shortly after dinner Tony's phone rang. The caller was looking for someone named Taylor. Sorry, said Tony. Wrong room. He hung up and immediately went downstairs to the casino. He found a seat at a slot machine that afforded him an unobstructed view of Taylor, who was seated alone at a $25 minimum table.

Ten minutes later, Taylor's dealer arrived at the plastic stop card. He shuffled, and Taylor inserted the cut card. A moment later, Taylor clumsily lit a cigarette.

That was Tony's signal. He strolled over to the table, introduced himself to a nearby pit boss, and asked for a $5,000 marker.

"Do you have credit with us, Mr. Austin?" asked the pit boss.

"No. I'm playing against front money I have in the cage. I'm on a junket with Jack Gordon."

The pit boss went to the phone in the pit, spoke briefly with the head cashier, and returned to the table with a clipboard and a broad smile.

"Sorry for the delay, Mr. Austin. Next time there will be no wait."

The dealer counted out $5,000 in black chips as Tony signed the marker with a flourish.

"Let's get started, shall we?" Tony said to the dealer. He glanced at Taylor and bet two hands of $1,000 off the top of the freshly shuffled shoe. The pit boss's already broad smile broadened. The MGM would be very good to Mr. Austin.

Tony played for four hours. He spread from $100 up to two hands of $1,000—a bet spread that would have gotten an ordinary counter barred in about ten minutes. But nobody was getting barred here. Tony's bets did not follow the count. He was a pretty good blackjack player, but he did make a number of "mistakes"—changes in Basic Strategy based upon the count of the clump he was playing. The bosses likely figured he was playing with a disadvantage of at least 1 percent—which meant he should lose several thousand dollars an hour in the long run.

By the end of the first session, Tony had been introduced to a dozen key employees. He gently hinted that his room wasn't exactly what he had expected. He pointed out that if his was the best room they had, then perhaps he should have stayed at Caesars after all.

When his first blackjack session was over, Tony discovered how much the MGM liked his action. He had been moved to a suite on the top floor of the tower, serviced by an elevator reserved exclusively for those few guests staying in the penthouse suites. A guard was stationed directly outside the elevator, checking the identification of each visitor who arrived on the top floor. Tony's view of the Strip was magnificent.

Tony was more interested in a different view. He called the concierge and requested the company of the woman he had barely met in the limo.

The first session went well. Tony won $6,000, and there was no heat. On the contrary, the bosses were falling all over themselves to make sure that everything was perfect. The following day, Brian played a session with Tony that netted $5,000. They were pulling money out at will, with no heat at all. This was going to be a slam-dunk.

On Christmas Eve Guppy went in to operate. By now the bosses were very familiar with the way Mr. Austin played, and hardly bothered to watch. When he arrived at the table, the bosses put out the "$100 minimum" sign. That meant all new players would have to bet a minimum of $100. Players who were already at the table—Guppy, in this case—were exempt from the new minimum. The high minimum kept average players from joining Guppy and Tony at the table, meaning they were getting the cut close to 100 percent of the time.

Although Mr. Austin spread his bets like a madman, the MGM's counters in the sky—watching the game via television monitors—clearly had determined that he wasn't spreading with the count. If they noticed, the counters may have found it curious that the count tended to drop when Mr. Austin made his big bets (a result of all those tens and aces emerging), but that could have been a simple fluctuation. The important point was—no way was he counting. The attitude from the pit couldn't have been clearer: let the man play.

Guppy's session began at 9:00 p.m. on Christmas Eve. By 11:00 p.m., Guppy had already returned to Brian's apartment.

"Barred?" Brian asked incredulously, when he saw the forlorn look on Guppy's face.

"We lost it all," Guppy said. "All the money we were up, and all the money in the cage."

"What went wrong?" Brian asked.

Guppy shrugged. "Bad fluctuation. The recap was good—over two percent." He flopped down on the couch. "Let's go someplace like Bolivia."

"Butch and the Kid!" said Reed from the couch.

"Look," said Brian, "you were playing with an edge. That means there is only one thing to do."

"What's that?"

"Go back in there and get it back! It's a good game, and you're losing. This is the best time to play. Come on! Go back tomorrow on day shift and win it back!"

If only life were that simple. Guppy went. When he returned from the next day's session, his teammates were waiting for him at Brian's apartment. Guppy entered, walked straight to the bathroom, and threw up. He and Tony had lost another $60,000. Merry Christmas, MGM.

"What the hell can go wrong next?" Taylor asked disgustedly.

"Look at the bright side of the fence," said Tony. "At least my disguise is working."

"You're going to have to do something about your eyebrows pretty soon," Brian advised. "The roots are beginning to show."

Tony examined himself in the mirror. Black roots faintly traced the outline of his blond eyebrows. Time for more Nature-Dye.

He removed the Nature-Dye box from his toiletry bag. For the second time in a week he squeezed some of the goop onto the plastic dish, sprinkled some of the powder on the goop, stirred the two together with the little plastic spatula, and then painted his eyebrows with the resulting mixture. Fifteen minutes later, he used the little plastic spatula and a washcloth to remove the goop.

Tony washed his face, toweled off, and turned toward his teammates.

"What's wrong with you guys?" he asked curiously.

Brian was of the opinion that the second mixture must have been stronger than the first. Taylor thought Tony had used too much of the stuff. And Guppy was convinced it was a message from God. Whatever the case, Mr. Austin's MGM holiday was over. His forehead was as bald as a doorknob. The second application of Nature-Dye had caused his eyebrows to fall out completely.

CHAPTER 12
THE DESERT INN FIASCO

Some days we win, and other days we win more.
~Smirking Pit Boss

The team was a study in depression after the MGM play. The recap showed that they had been playing with a substantial edge, but their bankroll had been hammered. Although they all hated losing, Taylor hated losing to the MGM most of all.

Tony wanted to be sure that the recap was recording the edge properly. Maybe the way the recap calculated the edge wasn't an accurate reflection of their actual edge at the table.

To test the accuracy of the recap, Brian dealt out hands at the kitchen table. Each round was counted manually, and the actual count edge was compared to the edge indicated by the recap. After three days and six thousand total hands, the recap agreed with the count edge to within 0.2 percent. They were indeed playing with an edge, and the recap was reflecting that edge accurately. The loss was nothing but a negative fluctuation. They took a vote, and decided to continue playing.

Manually tracking those thousands of hands taught them something. They were experiencing tremendous fluctuations because of the sheer number of large bets they were making. Instead of making eight or ten top bets per hour, they were making close to fifty. They were experiencing a day's worth of fluctuations every hour. As Brian had learned early on, you don't cut fluctuations by raising your expectation—you cut them by raising your edge. Shuffle tracking provided a high expectation and great cover, but the edge was only a little higher than a count edge. They would just have to learn to live with the swings.

Tony asked his friend Joey to come to Las Vegas and learn to operate the blackjack computer. Although this made the rest of the players uncomfortable, they were reluctant to argue. After all, Tony had provided the thirty grand to have the computers built in the first place, put up a substantial bankroll, and they had thanked him by costing him another ninety thousand dollars. How much worse could Tony's friend do?

Taylor and his teammates had learned to operate Butch as the program was being written, so they had had the opportunity to learn the commands one at a time. In its current form, however, the program was quite complicated. Learning to operate it from scratch wasn't going to be easy.

One of the more difficult aspects was the variety of toe inputs. Since only two buttons were used to produce fourteen different commands, the operator needed to perform a variety of overlapping sequences of button presses.

Joey, a player who years ago had learned to play blackjack with Tony, couldn't wait to become an operator. Since he didn't have a computer with which to practice, he rigged up a set of red and green lights and wires that attached to the buttons in a pair of playing shoes he had constructed with Tony's guidance. By watching the lights, he would know his button depressions were overlapping properly as long as the lights similarly overlapped.

As his wife steered their car from Chicago to Vegas, Joey practiced with his toes and his lights. If a Right-Left-Right sequence was called for, Joey would watch to be sure that the red light stayed illuminated until his left toe came down, lighting the green light. Once the green light came on, he then released and depressed his right toe. Obediently, the red light would blink off and then on.

By the time he arrived in Las Vegas, Joey had learned the toe commands. As soon as he learned to estimate packets of cards quickly and accurately, he would be ready to play. Having served their purpose, the wires and lights were stuffed in a corner of Joey's suitcase and forgotten.

Because Tony was reluctant to be seen in public with no eyebrows whatsoever, he phoned Julie—the waitress from Boomtown—and asked her to come to Vegas to be a Big Player. She agreed, and flew down the following day.

Since she had never before played a hand of blackjack, Tony wanted the rest of the team to help train her. To everyone's surprise, she learned the signals and the playing strategy quickly. And she did provide some built-in misdirection. It would be pretty hard for any male pit boss in the world to concentrate on her play when those top buttons came undone.

No one knew how comfortable she would be betting two hands of $2,000, so they decided to let Taylor break her in during a practice session at the Fremont. The Fremont dealt a six-deck game much like the one dealt at the Desert Inn. Following Taylor's signals, she spread from one hand of $2 to two hands of $20. The signals were undetectable, the computer functioned flawlessly, and Julie won $400. Good fluctuation.

The next evening, Taylor and Julie walked into the Desert Inn confidently. Taylor used the same program, operated the same miniature computer, and used the same signals. The six-deck game was virtually identical to the Fremont's. Everything was the same as the previous night's practice session, except for one detail. Now, instead of betting from $2 to two hands of $20, Julie bet from $200 up to two hands of $2,000. The signals were undetectable, the computer functioned flawlessly, and Julie lost $50,000. Bad fluctuation.

Son of a bitch. Taylor sorely wanted to kick something, but was afraid he would damage the shoes he had worked so hard to build. For the first time in more than a year, he walked straight to his car without checking to see if he was being followed. When he reached his car, he realized he had been careless, but dismissed it with a shrug. Why the hell would anybody bother following me? he thought disgustedly. The only reason he could think of was that the Desert Inn might want to invite him back to help Julie lose another fifty grand, any time at all.

He drove to Brian's apartment in a daze. Fifty thousand dollars. He had laughed when remembering the look on Guppy's face after his second MGM session, but now it didn't seem so goddamn funny. Taylor could have bought a Corvette for each member of his team with the money he had been instrumental in losing.

When he entered Brian's apartment, his teammates looked at him expectantly. Brian stood up, saw the look on Taylor's face, and sat down again.

"You'll never be a poker player," he said, and closed his eyes. After three weeks of play, the team was down over an eighth of a million dollars.

The phone rang, and Taylor moved woodenly to answer it.

"That'll be Tony," Brian said. "He's been calling every two minutes for the past half hour."

Taylor lifted the receiver to his ear.

"Was it Julie's fault?" Tony wanted to know.

"No," Taylor replied. "She played perfectly. She's still there, checking into a suite. They gave her a full comp."

"I know," Tony said. "I'm with her now. Was it Butch? The shuffle? What?"

"No. Just another bad fluc—are you calling from her room?"

"Yeah. When do you—"

Taylor hung up.

"Asshole. How many times are we going to have to tell him not to use hotel phones?"

"How much did you lose?" Brian asked, without looking up.

"Fifty grand," Taylor said wearily.

"You won twenty top bets last night, and tonight you lost twenty-five. You're down nothing—five top bets."

"Why couldn't we have had the negative fluctuation when we were betting two goddamn dollars a hand?" Taylor asked bitterly.

"Because life is tough," Brian said. "What was your recap?"

To no one's surprise, the recap indicated that Taylor had played with a healthy edge. The computer had done its job nicely. According to the recap, Julie's expectation for the session was about $6,000. There was only one thing to do.

The following evening, Julie went in to play with Guppy. There was no heat at all. The bosses fell over themselves making sure everything was perfect. There was no way they were going to risk losing this whale to another casino. Any player able to lose $50,000 in one night and then return the very next evening with another pile of cash gets whatever she wants. The fact that Julie was stunningly beautiful certainly didn't hurt. The bosses were overwhelmed, and acted the part of the most gracious hosts imaginable.

This time things went a little better, and Julie won $20,000. At $2,000 a hand, the bosses knew that $20,000 was a minor blip on the radar. No need to worry. There was no heat from the pit.

The following night Reed operated the computer, and Julie won a little over $40,000. Now the bosses were beginning to talk to each other behind cupped hands. It wasn't serious heat yet, but things were getting warm. Because of the way she played her hands, it was likely that they could tell she knew something about the game—for instance, she only took insurance with big bets out—but she should lose eventually. And they knew she wasn't counting, because she frequently bet big off the top of the shoe. Still...

Tony and Joey had moved into Julie's accommodations at the Desert Inn. It was a five-room suite with two bedrooms, a kitchen, a Jacuzzi, and its own swimming pool. It was the best the DI had to offer, and it was awesome.

Prior to this, Taylor and his teammates had resisted comped rooms. Brian felt it was too easy for casino personnel to keep track of players who had rooms in the very hotel in which they were playing. They accepted meals, but, as tempting as those suites were, they were just too dangerous.

Tony had convinced Brian otherwise. It wouldn't look normal for a gambler betting thousands of dollars a hand to refuse a suite. It was one of the perks big bettors expected, and it would be more suspicious to refuse. To his everlasting regret, Brian had caved.

At about 6:00 p.m., Tony called Brian from Julie's suite. They spoke briefly, and Tony invited Brian over for a meal.

At 7:00 p.m., Brian went over to the suite to eat. Tony had ordered about $300 worth of room service—courtesy of the casino, of course—and they feasted on cracked crab, broiled lobster tails, and filet mignon.

At 8:30 p.m., there was a knock on the door. Tony peered through the peephole, and all he saw was a sea of blue.

"Hotel security," said the voice behind the blue.

When Taylor received the phone call, he was at his girlfriend's apartment reading *Fools Die*, a novel by Mario Puzo, and thinking how unlike a real gambler he actually was. There was something dizzying about the consuming passion of the compulsive gambler; something with which he could not empathize at all. He answered the phone distractedly, his mind still on the novel.

"Yeah, they're holding us at the Las Vegas jail," Brian's voice was saying. "Julie, Tony, Joey, and me. You'll need twelve grand to bail us out."

Taylor squeezed his eyes shut. I have to stop getting so involved in what I'm reading, he thought, and glanced at the novel. It lay mute on the end table.

"Possession of a cheating device, possession of burglary tools, and lying to a police officer," read the desk sergeant. "Bail is a thousand dollars for each charge. If you need a bail bondsman, one can be here within an hour."

Taylor shook his head. He pulled $12,000 from an envelope and counted it out onto the desk. Then he frowned. "Possession of burglary tools?"

The officer glanced at the report. "Yeah, that's what it says here."

"Burglary tools, my ass," Brian grumbled. They were on their way home, wedged into Taylor's Maverick. "What a farce. They found the hotel keys on the coffee table, so they charged us with possession of burglary tools."

"What keys?" Taylor asked, confused.

"The keys to Julie's suite."

"They're claiming the keys to her own room are burglary tools?" Taylor asked incredulously. "How can they do that?"

"They can do whatever they want. Look at the cheating device charge."

"Whose bright idea was it to have a computer in the room?" Taylor demanded. "I thought we talked about that."

"We did talk about that. There was no computer in the room."

"So why the hell were you charged with possession of a cheating device?" Taylor asked, more confused than ever.

Brian stared out the window. "You'll see."

The next evening, the lead story on all three local news broadcasts concerned the apprehension of a major Las Vegas cheating ring. According to the anchorman on the ABC affiliate, a group of players had been cheating at the Desert Inn. Over a hundred thousand dollars in cash and chips had been confiscated, along with an "electronic cheating device."

Preston Hubbs, the department head in charge of gaming, stepped in front of the camera to explain how the "cheating device" worked.

"What the hell is that?" Reed asked, moving closer to the television screen.

"They have got to be kidding," Taylor said hollowly.

Preston Hubbs was holding the lights Joey had hooked to his shoes when he was practicing his toe inputs. With a pained expression, Hubbs outlined his theory of how the operation worked.

"A girl was positioned at one end of the pit. She made huge bets and lost a lot. This distracted the pit bosses. Meanwhile, at the other end of the pit, two other players were working. One player would position himself in such a way that he could monitor the hole card of the dealer." A shot of a dealer exposing his hole card from behind was replaced by Hubbs, who paused, squinted into the glaring television lights, and continued. "The player would signal his partner by illuminating the green light for 'hit' and the red light for 'stand.'"

"Thanks to quick action by Metro police," the anchor concluded, "the cheaters were thwarted. No money was lost by the Desert Inn."

Tony had difficulty making his attorney understand the charges. Losing thousands on purpose to gain a paltry two percent edge at the other end of the pit? Signaling with lights when a simple scratch on the side of the nose would do? Where were the lights? Sticking out of a hat, like rabbit ears? It was clear that no one involved in the case, not even the esteemed Preston Hubbs himself, bought the fanciful story. All charges were dropped two days later, and the money was returned. The police did keep the lights, however.

"How did they know?" Brian asked. He was sprawled out in Reed's reclining chair, his feet forming the ubiquitous V through which he viewed his corner of the world. Brian had moved out of his apartment. Having provided his address and phone number when he was arrested, his apartment and phone were officially burned. And Brian was distinctly unhappy. "That raid was no accident. They were specifically looking for some sort of device." He stared at Tony. "What tipped them off?"

"Maybe your phone was tapped," Tony suggested, clearly uncomfortable.

"I seriously doubt it," Brian said. "You want to know what I think?"

Tony already knew exactly what Brian thought. But he was going to hear it again.

"I think it was the phone in the suite at the Desert Inn. We told you fifty times not to use that phone, but you were too damn lazy to walk across the street to a pay phone. As a result, I had to flee my own apartment."

"Look, it happened and it's over," Tony said hurriedly. "But we oughta check out Reed's phone, just in case. I know a guy."

"There's nothing here," Brian said. "Tony, you screwed up. Period. Just don't do it again."

Then Reed came home with a hunched-over guy with thinning gray hair. Brian smiled. "Found him, eh?"

"His name's Jim," Reed said, enjoying himself. "Pretty good counter. I ran into him at the Castaway." Jim was twenty-eight going on sixty. His teammates called him "Pop."

Tony looked horrified. Pop was the guy with the wig who got him busted at Boomtown. "What the fuck is he doing here?"

Brian was thrilled. The symmetry was perfect. Pop was responsible for getting Tony busted, and Tony was responsible for getting Brian busted. Brian was stuck with Tony. Therefore…

"How long have you been playing?" Brian asked, handing Pop a deck of cards.

Pop shrugged. "Almost a year."

"Bet size?"

"One to five nickels."

Brian looked at Reed as Pop counted down the deck. There is a vast gulf between nickel bettors and players who have to face the music when they own the $300, or $500, or $1,000 bet sitting in front of them.

Pop finished in just under twenty seconds. "Ten," he said, and he was right. He tested out fine on Brian's counting program as well.

It was clear that Pop had the technical skills. Now what Brian needed was an explanation. Why was a player of this caliber—a player this *old*—shoving stacks of nickels across the layout? And, worse, getting barred?

It turned out that Pop had been riding a different curve from the players on Taylor's team. While they had started with modest bankrolls and built them up, Pop had come to Las Vegas with almost $20,000 he had collected from an insurance settlement. In six months, he had whittled that down to almost nothing. Then he met Arthur.

Arthur, a kindhearted, cartoonish character with curly hair and Coke-bottle glasses who had won $50,000 for himself during the late '70s counter convention in Atlantic City, decided to do his bit for mankind. He gathered together a group of players who were technically quite proficient counters, but were "down on their luck"—that is, they had all busted out in the recent past. Arthur bankrolled this sorry crew of five, who went out and in no time flat lost all of Arthur's fifty grand. So much for philanthropy.[20]

Pop and his unfortunate teammates had managed to lose Arthur's entire bankroll in less than 600 hours of play. And it was worse than that. Pop had become proficient in a rudimentary form of shuffle tracking. Although it wasn't nearly as powerful as the version Butch implemented, it worked.

---

20 That these counters had the technical ability to beat the game does not necessarily mean they were winning players who had simply experienced bad luck. Many technically proficient card counters can't win. Players who should win and don't often fail because they can't or don't disguise what they're doing. Casinos allow these players to play, so long as they lose. The moment they begin to win, they are unceremoniously tossed out the door. In the final analysis, the lesson Arthur should have learned from this fiasco is: there is no such thing as bad luck. The lesson Arthur actually learned was: if only I had some more money.

And it worked a lot better than counting. Yet the team had still managed to bust out.

"Bad fluctuation," said Brian.

"Maybe not," said Tony.

"Stealing?" asked Brian.

"Maybe," said Tony. "Listen. I know a guy..."

Tony knew a lot of guys. This particular guy was Milt, a reformed pit boss and drinking buddy who still had contacts in a number of casinos. It was Milt who had told Tony that his mug shot now adorned the Griffin Book. Tony thought Milt might be able to shed some light on Pop's troubles.

Brian was completely opposed to the idea. He wasn't sticking his snout out in front of a pit boss, retired or not.

"He's completely cool," said Tony. "Whatsa matter, you afraid you might learn something?"

More to prove Tony wrong than anything else, Brian agreed to go. Someone had finally figured out how to make Brian do something he didn't want to do.

At Tony's request, Brian strapped Butch to his leg before paying a visit to Milt. Tony told Milt they were trying something new, and that Milt was to try to figure out what it was.

Milt began to deal. Brian entered cards with his toes. Reed stood behind the table, pretending to read a magazine, but was actually spooking. And Guppy glimpsed the occasional hole card. In the midst of this carnage, Pop sat quietly at third, playing Basic Strategy.

After a few shoes, Tony asked Milt what he thought. "I don't know what he's doing," said Milt, pointing at Pop, "but I just know that guy's up to something."

Later, Tony asked Pop where he'd been barred. "Almost everywhere," said Pop.

"And your teammates?"

"Same thing."

"Bad fluctuation, you said," Tony told Brian.

Brian got it. Pop and his teammates were playing only very marginal games—they were barred everywhere else. Preferential shuffling and the occasional cheating meant they were probably playing with a disadvantage in those few joints that were still willing to let them play.

The team had some decisions to make. Brian was burned, Tony was burned, and the casinos' antennae had to be up. Everybody had to know there was more to the Desert Inn story, even if no one knew exactly what the rest of the story was. The best move would be to get out of town for a while and let things cool down.

They needed another player. Brian was going to stay put, changing the program when players found shuffles that differed from those Butch could handle. Nobody wanted to play with Tony—they were all too pissed off— and he was red-hot anyway.

Taylor and Guppy were going to pair up, but Reed needed a partner. They voted, and Pop came on board. Because he knew the fundamentals of shuffle tracking, he learned how to operate Butch quickly. Because he was a heat magnet, he would be an operator exclusively, which meant Reed would become a full-time BP. Reed couldn't have been happier with the arrangement.

"Where should we go?" Taylor asked.

"How about the Caribbean?" Brian suggested. "By the time you finish a sweep of the islands, it'll be springtime in Europe, and you can all go there."

"That sounds great!" Tony exclaimed. "Let's do it!"

CHAPTER 13

THE CARIBBEAN

Honey, pepper, leaf-green limes,
Pagan fruit whose names are rhymes,
Mangoes, breadfruit, ginger-roots,...
~*Agnes Maxwell-Hall*, "Jamaica Market"

Tracking cards with buttons in boots.
—*Tony Ricco*

The islands of the Caribbean extend eastward out into the Atlantic from Florida and then back toward South America like a boomerang. Taylor would start in Aruba—the bottom of the boomerang—and Guppy would start in the Bahamas. Brian stayed at home to receive word on the varieties of shuffles the players encountered.

Jack Gordon—the junketeer who had arranged Mr. Austin's truncated holiday at the MGM—proved to have connections in the Caribbean as well as in Las Vegas. With a few quick phone calls, Gordon arranged for Taylor's junket to Aruba and another junket to the Bahamas for Guppy.

The trips to Aruba and the Bahamas were fully comped. Players were required to deposit $15,000 in the casino cage and play at least three hours per day with a minimum bet of $50 to fulfill the requirements of the comp. In return, the casino paid their airfare, provided a suite, and supplied all they could eat and drink for a week. There was the risk that the program would not track the shuffles the players encountered on the islands, but they figured the odds were that they would find something. Besides, the alternative was to send a scout. Sending a scout to island-hop throughout the Caribbean would have cost a lot of money, and the team bankroll, while no longer in intensive care, was still in critical condition.

Guppy flew to the Bahamas and discovered that none of the casinos in Nassau or Freeport were trackable with the present program. The Cable Beach Club used two discard racks for the used cards, and the clubs on Nassau and Paradise Island shuffled the cards twice; thus, mixing the cards sufficiently and thoroughly so that clumps could not be tracked. Guppy reported back to Brian, played a break-even count game to qualify for the comp, and then flew to Puerto Rico.

In the meantime, Taylor had flown to Aruba and had located a great game at the Royal Palm Beach, one of five casinos located on the south shore of the island. Aruba, a small (six miles by twenty miles) coral gem located only fifteen miles off the coast of Venezuela, contains more casinos per square mile than any country in the world. Taylor called home with the news that the game was trackable, and Guppy left Puerto Rico on his own junket the following day.

Since their playing styles were identical, Taylor and Guppy never played at the same time. Taylor took the day shift, playing from three o'clock in the afternoon until about seven, and Guppy played in the evening.

For the entire week, Taylor rode a fantastic positive fluctuation. He was winning so fast he had to cut his bet spread in half to reduce heat. Even with a reduced edge, he was up a hefty $14,000 after only three days, betting up to $500 a hand.

During his fourth session, the casino manager—Mr. Kornberg—came over and sat next to Taylor. After watching Taylor play for a half hour, Mr. Kornberg told him he was a pretty good player.

"In fact, you're a very good player," Mr. Kornberg said. "Maybe too good for us."

Since Taylor had found out that the day shift boss knew how to count, Taylor thanked the casino manager for the compliment. "Yeah, I think I'm a damn good player," he boasted.

Taylor continued to play as the day shift boss took Mr. Kornberg aside. Taylor heard only stray bits of the conversation, but his blackjack antenna told him the day shift boss was attempting to convince Mr. Kornberg that

Taylor was not a counter and would lose eventually. Mr. Kornberg didn't look entirely convinced when he returned to watch Taylor play, but he didn't bar him.

"You know, there's a guy who comes in here at night who plays a lot like you do," Kornberg told Taylor. "It would be interesting to see the two of you play at the same table."

"That would be interesting," Taylor answered. Rather interesting indeed, he thought. Taylor was pretty sure Kornberg would never have the opportunity to learn exactly how interesting that would be.

The following day, Kornberg again sat down to watch Taylor play. Taylor was now up $18,000, and Kornberg was more convinced than ever that Taylor was a card counter.

"Boom!" Taylor exclaimed, using the trademark expression he had brought with him from Vegas. He now said it every time the dealer busted, as well as every time he was dealt a blackjack.

"I can count better than you can," Kornberg said, watching closely for Taylor's reaction.

"I'm sure you can," Taylor said distractedly, entering the last round into his computer.

"Yeah," Kornberg continued, raising his thonged foot and placing it on the stool next to Taylor. "I can count better than you because I'm not wearing any shoes."

The thud Taylor felt was like accidentally stepping off a curb. He stopped entering information and looked at Kornberg uneasily as his balls shriveled up and headed for the hills.

"Wha—?"

Kornberg smiled knowingly and waggled his toes. "You heard me. I can count better than you because I'm not wearing any shoes."

Taylor immediately sweated through his new *guayabera* and lost control of his toes. Shoes. No shoes. He thinks I need the shoes to count. He knows!

All right, Taylor thought. Calm down. Don't panic. You're not dead yet.

Taylor mentally inventoried his options. He couldn't run out the door because a) all of his stuff was in his room, including his airline ticket and his passport; b) he could barely walk, let alone run, with his ridiculous shoes on his feet; c) if he tried to leave they'd probably jump him; and d) the casino had over $30,000 that belonged to him.

Okay. Time to panic.

Taylor swallowed and looked at Kornberg's thonged foot, still perched on the stool next to him. Kornberg hadn't made a move to stop him from playing. The dealer was waiting patiently for his next bet. There wasn't a security guard in sight.

Something wasn't quite right. Taylor put a $50 bet out and waited for Kornberg to lower the boom. Kornberg didn't budge. Taylor played his hand, lost, and put out a $100 chip. There was no reaction at all from Kornberg.

The dealer busted. "Boom," Taylor said weakly, and smiled sweatily at Kornberg. Ignoring him, Kornberg was busily digging something out from beneath a toenail with a key.

Looking at Kornberg's gnarled toes, Taylor suddenly realized what he had meant. He had mentioned shoes not because Taylor's shoes were particularly suspect, but because Kornberg could use his ten exposed toes to help him count! It was a joke! Taylor breathed an audible sigh of relief and reset the computer with his now-functioning toes.

The Assault on Aruba netted Taylor and Guppy $26,500. They then booked separate fights to Curaçao. After discovering that the limits were only $100, they took a detour to Panama. They saw the Pope cruising through town in his bulletproof Popemobile and found a game with a low limit ($200), but with early surrender. Taylor won sixty-four top bets in only four hours. He managed to avoid massive heat by telling the pit bosses that he had spoken to the Pope earlier in the day, and that was why he was winning. It seemed they half believed him. How else could they explain that monster session?

Taylor and Guppy moved from island to island, sucking up American dollars like a huge vacuum cleaner. As was the case with the Royal Palm Beach in Aruba, most Caribbean casinos don't open until the afternoon or early evening. This meant the players had to find some way to occupy their days. Surrounded by beautiful white beaches, blue-green water, and brown women, they managed. Anything for the team.

They hit Antigua, where, with Butch's help, they quickly determined that the shoe was missing a number of tens and/or aces (the count was always positive when they reached the cut card, even after they presumably cut a massive clump of small cards to the back). So they moved on. Traveling south, they hammered St. Martin and St. Maarten (two sides of the same island), St. Kitts, and then Guadaloupe, where Guppy ran into a problem. A customs agent found Guppy's special shoes and fifteen or so decks of cards. Thinking quickly, Guppy told the customs man that he was a magician. The shoes, he explained, were part of an elaborate trick.

"A magician, eh?" said the customs man, and begged Guppy to show him a trick. When Guppy hemmed and hawed—he didn't know any—the customs agent performed a card trick. Thoroughly baffled by a trick designed to fool third graders, Guppy decided to retire his "magician" story.

They picked up visas in Guadaloupe, then flew north to the Haitian end of the island of Hispaniola. There, amid Haiti's incredible squalor, the players fully appreciated the meaning of a bad fluctuation. Being born in Haiti is a bad fluctuation indeed. They had a couple of good nights, and moved on to the Dominican Republic, where Gordon had set up another comped trip. They were treated like kings—lying beneath beach umbrellas and drinking rum concoctions by day, and serenaded by violinists and a piano player on a large rotating stage during dinner. They showed their appreciation by kicking ass in the casino at night.

After five weeks Taylor and Guppy were greeted as conquering heroes back in Vegas. They had won $55,000, enjoying a positive fluctuation that rivaled the negative fluctuation that had handed them their asses at the MGM. Because the limits in the Caribbean were lower than the limits in Vegas, the overall bankroll was still down, but no one was complaining.

Tracking was brand-new in the Caribbean; something none of the casinos had seen before. They had been barred in one of the casinos on the Dutch side of St. Maarten, but that was because the pit bosses thought they were counting. They discovered that a minimum level of savvy on the part of the casino personnel was necessary for tracking to be really effective. Pit bosses ignorant of how counting worked tended to think that a big bet spread alone was an indication of card counting. Ironically, the players played longer at the clubs with more informed personnel.

Brian wanted badly to travel with the team to Europe, but it just didn't make sense. After the variety of shuffles Taylor and Guppy had found in the Caribbean, they had to assume the shuffles they would encounter in Europe would be similarly diverse. Brian would have to stay home with his computer and make changes in the program so that his teammates could play the games they found.

Taylor made the first trip to Europe. Loews Monte Carlo offered a junket that paid for room, food, and airfare if the player qualified for the comp. Qualifying meant playing at least three hours a day with bets "up to the limit"; that is, bets up to 5,000 francs per hand (in early 1983, this was a little over $700). Taylor agreed to the requirements and flew Air France across the Atlantic to experience the worst jet lag of his life.

In the meantime, Reed and Pop flew to England. Initially they had been happy with the choice, because at least they wouldn't have a language barrier to compound the other problems inherent in finding oneself in a foreign land for the first time. (One minor issue: Reed thought England was "somewhere near New England, isn't it?")

They quickly learned that not everyone in England was as easy to understand as, say, Sean Connery. It took them several minutes to decide that the customs agent with the bizarre accent was attempting to ask them about the small computers they were carrying. Pop, following team rules, kept his mouth shut. Reed had set up his playing computer to attach to one of the Sharp calculators that had been eviscerated almost a year earlier. Reed told the customs agent that the computer was supposed to translate foreign languages, but that it must have broken down during the flight. The story worked.

It took Reed and Pop several days to familiarize themselves with the accents they encountered in London, Birmingham, and Manchester. If they were having this much trouble with one language, they thought, Taylor must be going through hell in France.

Several weeks after his teammates crossed the Atlantic, Tony—practicing with Butch in Vegas—decided to have a new pair of playing shoes built.

He brought a pair of shoes to a shoe repair shop located on Paradise Road near Tropicana, showed the shoemaker his buttons, and explained what he needed. While he was in the shop an attractive woman entered. Never one to pass up an opportunity, Tony decided to impress her. He showed her the buttons, and intimated that he and his magic shoes could take her to places she currently could only imagine. The woman smiled. She was quite impressed indeed.

When Tony returned to pick up his shoes a week later, there was quite a commotion at the little shop. It seems the woman Tony successfully impressed was a dealer at the Aladdin, and had reported the incident to her boss. He in turn had called the Griffin Detective Agency and the Gaming Commission. When Tony arrived at the shoe repair shop, he saw several agents belonging to these organizations waiting in force to see who showed up to claim those special shoes.

Fortunately, Tony had the presence of mind to leave without his newly minted magic shoes. Unfortunately, the Griffin agents were so impressed with the shoes that they put out a special "sheet" on them. A Griffin sheet is a bulletin containing any interesting information that cannot wait for the regular bimonthly publication. This bulletin is delivered immediately to Griffin subscribers all over the world.

In the meantime, unaware of the fan-splattering taking place in Las Vegas, Reed was busy playing blackjack in England. Casino gambling in England isn't the hard-driving, money-intensive business it is in the States. Before players can even enter a club in England, they must become members. The best way to become a member is to enter as a guest of someone who already is a member. Reed stood outside and waited for a club member whose nose did not appear to be lofted at too great an angle into the air, and asked if he could please enter as a guest. Reed proved to have a keen eye for relatively soft touches, and was rarely denied.

Upon gaining admittance with a member in good standing, Reed and Pop would apply for membership. The application procedure took forty-eight hours. So, two days after applying for membership at six different London clubs, Reed and Pop were afforded membership in five.[21] They were refused

---

21 These days, it would be a bad idea to apply for membership at this number of clubs at once. The inter-club communication is much better now than it was in the

at one club because the fellow who had gotten them in proved to be an obnoxious windbag, himself on the verge of being tossed out.

As is the case with almost everything British, the atmosphere in an English club is austere and stuffy. It would be unseemly for British croupiers to have to grub tips. Terribly gauche, you know. So tipping is strictly forbidden. Furthermore, gamblers who drink may exhibit an emotional outburst after a win or a loss. Well, that simply wouldn't do, would it? One shall maintain that stiff upper lip regardless, yes? Therefore, no alcoholic drinks are served in English casinos. In addition, the possibility exists that a player might attempt a particularly bad play and lose a certain amount of dignity in front of his tablemates. In order to prevent that from happening, the player in England is not permitted to split fours, fives, or tens, thank you very much.

This was Reed's little slice of heaven. While Pop operated Butch, Reed ordered ten drinks an hour, tried to tip on every other hand, and attempted to split every pair of fours, fives, and tens that came his way. It was quite good cover, and Reed was rather enjoying himself at the expense of his stuffy hosts.

By the time Tony's magic shoes had started generating heat in Las Vegas, Reed had already played at the London Park Tower, Stakis, and the Palm Beach, and was up just over £15,000. Pop then hopped aboard British Rail on a scouting expedition to Liverpool and Leeds, while Reed played on his own at the Cromwell Mint. After three days he had won a few thousand pounds, and there was no heat at all. Reed was keeping some of his money in the cage at the club, and was looking forward to another solid win.

Reed sauntered in to play the Mint one fine Tuesday, and the woman at the registration desk told him she was quite sorry, but the casino manager had informed her that she was not to allow him entrance to the club. She was apologetic but firm. Reed, recognizing a barring—albeit a mild one—when he encountered one, shrugged. He then asked for his money from the cage. Again, she was apologetic but firm. The casino manager had said that the money was not to be released from the cage until he himself had personally spoken to Reed. Reed cringed. This was not a good sign.

On the day that he was barred, Reed had come in to play wearing his playing shoes. These shoes, which Reed had constructed himself, were not the finest-

early '80s.

looking pair of shoes the world had ever seen. They were steel-toed work shoes that he had purchased at Gemco for $14. They were a size and a half too large (in order to accommodate the buttons) with enormous bulbous toes. Further, while Reed was constructing his shoes the miniature Dremel power saw had slipped, and a superficial gouge had been cut around the toe of the left shoe. When he installed the button and put the shoe back together, a little of the glue used to re-adhere the top of the shoe to the sole had oozed out and hardened. And, to top it off, there was some food.

A month or so earlier, Reed had been consuming a Dairy Queen vanilla ice cream cone after a play on a rather warm day, and a fair percentage of the ice cream had dripped onto his right shoe. The now-fossilized remnant of that dessert was still draped across his footwear.

The following day, Reed strode into the casino to get his money, wearing a sweat suit and Nike running shoes. He was met at the registration desk by the casino manager, a thoroughly proper gentleman who introduced himself as Mr. Rutland. Rutland, who presumably had never seen Reed before, looked him straight in the eye and asked, "And where are your shoes, Mr. Richards?"

Reed's balls, which had enlarged considerably over the course of the last few weeks, shriveled up and ran for cover. He shifted his weight from side to side and asked, "Uh, you mean my *dress shoes*?"

The next several hours were a complete waste of time. Rutland tried to convince Reed that it would be in the best interest of Northern Atlantic relations if Reed would just tell him what the shoes did. Reed adamantly denied the existence of any shoes at all. Finally Rutland sent Reed on his way, without his money.

Conceivably, Rutland could have made the argument that the casino had every right to the money Reed had won there. Rutland, however, kept the money that Reed had deposited in the cage as well. That seemed terribly unfair, but Rutland wouldn't budge. Tell me what the shoes do, he repeated, and maybe you'll get your money back.

Needless to say, this was the last time any team member deposited any money in a foreign casino. As it turned out, there is an archaic English law—apparently predating legal gambling—stipulating that gambling debts are not legally enforceable. In other words, if someone loses a bet, the loser may legally refuse to pay up.

"I didn't win the money gambling at the Mint," Reed insisted to his barrister, "and they admit that. They are keeping money I deposited there. That is money I brought with me from the outside."

"No matter," his barrister informed him. "That is considered a gambling debt, and we have no legal right to demand payment."

The Cromwell Mint never returned a dime of that money. Six thousand dollars bit the dust.

Reed was not at all fond of his British hosts. In the States, people generally ignored his disheveled appearance. In England, however, he was always made to feel uncomfortable. He spent most of his time wearing a crusty sweat suit, and the British, in their inimitable manner, managed to quietly convey to him their impression that he was utterly repulsive.

As sick as he was of the British, he was sicker of their food. After a thousand years of civilization—and the British were nothing if not civilized—their contribution to international cuisine seemed to consist of boiled meat and potatoes, soggy lifeless vegetables, warm beer, and chips. Oh, and vinegar.

While Reed was battling the British in London, Pop had found a couple of good games in Leeds. When the two players met back in London, Reed told Pop what had happened at the Mint. They decided to leave England and head for the Continent until things cooled off a bit. However, they were carrying too much cash. Before leaving England, they would have to purchase a number of traveler's checks and send them home.

This was the moment Reed had been waiting for. He knew banks generally kept only small amounts of foreign-currency traveler's checks on hand. Sporting his dirtiest sweat suit and his foulest baseball cap, he strolled into a Bank of England and asked to speak to the manager.

The teller frowned at him. "Perhaps I could help you with something," she said, with just the proper hint of distaste.

"I doubt it," Reed answered. "I need to speak with a *man*."

"What do you need?" the woman bristled, looking at a large coffee stain that almost covered the Adidas logo adorning Reed's chest.

"Just get me the manager."

The teller left, and returned moments later with a monocled gentleman bearing a stomach that was not to be trifled with. This was a British banker at his best.

"And what can I do for you, young man?" the banker harrumphed, glaring at Reed's attire.

"I want to buy some traveler's checks," Reed stated. "In real money."

"Real money?"

"Yeah. U.S. dollars."

The banker's neck began turning red. "And for what amount?"

"How many do you have?"

"How many do you need?"

Reed smiled, enjoying himself thoroughly. "How many do you have?"

"Young man, is this some sort of a game? If it is, I don't find it the least bit amusing. I can assure you we can satisfy the needs of the likes of you."

"How many do you have?"

The banker sighed and told the teller to bring the box of American Express Travelers Cheques. The teller brought the box (they actually kept them in a small cardboard box), the banker peered at the checks, and then glared at Reed.

"We have eight thousand American dollars' worth. How much do you require?"

"I'll take them all."

In the movie version of this story, the banker's monocle would now fall off.

When the transaction had been completed, Reed smiled at the deflated banker and said, "I need to change quite a large amount of money. Is there a real bank nearby?"

CHAPTER 14
EUROPE ON $2000 A DAY.

Excuse me. I would like...a rrhhhuuuummme.
~*Peter Sellers as Inspector Clouseau in* The Return of the Pink
Panther

While Reed was busy deflating the British banking establishment, Taylor was playing out every gambler's dream—full comp at Loews Monte Carlo.

The comp that Loews had arranged from New York covered everything—room, food, and drinks, and would even reimburse Taylor for his transatlantic airfare. All Taylor had to do was play a minimum of three hours per day, and bet up to five thousand francs per hand.

"No problem," he had said. Yeah. And now the jet lag was kicking his ass. In the morning, he felt like eating dinner and going to bed. In the afternoon, when the beaches were crowded with topless women, he was asleep in his room. And in the evening, when Taylor should have been drinking free champagne and eating lobster with the beautiful people of the world, he was scratching himself and ordering pancakes and eggs from room service.

Jet lag or no, Taylor had to play. Each evening he woke up, ate breakfast, and strapped the shuffle-tracking computer to his calf.

The shuffle at Loews was standard—the same shuffle the players had played at the MGM Grand and the Desert Inn. And, after the first two sessions, he was down seventeen grand. The negative fluctuation he started with in Vegas and had left behind in the Caribbean was back for the flight across the Atlantic. The British pit bosses—all Loews pit personnel above dealers were British—loved him.

On the third day the jet lag began to subside, and he staged a massive comeback. Spreading from one hand of two hundred to two hands of five thousand francs, Taylor almost got even. He continued his rally on the fourth day, winning over fifty thousand francs in one frenetic half hour burst of luck.

On the fifth day, Mr. Brocklebank—the day shift manager, who not forty-eight hours earlier had been commiserating with Taylor about his horrendous run of luck—appeared and told Taylor his comp status was being reconsidered. Passive tense. *Was being* reconsidered. Like it was some force of nature outside human control. Death, gravity, comp status. You know.

"I arranged my comp through Loews in New York," Taylor said, shoving out his first bet of the afternoon. "Talk to them."

The boss's upper lip stiffened. "The casino manager doesn't like your action. If you want to continue playing here, you will do so against half a shoe."

Taylor smiled. How quaint. In Vegas, a pit boss slithers up to the dealer and, with his back to the table and his hand over his mouth, tells the dealer to cut the shoe in half. Here, they tell you.

"Half a shoe? You mean two decks? Just for me?"

Brocklebank snorted. "Yes, sir. Two decks out of four."

Taylor shrugged. "Okay, as long as I get my comp. Loews in New York told me that I had to bet up to the limit to qualify. If my wife knew how much I'm betting she'd kill me, but I'm doing it just for the comp."

"We'll see about your comp," Brocklebank grumbled, and stalked off.

After only a few shoes Brocklebank was back, hovering over Taylor's game.

Ignoring him, Taylor continued to play and win. In one particularly unusual shoe, Butch signaled Taylor to alternate between one hand of 200 francs and two hands of 5,000. He lost almost every 200-franc hand, and won almost every 5,000-franc hand.

The dealer completed the shoe and shuffled the cards. He then offered Taylor the cut.

Taylor received the cut point from the computer and cut a moderately juicy clump to the front of the shoe. The dealer inserted the stop card in the middle of the pack, effectively cutting the shoe in half, and squared up the four decks.

"Wait a minute, wait a minute," Brocklebank said, and grabbed the pack of cards. He removed the stop card and reinserted it only one deck from the front of the pack. Now the dealer would shuffle after only one deck out of four had been dealt.

"There we are," he said, glaring at Taylor. "Play against that."

Taylor shrugged and continued to play.

After three of the short shoes, it became clear to Brocklebank that Taylor was willing to play this terrible game all night. He reached across the table and pushed Taylor's chips out of the betting circle.

"This is ridiculous," Brocklebank fumed. "We don't want your action."

Taylor shrugged. "Fine. Where do I go to get my airfare refunded?"

"Your comp has been revoked, that I can assure you."

"Why?"

"We don't like your action."

"Because I'm winning? Is that the problem? Is this how you treat everybody who happens to win?"

"It's not just because you're winning."

"Do you think I'm one of those card counters or something?"

Brocklebank glared at him. "We certainly know enough about card counters to recognize one when we see one. You are no card counter."

"What's the problem, then?"

Brocklebank squirmed. "Let's just say you're clever."

Taylor tried not to smile. He was getting barred for being clever!

"All right, I won't play anymore. Who do I see about my comp?"

"I told you, your comp has been revoked," Brocklebank glowered.

"Look," said Taylor, annoyed. "The woman at Loews in New York set up this comp, and she told me what I had to do to qualify. Now, it seems to me that I held up my end of the bargain, and you are reneging on your end just because I won. Give me the comp I earned, and I'll leave."

"The casino manager has decided not to honor your comp."

"Because I'm clever?"

Brocklebank steamed. He knew Taylor was up to something, and it was clearly killing him that he didn't know what it was.

"But the woman in New York—"

"I don't give a *fuck* what the woman in New York said!" Brocklebank exploded, finally losing his British reserve. "You're comp has been revoked, and that is fucking final!"

"Now, now," Taylor said, feigning shock. "We can discuss this like gentlemen, but I am not used to that sort of language. I won't stand for it."

Thoroughly chastened, Brocklebank regained his composure. "Ah, yes, of course," he stammered. "Terribly sorry."

Taylor argued a bit more, but he knew the comp was a lost cause. That wasn't so bad, since he had won more than enough to cover the cost of his stay and pay for his airfare. He was just giving Brocklebank the business. And he did want a souvenir.

"No chance," said Brocklebank emphatically. "Absolutely not."

"Come on."

"Forget it. We do not give our cards to anyone. When these cards are removed from the table, they are checked by the casino manager himself, and then they are destroyed. Very few people in the world have a deck of these cards. And I am certainly not going to sign them for you."

"You treated me poorly, you offended my sensibilities with your vulgar language, and you revoked my comp after I did everything required to qualify," Taylor argued. "It's the least you can do."

Brocklebank hesitated. He had lost quite a bit of face when his temper had flared earlier. Taylor was giving him the opportunity to make amends.

"Who's going to know?" Taylor persisted.

Brocklebank looked around, quickly grabbed the four decks in the shoe Taylor had just played, and handed them to Taylor. He never did sign them, however.

Taylor had plunged himself into several college-level French books before the team had left Vegas for the Caribbean. By the time he arrived in France, he could read and write French reasonably well, but hadn't yet had the opportunity to speak it. Speaking shouldn't be all that difficult, Taylor figured. After all, he was fluent in Spanish and Italian. French looked vaguely like a combination of the two.

Loews had insulated Taylor from having to deal with his home-cooked French. Every employee was fluent in English, so he never had the opportunity to embarrass himself. That would soon change.

After checking out of Loews with a couple of bathrobes stuffed in his suitcase, Taylor took a cab to Nice, where Guppy was scheduled to arrive in a couple of days. After shelling out the equivalent of $65 for the cab ride, Taylor decided that the team was going to need a car.

He found a cheap, two-star hotel near the center of Nice, walked in, and asked for a room.

"*Je voudrais une chambre*," Taylor said, pronouncing every letter.

The woman behind the desk looked at him curiously.

"*Je voudrais une chambre*," he repeated, a little louder.

"I'm sorry, monsieur," the woman responded in French, "but I don't speak Spanish."

Since he was able to read and write French, Taylor managed to get by with pen and paper until he got used to speaking through his nose. Writing for the girl cleaning the rooms, whose name tag said Nicole and who looked like Brigitte Bardot, Taylor managed to convey to her that he wanted to buy a car. She told him that her brother (father? ice cream cooler? Taylor wasn't sure) had a car for sale.

Nicole took Taylor to see the car the following day. Her brother was selling a two-cylinder Fiat automobile that might have fit into the trunk of Brian's Ford LTD. It seemed a bit small, but the price was right. At least Taylor thought the price was right. He made the guy write it down before he agreed to anything.

Taylor purchased the tiny Fiat with the remainder of the francs he had extracted from Loews. During his first trip in the car, Taylor was introduced to a couple of unpleasant facts. Traveling from Nice to Monaco—a long gentle upgrade—he found that the car had all the power of a Briggs & Stratton lawn mower. Mercedes, Renaults, trucks, and even caravans of guys on bicycles zoomed past him as if he were sitting still. Then, challenging the series of 180-degree switchbacks that lead from La Turbie down to Monaco, Taylor discovered that the car handled about as well as a shopping cart with a loose wheel. By the time he reached the bottom of the switchbacks, a long line of cars containing a good number of irate Frenchmen had piled up behind him. However, with gas priced at around ten francs per liter (over $5.00 per gallon), the miserable vehicle was good for something. It used almost no fuel whatsoever.

Taylor knew he would get some heat for the car from his teammates, so it was with some apprehension that he met Guppy at the airport in Nice. He needn't have worried. Guppy had been traveling for eighteen hours, and arrived with such a severe case of jet lag that he had no idea where he was or what kind of car Taylor had purchased. While Taylor tied Guppy's luggage to the roof of the car, Guppy shoehorned himself into the front seat and fell asleep.

While Guppy was recovering, Taylor played the beautiful casino in Beaulieu-sur-Mer, a small town on the Riviera between Nice and Monaco. It was in Beaulieu-sur-Mer that Taylor first had the opportunity to try out the French stop-card feature Brian had written into Butch's program. The French stop-card was something the players had read about in Arnold Snyder's *Blackjack Forum*—which by this time had become a clearinghouse for blackjack information from all over the world.[22]

---

22 The *Forum* had grown impressively since the days Reed and Taylor were providing Snyder information about games in Nevada. It was now indispensable, containing information about games throughout the world, as well as articles written by a number of blackjack experts.

In most of the casinos around the globe—and in all of the casinos Taylor had visited to this point—dealers deal until the plastic stop card emerges from the shoe. When it does, the current round is completed, the cards are scooped, and only then does the shuffle commence. This provides players with a natural break—a chance to visit the can, get up and stretch, or even to escape the table with what's left of their bankroll and their dignity.

To their credit, the French had come up with something rather interesting to keep those players from hitting the door. The shuffle starts the instant the stop card emerges. So, if three, or five, or ten cards have been dealt out when the plastic stop card comes sliding out of that shoe, the dealer stops. Immediately. The pack is shuffled, the player to whom the stop card was dealt cuts, and only then is the hand completed.

Quite clever. It keeps players who might otherwise escape riveted to the table. Once you have a hand (or half a hand, or even just a bet out), you're stuck. You can't leave until the round is completed. Having waited through the shuffle, most players opt to play a few more hands. You know, for the road.

The French stop-card rule impacted shuffle tracking in a couple of ways. First, it meant that the shuffle was taking place with less than the full six decks. No big deal—Brian had written in a special toe command that told the computer that the next n cards are lying on the table. Taylor entered the toe command, then the cards, and finally a Z-out. Time to shuffle. Butch removed the cards lying on the felt from the last packet, but did not add them to the cards in the discard rack. So, instead of assuming the stack consisted of 312 cards, it would contain 312 minus n cards.

A more problematic effect of this rule was that the hand would not be completed with cards from the packet with which the hand started. Let's say Taylor was playing a juicy packet, rich in tens. Eight cards come out, and it's the best of all possible worlds. Everybody has a ten, and the dealer has a five up-card. Then out comes the stop card.

Normally, the round would be completed from that nice rich packet of tens, meaning the dealer would have an even greater chance than normal of busting her five. But not in France. In France, the cards are shuffled and cut, and the round is completed with whatever random slug has been cut to the front. If Taylor got his mitts on the cut card, he would of course cut a juicy packet of tens to the front, and life would be good. But there was no *lean* in France—the player to whom the stop card was dealt was the player who cut, end of story. When Taylor had big money out he would put heat on the cutter, letting the cutter know in no uncertain terms that the fate of Taylor's 3,000-franc hand was in the cutter's hands, so to speak. Of course, Taylor was attempting to get the cut for himself, but most of the time he succeeded only in making the cutter cut *very carefully*. Big help.

Because of the French stop-card rule, Taylor and his teammates would become experts at estimating when the stop card was due to emerge. They would be very careful about betting big if the card was due to come out during the upcoming round. If possible, they would reduce the number of hands so they could complete the round before the stop card showed up (impossible at a crowded table, but something they could do if the table was sparsely populated).

Another oddity in the French game was a little number called the "European no-hole-card rule." This is a bit of a misnomer; the lack of a hole card mattered little to their playing strategy. What mattered was that the dealer had only an up-card until all of the players had finished playing their hands, meaning the dealer could not make a blackjack until then.

So what, you ask? Well, let's say the dealer has a ten up-card. You have a pair of eights, which you dutifully—and correctly—split. You get lucky—you hit each eight with a six and then a seven, giving you two twenty-ones. You sit back and count your money.

But wait. The dealer hits her ten with an ace, thus making a blackjack. Does the dealer take your original bet only, as in the early days of Atlantic City?[23] No. You lose both bets.

This does impact playing strategy. Because you lose both bets to a dealer's subsequent blackjack, Basic Strategy changes. You never double down or split against a dealer's ten or ace, except when you have a pair of aces against a ten.

---

23 In Atlantic City in the eighties, the dealer took a hole card, but didn't look at it until all the players had completed their hands. If she snapped (made a blackjack), the players lost their original bets *only*. So, doubling and splitting decisions were not affected by this idiosyncrasy.

The no-hole-card rule had a further negative impact on the shuffle trackers. It meant that the card that is to become the dealer's hole card comes out last. So, if they were playing toward the end of a rich packet, and the upcoming packet was laced with small cards, they had to be careful with their bets. They wanted the dealer to be hitting her hand from the ten-rich packet.

Yet another bit of strangeness was that players in France commonly played on each other's hands. If you stuck a hundred francs out, it was quite possible that someone else behind the table would plop a bet out next to yours. (This sounds like Wonging heaven, but the playing decision was up to the player who owned the spot. Once you saw the way the average Frenchman played, your so-called heaven would quickly become more reminiscent of one of Dante's circles of hell.) The only restriction was that the total amount bet could not total more than the table limit.

Taylor was introduced to this nicety in a way he would never forget. A tall, tanned, well-endowed woman was playing to his immediate right one night in Beaulieu-sur-Mer, and she couldn't help but notice that Taylor was rolling in dough. His session had started poorly—he was in for close to 100,000 francs. He had won that back, and more besides, so although much of it was his buy-in, he nonetheless had an impressive stack of "ashtrays" in front of him. (In Europe, the chips grow in size as they increase in denomination—at some point they cease to be round and become rectangular; hence, "ashtrays.") At one point he cut a monster packet to the front of the shoe, and shoved out two hands with three 1,000-franc ashtrays on each, the limit in Beaulieu-sur-Mer. The impressive woman to his right tapped him on the shoulder, smiled, and, in heavily accented English said, "Do you want to play on my hole?"

The dealer waited patiently as Taylor struggled to regain control of his faculties. What was he supposed to say? "Yes, I'd love to play on your hole, but perhaps now's not the time?" "No, thanks, I'm not in the mood?" What?

She patted the felt in front of her with her palm. "My hole," she repeated in that throaty voice of hers. "Please. Play on it."

What she meant, of course, was her *spot*. She was offering Taylor the opportunity to put more money out on her playing circle. Now what should he do? He was being tugged in at least three directions.

First, if he played on her hole, he would not be the one to decide how to play the hand.

Second, judging by the waggling eyebrows and knowing nods from the other males at the table, it was pretty clear to Taylor that when a woman of this … *magnitude* … made such an offer, one accepted.

Third, he had been in France for almost three weeks by this time, and… suffice it to say that Alexander Taylor played on her hole.

By the time Guppy had recovered sufficiently to play blackjack, Taylor had won about 50,000 francs and had been barred at Beaulieu-sur-Mer. They decided to return to Monaco. Taylor would play SBM—the other casino in Monaco—and Guppy would attempt Loews.

Since Taylor had been barred at Loews in part because of his monstrous bet spread, Guppy played Loews with a moderate bet spread of 1,000–5,000 francs. He hoped that his smaller bet spread, coupled with less attention— regular players are never scrutinized as carefully as comped players—would increase his longevity.

The plan worked. Guppy was able to play at Loews for almost a week before getting massive heat. He won over 100,000 francs, and left before getting barred officially.

Taylor played the smaller SBM casino carefully, spreading from 500 up to 3,000 francs. Since there were several other gamblers betting more than that, Taylor really didn't stand out. After a modest win, the two players decided to move on to Cannes.

It was in Cannes where Taylor decided it was inconceivable that any nationality could play blackjack more poorly than the French. They refused to hit any hand totaling fourteen or higher or split any pair, and any player who did so subjected himself to a certain amount of heat from the rest of the table. As bad as this heat got, however, it didn't approach the abuse regularly heaped upon the player at third base.

Generally speaking, third base is the worst seat in the house at any blackjack game in the world. Since the third baseman is the last player to make a decision before the dealer plays her hand, it often seems that this player is directly responsible for the outcome of the hand.[24]

For instance, suppose the third baseman hits his hand with a ten, busting it. Now the dealer turns up her hole card. She's stiff, and then makes a hand with the next card out. Obviously, if the third baseman had had any brains whatsoever he would have stood, the dealer would have busted, and everybody would have won.

Of course, the small card with which the dealer made her hand could just as easily have preceded the ten, but gamblers don't think that way. Especially non-third-basemen gamblers whose money is rapidly disappearing. So the abuse starts.

North American third basemen are immune to some of this abuse simply because the dealer often has a pat hand. If the dealer has a hand that doesn't require a hit, there is very little perceived damage the third baseman can do. Whatever he does (or doesn't do) will not affect the dealer's hand at all.

This is never the case in Europe. As mentioned, European dealers do not give themselves a hole card. They have one card up, and when all of the players have finished playing their hands, the next card out of the shoe becomes the dealer's second card.

This no-hole-card convention means that the third baseman seems responsible for the dealer's hand on every round. The dealer never has a pat hand, so the third baseman cannot relieve himself of blame by pointing out that the dealer had a hand anyway.

As the players soon learned, only a masochist would choose to play third base in Europe. And the player Taylor and Guppy met in Cannes seemed to define the term.

For a full week, Taylor and Guppy played Le Casino du Fleurs in Cannes. They arrived every evening at eight o'clock to packed roulette tables with

---

24 The belief that "poor" decisions by the guy at third base can cause everyone else at the table to lose is about as pervasive as the belief in luck. Taylor has long since given up arguing about this. Third basemen who play poorly negatively impact their own bankrolls, but in the long run, their mistakes will help the other players as often as they hurt. In other words, in the long run, it doesn't matter what they do. Now, best of luck trying to convince someone who currently believes otherwise.

massive action. The four blackjack tables, however, stood empty, save for a small man sitting at third base of Table 1, waiting for it to open. This guy, with his pinched face, scrubby beard, half frames, and badly nicotine-stained fingers, relished third base. Taylor quickly figured out what made the little man tick, and christened him Le Professeur.

Le Professeur absolutely believed that third base was the most crucial seat at the table, and further believed that he knew how to play the position. To say that the other players didn't agree with Le Professeur is to understate the case considerably.

The abuse would begin almost as soon as the table opened. Since Le Professeur had no better idea than anyone else at the table which cards were going to come out, he made "mistakes" on about half his hands. He had his moments, however, and it was for those moments that Le Professeur lived.

One evening Le Professeur was having a particularly bad night. He kept taking bust cards, and it wasn't necessary to speak a lot of French to understand that the other players' remarks weren't terribly complimentary.

To his everlasting shame, Taylor kept the players'—and the pit bosses'—attention squarely on Le Professeur. After each "bad" play Taylor groaned audibly, shook his head, and said, "No, no, no, Monsieur Le Professeur." The other players quickly adopted the nickname, and every several minutes "Ooooh, Le Professeur" rang out through the casino.

Then it happened. Le Professeur had a seventeen, and the dealer had a ten up-card. Le Professeur studied the other hands on the table for a full two minutes before deciding. Then, after milking the moment for all it was worth, he hit his seventeen.

> Never hit seventeen, when you play against the dealer,
> For you know, those odds won't ride with you.
> ~*David Bromberg*, "Summer Wages"

Before the other players could start throwing things, the dealer hit Le Professeur with a ten. That ten, the ten with which Le Professeur had selflessly busted his own hand, would have given the dealer a total of twenty. Instead, the dealer hit her hand with a five and then a ten. The table erupted in cheers.

Le Professeur leaned back, inhaled his cigarette, and serenely blew a cloud of smoke toward the ceiling. Led by Taylor, the others at the table stood and bowed, paying homage to the greatness that was Le Professeur. Le Professeur's evening—possibly his entire life—had been made.

It was during the course of the following evening that Taylor changed his mind about the world's worst players. The Cannes Film Festival had just begun, and Taylor and Guppy found themselves surrounded at a blackjack table by Japanese film producers.

Le Professeur had taken the night off—perhaps to bask in the glow of the previous night's triumph. The big bettor at the table—a guy Taylor referred to as Don Ho—was sitting to Taylor's left, one spot away from third base, and was flat-betting 10,000 francs per hand (about $1,500 at the time). A poor soul betting only 200 francs found himself stuck at third.

It didn't take long for the Japanese to wrest the "World's Worst" title from the French. Within minutes, Don Ho actually stood with a pair of aces. The third baseman was pat, and so it was up to Don not to take the dealer's bust card. Several hands later, Taylor tried to stand with a fifteen. Don Ho, whose double-down hand was next, actually bought Taylor's fifteen from him so he could hit it. Don Ho "knew" that the next card out would be small, and he wanted to get it out of the way of his double-down hand. (To his credit, Taylor was gracious enough to sell his fifteen at face value.) Don Ho hit the fifteen with a small card, received a ten on his double down, and looked like a damn genius. He looked at Taylor and calmly said, "See?"

Two rounds later, the misguided soul at third base decided to hit an ace-six (the correct play anywhere in the world). He hit it with a ten, and a Japanese-accented grumble traveled around the table. When the dealer made a hand, and the players realized that the third baseman's ten would have caused her to bust, the grumble rose to a roar. When the yelling subsided, Don Ho took it upon himself to explain to the unfortunate third baseman what had transpired. Taylor didn't understand a word he said, but his hand motions and his inflections made it abundantly clear that he was replaying the hand for the third baseman. "Ying yang whing bang," he explained patiently in Japanese, pointing first to the dealer's hand and then to the player's. The poor third baseman listened respectfully, head bowed.

When Don Ho concluded his dissertation, the chastened third baseman looked up, shrugged his shoulders, and said, "Solly."

By this time, Taylor and Guppy had become incredible computer operators. After hundreds of hours, they were now operating entirely automatically. The only time they had to hesitate at all was during the shuffle. The rest of the time they talked, clowned around, and otherwise looked like anything but professional players.

One indication of the incredible cover shuffle tracking was providing was that Taylor and Guppy had both been comped some excellent meals in Menton, Beaulieu-sur-Mer, and at both casinos in Cannes. This would have been unexceptional in Vegas, but, apart from Loews, comps were not part of usual business in European casinos.

Taylor had dated a few dealers in Vegas, and had learned quite a bit about the view from the other side of the table. Dealers stood on their feet for eight-hour shifts. It was terribly boring when there were no players at their tables, and worse when players arrived. Dealers got heat from the players when they won, and heat from the pit bosses when they lost. Throw in the obligatory sexual harassment,[25] and you had what amounted to one of the worst jobs in the world. Figuring this was likely a phenomenon everywhere, Taylor tried to be as entertaining as possible when he played. It was an act, yes, but it became more than that. Dealers actually liked it when he came to their table. It made everybody's job more pleasant.

In the game of blackjack, the eight is the least important card in the deck. It is absolutely neutral. Tens, aces, and, to a lesser extent, nines, favor the players. Sevens and below favor the dealer. And eights just sit there, favoring no one.

So, explaining how the eight ("*huit,*" pronounced "wheat" in French) was the most important card in the deck became a staple of Taylor's schtick.

---

25 This was not your bullshit "do you want to go out with me?" sexual harassment. This was the pre-enlightenment version, when sleeping with the boss was an integral part of keeping one's job.

Not incidentally, he could root either for ("*huit!*") or against ("*pas huit!*") an eight on almost every hand, thus seeming to prove his theory.

Taylor chose *huit* precisely because the eight is in fact the single most irrelevant card in the deck. Initially, Taylor thought that any pit boss who knew anything about card counting would realize that this *huit* business made no sense at all. However, there are precious few people outside the professional gambling community who know this, so Taylor almost certainly made believers out of a large number of French pit bosses. And it got the attention of the female dealers as well.

On those evenings that Taylor or Guppy managed one-on-one playing sessions with friendly dealers after hours, there was always a concern if the player in question was an operator. Because of the equipment, spontaneous tearing off of outer garments was not an option. The operator had to sneak off to the bathroom, untangle wires, batteries, and buzzers, carefully hide the stuff somewhere, and only then emerge, ready to consummate his night's work. This was an even more complicated proposition when they were staying in one of France's more pedestrian establishments where the bathroom was located down the hall.

After the run-in with Rutland at the Cromwell Mint, Reed and Pop left London and flew to Spain. Although Spain had been left behind much of Western Europe during Franco's reign, the casino industry quickly had made up for lost time.

The casinos were clean and thoroughly modern. Reed and Pop first visited a beautiful casino located in a castle just outside Madrid, but the shuffle was untrackable. They then rented the Spanish version of a Fiat (called a SEAT), and drove to Santander, in the north of Spain.

The casino at Santander offered a great game with relatively good limits. Reed converted a total of $500 U.S. to 62,000 Spanish pesetas, and, using the BP-Spotter Routine, Reed and Pop managed to win over three million pesetas. From Santander they drove to Bilbao, won four million, and then to Zaragoza, blasting the casino there for another six million pesetas.

They then drove to Valencia and took a ferry to Ibiza, a gem of an island floating in the Mediterranean about 100 miles away. The limit was only $80 U.S., but it would take a week before Reed and Pop could be pried off the island and back to a casino with a decent limit. The island was beautiful, and full of English-speaking tourists.

When they reluctantly returned to the mainland, they headed for El Casino de Barcelona. According to the pamphlet they had obtained at the hotel in Ibiza, the joint was about forty-five minutes outside of the city. They had no luck finding it. Whenever they stopped for directions, Pop pulled out his trusty Spanish phrase book and asked *"Donde esta cochino?"* Somehow, they continued to find themselves directed to the nearest farm. The confusion was cleared up weeks later when they learned that Pop should have been saying, *"Donde esta el casino?"* Pop had been asking "Where is the pig?" and the Spanish were only trying to help.

When they finally arrived at the casino outside Barcelona, they discovered that they had already been barred. Not barred from that casino. Barred from every casino in the country.

As in all European casinos except Loews, players must show a passport and pay a nominal fee (usually the equivalent of five to ten bucks) in order to get in. In France, the player's passport number is simply written on an index card and stored in a metal file cabinet. In Spain, however, the number is entered into a central computer. Every casino in the entire country has access to that information.

As Reed and Pop discovered, once they were barred in one casino, they were barred in all the rest. This was a system that even the casinos in Vegas would envy.

Neither player was particularly disappointed. While Taylor was reading books to teach himself French, Pop and Guppy had been watching Pink Panther movies over and over. Both could now speak English with a French accent better than Peter Sellers himself. Guppy had been telling Pop how well this was working with the girls at the beach, and Pop was eager to try it out.

Reed was similarly unperturbed. "Can you believe it!" he said to Pop. "We're so good, we got barred from the whole damn country!" This was the kind of story that could put Reed on par with the Czechs and other famous players. And he rarely missed an opportunity to remind his teammates that he was "into Spain for five hundred, out for thirteen million."

Since Spain was burned out for Reed and Pop, they decided to meet up with Taylor and Guppy in France. Taylor had been taunting Reed for weeks with stories of topless women frolicking on the beaches of the French Riviera. A volleyball game that Taylor had described in tantalizing detail had been causing Reed particular stress. He and Pop hopped on a slow train and, nineteen hours later, they were in Monte Carlo.

The first thing Reed did was hit a restaurant with Taylor. He wanted to show off his newly developed language skills, and he also was hoping for a Coca-Cola loaded with ice (it had been nearly impossible to get a drink with ice in Spain). The waitress came over and deposited a basket of typical rock-hard bread on the table.

Reed pointed to the bread. "*Mantequilla, por favor,*" he said, looking at Taylor proudly. The waitress just looked at him.

"Wrong language," said Taylor, and asked the waitress for butter in French. Reed was devastated. He had worked his ass off to learn a few words in a foreign tongue and now, just a few hundred miles away, the damn language didn't work anymore.

While Reed and Pop tried their luck at the two casinos in Monaco, Taylor and Guppy checked out the other casino in Cannes. There they found a shuffle that was hugely beatable, but one the program could not yet handle. Taylor phoned Brian, explained the shuffle in detail, and then continued down the Riviera with Guppy. They both played La Napoule for a short time, and were barred when the casino manager called Loews and described Taylor to Brocklebank. The call reminded Brocklebank of Taylor's unorthodox betting style, and he shortly thereafter barred Reed and Pop.

The barring didn't bother Reed at all. What was the good of traveling all the way to Loews Monte Carlo if you didn't get barred? Getting barred tells the world that you're too good for the casino. Reed tried to get some playing cards out of Brocklebank like Taylor had, but Brocklebank simply heaved him out. What the hell. (Taylor would torment Reed with his Loews cards for years.)

Guppy was thriving in France. When he first arrived, he had tried his Peter Sellers accent on some of the topless French women he found on the beach in Monaco. Of course, they didn't understand a word he said.

It wasn't a total waste, however. English-speaking women did understand his Sellerese. Guppy was quite successful with a number of the American and British women he met on the crowded beaches. Pop wasn't quite as successful until he set his sights on a slightly older demographic.

By this time, Brian had revised the program so that it could handle the shuffle Taylor had found in Cannes. He sent the new chip via Emery Air Express, and it arrived at the Nice airport two days later. Taylor practiced entering the new shuffle with his toes for a day and, with Guppy as the BP, they blasted Le Casino Municipal in Cannes, winning over a quarter of a million francs on the night of May 31.

Under ordinary circumstances, the team would not have pounded a joint that hard in one night. However, this was the last night Le Casino Municipal was to be open until the following November. The Palm Beach, located at the other end of the Marina and known locally as the "Summer Casino," would be open from June 1 through October 31.

Beyond the one-time aspect of the play, Guppy's action didn't even register on the radar on the night of the thirty-first. A roulette table nearby saw more action every spin than Taylor had ever seen. The green felt was completely buried in circular and rectangular multicolored chips. After every spin, the croupiers with their long wooden rakes worked like day laborers to scrape those stacks of losing chips from the layout.

On the first of June, Taylor and Guppy walked to the other end of the Marina to give the "Summer Casino" a try. They found a game similar to the one they had played down the street, except that for the first time in their experience, there was no casino-wide shuffle. There were three basic shuffles the dealers at this casino chose from. Fortunately, each dealer stuck with one of the three shuffles, so after Taylor had seen a dealer shuffle once, he knew how to set up Butch when that dealer arrived at their table.

It was at the Summer Casino that Taylor and Guppy experienced what was (at that time) the single largest negative fluctuation they had ever experienced on the turn of one card. They were in the middle of a monster packet, and

Guppy had shoved out two hands of 10,000 francs each on his spots, and another 10,000 francs on Taylor's hand. He received a blackjack, a pair of tens, and a pair of aces. (This packet was a *beast.*) The dealer had a ten up-card. Guppy split his aces (remember: with the European no-hole-card rule, the only time you split or double against a ten or an ace is a pair of aces against a ten). He received two tens, meaning he now had a blackjack, two twenty-ones, and a twenty. Even if the dealer hit her hand with a ten, he'd win 35,000 francs. If she hit it with a nine, or a "*huit,*" or anything but an ace, he would win 45,000 francs.

The dealer did not hit her hand with a ten. Or a nine, or even a "*huit.*" She hit it with an ace.

Instead of winning 45,000 francs, Guppy lost 30,000 francs, for a one-card swing of 75,000 francs (almost $11,000). Guppy did get a nice dinner comp, however.

It took them three full days to recover the loss from that single hand. And then they were barred.

The two pairs of players leapfrogged south along the French Riviera, hitting the beach during the day and playing at night. They were still getting barred occasionally, but they were getting barred for winning. Since the casino management never suspected them of anything while they were losing, they always had the chance to make a comeback before getting heaved out the door.

Because three or four months of hotel charges tended to seriously impact the bottom line, the players stayed at, well, dives. And in Europe, dives are several notches below your typical Motel 6. These were joints with bathrooms in the hall, and many of the elevators were so small the players literally couldn't fit inside them along with their luggage. When they first arrived, they would load the elevator with their suitcases, reach in, push the button, and then run up the stairs to meet the elevator at their floor. (Another thing: you considered yourself lucky if one of these elevators stopped within six inches of the actual surface of the floor. It took weeks for the players to stop either tripping over the floor sticking up like a curb, or stumbling like drunks as they stepped off the elevator to a floor that was several inches lower than it should have been.)

The late playing hours presented a couple of problems. Generally, European hotels locked their doors at around ten or eleven at night. There was always a doorman around to let stragglers in after that, but the guy was invariably asleep when the players arrived after a play at three or four in the morning. They'd bang on the door until the poor bastard woke up. He would then stagger over to let them in, and immediately go back to sleep.

The maid problem was more severe. European maids tend to go home by noon. Clearly, the "*ne derangez pas*" signs the players dangled from their doorknobs were merely suggestions (much like the speed limit signs, apparently). The maids would start banging on the door at around ten in the morning, about the time the players were just descending into stage four sleep. "*Suelment serviettes grandes!*" Taylor would shout ("Just towels!"). This would work for a couple of days, but ultimately the maids became aggressive. Apparently, their minds were working overtime imagining how filthy those rooms were becoming behind the locked doors (and they were right.) The maids desperately wanted to clean those rooms.

One morning a maid banged on Reed's door mercilessly. Taylor had taught him to say "*serviettes grandes,*" but Reed's pleading was having no effect on this woman. Finally Reed opened the door, wrapped in a sheet like some kind of debauched Roman, and peered out. The maid somehow let him know that he wouldn't get any more towels until she was allowed to clean his room.

"No towels, no *dinero!*" Reed yelled, again resorting to his one and only foreign language, and slammed the door.

It was around this time that the players ran into a problem none of them had anticipated, but everyone on the planet should have the pleasure of experiencing at least once. Currencies in Europe were physically large—the larger the denomination, the larger the bill (much like the casino chips). In Spain, the largest denomination was 5,000 pesetas—around fifty bucks at the time. The bill was about an inch longer and more than an inch taller than an American bill. French francs were similarly large. By now, their haul totaled almost thirteen million pesetas, and over a half million francs. When they had filled their wallets, pockets, socks, and shoes, they finally gave up. Reed pilfered a pillowcase from one of the fleabag hotels the team stayed in one night, stuffed it full of cash, and the pillowcase became *le bag*.

It's difficult to imagine how quickly *le bag* became just another piece of luggage. Maybe it was because the different colors made the money seem like it belonged on a Monopoly board; perhaps it was the outsized proportions of the bills that made them seem less than real. Whatever the case, they would take *le bag* into restaurants and Laundromats, and just plop it down somewhere as they went about their business. It sounds careless, and it probably was, but who would suspect that anyone in his right mind would carry that much money around in a goddamn pillowcase anyway?

After six weeks in Europe, the players had more than made up the loss they had incurred during that one bad fluctuation in Vegas, and had paid for the computers as well. After more than a thousand hours of play at greatly reduced limits, they were finally in the black. The system was working, and not one pit boss, not one dealer—*no one*—had any idea what was going on. It was blackjack heaven.

Surprisingly, Taylor's teammates didn't seem to share his elation when they all got together at a superb French restaurant in Bandol to celebrate. They were on a fantastic European holiday, cruising the French Riviera and earning their keep by beating casinos most people could only dream about visiting. Still, there was something wrong. Reed missed his car and his apartment. Guppy missed Burger King. Pop missed ordering a meal for himself without help. Taylor's teammates were actually homesick.

During this time, Tony and Brian were sitting in Vegas. Brian was periodically modifying the program so it would work on the new shuffles the players discovered on their trip through Europe, and Tony was just waiting for something to happen.

"What is this crap?" Tony fumed. "I want to play."

"You'll play when you learn how to operate the computer properly," Brian replied. "There's really no reason for you to play until you can play as well as the others."

"I'm really getting sick of your ass-holier than thou attitude."

Instead of practicing until he was good enough to beat any shuffle he happened to encounter, Tony decided to have some fun. He met Julie in Miami, and they began taking one-week Caribbean cruises. Not surprisingly, each of the cruises Tony selected offered blackjack aboard ship. After five such cruises, Tony had learned to operate the computer, had developed a tremendous tan, and had won over $20,000. What a way to make a living.

Brian just shook his head and kept working. Better to be lucky than good.

When the players reached Peripignan, a sleepy French town near the Spanish border, Taylor and Guppy bequeathed the tiny Fiat to their teammates and hopped a train to Spain. They took all of the pesetas, and Reed and Pop took custody of all of the francs. Upon their arrival in Spain, Taylor and Guppy christened *la bolsa*, the Spanish version of *le bag*.

They reached Valencia, beat the hell out of the beautiful casino there, purchased a dozen or so statuettes at the Lladró factory nearby, sent them home, and then continued south to Malaga. When they arrived at the casino, located just outside the city in a small town called Benalmádena, they were informed that they were not welcome. The Valencia win had been enough to convince the Spanish that these were no ordinary gamblers.

Next stop was the Malaga airport. With the two most recent issues of *The Blackjack Forum* under his arm, Taylor stood with Guppy, gaping up at the huge Solari departure board—the old-fashioned signboard on which white letters on black boards clattered rapidly around, magically creating destination names. They had their suitcases packed, and were deciding where to go next. The pure deliciousness of their circumstances was not lost on Alexander Taylor.

"A lot of what we did was interesting, or exciting, or maybe just crazy in retrospect," says Taylor now. "But this was different. We were standing in an airport with all our stuff and a pillowcase full of pesetas, deciding where to go next. We didn't have to be anywhere for any reason, and literally could have gone anywhere in the world we wanted for as long as we wanted. It just doesn't get much better than that."

Nairobi? Taylor found the game in one of the *Blackjack Forums*. Great rules, but only a $60 limit. Mallorca? Part of Spain; probably already barred. Zurich? No blackjack. Italy? No info on the games.

They settled on the Canary Islands. Although a part of Spain, the information they had indicated that the casino there wasn't hooked to the Big Brother computer system that oversaw the rest of the country. Hauling their stuff to the ticket counter, they reached into *la bolsa*, skimmed about a thousand in pesetas off the top of the stack, and bought tickets to Tenerife.

Good choice. The island was beautiful. They stayed in a hotel overlooking the ocean, where from their balconies they could see the Atlantic ferociously pounding the black volcanic rocks, shooting spray twenty feet or more in the air. Outside there was a series of concrete swimming pools that filled and emptied as the tide came in and out. Based on the hotel guests, one would have thought that this was an outpost not of Spain but of Britain, but Taylor found it nice to pick up girls in English for a change.

The game had low limits (around $200), but it was trackable, and the conditions couldn't have been better. They settled in, planning to play conservatively for as long as they could.

Meanwhile, Reed and Pop headed for Lake Geneva. There were three casinos on the French side of the lake they intended to play. Moreover, they could rid themselves of some of the francs in *le bag* by heading across the border to Switzerland. They figured they wouldn't have trouble finding fifty or sixty thousand in U.S. dollar traveler's checks in a country that is essentially a huge bank. They were right.

The drive was terrible. The French countryside, with its abundance of nuclear reactors, didn't charm either one of them. The fact that they were traveling in a riding lawn mower didn't help. Reed rarely missed an opportunity to curse Taylor and the Fiat, which he dubbed a Futile Italian Attempt at Transportation.

When they arrived at Lake Geneva, they started at the casino located in Évian-les-Bains. Pop took up residence at an empty table, and Reed headed toward the bar to wait for Pop's signal.

Reed plopped down at the bar. To his right, a Frenchman with an enormous nose was pouring a refreshing-looking liquid from a bottle. According to the label, the bottle contained "Pschitt."

"*Quelque chose à boire?*" the bartender asked Reed. Something to drink?

"*Oui,*" Reed replied. He had finally given up on Spanish and had learned a bit of French by this time. "*Qu'est-ce que lá?*"

"*C'est à qui?*" the bartender asked, indicating the bottle.

"*Oui.*"

"*Pschitt.*"

Reed was rolling on the floor.

From that point on, he ordered several bottles of *Pschitt* per day. He ordered it with a completely straight face, and then practically fell out of his chair when the bartender dutifully brought it to him. Of course, Reed's paroxysms of laughter completely mystified the French. So Pschitt was pronounced "shit." Big deal.

When Taylor called from the Canaries, Reed and Guppy had been playing around Lake Geneva for three weeks. Reed was gleefully relating the Pschitt story when they got word that Brian, Tony, and Julie were planning a trip to the Calgary Stampede in Alberta, Canada.

CHAPTER 15
OH, CANADA!

Canadians have an abiding interest in surprising those
Americans who have historically made little effort to learn
about their neighbor to the north.
~Peter Jennings

I don't even know what street Canada is on.
~Al Capone

Canada. The Great White North. A country with as many bears as people; a nation larger than the United States, but with a population less than that of California; a land with winters so cold you need another word for it.

Composed not of states but provinces; seeded not by revolutionaries but by loyalists; achingly beautiful and practically empty, Canada is one of the best-kept secrets in the world.

It is probably just as well the secret is kept. Any country this calm, this laid-back, this *fair*, would be viewed with acute suspicion by the little Big Brother to the south. To wit:

Exhibit I: Canada has a lottery, as do many U.S. states. The difference? If you win the Canadian lottery, you actually win *all* of the money. No twenty-year payouts. No taxes (!). If you win a $5 million prize, it isn't really $2.7 million, or $180,000 a year for twenty years. You get a check for $5 million. Period.

How can they do that, you ask? Well, the Canadian government figures a lottery is already a tax. After all, the money raised by the lottery is used as tax revenue (as it is in the States). It's only *fair* (there's that word again) that winners aren't taxed a second time.

Exhibit II: National health care. Enough said.

Exhibit III: The official policy statement of the Province of Alberta's Gaming Control Section of the Department of the Attorney General concerning card counters reads as follows:

> "Card counters who obtain an honest advantage over the house through a playing strategy do not break any law…Gaming supervisors should ensure that no steps are taken to discourage any player simply because he is winning."

What? *What!?* How can that be? What the hell is going on up there? Don't they realize that casinos are obliged to deter, harass, occasionally beat up, and ultimately bar skilled players? For crying out loud, what has the frozen tundra done to their brains?

Tony had filled in his teammates about the game. During most of the year, several Alberta casinos dealt a four-deck game with a $25 (Canadian) limit— about eighteen bucks U.S. And a tough game it was. Four decks, one cut off, double on ten or eleven only, no soft doubling, they hit soft seventeen, and no insurance offered. It was about 0.85 percent against the player off the top. The game was worth about seven bucks an hour. Canadian.

However, for the ten glorious days during the Calgary Stampede, and for another ten days during Klondike Days in Edmonton, the limits shot all the way up to $100.

Why would seven professional players converge from thousands of miles away on a game with a limit of $72 U.S.? Well…

Tony had visited the Stampede for each of the previous two years, and raved about it. He had had a blast. And he remembered the shuffle—it was very much like the one found at Caesars Palace, one Butch could already handle.

Reed, Guppy, and Pop were convinced. They voted to go. After four months in Europe, they would have voted to go to the moon, provided they could find (a) fast-food joints at which (b) they could place their order in English.

What about the bullshit limits? Taylor wanted to know. He was comfortably ensconced in the Canary Islands, and really didn't want to fly halfway around the world to play a game worth maybe fifty or sixty bucks an hour.

Tony argued. "Tracking should more than double our expectation. Plus, long hours, no heat, friendly people, and we can play on the other players' hands! I played at a table with the same group of players last year. Ten days. They bet nickels. When the count was up, they'd go to twenty bucks, and I'd put eighty bucks on each of their hands. That's a spread from ten to six hundred! And since they know we're card counters, they let us make the playing decisions."

Brian had sided with Tony, because the game was temporary. The players could return to Europe any time, he argued, but this game was ten days only, right now. And this would finally give Brian a chance to play.

"Come on," said Guppy to Taylor. "Think of it. Kentucky Fried Chicken. English-speaking cocktail waitresses. Baseball on TV. And wouldn't it be nice to just pick up the damn phone and make a call?" While Taylor was speaking to Brian, Guppy was standing next to him, feeding Spanish coins into the pay phone as fast as he could. The phone had a metal ramp down which the coins rolled, falling into the slot at the end of the ramp. By this time, Guppy had dropped one-third of the coins on the ground. From previous experience, he knew he didn't have time to pick them up before the last coin rolled down the ramp and Taylor's call was cut off.

"I'm almost out of change, and I want to go home. I'm as mad as hell, and I'm not going to take this anymore!"

"*Network*," Brian said through the phone.

Taylor caved. What the hell, he figured. They could return to Europe in the fall.

He and Guppy deposited most of their pesetas in several bank accounts, unceremoniously tossed *la bolsa* into *la basura*, and headed to the airport to buy tickets to Madrid and thence to Vegas. Reed and Pop—who had changed most of the team's French francs during a quick trip to Switzerland—packed up the Fiat and headed to Paris. They left the car in long-term parking, stuffed their remaining pounds, francs, dollars, and stray Swiss francs into their carry-on bags, and headed home.

For three days, the jet-lagged players woke up at two o'clock in the morning and waited for the sun to come up so they could play some tennis. Then, two days before the parade that opened the Calgary Stampede in July 1983, they headed north.

Brian couldn't wait to get there. Tony had raved about the place. The other players. The restaurants. The Stampede itself. The sun that didn't go down until 11:00 p.m., and came up again at four thirty in the morning.

After expending so much of their energy on their act, the other players figured it would be nice to focus on nothing but their play. They figured that Canada would be a wonderful change from the constant deflections of heat to which they had become accustomed their entire careers.

They arrived in the evening. Brian, Reed, Guppy, Tony, and Julie sailed through customs. Then the customs agent who was digging through Taylor's suitcase found Butch amid a bunch of wires and connectors. Using the story Reed had used when entering England, Taylor showed the guy how Butch hooked up to the useless Sharp calculator he was carrying. "To learn French," Taylor said.

This worked until the customs agent searching Pop's luggage pulled a pair of crusty socks out of the toes of his playing shoes and located the buttons glued inside. Pop was entirely unable to explain how in the world those buttons got there. Continuing to dig, the agent located Butch, the loader, and a few decks of cards. Flustered, Pop had no better explanation for these than he had for the buttons in his shoes.

Then the agent came across Pop's copy of the shuffle-tracking instruction manual Brian had written. Flipping it open, he read the first page: "Warning! Do not allow this manual to fall into the wrong hands." After some verbiage about keeping the manual out of the hands of pit bosses, Griffin agents, and customs agents, the following appeared in big black letters: "Remove This Page and Destroy It!" While a blunder, having the manual with him in the first place paled in comparison to the more egregious error of failing to remove that first page. Pop was now officially toast.

At this point, completely unaware of what was going on behind him, Taylor was giving his customs agent a song and dance that would have done Rodgers and Hammerstein proud, plugging the computer into the Sharp and explaining how it all was supposed to work. Unfortunately, Taylor's customs agent could see what was going on behind Taylor. He could see the aluminum-clad computer the other customs agent had extracted from Pop's luggage, and realized it looked an awful lot like the one Taylor had just connected to a broken-down calculator. Taylor finished his explanation, looked up, and the customs guy just shook his head.

After putting their heads together and flipping through Pop's manual, the customs guys realized the equipment had something to do with gambling. They decided that what Taylor and Pop were carrying violated a law that made it illegal to transport gambling equipment into Canada. The law was actually meant for things such as slot machines and equipment for bookie joints, but the customs guys figured what they had found was close enough. Their bags were confiscated, their bodies were searched, and the customs agents found more than $8,000 in pounds, dollars, and two kinds of francs tucked into the Comfort Carrier hanging off of Pop's right leg. Pop was about as successful in explaining the existence of the eight grand as he had been in explaining the buttons in his shoes. Despite Taylor's protestations, they were both thrown into a stinking, festering holding tank and left to rot.

But only for a couple of hours. Apparently, the customs guys didn't really know what to do with their prisoners, so they called the Calgary Vice Squad. They knew how to deal with hookers, drug dealers, and other such bottom-dwellers; surely they would know what to do with a couple of degenerate gamblers attempting to smuggle gambling equipment into their pristine land.

Taylor and Pop were led into a large, well-lit office and told to sit down in a couple of molded plastic chairs. In walked three members of the Calgary Vice Squad. Two bruisers the size of grizzly bears accompanied a blond-haired guy who looked like the Jackal from Forsyth's book. The Grizzlies stood by the door while the Jackal took up residence behind the desk.

The Jackal flipped through the shuffle-tracking manual and the rest of Pop's damning evidence, looked up, and said, "Okay, what's going on here?"

Taylor looked at Pop. Now, Pop had seen so many casino back rooms that he was considering writing a book on the subject. However, he had never been in jail before, and he looked as if he had been struck by lightning. It was going to be up to Taylor.

Taylor shrugged. "What do you mean, 'What's going on here?'"

Apparently, that was not the answer the Jackal was looking for.

"Look, wise guy," he said. "You are no longer in the States. Technically, you are no longer anywhere. You may think you have rights here, but you don't. Now, I'm prepared to offer you a few alternatives. First, maybe you'd like to spend a few days in that holding tank we dragged you out of. That may soften you up a bit. Or, we can put you on the next plane back to the States. Let me assure you, there will be a customs agent waiting for you when you land, and I'm sure he will be very interested to hear where you got all that cash. Or," he continued, eyeing the connectors emerging from the top of Butch's aluminum case, "perhaps you would like to tell me how this gadget works."

Taylor looked at Pop. Still unable to speak, Pop just shrugged. Taylor cleared his throat.

For the next hour and a half, Taylor gave the Calgary Vice Squad a harangue on card counting they wouldn't soon forget. He went through the theory, a variety of counts, the rules, and anything else he could think of. And, as he probably repeated twenty times, card counting is completely legal in Alberta.

He then loaded the program into Butch, hooked him up to his shoes, and showed the Jackal how Butch counted cards. (Because the players had to enter one complete shoe before shuffle tracking was of any use, Brian had added a routine that simply counted the first shoe; that way, the operators could at least take insurance if the count went up.) As the Jackal took notes, Taylor jammed his hands into his shoes, entered a bunch of big cards, and then pressed LRR to enter them. He then asked for the count, and Butch obediently output a long dash. "The signal for a large bet," Taylor explained. Taylor then entered a number of small cards, and asked for the count again. Butch output a couple of dots.

Every time the Jackal reached for Pop's incriminating manual, Taylor would make a point he hoped the Jackal would find interesting. "Here's the difference between blackjack and roulette," he'd practically shout, and then go off on an exciting tangent about independent trials, dependent trials, and roulette balls with no memories. This happened several times, and although the Jackal's eyes may have been on the manual, his mind clearly was not. Had the material in the manual traversed the connection between his eyes and his brain, the Jackal would have known Taylor's entire card-counting harangue was a load of...misdirection.

At one point, Taylor detoured to the intricacies of the game of craps after the Jackal had reached for the manual once more. When Taylor finished, one of the Grizzlies said, "Too bad Martin isn't here." The Jackal nodded. "Yeah, he's gonna kick himself. Looks like he took the wrong night off."

When Taylor finally stopped talking, the Jackal stared at him hard enough to separate truth from fiction. Then he said, "I don't know if I believe any of what you just said. But if you just made all of that up, you deserve to go." And so they took Taylor and Pop out to a bar for a few Molsons, introduced them to the waitresses, and told the players about their own annual trips to Reno. Surprised, Taylor could tell that they had been listening and they had understood much of his exegesis. After Taylor gave them a variety of playing tips, the Vice Squad guys gave the players their business cards, told them to call if they had any problems, wished them luck, and gave them a ride to their hotel. What a country.

The casino on the Stampede grounds was held in an exhibition hall that looked like an airplane hangar. There was oversized farm equipment on display in a section of the hall, but the area reserved for the casino dwarfed it. Hundreds of blackjack tables covered the smooth concrete floor, interrupted by a dozen or so roulette tables and several diceless craps tables. (Because dice were explicitly outlawed in Alberta, the craps tables used a customized Wheel of Fortune with two spinners and thirty-six numbers— one through six repeated six times—on the circular face.)

Looking over that sea of green felt tables, each manned by a friendly, fair Canadian, located in a province where skilled players cannot be barred, the players thought they had died and gone to blackjack heaven.

There were a few things to get used to. The largest chip was $25, and was not green but blue. (To this day, Taylor can still hear the Canadian-accented "blu-oat" in his head as clearly as he did the first four thousand times he heard it.) Tony was greeted like some kind of rock star by players and pit personnel alike. Many of the Canadian players were regulars at the year-round casinos, and so recognized the strangers in their midst. "Card counter?" they'd ask, and it was literally days before Taylor could nod before looking around to see who was within earshot. The Canadian players were smart enough to sit at a table with a card counter whenever possible, because this would allow them to spread with the count without performing any of the mental labor.

In many ways, these "locals" were the key to the players' success in Canada. The majority of the locals couldn't afford to bet $100 a hand, so it was the bets that the players made on the locals' hands that allowed the huge bet spread that made the game worthwhile. And the locals benefited because for the first time they could play with what was close to an edge.

Before the first day's play had ended, each member of the team had attracted a loyal following of local players. Tony played with Julie and five other players, all Filipino. Taylor's group consisted of two players from Taiwan, a Filipino, a young lady from Thailand, an Indian (from India—in Canada, those individuals Americans refer to as "Indians" are called "Aboriginals"), and a guy named Doug. The other players attracted groups of similarly mixed heritage. (The over-representation of Asians gambling at the Stampede was pretty hard to miss—in fact, after four days, Guppy commented, "I had no idea eighty percent of Canadians were Chinese.")

It turned out that, collectively, Canadian gamblers were polar opposites from their counterparts in Europe. These were the best players Taylor and his teammates had ever seen. Virtually everyone knew Basic Strategy. This was likely a typical response to a harsh environment—evolve or die. The Canadian game was so tough, players playing like your average Frenchman or Japanese film producer would see their bankrolls plummet like stones. Players either learned to play properly or moved on to roulette.[26]

This strength of play was not an unmitigated blessing. Because the local Canadian players knew Basic Strategy, they knew "mistakes" when they saw them. Many of the locals did not understand that Basic Strategy was only the best possible play for a given hand versus a given dealer up-card, nothing more. They thought the entire table had to play Basic Strategy in order for everything to work out properly.

Card counters occasionally change Basic Strategy as the count changes. It took a long time for the locals to stop grumbling when Taylor or one of his teammates stood with sixteen against a ten, and the dealer made a hand as a result. Their playing acumen notwithstanding, the locals were not immune to the notion that "mistakes" by the third baseman—and, by extension, mistakes by other players at the table—would cause the dealer to beat everyone.

Because they could count and play openly, Taylor and his teammates were able to explain their decisions to the locals. "I have a true count of plus four, and we stand with a true of plus three or higher with twelve against a two," Taylor would say. Initially, his tablemates responded by glaring murderously (especially when they lost the hand). However, as they realized that their bankrolls were actually holding their own (the locals weren't spreading enough to beat the game, but were betting with the trackers, giving them what probably amounted to a very small edge), they grudgingly started accepting the changes to the "correct" strategy.

It turned out that those locals who had played with Tony the year before were the hardest to convince. After all, they knew card counters waited for small cards to emerge, and only then raised their bets. What was this nonsense about betting off the top? Taylor told them they didn't have to

---

26 Although the players' disadvantage at the roulette table is greater than even the worst blackjack player's disadvantage, there are crucial differences. It is common to play 100 blackjack hands per hour; a typical crowded roulette table sees maybe fifteen to twenty spins an hour. Further, blackjack wins and losses are even money, whereas the multiple payouts in roulette mean the players can experience large upward fluctuations before their bankroll inevitably goes down the toilet. This is the long way of saying roulette players tended to stay in action longer than extremely poor blackjack players do.

bet if they didn't want to, but it doesn't take much to convince a gambler to stick more money out. They might not have known what was going on, but most of them were nonetheless along for the ride.

One of the more difficult aspects of the game was the sheer bulk of the chips they had to deal with. Because the largest chip was $25, and because they could easily have five or six thousand in chips in front of them at any time, the pit bosses kept them flush in white cardboard boxes, each of which held $1,250 in blue chips. It was pretty easy for any member of the team to see how a teammate was doing—if the boxes came up past the player's chin, he was doing well. The chips stacked up, yes, but there was to be no *le bag* issue in Canada. The Canadians have a pink $1,000 bill.

Four days into the Stampede, Brian, Tony, and Julie were walking down the midway where all the carnival games and the rides were. Tony chose this not terribly auspicious moment to have what looked suspiciously like a panic attack. He started walking in small, frantic circles, foaming at the mouth, tugging at his hair, and talking to himself. When Julie reached out to touch him, trying to calm him down, he lurched away violently.

There were a lot of kids around, and one parent was frightened enough to call the police. When they showed up, it took four officers to hold Tony down. During the struggle, a wire from Tony's computer pulled free and was visible hanging out of the bottom of his pants. At that point all hell broke loose, because the police were now convinced that Tony was a bomb.

Brian explained that Tony was not a bomb but a blackjack player, and that the wire simply ran to a computer that was operated by buttons in his shoes. The cops looked at Brian. "You've got some pretty big feet there yourself," one of them noticed.

So Tony was carried off to a hospital where he was given a sedative and sent on his way, and Brian was hauled off to jail. Having been told in great detail about Taylor's encounter with customs, Brian figured he would just use the same story Taylor had told to describe Butch's functionality. Brian had chosen to erase the program while seated in the back of the police car (the program had a special RLLLLL "kill" command that filled the RAM memory with zeros), so unfortunately he couldn't demonstrate anything. The police listened to his story, took a close look at the equipment, and shrugged. Now what? Because it sounded like this had something to do with gambling, and because the police were convinced that whatever this thing was, it sure wasn't a bomb, they decided to call the Vice Squad. Guess who showed up? The Jackal recognized the equipment immediately, and then drove to the Stampede to find Taylor.

When Taylor arrived at the jail, the Jackal made him an offer. The head of Calgary Vice, an avid craps player named Martin, had heard about Taylor and his equipment from the Jackal. It turned out Martin had a few questions of his own for Taylor. The Jackal would release Brian, he said, if Taylor agreed to make a videotape explaining how card counting works—basically a command performance, if you will—complete with a demonstration of the card-counting computer. And, he wanted a copy of the instruction manual they had found in Pop's suitcase. In the confusion, the Jackal had forgotten to copy it. He wanted the manual and the video in two days.

The videotape would be no problem. Taylor simply had to duplicate his performance of a few nights ago. The problem, of course, was Brian's manual.

The manual explained what the computer really did, with explanations of the various inputs and outputs, and also had seven or so sections on various shuffles the players had found around the world. Taylor didn't know how his new buddies on the Vice Squad would feel about shuffle tracking as opposed to card counting, but he did know that he damn well didn't want to find out. So he rented a typewriter, plopped it down on the nightstand in his hotel room, and began writing a new manual. Dusting off skills dormant since his college days, Taylor wrote seventeen pages of bullshit, divided up into sections just like the real manual. Because the Jackal had flipped through the manual several times, Taylor figured there was a pretty good chance that he would at least remember some of the names of the major sections, so he used the same section names. Therefore, the new manual still had a section entitled "Cannes Non-Split Game." However, instead of describing how to input the fantastic shuffle Taylor and Guppy had blasted in Cannes, it described a game in which splitting was forbidden, and explained how best to exploit this fictional game.

When he was finished, Taylor made copies of the typewritten pages (to cause the lumps of white-out dotting the original to disappear), carefully removed the cover from Pop's original, and had the new version bound using the very same slightly dog-eared cover. Taylor worked a full day on the project, but figured it was worth it. (His teammates agreed; they voted to give Taylor an entire day's worth of playing hours for the job.)

Taylor showed up the next day and was introduced to Martin, the head of the Vice Squad. He explained they wanted the tape so they could properly train their agents to spot card counters. That way, if someone was winning, they'd know he wasn't cheating. Then Martin began telling Taylor the details of his craps system.

Taylor listened patiently, and then asked, "How's your system working for you?"

"Pretty darned good. Pretty good. Not bad. Didn't lose much on my last trip, eh?"

One of the Grizzlies clipped a microphone to Taylor's collar while the other manned a camera mounted on a tripod. The cameraman pushed a button, and Taylor launched into his spiel. He spoke for a little over an hour, with the occasional prod from the Jackal. ("The thing about the roulette ball— you know, that it has no memory. Mention that.")

When Taylor finished they made a copy of the manual, took Taylor out to lunch, and once again wished him luck.

The next day, Tony wandered over to Taylor's table to see how he was doing. Taylor was busy inputting a shoe, so he couldn't turn around. The dealer recognized Tony and said, "Hey, are you all right?"

"Fine. Why?"

"I heard you were walking down the midway and had heatstroke or something, and there were wires sticking out of your stomach," she said.

Tony was behind Taylor and couldn't see his face, but smacked him in the head anyway. "What are you laughing at?" Tony demanded.

A final close call came when, on the last day of the Stampede, the Grizzlies showed up at Taylor's table just as he was pushing two hands of $100 and five hands of $80 onto the layout off the top of a shoe. "How you doing?" they asked, shaking hands. Then one of them noticed that the table was loaded up before a single card had been dealt.

"What's with the big bets?" one of them asked. "I thought you needed a true of two before you had an edge." (Apparently they had been studying the video.) Taylor hemmed and hawed a bit, and finally said, "Last day. You know. Last chance to get some money out."

The Stampede was a minor success—the seven players had won thirty grand in ten days, averaging a little over ten hours of play a day each. After airfare, food, and other expenses, they had cleared about $2,000 each. Canadian.

When the Calgary Stampede ended, they spent a couple of days in Banff to unwind, visited the toe of an enormous glacier, and then traveled north to Edmonton for the Klondike Days exhibition. The casino was much smaller than the Calgary version, but the game was exactly the same. Unfortunately, the Edmonton casino management did not share the tolerance for card counters that their Calgary counterparts had displayed. After three days, the team was up about $7,000, and they were all barred.

Although the barring of skilled players is expressly forbidden in the Province of Alberta, and although Edmonton is indeed located in Alberta, the management in Edmonton was gambling that, by the time the players won the fight to gain re-admittance, Klondike Days would be over. They were right. A television crew showed up, the players all did some yelling on TV, but no decision was made in time. They slunk back to Calgary, defeated.

Julie and Tony took a side trip to Jasper, while Brian traveled to Philadelphia to visit his sister. Guppy and Taylor had met a couple of female dealers during the Stampede, and decided to hang out for an extra week in Calgary. Reed and Pop headed back to the States immediately.

Before boarding their flight home, Reed and Pop had filled out the standard customs declaration form. (Traveling from Canada to the States, you clear U.S. customs before you leave Canada.) On the form was the question: "Are you carrying more than $5,000 U.S. in cash or monetary instruments?" Pop, who now had in his possession five different currencies that totaled less than $4,800 U.S., checked the No box.

When the plane made an unexpected landing in Montana, U.S. customs officials boarded and asked Reed and Pop to leave the plane. They were taken to a back room, and Pop's money was counted.

The customs officials used exchange rates valid perhaps on Mars, and decided that Pop was carrying the equivalent of $5,100 U.S. Did they give him a warning? Or perhaps confiscate the overage? Wrong! They took it all! They stole all of his money. When Pop protested, the customs officials said, "You broke the law. We can hold you here as long as we like. If you don't sign this form quitting any claim to the money we just confiscated, fine. We'll keep you here until you do." Nice to be home, eh?

When Taylor left Calgary a week later, he was ready, having been told what had happened to Pop. Taylor, his declaration form filled out, handed his passport to the U.S. customs agent in the Calgary Airport. The agent typed the passport number into his computer, and his face lit up along with the screen. "Well," he beamed, "let's have a look at your luggage, shall we?"

"Certainly," Taylor beamed back.

For the next forty-five minutes, this meaningless cog in a huge bureaucratic machine pulled, tugged, tore at, and examined every item Taylor was carrying that was large enough to hide a marble. Taylor could almost see the headline the agent's imagination was providing him: DILIGENT PUBLIC SERVANT SINGLE-HANDEDLY FOILS HUGE MONEY-SMUGGLING RING. After he had finished with everything in Taylor's luggage and was desperately unrolling the first of about twenty pairs of socks (embroidered holes and all), Taylor looked down at the agent's shining skull, with the seven long hairs plastered across it, and said, "You know, a friend of mine passed through here about a week ago and had all of his money confiscated because you people claimed he was carrying too much. Do you really think I look stupid enough to try something that dumb?"

The guy deflated like a balloon. He unrolled a couple more pairs of socks, but the fight clearly had left him. He hauled Taylor's belongings into a side room, added up his cash (even using the most novel exchange rates, he didn't come close to $5,000), and through clenched teeth informed Taylor that his plane was still at the gate. Taylor thanked him a little too politely, and then told him that a friend of his would be passing through in the next day or so, and he would be safely under the $5,000 limit as well. Harassing him would be equally unproductive, Taylor said. The guy looked like Taylor had kicked him in the stomach.

Guppy passed through customs the following day. He hardly drew a glance.

Because it had been seven months since the fiasco at the Desert Inn, the players decided to check out the game in Vegas for a while. There were still many good, trackable games, but an ugly trend was on the horizon.

The canary in the mine was the Fremont. The players had often practiced there because the Fremont dealt a six-deck game using a standard shuffle; a shuffle the players referred to as "The Hilton Shuffle." When Guppy and Pop returned from an assault on the buffet there one night, they reported the news. "Remember they used The Hilton Shuffle?" Guppy said. Then, as Clouseau: "*Not any more.*" The Fremont continued to perform The Hilton Shuffle, but they now did it twice. Technically this shuffle could still be tracked, but the edge would be diluted considerably.

This was not good news. Casinos don't change shuffles capriciously. Something had happened, and it was a year before the players knew exactly what that something was.

What had happened was this: a couple of the busted-out players with whom Pop had played had learned his rudimentary form of shuffle tracking. Their main focus was on the clump of cards behind the cut card, but they kept rough track of the cards in the discard rack using their chips. They would buy in for a large amount of silver and red, and move their chips around as cards were thrust into the rack.

They teamed up with Vince—one of the Americans on the infamous Czech team—and went out to play. When you combine (a) a system in which chips are moved around as cards are discarded; (b) players who could be out-acted by second-graders performing their Christmas Pageant; and (c) big money, what you have is a disaster waiting to happen. The casinos figured out roughly what these players were up to (it seems they thought the players were tracking the unplayed cards only), and began changing the shuffles as a countermeasure. Before long, virtually every shuffle in Vegas was untrackable.

By this time, there was some serious dissention in the ranks. Brian had been arrested twice courtesy of Tony, and had had enough. They had made an agreement to play until they doubled their original bankroll of $175,000, and so they would play until that happened. But no more. During his playing career, Brian had been very careful to avoid heat. Until the team hooked up with Tony, he had never even been barred. Now, as a direct result of Tony's behavior, he had been arrested—not just barred, but arrested!— twice inside of seven months.

Reed wasn't particularly happy with Pop. He blamed him for the original bust entering Canada, and definitely blamed him for the two-day hiatus in Montana. Pop claimed he had been under the $5,000 limit, and it was customs Reed should be pissed at. Reed said Pop should have known better, and shouldn't have been carrying anything close to the five-grand limit. "He's a goddamn accident waiting to happen," Reed grumbled, "and I don't want to be in the car when he hits the next tree."

Pop and Tony would move on. Pop started playing progressive slot machines—a game for which an act is entirely unnecessary—and Tony read a book about a team of roulette players. The book was titled *The Eudaemonic Pie*, and was the story of a group of physicists who focused their formidable intellect on the game of roulette. According to the book, the project ultimately failed because they were never able to develop reliable hardware.

We have reliable hardware, Tony thought, and it can run any software at all, not just shuffle-tracking software. Tony tracked down one of the individuals in the book, one contact led to another, and Tony ultimately found himself talking to Doyne Farmer, one of the founders of the original project. Not only would Doyne's group ultimately use the shuffle-tracking hardware— slightly modified and renamed "Oscar"—for their roulette project, but they would also use some of Tony's blackjack teammates as well. But the entire roulette escapade is another story for another time.

While his remaining teammates played carefully in Vegas, Taylor flew to Paris, bailed the Fiat out of long-time parking, and drove to Spain. He picked up a new pillowcase and went from bank to bank, withdrawing the pesetas he and Guppy had deposited several months previously. He visited La Hambra in Seville and La Mesquita in Cordoba before hanging out at the beach at Torremolinos for a week, living on gazpacho and paella.

This part of Taylor's trip was really a vacation. For the first time, he was able to stick to one language in his head without constantly translating for one teammate or another, and he loved it.

For Taylor, one of the delicious beauties of this part of his job was living in places that until then had been merely locations in books he had read. Taylor had read Michener's *The Drifters* when he was in high school, and now he was living on the very beach on which much of the action in the book had taken place. He had read *The Day of the Jackal* while in France, and had enjoyed traveling down many of the very same nonfictional roads through the nonfictional towns that the fictional Jackal had.

And it wasn't your typical vacation. There was no place he had to go; no place he had to be. He stayed in Torremolinos until he felt ready to drive to Portugal to play some blackjack. While hanging around waiting for a blackjack table to open one night at the casino in Estoril, he once again watched a European roulette game. The action was remarkable—the chips covered the green felt layout so thickly that not one number was visible. Watching the little white ball revolve around the spinning rotor again and again, Taylor began to think. If there was some way to predict where that ball was going to drop, they could play forever. Look at that action! Watching the ball fall into the spinning rotor and bounce along the numbers, he emerged from his reverie. The ball must have hypnotized him, he thought. Predict that bouncing ball? Come on. When the blackjack table opened, he found a seat and went to work.

CHAPTER 16
SLICING AND DICING

It slices! It dices! But wait…there's more!
~Ad for Ronco's Chop-O-Matic

Once in a great while a book comes along that is so remarkable you simply have to wonder how civilization managed without it for as long as it did. Peter Griffin's *The Theory of Blackjack* is one such book. First published in 1978, this slim volume contains more about the mathematics underlying the game of blackjack than anything ever published, before or since. Perhaps the ultimate compliment: among professionals, an appeal to "Griffin's book"[27] will immediately end any argument.

Brian read Griffin's book like someone else might savor a favorite novel. He enjoyed leafing through it, reveling in the beauty of the math that underlies the game that changed his life. Re-reading Griffin's book is like re-reading any classic—it gets better each time, because the more experience and knowledge you bring to the party, the more rewarding the event. Brian was already on his fourth copy of the second edition. Through overuse, the previous three had fallen apart.

If he had been looking for something in particular during a certain foraging expedition in late 1983, he never would have taken a second look at the small chart on page 146. Though Brian had seen it a hundred times before, its full implications had never registered—in part because it was there to bolster another point the author was making, in part because it is something

---

27 It is perhaps ironic that Peter Griffin shares his surname with a detective who publishes a very different kind of book. However, pros refer to the latter's book as "the Griffin Book," and there is no chance that anyone in the business will ever confuse one with the other.

even the least experienced player is intuitively aware of, but mostly because on the previous ninety-nine occasions Taylor hadn't recently shown Brian a card trick.

The trick had involved poker—a game Brian continues to play to this day. The trick began with Brian cutting the deck as many times as he liked. Then Taylor proceeded to deal seven full houses—one to everyone but himself. Taylor somehow managed to eke out a straight flush.

Taylor had shown Brian how to do the trick. It simply entailed setting up the deck. Allowing Brian to cut as many times as he wanted was purely misdirection. Cutting a deck of cards twenty times is exactly the same as cutting it once, as far as randomizing goes. (Try it. The two cards that were split by the cut are now on the top and the bottom of the deck. The next cut will bring those two cards back together and separate two new cards. And so on.)

So, with this tidbit tickling the outskirts of his consciousness, barely alive in his neural circuitry, Brian looked at the chart on page 146 for the hundredth time. And then it happened.

The name on her name tag was Rebecca. Her glory days—twelve years as a showgirl—were now behind her. She shuffled the single deck, squared the cards, and placed them on the felt in front of Taylor, who was seated in the middle of the table. Taylor hardly glanced at Guppy, cut the cards, and then rested his arm on the padded rail. Rebecca completed the cut, and burned the top card.

At first base, Guppy made two five-dollar bets. Brian, seated between Guppy and Taylor, bet one hand of ten dollars. Over at third, Reed bet two hands of five dollars. And Taylor shoved out two hands of $200—the table limit at Jerry's Nugget in North Las Vegas.

A sweaty pit boss crossed his arms and glared. But what could he do? Taylor was betting off the top and, given the rules at the Nugget, the best a perfect Basic Strategy player could hope for was to lose 0.2 percent of everything he bet. Not much, but certainly enough for the house to get the money in the long run.

Sometimes, however, the long run is a long time in coming. So, while waiting for its arrival, there was nothing the pit boss could do but sweat. Which he did. Admirably. Copiously. And with flair.

"Chips play to the limit," said Rebecca for the fiftieth time this day, and dealt. Each card was pitched perfectly, helicoptering directly to a waiting bet. Bang, bang, bang. Seven hands. Then, her up-card. Splat. The five of spades. Guppy touched his nose.

The pit boss's face tightened. When they named it "the *long* run," they weren't kidding. How much longer could his dealers continue to show so many stiff cards before the odds caught up with this big son of a bitch with more money than brains?

Rebecca dealt around the table once again, providing each hand with a second card, and then expertly, flawlessly, slid her hole card beneath her up-card. Whatever this lucky bastard was doing, he sure as hell wasn't seeing that hole card. Rebecca was as tight as a drum.

The players played their hands, and cheered when Rebecca busted. She paid the table, and the pit boss sidled up behind her, his back to the table and his hand covering his mouth. "Shuffle," he said.

Shuffle. The dreaded act. The dirty deed. If you want to stop professional card counters in their tracks, this is the ultimate countermeasure. After all, counters must wait until the second round before they can take advantage of a positive count. Now, there was no second round to take advantage of. Taylor couldn't remember the last time he'd seen one.

Shuffle, the pit boss said. And Reed failed to suppress a smile.

Dutifully, Rebecca shuffled, squared the cards, and placed them in front of Reed, who, because of his position at third base, didn't even have to move his eyeballs to see Guppy's signal. He cut, and placed his right arm on the rail as Rebecca completed the cut. Taylor shoved out another two hands of two hundred dollars.

"Thin to win," Reed said.

Brian stared at the unexceptional chart on page 146 of Griffin's book. It said that when the dealer has a five or six up-card, each player at the table plays with an average advantage over the house of a whopping 24 percent. The edge provided by fours is almost as good—18 percent. Twos, threes, and sevens are no slouches either—providing players with edges measured in the teens. Compared to the 1 and 2 percent edges counters struggle to achieve, playing against dealers with small cards showing is the ultimate.

Unfortunately, if you total the disadvantage with which the players play when the dealer shows a nine, ten, or ace, and add that to the edge they have when the dealer shows a small card, you simply arrive at the overall house advantage. Of course you do. You have to. After all, that's what the house edge *is*. It's the average edge the house enjoys, given all possible dealer up-cards, against all possible player hands.

If there was some way they could know when dealers were more likely to have one of those beautiful small cards perched in front of them, Brian and his teammates could bet big and play with an edge that positively dwarfed anything they had previously imagined. Of course, if they could develop the ESP necessary to know when the dealer was going to have a small up-card, they could simply skip all this nonsense and take their talent to the stock market. Much more straightforward, and there are no limits or sweaty pit bosses to worry about.

So it seemed Griffin's chart simply provided Brian with another interesting but ultimately useless bit of trivia about the game he loved so well.

But Taylor had just shown Brian a card trick.

Rebecca placed the deck on the felt in front of Guppy. He shook his head, declining the cut. Rebecca moved the deck in front of Brian. Guppy grabbed his chips with his right hand and began to shuffle them. Brian cut. Thin.

Brian put his hand on the felt. Guppy played only one hand this time. Brian and Reed put out their small bets, and Taylor shoved out his usual two hands of two hundred. Out came the cards. Splat. Four of hearts face up in front of the dealer. The pit boss reached for a handkerchief and wiped his forehead.

With Griffin's book spread-eagled on the desk in front of him, Brian shuffled a deck of cards and looked at the card on the bottom. It was the three of clubs. He then cut thin, and completed the cut by taking the thin pile he cut off the bottom and placing it on the top of the deck, just as a dealer would. Then he dealt the cards out, one at a time, face up. The three of clubs was the eighth card out. For the first time since he had seen Redd Foxx perform live at the Sahara, Brian almost lost control of his bladder.

Rebecca chatted about her career as a showgirl as she shuffled the cards. The four players had been sitting at her table all morning, and the big bettor in the middle was tipping well. The least she could do was talk. Anyway, he wasn't like most gamblers, who regularly took out their frustrations on her. Then again, he *was* winning. She had witnessed some pretty dramatic Jekyll-to-Hyde transformations when the cards turned.

As scintillating as it may have been, it wasn't Rebecca's conversation that kept Taylor and his teammates glued to their seats at her table. It was a particular characteristic of Rebecca's—one she shared with a number of dealers the players had scouted during the course of the last month. Rebecca had a horrible weakness.

Just before she offered the cards to be cut, Rebecca thoughtfully squared the deck. She did so by briefly holding the deck upright in her right hand and gently caressing the edge with the fingers of her left hand. And it was that move—not the chatter and not the quiver of her silicon breasts as they bounced gently beneath her blouse—that made Guppy's eyes light up. ("Well, maybe it was the breasts, a little," says Guppy.)

Maybe a little. But it was mostly this: As Rebecca held the deck sideways, Guppy could catch a glimpse of the bottom card.

If that bottom card was what the players referred to as "a big small card" (a four, five, or six), Guppy would grab his chips with his right hand. A regular small card—two, three, or seven—merited his right hand resting lightly on the felt. If it was a ten, he would put both hands in front of him on the table. And if it was an ace—oh, baby, if it was an ace!—Guppy would grab the rail with both hands and hang on.

So let's roll the action as lovely Rebecca squares the deck. Guppy spies the bottom card. It's the five of spades—just as big and as beautiful as they come. (There was something viscerally satisfying about black cards. Somehow—perhaps because of the way the black ink stood out in stark contrast to the shiny white background—they seemed, well, more *powerful* than their red counterparts.)

Guppy grabs his chips as Rebecca places the freshly shuffled deck in front of Taylor. Taylor notices Guppy's grip on his chips, and cuts thin. Quite thin. About nine cards. Rebecca lifts that small packet of about nine cards and places it on top of the rest of the deck, thereby completing the cut. And Taylor puts his arm on the rail to inform his teammates that he thinks the cut was indeed nine cards.

All seven spots are bet upon as Rebecca burns a card. That's one. Rebecca starts to deal, and we continue to count. Cards two and three go to Guppy's two hands. Card four goes to Brian. Five and six land in front of Taylor's two stacks of green chips. Seven and eight go to Reed's two five-dollar bets. And card number nine, that big, black five of spades that just moments ago adorned the bottom of the deck, is deposited right in front of lovely Rebecca like a big, wet turd. Splat.

And Guppy touches his nose. (Since he was the only one to see the bottom card, he is the only one who knows if Rebecca's up-card was indeed that card. After all, they could have been shooting for some other small card and gotten lucky.)

As a result of that five of spades, all seven hands now have an average advantage of 24 percent. Taylor's expectation *on this one hand* is ninety-six bucks. And they are playing fifty hands an hour. You do the math.

On average, Taylor's edge on the first round was about ten times greater than any count edge he could hope to get on a second round. And the casino's countermeasure was to give him nothing but first rounds!

And *that* is why Reed couldn't help but smile when the pit boss said, "Shuffle."

> Please, please, *please*, Br'er Fox, don't throw me in the
> briar patch!
> ~*Br'er Rabbit,* The Briar-Patch

So why are Guppy, Reed, and Brian betting so little? Well, nobody's perfect. The cutter doesn't pelt the dealer every time. Those times that the cut is a little thick or a bit thin, the card will go to one of the "buffer" hands—one of the hands with small money out.

This does several things. First, and most important, it prevents Taylor from getting smacked with that miserable small card, thus starting the hand with a huge disadvantage.[28] Second, that card is now for all intents and purposes out of play. If the dealer has a stiff hand, that card is not available to turn her stiff into a good hand. So, even when they miss the dealer, they aren't giving anything up. As far as Taylor's hands are concerned, that small card might as well be sitting in the bottom of the discard rack.

Last, and never least, is cover. Taylor is the out-of-town big-shot, his buddies live in town and are showing him around. Nobody who lives in Vegas bets big money for long unless they're doing something. So, Reed, Guppy, and Brian could talk like the locals they are, and only Taylor has to act like he is a tourist in town for a little bit of fun and a little bit of gambling.

Let's watch another round. The original pit boss has been banished to another pit—perhaps to avoid the lawsuit that surely would have followed the impending heart attack—and a less-menacing replacement is now hawking the game. He is watching the table—Taylor is out-betting the entire pit, for chrissakes, so he'd better watch—but his lack of emotional involvement

---

28 For example, a player whose first card is a five starts his hand with a disadvantage of 19 percent.

is apparent. Because of the one round and shuffle policy instituted by his predecessor, there really isn't a hell of a lot to see. A player who continues to flat-bet simply has to lose, and sweating will only serve to ruin a good shirt.

Rebecca squares the deck and places it in front of Brian. Guppy grabs the rail. Ace. Brian cuts thicker than usual, and places a hand on the felt. That means he thinks the cut was eleven or twelve cards. Leave one spot open. Guppy plays only one hand. Taylor shoves out two hands of the limit.

Burn card. That's one. A card to each bet makes seven. Rebecca's up-card is the eighth card. Nine goes to Guppy's hand, ten to Brian, and cards eleven and twelve go to Taylor's big bets. Two shots to get that ace and the monstrous 52 percent edge it carries in its back pocket.

Boom. The ace of diamonds is in his first hand (meaning the cut was eleven cards). Unfortunately, it hasn't mated with a ten this time. Too bad. Taylor hits a couple of times, and busts. Reality has collapsed the probability curve that represented the 52 percent edge, and turned this hand into an actual disadvantage of 100 percent. Nobody ever said an edge was a lock. *That* would be the ultimate.

Taylor shrugs and tosses in his cards. He'll get it back.

As beautiful as Slicing and Dicing was, the system wasn't the ultimate edge.

First, the players were limited to dealers who showed that bottom card at some point prior to offering the deck to be cut. By no means were all dealers as generous as Rebecca—even back in 1984.

Second, there was the sheer number of signals to contend with. Signaling the value of the bottom card required five different signals. The thickness of the cut—three more signals. Did the card pelt the dealer, or was the cut thick or thin? Three more. "You pelted the BP with a small card, you schmuck." Yet another. Add these to the standard "yes," "no," "I don't know," "follow me," "I'm going to the bathroom," "insurance," "heat," "massive heat," and the three "end of session" signals, and the players often looked like peripatetic third-base coaches. There were so many signals, in fact, that the players were forced to develop a signal that meant, "The next thing I do is *not* a signal," thus offering the victim of an itchy nose or a dry scalp the opportunity for a good scratch without throwing the team into turmoil.

Lastly, they had to get a table to themselves. This proved to be the most difficult task until Reed—always ready to lean in and take one on the chin for the team—took matters into his own hands.

Since they could play only those dealers who exposed the bottom card, the players often found themselves waiting around for hours before a particular dealer's table went dead. They learned to grab whatever spots were available and wait until the original occupants finally wandered off, muttering. Then, those team members who hadn't yet grabbed a spot could swoop in and take up residence.

However inevitable the eventual wandering off and muttering behavior of the original occupants, it often took quite a while for the house edge to manifest itself and grind those players down. Given the hourly expectation generated by Slicing and Dicing, the hours spent sitting at the bar drinking Coca-Cola were quite expensive.

Reed's first brainstorm was prompted accidentally. Brian, Guppy, and Reed occupied five of the seven spots at a table. Reed found himself wedged between a woman with bright red hair and a middle-aged man with an impressive stomach.

These two gamblers appeared to be permanently affixed to their stools. They were getting their asses kicked, but between complaints, a seemingly endless supply of twenty-dollar bills continued to emerge from their pockets. Finally the man with the stomach lit a cigar. The red-haired woman immediately started protesting, fanning the smoke away with her hands. The gentleman, living up to the terms of the moniker, agreeably ground the cigar out in an ashtray. And Reed's eyes lit up.

The rule was, Reed would give a player thirty minutes to vacate the premises on his or her own. After that, it was *mano a mano* with Robert Richards.

Reed accepted all challenges like the true professional he was. He scouted the entire city for the raunchiest cigars imaginable. He developed wracking coughs and phony sneezes indistinguishable from the real things. He ate meals that reeked of garlic. And he rarely showered.

In most cases, any one of the above worked well. However, Reed was to go up against some die-hard gamblers who were almost as tenacious as he. When the coughing and wheezing and smoking failed, Reed would make a trip to the gift shop for some beef jerky. Reed's digestive system reacted quickly and adversely to beef jerky. This intestinal distress would force all but the most intrepid of players from the table. Subtlety had never been Reed's strong suit.

To this day, Reed insists he showed admirable restraint. No matter how tempted he might have become, he never once asked a player to "pull his finger" before putting the exclamation point on his routine.

"We went too far," Taylor says now. "Those people had every right to gamble in peace. In fact, without the regulars, we'd all be out of work." However, talk is cheap. Neither he nor any of his teammates ever did anything to stop Reed. He was making them too much money.

Reed—never one to let philosophical hair-splitting get in the way of the size of the wad in his wallet—argued that it really didn't matter where a regular gambler played. "So what if a tourist has to move to another table? He'll still be playing with the same disadvantage. This way, he gets a change of scenery."

Philosophical issues aside, Reed was saving the team a great deal of time. Once he had perfected his technique, only one gambler had lasted as long as twenty minutes at the table with him. For once in his life, his teammates had to admit Reed was an unrivaled expert at something.

Slicing and Dicing provided unparalleled cover. One round and shuffle was the absolute minimum a casino could deal, so what more could they do? The only problem was when a relief dealer showed up who wasn't as generous with the bottom card as the regular dealer. The players routinely had to slog through unreadable relief dealers—just as they had when they were spooking and front-loading. If they had to live with betting big for fifteen minutes out of every hour with a slight disadvantage, they would have accepted it as part of the overhead. However, these guys were nothing if not professionals. If they could find a way to save money against the relief pitcher, they would. And they did.

As was the case with penicillin and Reese's Peanut Butter Cups, serendipity occasionally favors the good guys. The team was Slicing and Dicing at the Union Plaza when a Sherman tank disguised as the relief dealer came to the table—a dealer who protected the bottom card like a Brink's guard. The strategy was to play slowly—thus lowering the number of disadvantageous hands Taylor would have to play—but this woman had doubled her usual dose of caffeine, or Dexedrine, or something. She dealt so fast, the delaying tactics were obvious.

"Whatsa matter, y'all can't add alla sudden?" the dealer snapped, slapping a pudgy hand on the green felt in front of Taylor. "Make up your mind. Your cards ain't gonna change."

Taylor hit the bathroom a couple of times, but that looked as obvious as it sounds. Via hand signals, the players agreed that Taylor should just pull up his waders and slog through her shift.

Then, for some reason—perhaps a memory dredged up from his youth—Guppy began whistling the theme song from *The Andy Griffith Show*. The dealer was waiting for Reed to play his hand and, barely audibly, mumbled, "Andy Griffith."

"What?" said Reed, scratching for a hit.

"Nothin'," the dealer grunted, and busted Reed's hand.

Guppy smiled. He had heard what she said. As she began to shuffle the cards, he started humming something else. "*The Dick Van Dyke Show*," she said.

"Excuse me?" said Taylor.

"*The Dick Van Dyke Show*. I used to watch it every day after school."

Guppy touched his nose and began to hum another. After a few notes, Reed joined in.

"*The Brady Bunch*," said the dealer.

"You're good," said Guppy, "but how about this?" He began to hum another. One at a time, the other players joined in. Looking up, the dealer listened intently, still shuffling.

"Darn, I recognize it, but I can't think of what it is."

The pit boss leaned into the table, and the players instinctively recoiled slightly, preparing for the worst. The theme song tailed off.

"*Bewitched*," he said out of the corner of his mouth. Unable to take it anymore, Reed buried his face in his arms.

"Great!" said Guppy. "But you'll never get this one." And he hummed another.

"*Get Smart!*" said the dealer and the pit boss, at the same time.

And the dealer still hadn't dealt a hand.

One of the side benefits to Slicing and Dicing was that, for the first time in their careers, the players could acknowledge the fact that they were together at the table. They could talk, joke around, and openly discuss their wins and losses. It also meant they could play longer sessions. It is rare for players who don't know each other to remain at the same table for eight straight hours—one of the factors that limited spooking, front-loading, and shuffle tracking.

Beyond that, for the first time they could enjoy comps together. This was an unqualified bonus for Brian and Guppy, who were usually small players and therefore rarely had the opportunity to try to run up a bill in one of the better restaurants in town.

Although he had felt a flutter while shuffle tracking, this was the first time Taylor had experienced the full impact of the beauty of the game of blackjack. Brian had felt it briefly in Atlantic City, but for most professional players, the edge with which they normally play is so small, it is only in retrospect they can look back and appreciate the manifestation of their power and skill. During any given session—or any given month, for that matter—the game can be a terrible financial grind.

With Slicing and Dicing, however, the edge was so enormous that it manifested itself very quickly—so quickly, in fact, that the players would talk openly at the table about the arrival of "The Due Ship."

The overwhelming majority of gamblers and non-gamblers alike believe in something akin to "dueness." If a .350 hitter goes 0 for 4 and comes up in a clutch situation during a baseball game, the announcer will invariably say something about this guy being "due." Slot players are loath to leave a machine they've been playing because, to their minds, the longer they've played and lost, the closer they are to hitting that jackpot. Roulette players persist in playing the same number or numbers because they think a number that hasn't come up in eighty or ninety spins is "due"; that is, they believe it is more likely to come up now than it was when their terrible run of luck began.

Apart from the belief that voting actually makes a difference, this may be the world's most widespread misapprehension. And it isn't called "The Gambler's Fallacy" for nothing.

For the record, let's straighten this out. Dueness stands about the same chance of rearing its head at the gaming tables as does a unicorn. It just doesn't work that way. The odds of an event occurring do not change just because it hasn't occurred for a while. However, because the edge with which the Slicers and Dicers played was so huge, long losing streaks—like those that regular counters routinely experienced—simply didn't occur. The math precluded it.

So, when they did lose—pelting the dealer repeatedly with small cards and watching her pull out twenties and twenty-ones hand after hand—they knew the losing wouldn't last long. It just couldn't. So they would start to talk about "The Due Ship."

It began as a joke. The players knew full well there was no such thing as "dueness." That's why they used the word in the first place. It is one of those visceral semantic triggers that prove to a pit boss who knows the first thing about gaming that these players are morons. (As for those pit bosses who didn't know the first thing about gaming? Well, to those guys, Taylor and his buddies made perfect sense.)

The talk would start after Taylor won a few hands. Is this it? Has the due ship finally pulled into the harbor? Is it going to get stuck on a sandbar and stay awhile? Or is it going to float back out to sea?

What the players would never learn is what the hundreds of dealers, pit bosses, and cocktail waitresses who heard this meaningless prattle thought of it. What did they make of a guy who won a couple of hands, and then started pulling an invisible rope, making sounds like a tugboat horn, while his friends began the chant, "Due Ship! Due Ship! Due Ship!"?

And that wasn't the worst of the lunacy. Cutting an eight to the dealer was profitable, but only marginally—it provided a 5 percent edge. However, because the Slicers and Dicers hit the dealer on around half their cuts, they figured their overall edge with an eight was about 2.5 percent. Not bad, but if they were playing a joint with a big limit, they didn't want to slam two hands of a thousand out with that (relatively) small edge. Therefore, another signal was required so Guppy could indicate that the bottom card was an eight.

As we learned in the European chapter, "eight" is "*huit*" in French, pronounced "wheat." Since Guppy had worked so hard to learn to count to ten in a foreign tongue, it would have been a shame for all that schoolin' to go to waste.

It seemed like a good idea at the time. Whenever the bottom card was an eight, Guppy would signal a small card, and then mutter, "Wheat. Wheat. Good wheat crop this year." This quickly evolved into, "So, Taylor, didja eat your...*Wheaties* today?"

Asking Taylor about that morning's alimentary activities would have been okay once. Or maybe twice. But after the fifteenth or sixteenth time, what could the pit bosses have been thinking?

And, to this day, Taylor has never answered Guppy's question.

As bad as "Wheaties" was, "Ed" was worse.

There were times the Slicers and Dicers would miss a cut by a mile. Once, at the Aladdin, Reed cut a ten and gave it to the dealer in the hole. It isn't a terribly good idea to give the dealer a ten—it gives her an average advantage of 17 percent—but if you know it's there, the information can be of some value. If nothing else, it would be a good idea to take insurance if the dealer is showing an ace.

So they decided that, if Guppy saw a ten (this only related to tens; they'd never miss a small card that badly), and that ten didn't show up in anybody's hand, Guppy would signal his belief that it was now the dealer's hole card by saying, "Hey, anybody wanna go see Wayne Newton tonight?"

Why Wayne Newton? Because Wayne, his half-assed mustache, and his trunkful of musical instruments were appearing at the Aladdin at the time.

Well, Guppy saw a queen of spades, and Taylor cut fat. When Guppy didn't see the lady in anybody's hand, he got a little excited and said, "Anybody wanna see *Ed* Newton tonight?"

Which wouldn't have been so bad, except that for the next three years, whenever somebody cut fat, the other three players would taunt the cutter mercilessly, yelling, "Ed! Ed! Ed!"

At least Guppy hadn't said, "Fig Newton."

Once again, if the pit bosses had any opinion of this inanity, they were keeping it to themselves.

In most cases, joints were scouted thoroughly for those one or two dealers who showed the bottom card before offering the cut. However, during a ski trip in the spring of '84, Taylor found not the occasional gold nugget but a veritable mine.

The mother lode was located on the north shore of Lake Tahoe, disguised as an absolute toilet called the Nevada Lodge. Probably because it is more accessible from the Bay Area, Harrah's, Harvey's, and the other high-class Tahoe resort properties had clustered on the south shore of the lake, leaving the poor northern end with some pretty revolting dives. And the Nevada Lodge was bringing up the rear of this sorry wagon train.

The highest denomination chip in any of the racks was twenty-five bucks. On the blackjack tables themselves, only the occasional glimmer of green was visible between the coffee stains and cigarette burns. The formerly brown armrests were mostly silver now, courtesy of the duct tape used to hold them together. The carpet was of the perpetually moist and sticky variety; Reed guessed they probably bought it used from the local movie theater. And words simply can't do justice to the buffet. According to Taylor, the buffet was such that the Board of Health recommended customers wash their hands *after* they ate.[29]

But the dealers. My, oh my! You want to talk about beautiful. During the day shift, eight dealers out of ten were showing that bottom card to anyone within twenty feet of the table. Swing shift was almost as good, and graveyard—well, they *all* showed it on graveyard. This was the loosest joint any of the players had ever seen. They didn't even need Guppy's signals—it was impossible *not* to see the bottom card.

"After a while, it was just embarrassing," Taylor says. "Some of those dealers held the deck up so high, we were afraid the bastards in the sky were going to be able to see the damn card."

If they did, it didn't make much of an impression. For three days, Taylor pounded out two hands of the limit—two hundred dollars—in a joint that probably hadn't seen a bet over five dollars since the 1960s, when Frank Sinatra owned the Cal Neva across the street.

If you're a regular gambler, deciding when to stop playing isn't terribly difficult. You quit when you are exhausted or broke, whichever comes first. For professionals, however, life isn't that simple. Card counters have to make the most of excellent playing conditions, but a good rule of thumb is to leave before management has you thrown out, beaten up, or both.

Because of the huge edge generated by Slicing and Dicing, the decision was even tougher. Once the casino has taken its best shot—instituting their one round and shuffle countermeasure—it was simply a matter of deciding how much the joint could afford to lose without having to close the front door. Taylor and his teammates could literally have put the Nevada Lodge out of business, and they didn't want to do that.

It wasn't that they felt sorry for the joint. Casinos are run by people who routinely beat Social Security recipients out of their last dime, and then throw the poor buggers out into the street for taking up too much room. It was just better for business—*Taylor's* business—if the joints stayed around for a while.

---

29 Stolen with the utmost respect from Rodney Dangerfield.
—Alexander Taylor.

Circumstances presented the clear end of the first trip to the Nevada Lodge. After the session on day three—a marathon during which Taylor lost back everything he had won the previous two days, and then watched the due ship come in with an absolute vengeance, winning almost every bet he made for three straight hours—he went to the cage with mounds and mounds of green $25 chips. The woman in the cage gasped, and paid him in hundreds, fifties, twenties, tens, and finished up with over $300 in fives. Taylor had stopped just short of delving into the stash of singles.

He had won fourteen grand. Sticking with the ship metaphor, perhaps he had gone a bit overboard.

Taylor's windfall had made quite an impression on one pit boss in particular—a friendly enough sort who had the misfortune of being issued by parents who had seen fit to name him Ed. A bit on the lumbering side of large, and with a long face and widely set eyes, the players immediately started calling him "Mr. Ed." Whenever he came into the pit, Guppy would shake his jowls from side to side and say, "Wilber!" The dealers loved it.

The players all talked to Mr. Ed, and Mr. Ed was certainly civil, but despite the jokes and the songs, he wasn't buying the act. Not for a minute did Mr. Ed think Taylor was just some lucky gambler. He spent quite a bit of time circling the table like a vulture, but he never came any closer to figuring out what Taylor and his teammates were up to. He did, however, know what they *weren't* doing. They sure as hell weren't counting. And that may be why Ed let them play as long as he did.

Mr. Ed instituted the one round and shuffle after Taylor won his first big double down ten minutes into the first session. Then he stood, arms crossed, waiting for Taylor to put his tail between his legs and slink out.

When that didn't happen, Ed tried another standard countermeasure taught at The Nevada School for Sweaty Pit Bosses—changing decks. At one point, Ed changed the deck five times in twenty minutes. With each change, Ed would square the old deck by banging it on the top of the discard rack and then stare at it with one eye, conspicuously looking for bent cards. He would then glare at the players—usually with the other eye—to see how they would respond to this devastating countermeasure. Apart from some obligatory complaining ("Come on, Ed, we just had the old one broken in"), they didn't react much.

After about thirty such deck changes, Ed gave up—perhaps because Taylor continued to bet off the top against brand-new decks, before anybody would have had a chance to bend the cards. For the remainder of the play, Mr. Ed resorted to glaring, and little else. On the way out the door after that monumental cash-out, Taylor thanked Ed for his hospitality, and especially for the comps to that extraordinary buffet.

Just less than a year after the first visit, Taylor watched a weather report from his house in Vegas. A storm had dumped four feet of fresh snow on an already deep base in the Sierras. Out came the skis, and the team made a second trip to their private North Shore Gold Mine.

Taylor started winning immediately. One of the dealers, remembering Taylor's performance of a year ago, asked Taylor if he was always this lucky. "Nope," Taylor told her. "Only here."

Surprisingly, Mr. Ed was glad to see them. It was clear he had thought about the play more than once over the course of the intervening year, and was more convinced than ever that Taylor's good fortune had nothing to do with the gambling gods smiling down upon him. Plopping his carcass on a stool next to Guppy, Ed informed the players he was going to figure out what they were up to. Taylor shrugged and said, "Fine. Let me know what makes me so lucky here, and I'll put it in a bottle and take it to Caesars." Mr. Ed wasn't particularly amused, but did spend quite a bit of time at the players' table, listening to their jokes and desperately trying to look like he knew more about what was going on than he actually did.

They quit after four days—up ten grand. Keep the egg-laying goose alive, Brian always said, and quitting too soon was always preferable to quitting too late.

In early '86, the players returned to the Nevada Lodge for a third trip in as many years. They had already taken up their positions and rolled the artillery in place when Mr. Ed returned from his break. He did a priceless double take, looked at his watch, and said, "Must be that time of year again."[30]

During the first two trips, Mr. Ed had been surprisingly decent in his interaction with his dealers. Because so many pit bosses fundamentally

---

30 Why Mr. Ed had to look at his watch to determine what season it was is a question best left unasked.

misunderstand the game it is their job to oversee, they frequently blame the dealer for a player's good fortune at the gaming table (but rarely credit her when she kicks a player's ass). To his credit, Mr. Ed had not resorted to that. Until now. And he could not have picked a worse time to start.

Maybe something unpleasant was going on in Ed's personal life. Whenever Taylor did particularly well against a dealer, Ed would harass her mercilessly. Comments such as "Stupid bitch, can't make a hand," and "I hope you enjoy unemployment, you worthless loser," would be lobbed periodically from the pit. He went after one girl so viciously she handed off the deck to her relief and burst into tears.

Of all the behaviors engaged in by pit bosses, the way they treat their dealers is perhaps the most despicable. Most dealers in Nevada have no unions, no rights, no recourse if they lose their jobs. And they are frequently fired for—are you ready?—losing.

When a dealer beat the pants off a player, winning over expectation, she has to take massive heat from the victim. Is she rewarded by the pit? Is she congratulated? Does this get posted to someone's mental ledger so that at some time in the future this big win will offset the occasional (and inevitable) loss? No. When a dealer kicks a player's ass, she is simply doing her job. And, when the totals are tallied at the end of the shift, it is often the *pit boss* who gets credit for the win.

However, if a player happens to get lucky, suddenly it is the dealer who is responsible. As incredible as it may sound, dealers can still lose their jobs because players sometimes win.

After two days on this third trip, Taylor had beaten the Nevada Lodge dealers out of six grand, but no jobs were at risk. Unless the management was willing to fire the entire staff, there was very little they could do.

When Ed came in to start his shift on the third day, the team had been treading water for a couple of hours. Ed looked at the clipboard with the rubber band cinched around its waist, perused the names of the dealers, and came over to Taylor's table. "Good news, boys," he said. "We're short-staffed. I'm gonna get to deal to you later."

"That's great," Taylor said, "because you're my favorite pit boss of all time."

There were some joints—like the MGM Grand in Vegas—where everything always seemed to go wrong. And there were other places where everything simply went right. The Nevada Lodge was a member of the latter group.

In the next hour, Taylor lost four of the six thousand he was up. It was clear the due ship had set sail, deserting the team. And it was then, in their hour of desperate need, that relief arrived—in the form of a certain pit boss named Ed.

When Ed took the deck from the dealer, Taylor was in the process of buying in again. He had exactly two green chips left in front of him. Ed gladly exchanged Taylor's six hundred dollars for twenty-four green chips, and jammed the thick wad of cash down the slot into the drop box. It was beginning to look as if Taylor's incredible run of luck had finally expired. Ed shuffled the cards expertly, squared the deck, and then made sure everyone within a one-hundred-yard radius of the table saw that the bottom card was the four of diamonds before he plopped the deck down in front of Taylor.

Ed couldn't have been more effective if he had waved an automatic weapon around the pit. Everybody on the team ducked.

"It was like talking to someone with some glaring deformity," says Brian. "You try very hard *not* to look. But you can't help it."

But that wasn't all. After showing half the population of the North Shore the bottom card, Ed did Taylor the favor of showing everyone his hole card as well.

They killed him. They murdered him. They absolutely sliced the man apart. Poor Ed hardly won a hand. Given the abuse he had been heaping on his dealers for the last few days, to say that this was gratifying would be an understatement.

When Ed slunk away from the table forty-five minutes later, the dealer who replaced him took the deck with one of the broadest smiles the world had ever seen. Ed had dumped five thousand dollars—over a hundred bucks a minute. And the dealer to whom he handed off the deck was one he had reamed out just the day before.

An hour later, Ed had to deal again. For some reason, he didn't return to Taylor's table. But he had stopped verbally abusing his dealers.

To a person, every dealer the players ever encountered thought it was her responsibility to do something if a player started to win. If the players lost, well, too bad. That was supposed to happen. If, however, a player started winning big, something had to be done. And the dealers very often didn't wait for instructions from the pit to intervene. The dealers' countermeasure of choice was to change the way they shuffled. And the dealers at the Nevada Lodge were no exception. Taylor and his teammates were treated to more shuffling than a nurse on a geriatric ward.

The dealers are right, of course. Changing the shuffle does in fact change the order of the cards. It changes them from one random ordering to another.

This is something that has to be seen to be fully appreciated. Ordinarily, a single deck is riffled a couple of times, stripped once, and perhaps riffled again. The entire process takes about forty seconds—a minute at the outside. However, as Taylor began to win, the dealers would begin riffling and stripping as if life itself was at stake.

In downtown Reno, the Nevada Lodge had itself a big-city cousin—the Nevada Club. It wasn't quite as complete a dump as the joint up the hill, and the dealers weren't quite as generous with the bottom card, but it was still worth playing. "Hell," says Taylor now, "if all we got was the following story, it would've been worth it."

The story, it turns out, involves a detour that leads into a seriously deep, politically incorrect ditch. However, reality is reality, and all seriously successful professional blackjack players learn to view it as such, even if they wish certain things weren't so.

There is an interesting behavior exhibited by a certain percentage of dealers. They take losing personally. If they lose, they believe *they* lost. Not the casino—*them*. You'd think that most dealers would like to lose periodically; after all, they don't generally get tipped particularly well for handing a player his own ass on a platter. However, there are those dealers who react so adversely to losing that it is clear that they genuinely believe they themselves have something to do with the result.

The politically correct way of saying this is that some dealers take losing personally, and some don't. A less politically correct way of saying this is that more male dealers than female seem to take losing personally. The most accurate and least politically correct way of saying the same thing is to say that the vast majority of Asian dealers seem to react this way.[31]

There is probably a combination of factors that underlie this phenomenon. Part of it is the lack of social ostracism of gamblers in Asian cultures (perhaps because these cultures were not bludgeoned into submission by Puritans and their ilk). Certainly a large piece of this puzzle is what Brian refers to as the Tangible Theory of Luck.

The Tangible Theory of Luck is reasonably self-explanatory. Perhaps the best example of this was witnessed at a roulette table during Klondike Days in Edmonton.

A whale of a roulette player was experiencing a tremendous positive fluctuation. In three hours, he won more than twenty thousand dollars at a table with a $10 limit.

What was most telling was the behavior of members of his entourage. They would get as close to him as possible, often touching him, before they themselves started to play. It was as if the luck he was experiencing was somehow tangible—so tangible that they could get a little piece simply by coming into physical contact with someone so endowed.

If this belief is widespread, then it is easy to see why so many Asian dealers take losing personally. It is, after all, intimately connected to *them*. We aren't simply talking about randomly rearranging cardboard cards with pips

---

31 If you don't believe this generalization, go out and play against 10,000 dealers in 400 casinos around the world. Then we'll talk.—Brian Manning

printed on one side. We are talking about the essence of someone's being. Or something.

The Nevada Club had a fair sampling of Asian dealers. During one trip, Taylor was up about six grand when Kim showed up. And whatever the Edmonton whale had, it seemed Kim had it, too. She kicked Taylor's ass. After forty-five minutes, he was back to even.

Kim went on break. Taylor won some back against her relief. And then, despite the fact that the Nevada Club was a rubber-band joint, Kim was returned to Taylor's table for round two.

It was uncanny. Reed would cut thin. Taylor would shove out two hands of two hundred. Kim would deal, get pelted with a small card, and make a hand anyway. Taylor would then lower his bet for the second round.

On one of these second rounds, Taylor got a blackjack on a fifty-dollar hand. "Boom!" he said automatically, and slammed the cards on the felt. And Kim then provided the phrase they all use to great effect to this very day.

"I no care," Kim said. "Only fitty dollah."

One testament to the power and invisibility of Slicing and Dicing was that it fooled more than dealers and pit bosses. During a play at the Pioneer Club in Laughlin, Reed recognized a player he had met during one of his forays to the bar in which his dreaded encounter with the Czech had taken place. "It's the Englishman!" Reed said.

The Englishman was fairly well-known in the subterranean world of professional blackjack. He was best known for three things—his purse, his over-the-top act, and his ability to multi-parameterize. ("Multi-parameterize" means to keep track of individual cards in addition to the count in a single-deck game.) Brandishing a distinguishing mop of unwieldy hair and sporting the quintessentially British dentition that Austin Powers has since made famous, the Englishman carried a black purse-like object in which he kept his bankroll. Clearly, this was a player who did not disappear into the woodwork.

If for some reason the accent, hair, and purse were not noticed by the pit, his antics could not be missed. When he lost a big hand, he would yell, scream, wave his arms around, and—if a pit boss was nearby—pour a glass of orange juice over his head.

On this day at the Pioneer Club, Taylor was up a ton. He was betting up to two hands of two grand, and he had over $60,000 in chips in front of him. The Englishman spent some time watching from behind the table, so Taylor made sure he dropped his bet from two hands of two thousand to one hand of two hundred when the count went up. The Englishman shook his head and walked off.

It wasn't hard to figure out what the Englishman was thinking. "Here I am, a professional player, nearly bursting with knowledge and skill, struggling to eke out a living. And there sits that boneheaded bloke, who not only cannot recognize an edge when he has one, but actually lowers his bet when one appears. And he's winning! How terribly unfair."

It was one thing to fool pit bosses, dealers, and the guys in the sky. It was even more rewarding to put it over on other professional players.

During a visit from a relief dealer, Guppy wandered over to the Englishman's table to watch a few hands. He watched as the Englishman stood with a fourteen against a ten, actually telling the dealer, "No more sevens, doll." Seems the Englishman had a bit of a Reed thing going—he wanted to be sure others knew how good he thought he was. This time, the dealer could not have been very impressed with his playing prowess; she had a three in the hole and hit her hand with one of those nonexistent sevens. Guppy winked at the dealer and returned to his table.

Just to stick the knife in the rest of the way, Taylor waited until the Englishman once again returned to watch him play. Taylor cut thin, pelted the dealer with a four, and won his two hands of two grand. The count was plus seven. "That's it for me," Taylor said, gathering his stacks of black. The Englishman practically trampled Brian getting to the table for a shot at that monstrous second-round edge of about 3 percent. Alas, the dealer shuffled. Life, as they say, is tough.

One night at one of his regular watering holes, Reed met a player who owned one of Keith Taft's David computers. Reed then contacted Keith, and for $10,000 purchased a small red model. He and Taylor learned how to operate the thing. It was much more difficult than running Butch, but allowed them to beat single-deck games with a very small bet spread.[32]

Although Reed and Taylor no longer wrote for *The Blackjack Forum*, Reed stayed in contact with Arnold Snyder. During one communication, Reed learned that Snyder was going to begin selling a playing computer called a "Casey"—a computer that sounded suspiciously like Keith Taft's David.

Reed called Keith, and Keith filled him in. He had worked briefly with a slimebag named Steven Goldberg. Goldberg had pirated Keith's software, duplicated his hardware, and was now going to sell the counterfeit Davids through *The Blackjack Forum* and Stanford Wong's publication, *Current Blackjack News*.

Taylor sat down at the typewriter and wrote the equivalent of a short, devastating legal brief. It said the following:

(1) Keith Taft's *David* had been around for at least six years. David was a functioning blackjack computer in 1978, when Keith was interviewed by *Sports Illustrated*. However, no one had ever heard of a Casey until recently.

(2) The Casey had *exactly* the same inputs as David. Four buttons.

   (a) Right toe up: 1

   (b) Right toe down: 2

   (c) Left toe up: 4

   (d) Left toe down: 8

      (i) Although unlikely, the fact that Casey and David shared the same inputs admittedly could be a coincidence.

(3) The Casey had *exactly* the same outputs as David.

   (a) Short dot: 1

---

32 Taylor's first foray with David was in the MGM Grand, where in two sessions, betting one to two in blacks, he lost $10,000. There was just something about the MGM...

(b) Short dash: 3

(c) Long dash: 0

　　(i) Although unlikely, the fact that Casey and David had the same outputs could also be a coincidence. However, that the two machines would have exactly the same inputs *and* the same outputs was *extremely* unlikely.

(4) The Casey had exactly the same *bugs* as David.

　　(a) Enter a twelve against the dealer's four off the top of a single deck playing with downtown Vegas rules. Both David and Casey will tell you to hit, which is incorrect.

　　　　(i) The likelihood that this was a coincidence had now plummeted to zero. Casey is David, or David is Casey.

(5) Given David's documented existence in 1978, it is fair to conclude that Casey is David.

When Arnold Snyder received Taylor's letter, the upcoming issue of *The Blackjack Forum* was ready to print. In it was an article about Casey. To his credit, Snyder covered the article with a piece of paper on which was scrawled, in essence, "Hold the Presses!"

Snyder would go on to sell Keith Taft's David computers, but Casey was relegated to the dustbin of history. End of Casey. End of story.

For the roughly three years following the advent of Slicing and Dicing, the players found themselves in a comfortable rut. They sliced 'em up when they could, spooked occasionally, used the David infrequently, and broke out the shuffle-tracking computers when they came across a trackable multiple-deck game. And they might have continued to do so for a long time. But they didn't.

Fluctuations driven by the Butterfly Effect once again showed their omnipresent winning hands. A series of entirely unrelated and unlikely events converged and propelled the players inexorably toward The Ultimate Edge.

CHAPTER 17
THE MARINA

Cleopatra's nose, had it been shorter, the whole face of
the world would have been changed.
~Blaise Pascal, Pensées

On Tuesday, April 24, 1984, while the Slicers and Dicers were happily humming theme songs and playing their hearts out at the Tropicana, Taylor's future was being shaped across the street. Thick, greasy tentacles that would ultimately reach out and touch Taylor and his teammates were being spawned from a monstrous negative fluctuation—a fluctuation that would reverberate throughout the industry for years.

At around 8:00 p.m., someone—perhaps a random bastard disgruntled gambler—phoned in a bomb threat to the Marina Hotel and Casino. Ordinarily, you might expect an immediate evacuation of the premises. However, the operative word in this scenario is "Casino." Because evacuating the joint would have involved great financial cost—people tend not to gamble much as they are fleeing toward the exits—the Marina management decided not to tell their customers that they all might be treated to an aerial view of the Strip at any moment. Instead, security guards quietly combed the property in an attempt to locate the bomb.

No bomb was ever found, but while searching the parking lot, a pair of sweaty guards did notice a small pickup truck with a camper cap on the back. And for some reason, they decided to investigate.

Two professional blackjack players were in the truck, completely oblivious to the fact that their lives were about to become far more interesting than they possibly could have imagined. They were preparing for a front-loading play.

As far as anyone knows, front-loading has been around for as long as casinos have been dealing single-deck games. And there is no reason to believe it will die out anytime soon.

As we learned in chapter 8, front-loading demands two necessary—but not sufficient—conditions. First, the deck must be handheld. There is no such thing as front-loading a shoe. Second, the dealer must take a hole card. In 1984, both of these conditions existed in just a handful of casinos in the world. Almost all of those casinos were located in Nevada.

Once the necessary conditions are met, a dealer with a horrible weakness must be located. Perhaps one dealer in three hundred exhibits this particular weakness.

Here is how it works. A right-handed dealer holds the deck in her left hand and pitches with her right. The cards are dealt to the players clockwise around the table, and then the dealer provides herself an up-card. After the dealer has dealt the players their second card, she gives herself a hole-card; that is, a card that rests face down beneath her up-card. In order to give herself a hole card, the dealer must remove a card from the top of the deck, lower it to table level, and jam it face down beneath her up-card. It is this move that has inspired visions of fame, glory, and yachts in the minds of blackjack players everywhere.

You see, in removing the card from the top of the deck and jamming it beneath the up-card, the dealer must expose this soon-to-be hole card. It may be exposed to the front (hence the term *front-loader*), it may be exposed to the side, or it may simply be exposed to the blind green felt directly beneath the card. This last exposure is the one most desirable to the casinos.

But it is the first two possibilities—exposure to the front or to the side—that most interests players. If it can be seen, that card drips with information— information that can give the player an advantage over the casino of up to 8 percent. To a professional card counter used to performing the labors of Hercules to achieve an edge of perhaps 1 percent, this is manna from heaven.

To the uninitiated, this sounds like an extremely slimy business practice. After all, if someone were to do this at a home poker game (and there are endless front-loading opportunities at home poker games, but that is another matter), he would immediately be drummed out of the game and rightfully referred to as a goddamn cheating bastard for as long as any of his victims lived.

But casino blackjack is not home poker with the boys. The system of morals we learned at the knees of our elders bears no resemblance to the one that must be adopted when dealing with entities as nasty and as tough as Nevada casinos. The question is not one of morality. It is one of legality.

In 1981, a decision was handed down by the Nevada Supreme Court. Front-loading is perfectly legal. Casino protestations to the contrary notwithstanding, it is the casino's responsibility to hide the hole card. It is not the responsibility of the players to look the other way.

Front-loading requires a unique constellation of skills. First, very few dealers expose the card at all, and those who do usually expose it only occasionally. So, potential front-loaders must be scouted thoroughly.

Second, the hole card is usually jammed beneath the up-card at a high rate of speed. The reader typically needs extraordinary eyesight.

Third, and perhaps most important, the card is almost always exposed very low to the table. The reader must get his head down to or near table level to get a decent view of the exposed card. This eliminates almost everyone over five foot six.

Given the above, it is not terribly difficult for casinos to identify front-loaders. Here is their instruction set:

1) Look for a short guy who keeps his head on or near the table, and pays particular attention not to his cards but to the dealer as she shoves her hole card beneath her up-card.

2) If he seems to hit his stiffs when the dealer is pat and stand with stiffs when the dealer is stiff, you have your man.

3) Drag him into the back room, photograph him, beat him up a little, and bar him.

It's easy and it's fun.

If professional blackjack players are aware of anything, they are aware of their vulnerabilities. Counters know their bet spread is a dead giveaway, which is why Taylor and his teammates labored mightily to limit or eliminate it. Most of the players who lasted in the business were equally cognizant of the weaknesses in whatever system they were using.

Keith Taft was almost six feet tall, and his eyesight was average at best. He knew he couldn't front-load, and, most importantly, he knew the casinos knew it, too. Therefore, if he somehow *could* front-load, he might have been able to get away with it until some time in the next decade, when he could have retired with enough money to buy himself his own country, where he could have made his own rules.

And he might have. Except he didn't. That's life.

The Marina security guards asked the two players to step out of the truck. They acquiesced. One of the players pulled his pants up as he hopped out. The guards looked at each other, smirked, and proceeded to check the truck.

"What's all this, then?" one of the guards asked, aiming his flashlight around the cab of the pickup. Bearing in mind that it was clear the guard had no idea what he was looking at, and in fact only cared that whatever he was looking at wasn't a bomb, the players could have told him anything. Anything at all.

To the astonishment of the guards, and to the disbelief of players the world over, the players told the truth.

They were front-loaders, they said, and they were getting ready to play.

One of the players—the Big Player—had a small, modified surveillance camera strapped to his stomach. The camera lens peeked out at the world through the capital letter P on his belt buckle. Once in the casino, he aimed the camera at the spot where the dealer exposed her hole card as she jammed it beneath her up-card. The signal traveled from the camera to an amplifier the player wore on his back and then out a small antenna.

The signal was picked up by a satellite dish mounted in the back of the pickup truck, hidden by the camper cap. A high-resolution video recorder mounted beneath the dash recorded the action. The player in the truck then played the tape back in slow motion, watching the action on a six-inch monitor mounted alongside the recorder. When he identified the hole card—a true Kodak moment—he sent a signal to the BP, enabling him to play perfect front-loading strategy.

The BP would never be suspected of front-loading while standing up, because everybody knows that front-loaders have to get their eyeballs as low as possible to see that hole card.

They had been playing for six weeks, and had been winning steadily. If a bomb threat hadn't been called in to the Marina, they might have continued to play unmolested for years. Instead, the two players were on their way to jail. Bad fluctuation.

Why in the name of probability did these guys tell the security guards what they were doing? They did so because they honestly believed their system was legal. And, if Nevada had been any other state, their argument might have had a chance.

Nevada has specific laws to allow for the prosecution of cheaters. These are commonly referred to as the Bunco Steering Statutes, and the salient part for card games reads as follows:

> Any activity that serves to change the frequency of occurrence of
> payouts in a series of gambles shall be deemed unlawful.

There is only one legitimate response to a reading of this statute; one response upon which both the prosecution and the defense can agree:

"I beg your pardon?"

There is an aspect of due process which states, "A statute must be sufficiently clear so as to allow persons of 'ordinary intelligence' a reasonable opportunity to know what is prohibited." Laws making it illegal to act like a bonehead in public are not passed, because your opinion of what constitutes acting like a bonehead may not jibe with Reed's opinion or, more importantly, with the opinion of the cop who arrests you, the judge who arraigns you, or the jurors who judge you.

If passed in any other state, Nevada's Bunco Steering Statute would likely have been declared unconstitutionally vague and unceremoniously tossed out of the law books. There is simply no way to read the statute and then determine whether or not what you plan to do contravenes that law.

The sovereign state of Nevada, however, is guided by a different light. Players are treated to a Kafkaesque journey through a legal limbo that most resembles Dante's descent into hell, or perhaps a Keystone Kops episode. The sequence of events runs as follows:

1) A player enters a casino and counts, spooks, front-loads, or in some other way obtains an edge over the casino.

2) The player is dragged into the back room, photographed, and usually beaten up a bit to help remind him of his place in the overall scheme of things.

3) The player is arrested and charged with Bunco Steering.

4) The court decides whether or not what the player was doing was in fact cheating.

   a) If the court decides that what the player was doing was not cheating, the player may go home.

   b) If the court decides that what the player was doing was cheating, the player goes to jail.

5) Whatever the court decides, the player spends a small fortune in legal fees, while the cost of the casino's prosecutorial vendetta is borne by the good citizens of Nevada.

Fortunately for individuals like Alexander Taylor—and much to the chagrin of the casino industry—the courts have been consistent in their interpretation of this section of the Bunco Steering Statute. In decisions going back as far as there are records, the courts have consistently ruled that players who use information made available to them by a casino or its agent (the dealer) are not cheating. In the 1981 ruling concerning front-loading, the court said, "It is the responsibility of the casino to make sure a dealer doesn't expose the hole card. It is in no way incumbent upon the player to look the other way."

Beginning with the original 1976 decision permitting players to use their brains while playing blackjack, through the decisions that allowed spooking, front-loading, and signaling, the courts have stuck doggedly to the following interpretation of the Bunco Steering Statute: players may make the best use they can of information made available to them by the casino. They may not, however, make information available to themselves.

If a casino chooses to deal the players' cards face up so that everyone can see which cards have been dealt out, the casino is voluntarily lavishing this information on any player willing and able to take advantage of it. Whether or not players choose to do so is, of course, up to them.

Players also may take advantage of any information provided them by the dealer, as long as the dealer doesn't know she's providing it. If the dealer picks up her ten a little higher than she should, and Guppy glimpses the hole card from first base, that is not cheating. However, if Guppy begins to tip her, and she lifts her hole card higher *on purpose*, that is collusion—a Class 1 felony in the state of Nevada that will rightfully get you ten years in the Carson state pen.

This may sound like splitting hairs, but there is a real line here, and nothing focuses that line better than something called warp play.

According to some authoritative accounts, playing cards were invented in China during the T'ang Dynasty about 1,300 years ago. And, according to this authoritative account, cheating was invented about five minutes later.[33]

The most common method of cheating in a card game is to somehow mark the cards so that the cheater can tell which cards are which by looking at their backs. There are dyes, daubs, and shines, but the easiest method—the method that has been with us since the Chinese started this game rolling—is bending. Bending cards requires no equipment, no real expertise, and is the method that readily comes to mind to anyone with an IQ above room temperature.

Bending cards is cheating. Period. It falls squarely on the wrong side of the statutory line. When a player bends a card, he is providing himself with information that is not provided by the casino or the dealer.

---

33 Loaded dice have been found in Egyptian tombs, dating back 5,000 years.

But, get this. Dealers used to peek under tens to see if there was an ace in the hole. To accomplish the peek, they would bend both the ten up-card and the card beneath it away from themselves (see Photo 1). After a few hours of this, the tens in the deck tended to get bent (or "warped") so that when they were lying face down on the felt, their bellies bowed up. There would be a tiny space between the middle of the face down ten and the table, as indicated in Photo 2.

Photo 1: The dealer peeks beneath a 10.

Photo 2: A warped 10-value card, side view.

It was possible for a skilled player to read these "warps" and determine to a reasonable degree of certainty if the dealer had a ten or a non-ten in the hole. Since the player was using bent cards to obtain his advantage, this method of play might seem to fall on the wrong side of the fine line. But it does not. Just as in counting, front-loading, and Slicing and Dicing, warp play used information provided—albeit inadvertently—by the *casino*. Playing warps was a perfectly legal way to obtain an edge.

So, although the means by which the information is gleaned—via bent cards—is the same, the method by which the cards develop bends differs. And therein lies the difference. As of this writing (2008), this difference has held up in court.

So, since the electronic front-loaders were using information made available by the dealer—after all, she still had to expose her hole card for the camera to see it—they thought they were treading on the right side of that fine legal line. But that's not all they had going for them.

In 1977, playing in beautiful Lake Tahoe, one of Keith's teammates was caught with a David computer on his leg. The player was charged with cheating, but the prosecution couldn't make the charge stick. It was decided that a computer is not a cheating device because it is simply an extension of the human brain; that is, a computer does nothing more than what card counters already do in their heads. And what card counters do in their heads is perfectly legal.

So, casino protestations to the contrary notwithstanding, it was determined that nothing a computer did contravened the Bunco Steering Statutes.

Keith Taft—an eminently logical man—used his logical brain to come to a logical conclusion. If a computer is legal because it is nothing more than an extension of the brain, then a camera should also be legal because it is nothing more than an extension of the eye.

Completely logical, except it begs a question of metaphysical proportions: Is the man who makes logical assumptions about an illogical world truly logical?

The front-loaders nailed by a couple of overweight security guards and a bad fluctuation in the Marina parking lot were found guilty by a jury of the casino's intellectual peers. The argument that won the jurors over was the closing words of the prosecuting attorney.

"If you're playing Old Maid and you peek at the other guy's cards, even a five-year-old knows it's cheating."

The players were fined ten grand and thrown in jail for four months, where, presumably, the other inmates hid their cards while playing Old Maid.

If the story had ended there, these players simply would have remained a dangling participle. Except it didn't.

CHAPTER 18
…AND THE LAW WON

We live in the most probable of
all possible worlds.
~ Steven Hawking's corruption of Voltaire

I long ago come to the conclusion that
all life is 6 to 5 against.
~Sam the Gonoph, in A Nice Price
by Damon Runyon

Although the moral question may remain the purview of philosophical discourse forever, the legality of computers versus brains and cameras versus eyes was settled with brutal finality on July 1, 1985. On that day, the Nevada state legislature used all the subtlety and grace of a black boot to stomp the argument into the ground forever. N.R.S. 465.075 was passed, and reads, in part, as follows:

It is unlawful for any person at a licensed gaming establishment to use, or possess with the intent to use, any device to assist:

1. In projecting the outcome of the game;

2. In keeping track of the cards played;

3. In analyzing the probability of the occurrence of an event relating to the game; or

4. In analyzing the strategy for playing or betting to be used in the game, except as permitted by the commission.

Clearly, a computer is a device that can perform some or all of the above tasks. But so are a pen and a piece of paper. Will we see card counters arrested on the grounds that a pen is a device that can be used to keep track of cards played, or to analyze probabilities? As ridiculous as it sounds, it's not inconceivable. These are the same people who in 1976 arrested a card counter for thinking at the table.

Unlike most of the bills passed by the legislature during that session, N.R.S. 465.075 was passed with an emergency measure appended to it, meaning it would take effect immediately upon the governor's signature, instead of ninety days after the conclusion of the legislative session. The emergency? Through what was no doubt moral suasion, the casinos managed to convince the legislature that Taylor and his ilk represented an "economic threat to the State of Nevada."

And the Bahamian Navy represents a military threat to the coastal integrity of the United States.

Because of the new statute, shuffle tracking with Butch was now illegal. Since most of the trackable shuffles were available in other countries anyway, the new law was largely irrelevant insofar as shuffle tracking was concerned. However, Butch's development had spawned some interesting outgrowths.

The team's spooking strategy had improved dramatically since Taylor's first session with Brian and Guppy at the Mint. Using the signaling equipment that had been developed for use with the shuffle trackers, they could now dispense with a relay and all physical signals. All they needed was a more or less clear line of sight for the signal. Since the spook himself needed a clear line of sight to see the dealer's hole card, this wasn't an additional burden.

While spooking wasn't as lucrative as shuffle tracking, it was legal. Although the players knew that playing with an edge entailed assuming certain risks, jail was not one that any of them was willing to take.

And so, in the summer of 1987, Taylor traveled to Lake Tahoe. The game at the Nevada Lodge was long gone—after Taylor kicked Mr. Ed's ass from one side of the pit to the other, the casino finally had had enough—and the other games were pretty weak. Then, Taylor found a couple of spookable dealers on the south shore, and phoned Brian in Vegas. Brian immediately flew up, Taylor picked him up at the tiny Lake Tahoe Airport, and they attempted a spook play in Harrah's. Taylor was mistaken for Rick Sandler, and you know the rest.

The long string of fluctuations and contingencies that had brought Taylor to this point by no means ended with his beating at the hands of the security guards at Harrah's. The player the guards thought they were beating the crap out of just happened to be the son of a certain Frank Sandler—the same Frank Sandler who had developed the BP-Spotter Routine, and had originally trained Ken Uston.

And the device the Harrah's guards missed but the police found secured to Taylor's leg could in no way perform even one of the four functions that would have made its possession illegal under N.R.S. 465.075. It could do nothing but receive signals. For that reason, all charges against Taylor were summarily dismissed after a preliminary hearing.

But that didn't improve Taylor's mood much. Not much at all.

CHAPTER 19
A BRIEF BIBLICAL INTERLUDE

And God saw that it was good.
~Genesis 1:1

In the beginning there was gambling. There was an enormous abundance of games, and different kinds, too. And the multitudes played them gladly, and derived great pleasure from them. But the pleasure was always short-lived, because the games all had one thing in common: the players always lost.

Until Thorp said, let there be counting.

And small groups of players learned to count, and to spread their bets. And they traveled the world beating the casinos at their own game. And Thorp did grin, and saw that it was good.

And Thorp begat Revere, who begat hundreds of players, including Brian, who begat Reed and Guppy and Taylor, who begat Tony. And Thorp begat Wong, who begat Vince and the Czechs, and hundreds of other players.

And Thorp begat Robert Stanley, who begat hundreds of losers.

And Revere and Wong did frown upon Stanley, but there was nothing they could do.

And the players found themselves in a lush garden of games, including single decks with Vegas Strip rules. And there were front-loaders, and spooks, and first-basers, and various and sundry dealers, none of whom could count.

And the players played and won, and frolicked about with great joy. And there was great happiness in the land for a number of years.

But soon there came a pestilence upon the land, and it appeared in the form of blackjack players who wrote books about the game. And these books told laymen and pit bosses alike what these frolicking players were doing. And the bosses did learn, and changed the games so that it was harder and harder for the players to win.

And many hundreds of players—especially those players begotten by Robert Stanley—watched as their bankrolls dwindled, and then returned home to work at McDonald's.

But Brian looked at the barren wasteland created by the blackjack books and said, let there be shuffle tracking.

And the players looked about, and lo! there were opportunities galore and money to be made. And Brian did grin, and saw that it was good.

And Brian and his teammates built small computers that strapped to their legs and tracked the shuffles. And the shuffles succumbed, and Brian and his teammates won great stacks of currency traveling the world with computers on their legs and buttons in their shoes.

But soon there was another scourge upon the land, and it came in the form of Vince and his teammates. While the Team of Brian tracked the shuffles with technology that was great and fair, the Team of Vince tracked the shuffles with crudeness befitting the Philistines, whom they greatly resembled. And soon the bosses learned what ill befouled the land, and changed the shuffles, putting an end to it all.

And it came to pass that the end of shuffle tracking cast a long shadow over those few players who remained. But Brian did not despair. He looked about, viewed the barren wasteland that the Team of Vince had left, and said, let there be Slicing and Dicing.

And the sky opened wide, and out poured green from the coffers of the casinos. And Brian did grin, and saw that it was good.

But the grin of Brian lasted not long, for the long arms of the beastly Griffin extended farther and farther, until the casinos at which Slicing and Dicing could be performed with impunity were rarer than hen's teeth.

Then, in a far-off land called the Marina, an innocent pair of players laden with the latest technology were preparing to play. Unbeknownst to them, a curse was cast upon the Marina; a curse in the form of a bomb threat. And in searching for this evil bomb, the Marina security guards did stumble upon these technological players, and had them arrested, and thrown in jail, where horrible, grisly birds did peck at their livers. And it was terribly unfair.

And so it came to pass that Brian learned of the miscarriage of justice, and attempted to turn the Nevada casinos into pillars of salt. Failing that, he tried a flood. When that didn't work, Brian gnashed his teeth, burned myrrh and frankincense, and cast a curse upon the casinos of Nevada. This curse took the form of The Ultimate Edge.

And Brian did grin, and saw that it was great.

CHAPTER 20

THE ULTIMATE EDGE QUARTET

Life is a game to be played, not a puzzle
to be solved.

~Anonymous

As with Slicing and Dicing before it, the journey that led to The Ultimate Edge began with one of Taylor's magic tricks.

The trick involved a deck with a stick figure drawn on the back of each card. The stick figure began in this position:

A card was chosen and placed on the table. Taylor then riffled the deck, face down. As the backs of the cards sped by, the stick figure appeared to reach into his hat, withdraw a card, and behold! It was the chosen card. The trick was particularly popular with kids, but it wasn't the guy with the hat that got Brian's attention. What got Brian's attention would become the heart and soul of The Ultimate Edge.

Something as powerful as The Ultimate Edge deserved—nay, *demanded*—world-class misdirection. This misdirection would be layered, and would be the best kind—misdirection that existed below the psychological radar.

The types of misdirection used by the team parallel that used by magicians. Straight misdirection—acting drunk, acting stupid, acting obnoxious—was the equivalent of a magician distracting the audience by igniting gunpowder on the left side of the stage while doing something on the right. Subtler misdirection—betting off the top while shuffle tracking or Slicing and Dicing—was analogous to showing another magician a magic trick. It used the victim's knowledge against him. The best misdirection, however, was the hardest to pull off. It was misdirection caused by the limits the spectator put on his own imagination—limits provided at a subconscious level by the magician himself.

Taylor's best trick—a trick called The Invisible Deck—involves a gaffed (rigged) deck. But the trick rarely works on its own. Do the trick, and the first thing most spectators say is, "Let me see that deck."

Taylor solved that problem when he was just twelve years old. He first did a separate trick with a normal deck that looked exactly like the gaffed deck. And he let the victim shuffle the cards. No hand-waving. No explosions. He NEVER said, "Notice that this is a normal deck." He never said anything about the deck at all. The victim "got" that it was a normal deck, and got it at a profound level—a level so deep that the thought of a gaffed deck really wasn't available to his consciousness. Why not? He handled the cards himself. That the deck was normal was like part of the furniture. It just was.

Once the first trick was done with the regular deck, Taylor secretly switched in the gaffed deck and performed The Invisible Deck. Boom. Knockout.

The entire first trick—which allowed the spectator to handle the cards—was a setup; a trick performed simply to implant the "normal deck" notion below the level of the victim's consciousness. That is *serious* misdirection.

The first layer of misdirection employed for The Ultimate Edge existed at this same deep level. One delicious irony was that the impetus for it would come from Preston Hubbs—he of the absurd explanation regarding Joey's red and green lights after Tony was busted at the Desert Inn.

The second layer was the way in which the system itself was executed. This was *The Ultimate Edge.*

Even at night, the heat is intolerable. At the far end of the Strip the lights shimmer and dance, driven by the heat emanating from the asphalt. The van's tires hiss as they roll along the street. Reflections from signs made up of thousands of flashing lights start at the center of the windshield, split, wander sideways, and exit around the smooth curves of the glass. A disemboweled casino fun book helicopters across the street in front of the van, propelled by a hot wind. None of this makes a noticeable impression on the Driver.

What were the chances of ending up here? the Driver wonders. What were the odds? A thousand to one? A million? There had been so many possibilities over the course of the last six years; so many alternatives that would have led elsewhere. Only one highly unlikely sequence of events led to The Ultimate Edge. One long string of accidents. Fluctuations. Five minutes earlier somewhere, ten minutes later somewhere else, and maybe he would be a millionaire now. Or busted out completely. Or, perhaps, not around to think about it at all.

Now the van slows as a herd of gawking, camera-toting tourists crosses the Strip. To the left is Caesars Palace—a sprawling, bluish-green structure surrounded by lighted fountains, statues, and tall evergreens. To the right, a magnificent spray of pink neon announces the Flamingo Hilton.

Silently, the Driver watches the impressive display. A cascade of memories collides with the glittering lights that introduce casino after casino on the Las Vegas Strip.

A sharp burst of static emanating from the two-way ICOM 4-AT handheld radio perched in his lap breaks the Driver's reverie. "Big Cheese standing by at location number one," barks a familiar voice. The end of the communication is announced by another burst of static.

"Ten-four, Cheese," responds the Driver, depressing the talk button. "Golfers are about a minute from location."

"C'mon, Golfers." It is the Big Cheese again. "What'd you do, stop for a six-pack?"

The Big Cheese is a real comedian. Dramamine has already cast the Putter's eyes with its unmistakable dull sheen, and at this point a beer would knock him flat on his ass.

The Driver grins. "Ten-four, Big Cheese. The Putter was a little too sharp earlier. We can't have that."

The Driver changes lanes slowly, mindful of the poor bastard riding along in darkness in the back of the van. The Castaways, Sands, and the Desert Inn ease by. When the Driver and his teammates started playing six years ago, each of those casinos had been beatable by conventional means. Now those means had become decidedly unconventional. Of course, they used to struggle to eke out an edge of 2 percent. Now their edge rivals the temperature. This evening it's in the low nineties.

The van turns slowly into a parking lot and rolls beneath an enormous sign announcing a cheap buffet, loose slots, and mediocre entertainment. The Driver leans back in his seat and speaks over his shoulder to the curtain separating him from the rest of the van. "We're ready. It'll be about four o'clock."

"Ten-four." The Putter's disembodied voice floats forward from the back of the van. The Driver can hear the hum of an electric motor as the Putter maneuvers the small satellite dish into position. "Ten-four," the Putter announces. "I'm ready."

The radio in the Driver's lap crackles to life again. "Geezer standing by at location number one."

"Ten-four, Geezer," the Driver responds immediately. "Golfers are standing by. Here comes a little test."

As the Putter rattles around in the darkness in the back of the van, the Driver is reminded of the Wizard of Oz working his magic behind his secret curtain. There are two audible clicks as a pair of switches are snapped on. Seconds later, the feedback from the Putter's encoded signal squawks over the radio in the Driver's lap. At the same time, about a quarter-mile away, those signals are received and decoded by modified 4-ATs, and are then transformed into a series of very specific vibrations.

"Loud and clear," the Big Cheese reports.

"Ten-four," the Geezer agrees.

"Goddamn Dramamine," complains the Putter.

"Go ahead, guys," says the Driver into his radio. "Pop is already inside, dining. Cough us in, wait for us to acknowledge, and don't forget to tell us where you are."

"Ten-four. Geezer out."

"The waitresses have great busts here, Putter," the Big Cheese says pointedly. "Cheese out."

In a nearby parking lot, the door of a red 1984 Porsche 911 SC opens, and the Big Cheese climbs out. As he does, his body is assaulted by a wave of hot air that makes him feel like he opened an oven door to check the baked potatoes. He hesitates a moment, allows his body to adjust to a temperature increase of twenty-five degrees, and starts toward the casino.

A quarter-mile away, a slight figure emerges from a rented 1987 Chevrolet Corsica. His gray hair is a bit too thick, and his gait is brisk. A cane is wedged uselessly beneath his arm. As he approaches the main entrance to the casino his stride shortens, and his back bends as a seeming concession to gravity and years. The cane is now necessary. The Geezer struggles with the door and manages to enter the casino with difficulty. A bead of perspiration breaks from his forehead and trickles down his face.

Once inside, he is met by a blast of Arctic air. Chills run over his body as perspiration cools and evaporates. The sights and sounds of a very active casino fill the room as thoroughly as the over-conditioned air, but to this the Geezer is oblivious. His senses are focused, filtering everything but potential targets.

The Geezer finds Pop, and two of Pop's former teammates from years ago, manning a table in the main pit. There are three pit bosses behind Pop's dealer, arms crossed, glaring. The Geezer smiles. Pop, the heat magnet, still has the ability to attract unwanted attention. Time to roll.

The Geezer finds a potential target toward the other end of the pit. Furtive eye contact is established across the pit with the Big Cheese, and the Geezer scratches his head. Casually, the Big Cheese touches his nose. The Geezer reaches for the button located in the pocket of his baggy pants, coughs softly, and says, "Main front. Front."

Almost immediately, a series of long and short vibrations announce the presence of the Golfers, as well as a great many nerve endings in the Putter's right calf. These vibrations are unmistakable, and not exactly unpleasant.

Having received the same series of vibrations—in the same sensitive area— the Big Cheese pulls out his wallet and extracts a few small bills. The Geezer appraises the situation quickly: a young, attractive dealer with no players at her table. Time to move in for the kill.

The Big Cheese touches his nose again and moves toward the empty blackjack table. The Geezer acknowledges by scratching his nose; he then reaches into his pocket and coughs again.

Using his cane for support, the Geezer hobbles toward the target. The Big Cheese is talking to the dealer as he pushes a stool out of the way. The dealer is smiling as she shuffles the cards. When the Big Cheese buys in for twenty dollars, the dealer looks over her shoulder.

"Changing twenty!" she calls out.

A pit boss hovering near Pop's table glances over. As is almost always the case, the pit boss pays scant attention to the dealer's call. A player who buys in for twenty dollars is probably just another degenerate gambler—certainly no threat to the casino. The Big Cheese's cash disappears down a slot in the table to the dealer's right, and he is given four red chips.

By now the Geezer is in position, standing to the left of the Big Cheese. While leaning on the cane with his right hand, he digs through his pockets and fishes out a ragged wallet. Although he appears to be busy searching for something in it, he is actually concentrating on the string of long and short vibrations being sent to him by the Putter from the back of the van. Obeying the instructions flawlessly, the Geezer swivels the cane slowly to the right, and suddenly stops.

Still talking animatedly, the Big Cheese receives the three short bursts of vibrations a moment before the cane comes to rest. His hand moves forward exactly one second later and cuts the cards.

"Geezer here." The voice coming from the Driver's 4-AT interrupts the silence in the van. The Driver grabs his radio and depresses the talk button.

"Ten-four, Geezer," answers the Driver. "Golfers here. How did it go?"

"A big ten-four," the Geezer responds. "It was a gourmet table."

"Way to go!" exclaims the Putter from the back of the van.

"The Putter sends his regards," says the Driver to the Geezer.

"Ask him why he didn't cough a second time," the Putter requests.

"I did," says the Geezer in response to the Driver's question. "Didn't you get it?"

"Negative," says the Driver. "We received only one cough."

"I'm checking my mike now. You should start receiving in two seconds."

"I'm not getting anything," reports the Putter from the back of the van.

"Negative, negative, no dice," the Driver says into his radio. "You're dead. Proceed back to base. We'll stand by for the Big Cheese."

"Ten-four. I'm going to stop for something on the way back. You guys want anything?"

"Get me a coffee and a glazed doughnut," says the voice from the back of the van.

"Coffee and a glazed for the Putter," says the Driver into his radio. "Get the Big Cheese a coffee, and the usual for me."

"Ten-four. See you at base. Geezer out."

"What did it come out to?" the Putter asks the Driver.

The Driver looks at the work sheet perched in his lap. "I have two of one and three of one, and then two of three in flux mode. Is that right?"

"I think so." The Putter pauses. "Do you want me to play it back again?"

"No, that's all right." The Driver scribbles on his work sheet for about thirty seconds.

"We should have won five grand, plus or minus whatever happened on the flux mode."

"Not bad," says the Putter dryly. "Almost worth the Dramamine."

"Big Cheese here," the radio interrupts.

"Ten-four, Cheese," answers the Driver. "Go ahead."

"Was that two of one with a ten, and then three of one with an eight?" asks the Big Cheese.

"We think that's a big ten-four, Cheese, and it was followed by two of three in flux mode. How was it?"

"Never saw the flux," says the Big Cheese. "However, the rest…" The Big Cheese pauses for effect, and then says, "Boom!"

"Nice job," says the Driver. "We are proceeding back to base. The Geezer has a malfunction."

"No doubt. Cheese out."

"Pop here," a new voice crackles over the Driver's radio.

"Ten-four, Pop. Good job. Everybody's out. We're headed back to base. Technical difficulties beyond our control."

"Ten-four. Should we accompany, or stand by?"

"Proceed to location two and take up residence. This shouldn't take long."

"Ten-four. Pop proceeding to location number two."

To avoid the thick tourist traffic on the Strip, the Golfers travel a block east to Paradise Road before heading south. They cruise past the massive Las Vegas Hilton and the infamous Crazy Horse Saloon. The Big Cheese turns left on Harmon and loops through the UNLV campus to make sure he isn't being followed. The Golfers continue south on Paradise and turn into the Airport Inn parking lot. The van bounces softly as the Driver carefully negotiates several speed bumps, and then steers into a parking space. The Golfers wait in the van until they see the Big Cheese's red Porsche screech into the lot.

The Big Cheese climbs out of the Porsche and reaches into the glove box, extracting a thick brown envelope. The Golfers are already waiting at the door to room 21. It's their favorite room.

"How'd we do?" the Putter asks, producing a key to the room.

"Pretty well," the Big Cheese replies. "Let's wait until we're inside, and I'll give you the good, the bad, and the rest."

The Driver snaps the lights on in the room, and the Putter walks to the television and finds a station broadcasting the news. The Big Cheese sits on the bed and begins to pull wads of hundred-dollar bills out of several different pockets. He then opens the brown envelope and dumps more cash onto the bed. The Big Cheese tells the Golfers they just cleared $5,925. The Golfers nod. That's about what they figured.

Someone bangs on the door twice, pauses, and bangs again.

The Driver pulls the curtain aside, looks out, and then unchains the door. An old man steps into the room with a cane wedged under his arm, carrying a Winchell's doughnut box and a cardboard coffee carrier holding several steaming Styrofoam cups. It is the Geezer.

"How much we owe you?" asks the Driver.

"I no care. Only fitty dollah," replies the Geezer, and distributes the snacks.

The Putter looks at the old man and begins to laugh.

"What the hell's so funny?" the Geezer scowls. "Are you lookin' at me? Are you lookin' at me?"

"Your hair, De Niro," the Putter says.

"What is it?" the Geezer demands, and strides into the bathroom to examine himself in the mirror.

"Jesus!" he exclaims. "That makeup woman said this stuff should last through an entire night."

The Geezer stares at himself in the bathroom mirror. Perspiration has caused some of the dye in his hair to run, and he now has a number of gray streaks running down his face, over his ears, and down his neck. He turns the water on in the sink and begins to wash his face.

"I hope you didn't look like that in the casino," calls the Driver from the other room.

"No, I checked before I went in. I looked fine."

"A matter of opinion," says the Putter from the bed.

The Geezer towels off and leaves the bathroom, snapping off the light switch behind him. By this time, the Driver has pulled a toolbox out from under the bed and has plugged the soldering iron into the wall socket. He holds a small, pen-like continuity tester in his hand.

"Relax," the Driver says. "This will only hurt for a minute."

The Geezer opens the top three buttons of his shirt, exposing a condenser microphone the size of a pencil eraser. It is angled toward his mouth, stuck to the left shoulder of his T-shirt with duct tape. The Driver examines the wires leading to the microphone, and then tests the continuity across its back.

"The mike's fine," the Driver says. "We'll have to check it further down."

With each button the Geezer unfastens, more wire becomes visible. When he reaches the bottom button and pulls his shirt off, a white medical bandage pops loose, and four feet of coaxial cable dangles to the floor. The Geezer's upper body is almost entirely straitjacketed in tight medical bandages—one of the reasons he had been perspiring so profusely.

The Driver follows the white and blue microphone wires down to the Geezer's waist, where they merge with a thick multicolored cluster of wire. This cluster winds its way around the Geezer's back and down his leg, disappearing into a homemade Ni-Cad battery pack strapped tightly to his calf.

The Driver carefully follows the microphone wires through the multicolored cluster around the Geezer's back. Finally he locates the problem.

"Yeah, here it is," the Driver says, pinching the broken, frayed ends of the blue wire between his fingers. The wire has broken off against the edge of the black metal box strapped to the Geezer's body. "Shrink tubing, Cheese?" the Driver asks.

The Big Cheese digs through the toolbox and finds a small, tubular piece of black plastic, about as big around as the lead in a pencil. He hands it to the Driver.

"It's a good thing we found this problem now," says the Big Cheese. "A stitch in time is worth two in the bush."

The Driver is too busy to respond. Carefully, he threads one end of the blue wire through the black plastic shrink tubing, and then slides the tubing well up the wire and out of the way. Then he twists the frayed ends of the blue wire together.

"Hold this right where it is," the Driver instructs the Geezer, handing him the blue wire. The Geezer takes the blue wire in his wrinkled, spotted hands, which contrast sharply with his smooth arms.

"Jesus, your hands look terrible," comments the Driver.

"It's Palmolive liquid," answers the Geezer.

"Soldering iron, solder, and flux," says the Driver.

"The only flux we have comes in a can," the other three players recite in unison, articulating the motto of The Ultimate Edge Quartet.

The Big Cheese hands the Driver the hot soldering iron and a spool of solder. The Driver uses the hot iron to cut himself a small piece of solder, dips it in the flux, and turns toward the Geezer.

"Don't touch me with that," jokes the Geezer. "You touch me, I'll kill you."

The Driver touches the tip of the soldering iron to the twisted ends of the blue wire. Then, he touches the solder to the wire and quickly removes the iron. The solder runs along and through the twisted strands of copper, drying to a shiny grayish-silver.

"Perfect," says the Driver, mostly to himself. "Just like Mitch."

He runs his fingers along the blue wire, finds the length of shrink tubing, and slides it back down the wire and over the new connection. While the Geezer holds the blue wire away from his body, the Driver lights a match and waves it beneath the shrink tubing.

Like a struggling insect, the shrink tubing wrinkles and curls, shrinking around the newly soldered connection. When the tubing had shrunk tightly, insulating the new connection, the Driver blows out the match and stands.

"Try it out."

The Putter removes the Driver's handheld 4-AT from the nightstand and dials to the Geezer's microphone frequency. The Geezer reaches into his left pocket and turns his power on. Then he reaches into his right pocket and coughs. The Geezer's cough crackles over the radio the Putter holds in his hand.

"And there you have it," the Driver says, tossing the book of matches into the toolbox. "Good as new."

"What about my hair?" asks the Geezer. "As soon as I start sweating, this gray stuff is going to run all over the place again."

"How about wearing a hat?" the Big Cheese suggests.

The Geezer shakes his head. "I think that will make me sweat even more."

"Why don't you bring a few handkerchiefs along," recommends the Driver. "As soon as you walk in, go to the men's room and clean up a little. You don't perspire in the casino, do you?"

"I sure do," the Geezer says insistently, "and you would too, if you walked into a casino with all this crap strapped to your body. Shit, I start sweating even if an old lady playing a slot machine looks at me."

"You don't want anybody looking at you? Try this," says the Putter, and jams his index finger up his nose.

"Jesus," says the Big Cheese turning away.

"See?" says the Putter.

The other players attempt to ignore the Putter while the Geezer straps the newly soldered wire and the dangling coaxial cable to his body with the white medical bandage. The Driver hisses the soldering iron clean with the wet washcloth and places it on a glass ashtray to cool. When the Putter finishes his doughnut, the team follows the Geezer outside and into the cars. Back to work.

"Golfers proceeding to location number two," the Driver broadcasts, glancing at the list hanging from the visor of the van. "Let's go."

"Geezer proceeding," answers the Geezer.

"Ten-four, Big Cheese proceeding to location number two." The Big Cheese looks at his list, taped to the dashboard of the Porsche. According to the list, location number two is Hemingway's.

The location names used by The Ultimate Edge Quartet are doubly coded. First, each target casino is given a name that the players can remember.

Each location is then given a number the players will use on the air. Only in the event of an emergency are the casinos referred to by their code names. Under no circumstances are casinos ever referred to by their proper names on the air, or even acknowledged as casinos. They are referred to as restaurants.

If anyone happened upon the Big Cheese's list, he would find the following:

1. Apple Pie

2. Hemingway's

3. Anita Bryant's

4. Bailey's

5. Larry Flint's Place

6. Domino's

7. Charlie Brown's

Pretty innocuous stuff. Here is the translation:

1. Apple Pie (Dessert – Desert – Sahara)

2. Hemingway's (Spain – Flamenco dancers – Flamingo)

3. Anita Bryant's (Orange juice – Tropicana)

4. Bailey's (Ringling Brothers and Barnum & Bailey Circus – Circus Circus)

5. Larry Flint's Place (Sleaze – Sleazers – Caesars)

6. Domino's (Pizza – Onion Pizza – Union Plaza)

7. Charlie Brown's (Peanuts – Peppermint Patty – Mint)

Each player has his own mnemonics, so none of the lists are the same. Further, the numbers change daily. If others are listening in on The Ultimate Edge Quartet's radio traffic, they would find it difficult indeed to figure out where the players are or what they are doing.

"The waitresses do have great busts at location number two, correct?" the Geezer asks.

"Ten-four, Geezer, great bustage confirmed at all locations except the double-helping buffet at location number four," the Driver says.

The Driver is verifying that the policy at all the above casinos except Circus-Circus is to burn a card before commencing the deal. The double helping at the Circus is a reference to the double-deck games there. The Driver is telling the Geezer that the Putter will assume a burn card at every potential situation on tonight's list, except the double-deck games at Circus-Circus. Anything different, and the Geezer must notify the Putter of the change. If the Putter assumes a burn card and there isn't one, the results can be disastrous for The Ultimate Edge Quartet.

"Big Cheese standing by at location number two," squawks the Driver's radio. Zipping around in the Porsche, the Big Cheese usually arrives on location first.

"Ten-four, Cheese," the Driver replies. "We're almost there."

It is amazing that we make any money doing this, the Driver marvels. In order for The Ultimate Edge to work, a large number of elements must mesh together perfectly. If any one element isn't exactly right, the play must be aborted.

The Ultimate Edge Quartet does face a number of aborted efforts every day. Given the massive edge they are able to develop with their system, however, it doesn't have to work often.

When the Golfers and the Geezer arrive at location number two, the Putter requests one last test. Satisfied that the equipment is working perfectly, he gives the order to go.

The Geezer enters location number two and stands on the east side of the main pit. He faces the enormous tinted windows that block out the view of the Strip and the beautiful blue-green fountains that introduce location number five.

The Big Cheese stands with his back to these windows. He faces the Geezer as he surveys the pit.

A security guard marches past the Geezer. The Geezer looks at him, the index finger of his left hand jammed so far up his nose he conceivably could be cited for excavation without the proper permit. The security guard passes without a second look.

The Geezer scans the pit and quickly locates Pop at the north end. It's not difficult. His is the table surrounded by pit bosses. Although Pop isn't giving the bosses much to see—he is flat-betting $100 a hand—they are nonetheless giving him heat. There is just something about the guy…

The Geezer establishes eye contact with the Big Cheese and glances toward the south end of the pit. The Big Cheese looks down the length of the pit and locates the Geezer's target. Calmly, the Big Cheese scratches his nose.

The Geezer reaches into the right front pocket of his slacks, depresses the button located there, and speaks into his now-functional condenser microphone.

"Situation main south. Main south."

The signal leaves the casino and is picked up by the 4-AT perched in the Driver's lap. The Golfers are lurking near the entrance of the parking structure located at the rear of location number two.

The Driver starts the van while the Putter flips an array of switches. One button sends a signal on a frequency different from the one the Geezer used to contact the van. That signal tells both the Geezer and the Big Cheese that the Golfers are moving into position.

Meanwhile, the Big Cheese is making his way toward the target table. The dealer is a young female, and the table minimum is $25. Her table is empty.

Suddenly, three sets of signals tickle the calves of the two players in the casino. The signals mean that the Golfers are in position, and the Geezer should turn his equipment on.

The Geezer slides his forefinger along the underside of his cane. Seven seconds later, a picture appears on one of the Putter's three television screens located in the back of the van.

After making some minor adjustments to his satellite dish, the Putter sends another series of signals to the players. Picture quality is good, the signals say. Proceed.

The Big Cheese steps up to the table and smiles at the dealer. The dealer returns his smile and scoops up the cards that are spread face up in a smooth arc on the felt in front of her.

"Why isn't anybody playing at your table tonight?" asks the Big Cheese, as he pulls a stool out from the table. "Have you been hot?"

"Yes, I have," the dealer replies quietly. "I'm beating everybody."

"That's good," says the Big Cheese. "That means it's someone else's turn."

Still talking, the Big Cheese pulls a twenty from his pocket and places it on the felt.

"Changing twenty!" calls the dealer. A pit boss at Pop's table grunts without looking up.

The Geezer wanders over to the table and stands in the spot vacated by the stool the Big Cheese has moved. There is a clear line of sight to the table. He places his cane firmly on the floor. With his left hand he digs his wallet out of his back pocket and begins to fish through it.

The Big Cheese continues conversing with the dealer. She answers, finishes shuffling, and places the cards on the felt in front of the Big Cheese.

Immediately, the buzzer pressing against the Geezer's calf begins vibrating. He swivels the cane a little to the left, and then tilts it back a bit. That's it. The Geezer receives three short dashes. His right hand freezes the cane. His left hand, however, continues to search through his wallet.

"And how long have you lived in Vegas?" the Big Cheese asks, reaching forward to cut the cards.

Moments earlier, two casino workers had strapped a dysfunctional slot machine to a hand cart. At this instant, they are wheeling the heavy metal machine through the casino, and pass between the Geezer and the van waiting outside.

A huge, jagged spike of interference bolts across the Putter's television screen just as the Big Cheese performs his move. The Putter curses softly and sends the abort signal.

This is nothing new to the players. With so many things that can go wrong, something often does. The Big Cheese smiles at the dealer and places a $5 chip on the felt in front of him.

The Geezer is scratching his head. The Big Cheese touches his nose and glances at his watch, signaling the Geezer to wait around. They'll try again. The Geezer touches his nose and continues searching through his wallet for something he'll never find.

As the dealer nears the middle of the double deck, the Big Cheese establishes eye contact with the Geezer. The Geezer touches his nose. He's ready.

The dealer depletes the deck, reaches into the discard rack, and removes the discards. She then proceeds to shuffle.

The Geezer reaches into his pocket again, depresses the button, and coughs. Almost immediately he receives a series of vibrations. The Golfers are ready.

The Big Cheese chats about the problems he is having with his ex-wife. She seems to be more interested in the kind of car she drives than in the schools they send their children to, the air they breathe, the neighborhoods they live in, or anything else that affects their lives. The dealer is nodding sympathetically as she places the cards on the felt in front of the Big Cheese.

Back in the van, the Putter's view of the world is limited to the picture provided by a nineteen-inch black and white Zenith television set. The cards that the dealer has just placed on the felt are barely visible in the extreme lower right-hand corner of the screen. Without removing his eyes from the screen, the Putter flips a switch and depresses two of four buttons on a modified keypad. These four buttons operate the Putter's David playing computers every bit as well as they did when they were in a pair of shoes. A buzzer glued to the table vibrates as the computer outputs a short dash.

Simultaneously, the signal travels through a specially engineered circuit board and into a 4-AT. The radio signal is then broadcast outward on the edge of a sphere traveling close to the speed of light.

The modified 4-AT strapped to the Geezer's body picks up the wave front generated by the Putter's 4-AT. Another specially engineered circuit board translates the radio signal and changes it to an electronic pulse. That pulse causes the buzzer strapped to the Geezer's calf to vibrate.

Obeying the vibrations, the Geezer begins to swivel his cane to the right. An instant later, the Geezer receives a dash followed by two dots. The Geezer stops swiveling the cane and begins to tilt it away from the table.

The cards are now perfectly centered on the Putter's nineteen-inch black and white Zenith television set. The Putter depresses a different pair of keys on the modified keypad, and the signal they've all been waiting for is transmitted.

The Geezer receives the signal as three short dashes and freezes his cane. Having received the same signal, the Big Cheese continues to talk.

The Big Cheese has practiced what he is about to do perhaps five thousand times. It is something he can do remarkably well. Holding the deck down firmly with his forefinger and lifting the lower left-hand corner with his thumb, he must riffle the individual cards evenly. If two cards fall together during the riffle, the consequences can be disastrous. If he riffles too rapidly, the consequences can be disastrous. If the dealer hears the riffle, the consequences can be disastrous. The riffle must be smooth, even, and look like a completely normal cut.

The Big Cheese maintains eye contact with the attractive dealer as his hand reaches out, grabs the double deck firmly, and riffles through about thirty cards before actually cutting. He does so in just under a second. The riffle is perfect.

The Geezer slides the switch underneath the handle of the cane, returns his wallet to his baggy pants, and starts slowly toward an exit. The Big Cheese smiles as the dealer completes the cut, burns a card, and prepares to deal. She would never betray him. Sodium pentothal couldn't force the truth out of her. She didn't see a thing.

Back in the van, the Putter is working frantically. The scene—every bit as beautiful as any Hollywood director could ever hope to capture—had been picked up by the tiny lens located in the handle of the Geezer's cane. It then traveled up the Geezer's arm through four feet of cable to the camera body.

There, it was translated into a video signal and sent to the miniaturized microwave amplification unit strapped to the Geezer's back. The signal was transformed into microwaves, amplified, and sent to a directional microwave antenna located under the Geezer's right arm. The antenna sent the signal out of location number two in the general direction of the Strip.

Sitting between the Geezer and the Strip is the van containing the Driver, the Putter, and about $60,000 worth of electronic equipment. The satellite dish located in the back of the van captures enough of the signal to obtain a picture. The microwaves are then transformed back into a video signal and sent to a SONY 5800, a video recorder with the best frame-by-frame replay capability money can buy in 1987.

The Putter quickly rewinds the tape back to the end of the Big Cheese's riffle, ignores the last card to fall (which at this very moment has become the burn card), and stops. He then begins reviewing the tape frame by frame on a twelve-inch black and white television screen. At this speed, individual cards are easily discernible. Each card lives for about three frames, and is then replaced by the next card in the deck from which the dealer will soon deal. Using the modified keypad, the Putter enters the card values with his left hand as his right hand controls the tape speed on the 5800.

At this moment the Big Cheese is earning his money. He must stall for the approximately sixty seconds it will take the Putter to rewind the tape, find the riffle, and input a sufficient number of cards to complete one round. The stall cannot appear contrived or artificial in any way. This is the longest minute of the Big Cheese's life.

The Big Cheese looks at his watch. "You know, I had no idea it was this late. My plane is scheduled to leave in less than an hour!"

"I'm sorry to hear that," the dealer replies. "You'd better get going."

The Big Cheese looks the dealer right in the eye. "You know, I have a good feeling about you. I'm going to make or break this trip right now. What's the limit here?"

The dealer indicates the green sign on the table. "Five to a thousand," she says.

"So the most I can bet is a thousand?" the Big Cheese asks. The dealer nods.

"What if I have to double down or split?" asks the Big Cheese.

"Then you can put more money out," the dealer answers. "The limit refers to your original bet only."

The Big Cheese reaches into his pocket and extracts a thick wad of bills. "I'm going for it. What do you think?"

The dealer shrugs, but the Big Cheese can see she doesn't think it's a very good idea. She likes the Big Cheese, and, as is the case with virtually every Vegas dealer, she has seen this too many times before.

She's never seen this, the Big Cheese thinks as he counts out several stacks of a thousand dollars on the table in front of him.

By now the Putter has entered twenty of the approximately thirty cards the Big Cheese riffled when he performed his cut. He presses a certain combination of buttons on the keypad, and the new program running in the David playing computer kicks into action.

Dot, dot, dash, dash, dot, dot, dash-dash-dot-dot, the computer responds. The signal travels at the speed of light to the Big Cheese's right calf, the owner of which is beginning to wonder what the hell is taking so long.

Three hands of strategy one, eight up-card, the Big Cheese thinks, and places three piles of a thousand dollars each on the table in front of him. He also places a twenty in front of each pile for the dealer.

"Money plays!" the dealer calls. "Three hands of the limit!"

A pit boss leaves Pop's table and arrives at the table in an instant. He glares at the Big Cheese, the dealer, the empty discard rack, the Big Cheese again, and shrugs. There is nothing to see. Like any good magic trick, the move is done before anyone thinks to start looking.

The pit boss offers his hand and a business card. "Name's Pete Murphy," says the pit boss. "If there's anything I can do for you, let me know."

"Thanks," replies the Big Cheese. "I'm Tony Freeberg, and I'm in a bit of a hurry. My plane leaves in less than an hour."

"Deal," says the pit boss.

The dealer deals to the three piles of money in front of the Big Cheese. She gives herself an eight up.

Right so far, Putter, thinks the Big Cheese, and looks at his first hand. Thirteen. He shows the pit boss the hand, and scratches for a hit. She hits him with a two. The Big Cheese shrugs and stands. The pit boss smiles. Bad play. This guy doesn't even know Basic Strategy. And he's not seeing the hole card.

The Big Cheese's second hand totals eighteen. He stands. His third hand is an eleven. He pulls out more money.

"You said I can double my bet, right?" he asks the dealer. The dealer nods.

The Big Cheese counts out another ten hundreds and plops them crossways on top of his original bet. The dealer deals the double-down card face down. Without looking at it, the Big Cheese shows the card to the pit boss. The pit boss fails to suppress a smile. Small card, thinks the Big Cheese. So what.

The dealer flips her hole card up. It is a seven. She then busts her hand with a ten.

"Thank you very much," says the Big Cheese. The dealer proceeds to pay the Big Cheese $4,000, and herself $60. The pit boss is no longer smiling.

While the Big Cheese is playing his hands, the Putter is busy replaying and inputting the remaining cards exposed during the riffle. When he finishes, he pushes a button sequence and outputs further information to the Big Cheese.

The Big Cheese receives the signals while the dealer is paying his winning hands. Dot-dash, dot, dot, dot-dot, dot-dot, dash, dash.

The last card is a ten, and two hands of basic, thinks the Big Cheese. The Putter is right on so far. The last card—the dealer's bust card—was indeed a ten.

"Let's try again, shall we?" says the Big Cheese, gathering his money together and leaving two tall stacks of black chips in front of him. "Just two hands this time." He pushes the extra forty bucks he won for the dealer toward her. "Take this, and let the rest of yours ride."

As the dealer begins to deal, the Putter outputs more information. It's too soon, but the Putter has no way of knowing that.

The last card of this round should be a seven, the dots and dashes say, and the Big Cheese should bet three hands of strategy three on the subsequent round.

The Big Cheese smiles as he memorizes his instructions. He loves strategy three. It always makes him look like a complete moron.

The dealer has a five up-card. The Big Cheese lifts his first hand and shows it to the pit boss. Twenty. He stands. He lifts his second hand. Blackjack.

"Boom!" exclaims the Big Cheese. The dealer pays his bet $1,500, and her bet $60.

While the dealer is paying the Big Cheese for his blackjack, the Putter outputs the final round. Again, it's far too soon. The final round will be a flux round—not all of the cards are known—and the Big Cheese is to play two hands.

The Big Cheese rehearses the next two rounds in his mind. The last card on this round will be a seven. He will play three hands of strategy three. The dealer's up-card will be a four. The last card at the end of that round will be a ten. He will then reduce his bets and play two hands of Basic Strategy. The Big Cheese smiles. Now *this* is like having an X-ray machine at the table.

The dealer flips up her hole card—a six—and hits her eleven with a seven. So far, so good.

She pays the Big Cheese another thousand dollars, and herself another forty.

The Big Cheese moves a thousand in chips and half the dealer's win over to a third hand. The dealer deals. The pit boss turns a different shade of green.

The dealer's up-card is a four. Right on, Putter, thinks the Big Cheese. He lifts his first hand and shows it to the pit boss. He has a fifteen.

"Hit it," says the Big Cheese, scratching the felt.

The dealer looks at him, horrified. She has $100 riding on the hand. She hesitates.

"You heard him," the pit boss growls. "He wants a card."

Reluctantly, she hits the Big Cheese's hand. Five. He stands. The dealer is visibly relieved. Not so the pit boss. Relieved is not a word normally associated with one so green.

The Big Cheese's second hand totals seventeen. He stands, and lifts his third hand. Fourteen. The Big Cheese scratches for a hit.

This time the dealer doesn't hesitate. The Big Cheese may be one of the worst players she has ever seen—randomly standing with stiffs against big cards and hitting stiffs against small cards—but today seems to be his day.

Indeed.

She hits his fourteen with a six. He stands.

She flips her hole card face up. It's a ten. She hits it with another ten.

"Whew! Good thing I took those hits!" says the Big Cheese, wiping his forehead with his sleeve. "Otherwise, I would have lost them all."

By now the pit boss can't even force himself to smile. Even the green has drained from his face.

The Big Cheese drops his bets to two hands of four hundred, and shoves all of the dealer's tips toward her. Everything has been perfect so far, but this is the flux round—not all of the cards are known. The dealer has made $400 in the past two minutes, and the Big Cheese doesn't want her to risk it.

The dealer deals the cards. The Big Cheese wins one hand and loses the other. Push. He looks at his watch.

"Well, time to get out of here. If I hurry, I still might make my flight. Do you have a bag or something I can use to carry all these chips?"

The pit boss manages to get to the podium, and returns with a Plexiglas chip rack. The Big Cheese racks his chips, winks at the dealer, and heads for the cage.

The dealer and the pit boss watch the Big Cheese depart. The dealer thinks she is in love with the Big Cheese. The pit boss is holding on to the blackjack table for support.

The Big Cheese wheels his balls toward the cage. He just won $9,500. Less the bets he made for the dealer, he and his teammates have cleared $9,440 in ten minutes. Not bad. Not bad at all.

Perhaps next time they'll beat up the right guy.

CHAPTER 21

AND WE'LL NEVER SEE THE LIKES OF THEM AGAIN

And, poof! He's gone.
~Kevin Spacey in The Usual Suspects

The Ultimate Edge Quartet stayed in action for only six months. In that short stint, the quartet logged more monster wins than most players see in a lifetime. It isn't often that players know almost beyond the shadow of a doubt that they are going to win every hand they play, and both Big Cheeses—the Driver and Big Cheese roles switched regularly—made the most of their unique situation. As a smirking pit boss once said, "Some days we win, and other days we win more."

The Big Cheese opened a dead table in a location in Reno, buying in for the usual twenty-dollar bill. Frowning, the dealer scooped the cards and began to shuffle. The Geezer wandered over to the table, hesitated for less than three seconds while the Big Cheese performed a lovely twenty-five card riffle, and continued on toward the door.

The dealer quickly completed the cut, burned a card, and stood, ready to deal. Before the Big Cheese could begin his stalling tactics, however, a security guard carrying a rack of $5,000 in black chips arrived at the table accompanied by a pit boss. The security guard placed the chips on the table, and the dealer began to fill her depleted tray. Knowing that the fill would take at least a minute, the Big Cheese recognized that his stall had just been handed to him on the proverbial silver platter.

"Is that for me?" the Big Cheese asked innocently, pointing at the stacks of black chips.

The pit boss looked at the four pitiful $5 chips in front of the Big Cheese and laughed. "Yeah, right," he scoffed, "this is for you."

"Great!" the Big Cheese exclaimed, reaching into his pocket and extracting a thick wad of hundreds. As the pit boss watched, thunderstruck, the Big Cheese shoved out three hands of a thousand, won, played another three hands of a thousand, and won again. "Thanks," said the Big Cheese, and headed for the cage with six thousand dollars in black chips. The pit boss and the security guard stood motionless, their mouths hanging open.

On his way out of the casino, the Big Cheese noticed that the pit boss had managed to get to a phone. He was calling for another fill.

When they were on, The Ultimate Edge Quartet performed like a well-choreographed ballet. When they were off, they were more reminiscent of Laurel and Hardy.

One of the more memorable hands the Big Cheese played transpired after The Ultimate Edge Quartet had been in action for about a month. At the time, they were experiencing some problems breaking in a new Geezer.

The Big Cheese chose a high-limit table in the middle of the main pit at a downtown Vegas location. The Geezer contacted the Driver, who pulled the van into position. The Putter then signaled the Geezer to turn his camera on.

At that particular moment, the Geezer was standing about six feet from an open security booth. A large, sweaty security guard was manning the booth, which contained a television monitor perched on a desk, a stool, and (the new Geezer imagined) seven or eight semi-automatic weapons.

The semi-automatics notwithstanding, the Geezer bravely turned his camera on. Apparently, his microwaves didn't agree with something in the casino, because the television monitor in the security booth started buzzing loudly. The Geezer inconspicuously jumped about four feet in the air and fled.

By the time the Geezer arrived on the side of the pit where the Big Cheese was waiting, the buzzing had stopped. At least it appeared to have stopped.

The security guard had stopped fiddling with the knobs on the television monitor and had resumed staring off into space.

The Big Cheese stepped up to the empty blackjack table, moved a stool out, and smiled at the dealer. She smiled back, and began shuffling the cards.

"Twenty-five-dollar minimum, eh?" said the Big Cheese, eyeing the two-thousand-dollar limit.

"Yes, sir," said the dealer.

"Can you make this a hundred-dollar-minimum table?" asked the Big Cheese, placing a hundred-dollar bill on the felt.

"I'm not sure," the dealer replied, and called a pit boss over to the table.

At that moment, the Geezer had arrived at the table and was planting his cane firmly on the carpet. When he saw the pit boss approaching the game, however, he lifted his cane and hobbled off, leaving the Big Cheese standing there with his dick in his hand.

"He wants to know if he can have a hundred-dollar-minimum table," the dealer told the pit boss.

"I think we have one in the other pit," the pit boss replied. "Let me check."

"Don't bother," called the Big Cheese, but the pit boss had already left.

The Big Cheese didn't want to play in the other pit. He knew from experience that the Geezer's microwave signal couldn't plow through all of the slot machines, change booths, and other assorted crap located between the other pit and the van. Additionally, Pop had already taken up residence in this pit, and was currently occupying the undivided attention of two pit bosses.

"It's just that I don't like playing with other players at the table, and I can usually play alone at the hundred-dollar minimums," said the Big Cheese, and cut the cards cleanly.

The Big Cheese began playing quarters, keeping an eye on the Geezer. He wanted the Geezer to come up to the table after the next shuffle. The Golfers were still reporting good picture quality, and the Big Cheese had not yet been joined by other players.

When the deck had been depleted and the dealer began to shuffle, the Big Cheese touched his nose. The Geezer acknowledged and moved into position. As the dealer placed the cards on the felt for the Big Cheese's cut, the pit boss returned. And the goddamn Geezer took off again.

"I can't raise the minimum at this table, but there's a high-limit table in the other pit," the pit boss said helpfully.

"Thanks," said the Big Cheese, again cutting the cards cleanly, "but I like this dealer. I'll stay here."

The Big Cheese slogged through another deck, alternately flirting with the dealer and glaring murderously at the Geezer. The Geezer studiously avoided eye contact.

The problem was, the Geezer was afraid to come up to the table while the pit boss was standing nearby. What the inexperienced Geezer didn't understand was that the pit boss would be able to see absolutely nothing from his vantage point inside the pit. The Big Cheese knew that The Ultimate Edge Quartet would be highly likely to pull off a successful blast with the pit boss standing there, because he would have seen nothing, and would have absolutely no reason to suspect anything. Unfortunately, the inexperienced Geezer was being about as cooperative as a balky mule.

Finally, the dealer completed the deck and began to shuffle. The Big Cheese had already lost about $200, largely due to the fact that he was paying virtually no attention to his cards whatsoever.

The dealer finished shuffling and placed the cards on the felt. The pit boss, who was enjoying the banter between the Big Cheese and the dealer, was still at the table. The Geezer approached the table reluctantly, placed his cane on the floor, searched his wallet for a moment, and then left.

The Big Cheese sighed as the Geezer wandered off. The riffle had been short, but sweet.

He leaned forward. "Whew!" he said to the dealer. "I thought that poor bastard was going to play here."

The dealer smiled. The Geezer looked like a degenerate gambler who had long ago lost his last dime.

"That always brings me bad luck," the Big Cheese continued. "I don't get a chance to play alone too often, so I'd better take advantage of it." He reached into his pocket and extracted the wad.

While the Big Cheese was stalling, counting out piles of $2,000, he noticed a group of relief dealers heading into the pit. If a relief dealer came to the table, she would shuffle the cards, thus destroying forever the precious information the Putter was presently recovering from his video recorder and entering into his computer.

The Putter's signal arrived while the relief dealers were gathering at the podium in the middle of the pit, getting their table assignments. The Big Cheese was to play three hands of basic.

He threw six thousand dollars on the table. "Play it," he said. "Three hands of the limit."

The dealer scooped the sixty hundred-dollar bills and began placing each face down on the layout, so that each bill was discernible to the eye-in-the-sky above. Come on, thought the Big Cheese, deal the cards!

She made a large square out of twenty of the bills. "Two thousand," she said.

Hurry!

The dealer formed another large square. "Another two thousand," she said.

Come on!

Too late. The relief dealer was approaching the table, and the dealer had just started counting out the remaining twenty bills. If the relief dealer got her hands on that deck, the Big Cheese would face two alternatives, both unpleasant. Either he would have to risk the six thousand dollars playing with no advantage, or he would have to pull the money back and look like a complete moron.

The Big Cheese leaned forward. "Can she please deal the cards?" he asked the pit boss plaintively, indicating the original dealer.

The pit boss smiled. "Why?"

"Well, I really like her, and…superstition, I guess."

The Big Cheese held his breath. The pit boss looked at the dealer and shrugged. "Why not?"

Why not, indeed, thought the Big Cheese triumphantly as the dealer finished spreading his remaining $2,000. By now, two-thirds of the table was covered with $100 bills, and a crowd of curious onlookers had started to gather. With a flourish, the Big Cheese added $100 to each of the three hands for the dealer. He really did like her.

The dealer dealt the cards, dealing herself a five up. The Big Cheese looked at his first hand, a six and a four. He counted out another two thousand and doubled down. The dealer dealt him a card face down, and he lifted it. The crowd groaned. A three.

He looked at his second hand. Fourteen. Another groan. He stood.

His third hand was a pair of eights. He pulled out the rest of his money, and discovered that he only had $1,820 left.

When a player doubles down, he has the option to double down for less than the amount of his original bet. So, if the Big Cheese had received another double-down hand, he wouldn't have had a problem. He simply would have doubled down by placing $1,820 alongside his $2,000 bet. However, if a player wishes to split a pair, he must match his original bet exactly. There is no such thing as splitting for less than the amount of the original bet.

As the Big Cheese later recounted, he felt like the biggest fucking moron the world had ever seen. He was sitting there with $8,000 on the table, and was unable to play the strategy the Putter's computer had told him to play. Because of that $180 shortfall, he would in all likelihood lose eight grand.

The Big Cheese counted his money again. It still totaled $1,820. He eyed the $300 he had put out for the dealer and reminded himself to have someone kick him in the ass later.

Several options surfaced in his brain and were immediately discarded. He could run out to the van and get some more money. He could ask the pit boss if he could move $180 from his double-down hand to his third hand. He could ask the dealer if he could pull back her tips. He could ask one of the forty rubberneckers behind him for a couple hundred bucks. All no good. Then it hit him. The pit boss hadn't seen how shitty his first two hands were.

Summoning nonchalance from the very depths of his soul, the Big Cheese turned to the pit boss and said, "Can you mark $180? I'm sure I'll win at least one of these hands."

The pit boss eyed the Big Cheese's cash covering most of the table, looked at the crowd of forty or so rubberneckers straining to hear every word, and made the right decision.

"Mark one-eighty," he told the dealer.

The Big Cheese split his eights. He received a five on the first eight, stood, received a four on the second, and stood again. The Big Cheese had ten thousand dollars covering the entire blackjack table, and his best hand was a goddamn fourteen.

The dealer flipped up her hole card. She had a ten lurking beneath her five, and hit it with the biggest, fattest nine of spades the Big Cheese had ever seen.

"Boom!" exclaimed the Big Cheese, but was entirely drowned out by the cheering from the forty or so rubberneckers.

The Big Cheese slumped in his stool and ordered a Chevis from the cocktail waitress. "Better make it a double," said the Big Cheese, and he meant it. The waitress returned with the drink before the dealer had finished paying his hands. The Big Cheese gulped it down, flipped the waitress a quarter chip, gave the dealer her $600, and headed for the cage.

The forty rubberneckers disappeared into the crowd, buzzing about what they had just seen. Advertising isn't cheap. The Big Cheese figured his version was easily worth ten grand.

Often, The Ultimate Edge Quartet would spend hours hanging around a location waiting for a situation to develop. On one such afternoon, a number of situations had opened up periodically. The Big Cheese had approached the table, the Geezer had turned his equipment on, and another player had sat down at the table to play. In all such situations, the attempt was aborted.

Once, the Big Cheese had actually performed a riffle. However, the dealer had looked down at the cards as the Big Cheese was completing the riffle, and might have seen a card or two fall. The Ultimate Edge Quartet adhered to one rule that was unbending: they were to take no chances. The fact that the dealer might have seen the tail end of the riffle was enough for the Big Cheese to abort the play. He played a few hands, lost, and left. Since he had played only a few hands at the table minimum, the dealer would never give what she might or might not have seen a second thought.

By five in the afternoon, the players had aborted twelve or thirteen attempts, and the Geezer's battery power was getting low. He and the Big Cheese decided to hang around for another fifteen minutes. If nothing opened up, they would break for dinner and attack swing shift.

A situation opened. The Big Cheese touched his nose and headed toward the empty table. The Geezer showed up moments later and aimed his cane. The Big Cheese performed a beautiful riffle, and the Geezer left. The Big Cheese then began his stall.

In the meantime, the Putter was struggling in the back of the van. The Geezer's low battery power had caused the picture on the Putter's all-important twelve-inch screen to shrink and darken. The cards were difficult to discern. The picture quality on the Putter's six-inch auxiliary screen was no better.

After slightly more than a minute, the Putter output instructions to the Big Cheese. He was to play three hands of strategy one.

The Big Cheese plunked three hands of $3,000 each out on the table. The dealer dealt herself an eight up, and dealt the Big Cheese a fourteen, a fifteen, and an eleven. As per strategy one, the Big Cheese stood with his stiffs and doubled down on his eleven. On his eleven he was dealt a two.

The dealer flipped up her hole card. She had a nine beneath her eight. On the Putter's dark, shrunken picture, the nine had looked like an eight. The Big Cheese lost $12,000 on one hand.

"I had practiced acting excited when I won," said the Big Cheese later, "but I never practiced how to act when I lost, so I didn't know what to do. As the dealer was taking my money, I almost said, 'Hey, wait a minute. That wasn't supposed to happen.'"

On another, happier occasion, the Geezer and the Big Cheese had been waiting for a situation to develop. For two hours, the Geezer had been signaling and aborting the Golfers. Every time the Geezer called the Golfers in, the Driver drove the van around the corner and into position. Every time the Geezer aborted the play, the Driver drove the van back to the spot where the Golfers lurked.

The Putter, susceptible to motion sickness under the best of circumstances, was dying in the back of the van. Going around in circles for two hours in complete darkness was wreaking havoc on his stomach, and he had swallowed seven Dramamine tablets to combat his queasiness.

The Dramamine had done an admirable job of combating the Putter's motion sickness. His stomach felt fine. Unfortunately, he was half asleep.

Meanwhile, inside the location, the Big Cheese was getting impatient. When a situation opened up at a table with a male dealer, the Big Cheese decided to move.

One of the reasons The Ultimate Edge worked so well was the Big Cheese's ability to communicate with female dealers. As the Big Cheese would soon discover, however, this talent didn't extend to their male counterparts.

The Big Cheese moved into position, the Geezer wandered by, and the Big Cheese performed his move.

He then began his stall.

The Putter immediately began to input cards. Unfortunately, in his Dramamine-induced stupor, he had forgotten to reset the computer. It still contained information from a riffle the Big Cheese had performed three hours earlier.

At the same time, the Big Cheese was having trouble with his stall. Two players had attempted to join the game. The Big Cheese had managed to talk them into waiting just one round, but now it was almost a minute later and he was still standing there, waiting for instructions from the Putter.

Finally, the Putter output instructions. Three hands of basic. The Big Cheese put two hands of a thousand out on the layout, and reached into his pocket for more money.

The dealer immediately began to deal to the two piles of bills.

"Wait!" the Big Cheese exclaimed. "I want to bet another hand."

"Too late," the dealer said curtly.

"Don't worry," said one of the players waiting for the Big Cheese. "You did the right thing. He has a six up."

The Big Cheese sighed and played his hands. Luckily, he won them both. Pissed, he took off without tipping the dealer. Who knows how much he might have won had he played three hands?

"You're not going to believe what happened," said the Big Cheese into his radio when he had returned to his car.

"We already know," responded the Driver. "Indigestion."

"What?"

"We know. Sorry."

"What are you talking about? How'd you know I got sick?"

"What are *you* talking about? *We* got sick."

They finally sorted it out back at the room. Because he had forgotten to reset the computer, the information the Putter output was completely bogus. If the dealer had allowed the Big Cheese to play a third hand, he would have lost three thousand dollars. Instead, he won two thousand.

"See?" said the Big Cheese. "We've kept our elbows to the grindstone for a long time, and we finally had a positive fluctuation."

An enormous amount of thought and practice had gone into every aspect of The Ultimate Edge. Each player fully appreciated the ramifications if something were to go wrong. Each member of the team was quite pleased with the layers of misdirection built into the system. But it wasn't until they started their search for a new Geezer that they fully appreciated how invisible their performance actually was.

They had located a promising prospect and nicknamed him "the Flounder." The roles of the front men—the Geezer and the Big Cheese—had been described to the Flounder in great detail. Now it was time to go into a casino and show the Flounder what The Ultimate Edge looked like in real life.

The Flounder entered first and took up residence at the bar. The Geezer and the Big Cheese entered separately, established eye contact, and crossed paths at an empty table. The move was done, the Big Cheese won a quick five grand, and they headed for the door. The entire escapade had lasted maybe three minutes.

When they arrived back at base in their separate vehicles, the Flounder had only one question. "What went wrong?" he asked.

The Big Cheese asked what he meant.

"Why'd you call off the play?"

Even knowing what to look for and when, the Flounder had seen nothing. He had blinked, and missed the whole show.

That is misdirection.

After The Ultimate Edge Quartet had been in action for six months, an incident in what had been historically one of their most profitable locations convinced them that it was time to stop. They knew they could continue playing for a little while longer, but all of the players agreed that stopping too soon was infinitely preferable to stopping too late.

The Big Cheese walked into his favorite Reno location at four o'clock in the morning. The gait of choice at that time was weaving dramatically, and the Big Cheese fit in rather nicely. He steered himself over to an empty table, greeted the dealer, and almost knocked over a bar stool.

"Cut that stool off!" slurred the Big Cheese. "It's had enough."

The Big Cheese bought in for the usual $20. The dealer shoved four nickels toward him and shuffled the cards. She then offered the Big Cheese the cut.

The Geezer wandered by the table, the Big Cheese riffled like a champ, and the dealer completed the cut. The Big Cheese reached into his pocket, pulled out his wad of bills, and began his stall by buying in for three thousand dollars in chips.

"It's you!" the dealer said excitedly. "I can't believe it! You're back!"

"Huh?" The Big Cheese froze in mid-buy.

"It's him!" the dealer said to the dealer on her right, pointing at the Big Cheese. "Remember I told you about that guy who bought in for a little, and then bet, like, thousands of dollars? And then left? It's him!"

The Big Cheese grimaced. "Ah, are you sure—"

"Don't you remember?"

"Ah, I'm not sure. How did I do?"

"You did great!" She hesitated. "In fact, *we* did great."

"Well, let's do great again, shall we?" In his mortified state, the Big Cheese forgot that he was supposed to be drunk.

The Big Cheese won $6,000 for himself and $300 for the dealer. She was astonished.

"You are amazing! Are you, like, the luckiest person in the world or something?"

The Big Cheese smiled. He just might be.

The incident pointed out a problem: the *modus operandi* had been identified. The next time, the clever individual might be someone who didn't appreciate the Big Cheese's uncanny luck, and would examine the situation a little more closely. It was time to pack it in.

A little sadly, the Geezer hung the cane on its hook for the last time. It had been fun, but it was time to move on. The Ultimate Edge Quartet had played its last note.

About a year after the team had split up, Taylor received something in the mail from Tony. Apparently, Tony had come across Thayer's *Casey at the Bat.*

TONY AT THE DECK

The outlook wasn't brilliant for the Reno team that day;
Their bankroll hit an all-time low with one place left to play.
When someone finally won a hand, the dealer would win two;
Those few wins they did eke out were far between and few.

The players simply shook their heads, and looked about in awe;
Their fortune had just disappeared in the casino's voracious maw.
They said, "We know that Tony could give those bastards heck;
We'd put up some more money, with Tony at the deck."

Now Wong preceded Tony, and so did L. Revere;
But both had taken beatings; their losses quite severe.
So in the players' eyes was the vision of a wreck;
It seemed to be impossible to get Tony at the deck.

Then Geezer strapped the camera on, and stood there with a grin;
And Putter learned to work the van, and thought that he could win.
So when the players came to town, they saw what had occurred;
The BP played the middle, while the Geezer stood at third.

The players' minds were racing; their mouths did salivate;
They'd make a pile of money, if the dealers took the bait.
But they all had to wait to see if the dealers would reject
Tony—mighty Tony—advancing toward the deck.

Tony's stride was swift and sure as he approached the game;
He said, "This is the game for me, and Tony is my name."
So quickly did the crowd rush up a woman broke her neck,
To get a glimpse of Tony—Tony at the deck.

THE ULTIMATE EDGE

The dealer's eyeballs widened, and the crowd saw what she saw;
Their murmurs grew quite deafening; their voices filled with awe.
For Tony flashed a wad of bills that could have choked a Czech;
And all remaining doubts were gone—'twas Tony at the deck.

The dealer glanced around the pit, and saw the floor man's fright;
She turned to ask him for advice, but he stayed out of sight.
Her knees began to tremble; her hands began to shake;
She didn't want to deal the cards; she dreaded a mistake.

At last a pit boss showed his face, and stepped up to the game;
He smiled up at Tony, and said, "I'm glad you came."
He said, "You want some dinner? The tab will be on me."
They were good to Tony—Tony always ate for free.

The dealer mixed the cards up well, and offered him the cut.
He knew his cut would be just right—he felt it in his gut.
But as he reached to cut the cards, the pit boss jumped right in;
And said, "I think we'll try a brand-new deck. Now let's see you win."

The crowd began to hiss and boo; security was called.
Tony had to do something, before that boss was mauled.
Yes, Tony had to say the word to keep that crowd at bay;
He looked about and raised his hand and simply said, "Okay."

The dealer mixed the brand-new deck, and placed it on the felt;
It all was up to Tony's cut to determine what was dealt.
One could hear that classic sound—a pin at fifty yards;
The crowd grew still, their voices hushed, as Tony cut the cards.

Oh, somewhere players gamble; they count and spook and cheat;
Some win lots of money, and others just get heat.
Yes, counters are a happy lot; they win and dance about;
But there is no joy in Reno—mighty Tony busted out.

Three months later, Tony showed up at Taylor's condo bearing a thick manuscript. "I'd like to know what you think," he said.

"Whose style is this?" Taylor asked.

Tony smiled. "I hope you don't mind. I found a letter you sent to that dealer after the Canadian trip."

Taylor felt the heft of the manuscript. "How long is it?"

"In book form, it'll be about four hundred pages." His smile broadened. "After they read this, they might name a statute after me."

Taylor laughed. "You mean a statue. They might name…"

Tony Ricco was grinning at him.

"You said that on purpose."

"Of course."

"Were they all on purpose?"

"What do you think?"

"But why? What for?"

"People think I'm an idiot. They underestimate me." Tony shrugged. "It gives me an edge."

EPILOGUE

Since Taylor hooked up with Brian, Guppy, and Reed on that fateful day in 1981, casino blackjack has undergone some significant transformations. In many respects, today's version of the game isn't at all the same.

The most significant change has been the way in which the casinos deal with the hole card. When the players began their blackjack careers, virtually every dealer in the state of Nevada peeked beneath tens and aces to check for blackjack. It was this peek, of course, that made spooking, tells, and warp play possible. Today, there are virtually no casinos in which the dealers check beneath tens for aces. A small device is used with special cards. A dealer can determine if a card is an ace; however, if it is not, the actual identity of the card remains hidden. These dealers can be neither spooked nor read.

Shuffles have increased in complexity by several orders of magnitude. Since the casinos never really understood shuffle tracking, they never figured out how to develop a short, elegant untrackable shuffle. What they failed to accomplish with subtlety they attempted to accomplish through brute force, and now all players are forced to wait through shuffles that can take several minutes to complete. Ironically, a number of these monumentally time-consuming shuffles are still trackable, but the new device law has effectively eliminated computerized shuffle-tracking teams. Still, regular gamblers must wait for several minutes for an activity that should take only a minute or so, which means these back-breaking shuffles are costing the casinos a lot of money. Remember: casinos make no money while players sit around watching the dealer shuffle.

Of the original members of the team with which Taylor traveled the world, only Guppy and Tony are gambling exclusively today. (You may have noticed that their biographical information was sketchy at best. This is why.) However, the others are all still involved peripherally. If there is the possibility of an edge somewhere, they can probably be found attempting to exploit it.

Brian is a serious NFL football fan, but long ago gave up on trying to beat the game. He learned that a schedule consisting of only sixteen games allows the fluctuations caused by major injuries, weather, psychology, etc., to swamp regular results.

Brian did, however, begin to watch baseball games attentively. With 162 games and more statistics than anyone has the right to collect, baseball could be his little corner of heaven. If he could just cull the chaff from the meaningful statistics, and then weigh those meaningful statistics properly…

Guppy had always been fascinated by roulette. To him, it represented the ultimate video game. He knew there was a way to beat it with skill, and spent hours staring at that little ball spinning around and around. Unlike most gamblers, Guppy recognized that in the usual sense every spin of a roulette ball is a brand-new universe—that is, the results of previous spins would have no bearing on upcoming results—but he also knew that certain physical laws carried over from universe to universe. For now, Guppy will allow the author to say no more than that.

Taylor consults part-time with a software firm, but still exploits the occasional hole card. When he heard that there was a good game available in Korea, he bought a ticket on Korean Air, hopped aboard, and spent three weeks playing what was perhaps the best game on the planet.

The point of view of these professional gamblers has colored their view of life forever. For the rest of their lives, the players would examine everything with the hope—nay, the conviction—that there was a solution. Somehow, information could be organized in such a way that it could be deciphered; the extraneous trash could be stripped away, revealing a gleaming naked core. An edge.

After the body of this book was completed, Taylor related the following to the author:

As a teenager during a ski trip to Vermont, Taylor's mind provided him with the first edge he can consciously remember. After skiing to the bottom of the slope, he headed toward one of the three lift lines converging on the double-chair that would lug him back up the hill. The three lines were the same length. In which line should he wait?

Well, if all three lines were the same length, it didn't matter, right?

Wrong.

Taylor realized he should get in the line with the tallest people. Why? Because taller people tend to have longer skis than shorter people. Because of this, each tall person takes up more room in line than each shorter person. Therefore, the line with the taller people would actually contain fewer skiers than a line consisting of shorter people. Therefore, it should move faster.

Admittedly, this isn't exactly the stuff of Nobel Prizes. But it does exemplify the kind of thinking that comes in mighty handy to the professional gambler. And, Taylor insists, it is not something he consciously tries to do. His brain is simply wired that way.

After a couple of years without seeing each other, Taylor ran into Reed in a supermarket checkout line. Reed told Taylor he was playing poker, and that he was distracting the hell out of the other players with his gorilla act. As for Taylor, he was spending a lot of time sitting in his lawn chair in his back yard, reading everything he could get his hands on and enjoying the fact that he had done what he had done, and still nobody knew who he was.

As Reed rambled on, Taylor watched the cashier pass a box of frozen broccoli over the laser scanner built into the counter. The scanner read the International Product Code on the side of the box, and the price flashed on the register.

If that thing can discern differences between those tiny little lines, Taylor thought, surely it could tell the difference between an eight and a nine.

And in the back of his mind Taylor heard Guppy say, "Of course it could. And don't call me 'Shirley.'"

APPENDIX I:

BLACKJACK BASICS

The game of blackjack as dealt in casinos all over the world has become reasonably standardized. Although there are differences in rules, differences in the number of decks, and differences in the way those decks are dealt, the following two fundamentals remain the same:

1. All players at the table play against the dealer. The game is not like poker, where players at the same table play against each other.

2. The dealer makes no playing decisions. The rules for the dealer are fixed, immutable, and should be known to all before a hand is dealt.

The game is played with a multiple of regulation 52-card decks. Taylor and his teammates have played games dealt with one, two, four, five, six, and eight decks. (Although they've never played a game dealt from three or seven decks, there is no technical reason why such games could not exist.)

The dealer shuffles the cards, more or less randomizing the order. In some casinos, brand-new decks are "washed," meaning the cards are spread out over the felt layout and mixed by hand. The cards are then reconstituted and shuffled.

Casino shuffling consists of two basic moves: *riffling* and *stripping*.

Riffling is the kind of shuffling familiar to most people who play cards at home. A stack of cards is divided roughly in half, and the two halves are riffled, end to end, so that cards from one packet are interleaved with cards from the other. In the casino version, only the corners of the cards are lifted with the thumb, and the riffling cards are tilted back toward the dealer. This is so the cascading cards are hidden from the players.

After two or three riffles, a dealer will normally *strip* the deck. This involves lifting the stack of cards with one hand, and pulling clumps of cards (normally between one and ten cards) off the top and plopping them down on the felt. This serves to more or less reverse the order of the cards. (Note that a dealer who stripped by grabbing exactly one card at a time would precisely reverse the order of the cards.)

In some casinos, the order and quantity of riffling and stripping appears to be strictly controlled (e.g., two riffles, a strip, and two more riffles); however, in most it seems to be up to the dealer. (A common countermeasure—if you can call it that—employed against players who are winning is additional stripping. It seems many dealers believe changing one random sequence of cards to another random sequence will somehow change a player's luck.[34] Why they think extra stripping is more effective than additional riffles remains an open question. Whatever the reason, Taylor and his teammates have been treated to stripping impassioned enough to start a fire.)

The entire idea of shuffling is to more or less randomize the order of the cards. And normally this riffling and stripping does a pretty good job of just that.

The dealer then offers one of the players the cut. It is up to the dealer to decide who cuts (except in games with the French stop-card rule—then the cut automatically goes to the person to whom the stop card was dealt at the end of the last round). In low-limit games, the dealers tend to rotate around the table, giving everyone a chance to cut. In games in which someone is betting big, the big bettor tends to get the cut card more often than other players. (There are at least two reasons for this: the dealers want tips, and they don't want the big bettor to have anyone but himself to blame when he [inevitably] loses.)

---

34 The irony, of course, is that more often than not, this appears to work. Since the house has an edge over regular players, anything the dealer does—standing on one foot, whistling, shuffling, etc.—will eventually result in the player losing, just as standing on one foot at night will eventually result in the sun coming up the following morning.

If the game is played with one or two decks, the deck may be cut by hand or with a plastic cut card. If the game is played with more than two decks, a plastic cut card is almost always used.

If a player declines to cut, the dealer will offer the cut to another player at the table. If all players decline, the dealer herself will cut.

Once the cards are cut, the dealer reconstitutes the deck, moving the chunk of cards cut from the top to the bottom, as follows:

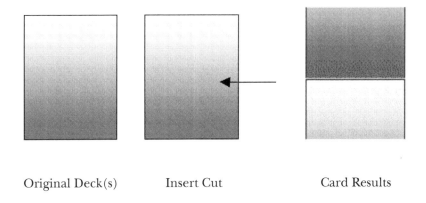

Original Deck(s)   Insert Cut   Card Results

This move is referred to as *completing* the cut. For regular players, the cut simply changes one random ordering of cards to another random ordering of cards.

If the game is played with one or two decks, the dealer will then grab the deck with her nondominant hand (e.g., right-handed dealers hold the deck in their left hand). This is known as a "handheld game." If the game is played with more than two decks, the stack of cards will be placed in a contraption called a "shoe," and is thus referred to as a "shoe game" or a "multiple-deck game."

In most casinos, the dealer will then "burn" one or more cards. "Burning" simply means removing the top card from the deck or decks and sticking it either on the bottom of the deck or in the discard rack.

In a handheld game, this will almost always be one card only, and the card will almost always be hidden from the players. In multiple-deck games, this can be more than one card. (In some casinos, the first card out is shown to the players, and that number of cards are then burned. For example, if a six is drawn, six cards are burned.)

The dealer then deals clockwise to the money on the table. One card goes to each betting circle containing a bet, and then the dealer gives herself her up-card. In a handheld game, this card is placed face up on the felt. In a shoe game, this card is (temporarily) positioned face down in front of the dealer. The dealer then provides a second card to each hand.

In games in which the dealer takes a hole card, she now gives herself a hole card. In handheld games, the hole card is jammed beneath the face up up-card. In shoe games, the hole card is pulled from the shoe and slid face down across the felt until it is next to the dealer's (currently) face down first card. The first card is then flipped face up on top of the hole card.

In most handheld games, the cards are dealt face down. In almost all multiple-deck games, the cards are dealt face up. Because the dealer makes no strategy decisions, and because the players are playing not against each other but against the dealer, it doesn't matter if the cards are face down or face up. However, it does matter in terms of table etiquette.

Face Down: You may touch your cards (you have to in order to see them, no?). You must lift both cards with the same hand, and you must keep the cards over the surface of the felt at all times. If you are playing more than one hand, you must complete your first hand (the one farthest to your right) before looking at the cards that constitute your next hand. The only exception to this is when the dealer has an ace up. Then you are allowed to look at all of your hands to decide whether or not to take insurance.

In the United States, dealers generally will not accept verbal signals like "hit" or "stand." The reason is that the guys in surveillance can't tell what's going on. Physical signals are used, as follows:

> **Hit**: Gently scratch the felt in front of you with your two cards, keeping your cards between you and your bet.
>
> **Stand:** Secure the two cards as one, and tuck them beneath your bet.
>
> **Double Down or Split:** Flip the cards face up on the felt, and shove a bet equal to your original bet next to (not on top of!) your original

bet. (In Europe, the dealer may place your new bet on top of your original bet if you double down.)

Blackjack: Immediately[35] slam the two cards face up on the felt and yell "Boom!"

Bust: Flip your two original cards face up and watch morosely as the dealer removes your cards and your money. Muttering is optional.

Face Up: You may _not_ touch your cards.

Hit: Scratch the felt behind your bet gently with your fingernail, or just sort of poke at the felt. (If you want a big card, poke _emphatically._)

Stand: Wave your hand parallel to the table top, palm down. (If you have a crappy hand, you might wave at the dealer as if shooing away a fly.)

Double Down or Split: Shove another bet out next to your original bet. The dealer will separate the two cards if you want to split, or simply give you a double-down card if you want to double. If there is any question (e.g., if you have a pair of fours or fives), the dealer will probably ask, "Double or split?" (To which the only correct answer is "Yes.")

Blackjack: Celebrate as the dealer pays you time and a half.

Bust: Dig around in your pocket to see if you have any more money.

Once all of the players have completed their hands, the dealer will then complete her hand. If she has 16 or less, she will take another card. If she has 17 or greater, she will stand. If she has soft 17 (A-6, or equivalent, such as A-3-3, or A-4-2, etc.), she will do whatever the rules of the casino dictate. Some joints hit soft 17; most stand.

The dealer then pays winning bets, takes losing bets, and pushes tie bets. Dealers often indicate pushes by patting the felt near the bet.

---

35 This is important. In some joints, if you tuck a blackjack, it may be treated as a regular 21, meaning (1) you will push if the dealer makes 21; or (2) you will win even money instead of time and a half if you win.

Casinos use two different methods for resolving hands: *lay and pay*, and *pick and pay*.

Lay and Pay: The cards remain on the layout until the dealer has resolved all of the hands. Then all of the cards are scooped from the layout and thrust into the discard rack. This method is used in most casinos, and at the vast majority of multiple-deck games.

Pick and Pay: The cards constituting each hand are removed from the layout and thrust into the discard rack as the hand is resolved. This method is used largely in handheld games.

Do *not* touch your bet until the dealer has paid you. If you think the dealer has made a mistake (e.g., she pushes your bet, but you think you won, or she didn't pay a blackjack correctly), do *not* touch your bet. It is good to get in the habit of keeping your hands in your lap—or at least on the rail—until the dealer has finished resolving all bets, and you are satisfied that she did everything correctly. Dealers are not automatons—they *do* make mistakes. It is up to you to catch any mistakes made in the casino's favor.

APPENDIX II:
BASIC STRATEGY

If you want to learn to play blackjack well, you must first learn what is called *Basic Strategy*. Although you will not be able to beat the game of blackjack by playing Basic Strategy, you will reduce the house advantage to a minimal level. Moreover, if you ever hope to make money playing blackjack, Basic Strategy is the foundation for everything that is to come later.

None of what follows is a matter of opinion. If you start playing blackjack seriously, you are going to learn that there is an absolute reality out there; one that is completely independent of opinion. There is a right way to play a hand, and a wrong way. If you persist in playing the wrong way, you will lose more money than you should. Period.

Basic Strategy is simply what you do with any given hand versus any given dealer up-card. The number of decks used and the particular rules for a given game can change the Basic Strategy for the game. However, as you will see, those differences will be relatively minor.

Terminology

Notice the terminology used for a two-card hand that contains an ace. An A-5 (that is, an ace and a five) is not referred to as "six or sixteen," despite what the dealer says. It is not played as a six; nor is it played as a sixteen. You should learn to refer to this hand as "ace-five." Once you learn to refer to soft hands this way, it will be easier to learn how to play them.

Similarly, pairs are referred to uniquely, not as the amount they total. An 8-8 is not "sixteen." It is "eight-eight," or, if you like, "a pair of eights." This hand is very rarely played as a sixteen, and therefore should not be referred to as such.

The Charts

For all of the following charts, the following legend applies:

H – Hit

S – Stand

D – Double Down

SP – Split

The rules that are assumed are referred to as Vegas Strip Rules. These are:

- Hit or stand with anything
- Double on any two initial cards
- No doubling after splits
- Split any pair
- Dealer stands on soft 17

Note that you are looking at Basic Strategy for any given two-card hand versus any given dealer up-card. What do you do when you have a multiple-card hand and are not allowed to make the correct play? This impacts double-down hands and, rarely, splits (splits are impacted when re-splitting is limited or forbidden).

For all multiple-card hands that total:	Play
11 or less	Hit
A-3, A-4, A-5, A-6	Hit
A-7, A-8	Stand
2-2	Play as 4
3-3	Play as 6
6-6	Play as 12

7-7	Play as 14
8-8	Play as 16
9-9	Stand

The way different rules impact various decisions will be explained at the bottom of each chart.

BASIC STRATEGY – SINGLE DECK

DEALER'S UP-CARD

♣	2	3	4	5	6	7	8	9	10	A
< 8	H	H	H	H	H	H	H	H	H	H
6-2	H	H	H	H	H	H	H	H	H	H
5-3	H	H	H	D	D	H	H	H	H	H
9	D	D	D	D	D	H	H	H	H	H
10	D	D	D	D	D	D	D	D	H	H
11	D	D	D	D	D	D	D	D	D	D
12	H	H	S	S	S	H	H	H	H	H
13	S	S	S	S	S	H	H	H	H	H
14	S	S	S	S	S	H	H	H	H	H
15	S	S	S	S	S	H	H	H	H	H
16	S	S	S	S	S	H	H	H	H	H
>16	S	S	S	S	S	S	S	S	S	S
A-2	H	H	D	D	D	H	H	H	H	H
A-3	H	H	D	D	D	H	H	H	H	H
A-4	H	H	D	D	D	H	H	H	H	H
A-5	H	H	D	D	D	H	H	H	H	H
A-6	D	D	D	D	D	H	H	H	H	H
A-7	S	D	D	D	D	S	S	H	H	S
A-8	S	S	S	S	D	S	S	S	S	S
A-9	S	S	S	S	S	S	S	S	S	S
A-A	SP	SP	SP	SP	SP	SP	SP	SP	SP	SP
2-2	H	SP	SP	SP	SP	SP	H	H	H	H
3-3	H	H	SP	SP	SP	SP	H	H	H	H
4-4	H	H	H	D	D	H	H	H	H	H
5-5	D	D	D	D	D	D	D	D	H	H
6-6	SP	SP	SP	SP	SP	H	H	H	H	H
7-7	SP	SP	SP	SP	SP	SP	H	H	S	H
8-8	SP	SP	SP	SP	SP	SP	SP	SP	SP	SP
9-9	SP	SP	SP	SP	SP	S	SP	SP	S	S
10-10	S	S	S	S	S	S	S	S	S	S

P L A Y E R' S   H A N D

If Double After Splits is allowed:	If Conventional Surrender is allowed:
Split 2-2, 3-3, 6-6 vs. 2, 3, 4, 5, 6, 7 up	Surrender 16 (not 8-8) vs. 10, A
Split 4-4 vs. 4, 5, 6 up	Surrender 15 vs. 10
Split 7-7 vs. 2, 3, 4, 5, 6, 7, 8 up	Surrender 7-7 vs. 10
If you lose all to dealer's blackjack:	**If Soft Doubling is not allowed:**
Do NOT split 8-8 vs. 10 or A	Hit A-2,A-3,A-4,A-5,A-6 vs. 3, 4, 5, 6
Do NOT split A-A vs. A	Stand A-7 and A-8 vs. 3, 4, 5, 6
Do NOT double 11 vs. 10 or A	
If the dealer hits soft 17:	
Hit A-7 vs. A	

BASIC STRATEGY – MULTIPLE DECK

DEALER'S UP-CARD

PLAYER'S HAND

♣	2	3	4	5	6	7	8	9	10	A
< 9	H	H	H	H	H	H	H	H	H	H
9	H	D	D	D	D	H	H	H	H	H
10	D	D	D	D	D	D	D	D	H	H
11	D	D	D	D	D	D	D	D	D	H
12	H	H	S	S	S	H	H	H	H	H
13	S	S	S	S	S	H	H	H	H	H
14	S	S	S	S	S	H	H	H	H	H
15	S	S	S	S	S	H	H	H	H	H
16	S	S	S	S	S	H	H	H	H	H
> 16	S	S	S	S	S	S	S	S	S	S
A-2	H	H	H	D	D	H	H	H	H	H
A-3	H	H	H	D	D	H	H	H	H	H
A-4	H	H	D	D	D	H	H	H	H	H
A-5	H	H	D	D	D	H	H	H	H	H
A-6	H	D	D	D	D	H	H	H	H	H
A-7	S	D	D	D	D	S	S	H	H	H
A-8	S	S	S	S	S	S	S	S	S	S
A-9	S	S	S	S	S	S	S	S	S	S
A-A	SP	SP	SP	SP	SP	SP	SP	SP	SP	SP
2-2	H	H	SP	SP	SP	SP	H	H	H	H
3-3	H	H	SP	SP	SP	SP	H	H	H	H
4-4	H	H	H	H	H	H	H	H	H	H
5-5	D	D	D	D	D	D	D	D	H	H
6-6	H	SP	SP	SP	SP	H	H	H	H	H
7-7	SP	SP	SP	SP	SP	SP	H	H	H	H
8-8	SP	SP	SP	SP	SP	SP	SP	SP	SP	SP
9-9	SP	SP	SP	SP	SP	S	SP	SP	S	S
10-10	S	S	S	S	S	S	S	S	S	S

If Double After Splits is allowed:	If Conventional Surrender is allowed:
Split 2-2, 3-3 vs. 2, 3, 4, 5, 6, 7 up	Surrender 16 (not 8-8) vs. 9, 10, A
Split 6-6 vs. 2, 3, 4, 5, 6 up	Surrender 15 vs. 10
Split 4-4 vs. 5, 6 up	
Split 7-7 vs. 2, 3, 4, 5, 6, 7, 8 up	**If Early Surrender is allowed:**
	Surrender 5, 6, 7, and 12–17 vs. A
If you lose all to dealer's blackjack:	Surrender 14, 15, 16, 7-7 and 8-8 vs. 10
Do NOT split 8-8 vs. 10 or A	Surrender 16 (not 8-8) vs. 9
Do NOT split A-A vs. A	
Do NOT double 11 vs. 10	**If the dealer hits soft 17:**
	No changes
If Soft Doubling is not allowed:	
Hit A-2 – A-6 vs. 3, 4, 5, 6	
Stand A-7 vs. 3, 4, 5, 6	

Note: Full-color versions of these charts can be found at http://www. markbillings21.com.

Practice

What follows is the way in which Taylor and his teammates trained prospective players to play Basic Strategy. There were three steps:

1. Index Cards

To learn Basic Strategy, first create index cards for the game you wish to learn—one card for every possible hand versus every possible up-card (you'll end up with about 280 cards). Put a hand in large digits on the card, and the correct play in the lower left-hand corner (right-hand corner if you are left-handed), using letters small enough so they will be hidden by your thumb when holding the cards normally, as follows:

```
┌─────────────────────────┐
│                         │
│     9-9 vs. 3           │
│                         │
│  SP                     │
└─────────────────────────┘
```

Note: Complete sets of index cards can be found at http://www. markbillings21.com.

Once you can flip through these cards virtually without hesitation, getting every play correct, you are ready to move on to the next step.

By now you will have implanted in your mind such plays as "thirteen against a four, stand." Now you have to recognize what that "thirteen" really looks like.

2. Practice Deck I

Remove 12 of the 16 tens from a regular deck and set them aside (this will greatly reduce the number of pat hard hands you receive). Find a 2 in the deck, and place it face up on the table. This will serve as the dealer's up-card. Now deal pairs of cards in front of you, announcing the correct play for each. Once you've completed the deck, find a 3 to use as the up-card, and go through the deck again. Do this for each card value in the deck.

As you already know Basic Strategy, it should not take long before you progress from the "thirteen against a four, stand" that already exists in your head to recognizing what "thirteen against a four" looks like when it is sitting in front of you on the table.

3. Practice Deck II

The last thing to do is make a practice deck that will provide many of the hands that tend to give novice players trouble ("soft" hands, and pairs). Add eight aces and four nines to the deck that currently is missing 12 tens. This will provide many soft hands, as well as a greater-than-normal number of pairs of nines. Go through the workout under Practice Deck I using this deck. However, this time, keep hitting hands until you get to the point at which you should stand.

For example, if you have 6 vs. 4, you think "hit." Give yourself a card. Let's say you hit with a 3. You now think "nine vs. four, hit." (Note that you can't double, because you have more than two cards.) Hit it again. Let's say you hit with a 5. You think "fourteen against a four, stand." You are done with the hand.

This will provide practice with multiple-card totals and soft totals, as well as help you recognize the difference between soft and hard hands.

Once you can get through the deck rapidly with each dealer up-card, you are ready for the final drill.

1. Shuffle Practice Deck II.

2. Deal out an up-card, and give yourself a two-card hand.

    a. Always put the dealer's up-card out first. This way, you will get used to looking at the dealer's card first.

3. Play out your two-card hand.

4. Check your work.

5. Sweep the cards aside, and deal another hand.

Once you can do this quickly and accurately, you are ready to play Basic Strategy in a casino.

Insurance

When playing Basic Strategy, never take insurance.

Why not, you ask? Well, the logic that underlies the insurance decision is a microcosm of the logical underpinnings of Basic Strategy itself, and a microcosm of the fundamentals that underlie card counting as well.

First, the name "insurance" is a misnomer. A more disingenuous name has never been affixed to a betting proposition.

Most blackjack players think that the insurance bet is just that—a way to "insure" one's hand against the dealer's possible blackjack. Most players draw the casino-inspired analogy between blackjack insurance and insurance in the everyday sense of the word, such as automobile insurance, for example. One insures a shiny new Mercedes. One does not waste one's money insuring a broken-down Oldsmobile.

Likewise, many blackjack players feel the urge to insure good hands. A hand that totals 20 seems to be worth protecting with an insurance bet. Insuring a miserable hand totaling 13 is like spending good money to insure a rusted-out Dodge Colt.

This is how the majority of blackjack players view the insurance bet, which is precisely why the casinos named the bet "insurance." However, from this moment on, you should no longer think of the insurance bet as "insurance."

From this day forward, you should think of insurance as a *completely separate bet*. When you take insurance, you are betting that the dealer has a ten beneath her ace (in Europe, you are betting the dealer will hit her ace with a ten). That's all. Whether your hand totals 15 or 20 is completely irrelevant. Insurance is a *side bet*, and has *nothing* to do with your original hand. Your original hand will sink or swim on its own.

Here's how insurance works: if the dealer has an ace up, you are allowed to bet up to half the amount you have bet on your hand. If you win (that is, if the dealer has a ten in the hole), you win twice your insurance bet. If you lose, you lose your insurance bet.

Because insurance pays 2 to 1, you would have to win one insurance bet out of three to break even. This can be demonstrated as follows:

- Hand #1 – bet $10, insure for $5, lose. You have made one insurance bet, and are down $5.

- Hand #2 – bet $10, insure for $5, lose. You have made two insurance bets, and are down $10.

- Hand #3 – bet $10, insure for $5, win. You are paid 2 to 1 ($10). You have made three insurance bets, have won one bet out of three, and are now even.

Hence, insurance is an even bet if you win one out of every three bets. If you were to win more than one out of three bets, insurance would be a profitable bet; that is, you would have an edge. If you were to win less than one out of three bets, insurance would not be a profitable bet; that is, the house would have an edge.

Question: When would you win more than one insurance bet out of three?

Answer: You would win more than one insurance bet out of three when the dealer's chance of having a ten in the hole is greater than one out of three (i.e., when the dealer will have a ten in the hole more than 33.33 percent of the time).

A deck of 52 cards contains 16 ten-value cards and 36 non-tens. In the long run, the dealer will have a ten in the hole 30.77 percent of the time (16/52). As this is less than 33.33 percent, the house has an edge off the top of the deck.

However, we haven't yet considered the dealer up-card or the cards that constitute your hand. Let's give the dealer her ace up-card, and give you a pair of twos. Now 49 cards remain, consisting of 16 tens and 33 non-tens. With this subset, the dealer will have a ten in the hole 32.65 percent of the time (16/49). This is still less than 33.33 percent; so insurance is never the proper play off the top of a single deck.

And we are looking at the best possible situation for insurance—three non-tens have been removed. If you had a pair of tens (a "good" hand that you might think is "worth insuring"), you can see that the dealer will now have a ten in the hole 14/49 times, or only 28.57 percent of the time. Now do you see why they call it "insurance"? Good hands—those of 19 and 20—tend to contain a ten or two, meaning the insurance bet is even worse when you have a good hand than it is normally.

However, get this. Let's say you once again have your pair of twos. The dealer has an ace up. You lean over and "happen" to see the cards belonging to the player to your right—he has two non-tens (assume he has a pair of eights). Now let's do the math.

There are 47 unplayed cards left, of which 16 are tens. The dealer's chances of having a ten in the hole are 16/47, or 34.04 percent. This is in fact greater than 33.33 percent, meaning that you will win your insurance bet greater than one time in three, meaning you have an edge. Take insurance.

So, why did this section begin with the admonition never to take insurance when playing Basic Strategy? Because Basic Strategy always assumes knowledge of the two cards that constitute your hand, the dealer's up-card, and *that's all*. When you start bringing the effects of removing other cards into your decision-making process, you are now spilling over into the bailiwick of card counting. And that is what appendix 3 is all about.

Note: When playing Basic Strategy against a four-deck shoe, there is never a time when your insurance bet has an edge, even if (a) you are playing at a full table; (b) you can see everyone's cards; and (c) not a single ten has been dealt out.

A four-deck shoe contains 64 tens out of 208 cards. A full table consists of seven hands, each of which contains two cards. That's 14 non-tens. The dealer's ace up-card makes 15 non-tens, meaning the remaining subset contains 64 tens out of 193 cards, giving you a percentage of 33.16 percent tens to non-tens. As this is less than 33.33 percent, insurance is not warranted.

However, assume you saw the burn card, and it also was a non-ten. Now you have a ratio of 64/192, giving you a percentage of 33.33 percent. Insurance is now a dead-even bet. Flip a coin.

Better yet, here's your opportunity to insure good hands! Brian and Taylor had this argument back in 1984, and it was settled—as were so many disputes of this sort—by the great Peter Griffin himself.

Bear in mind that insurance at this point is an even bet, so the issue is not profit. In the long run, you will break exactly even on insurance when the ratio of tens to non-tens is 1 to 2. So the argument has nothing to do with making money. It has to do with fluctuations.

Brian argued that any time you put extra money out on the layout, you increase fluctuations. Taylor argued that insuring good hands would reduce fluctuations, because you reduce the number of times you lose a full bet. You will occasionally lose a bet and a half (when you lose both your insurance bet and your hand), but most of the time you will either (a) push; that is, you lose your bet but win 2 to 1 on insurance, effectively pushing; or (b) lose your insurance bet and win your hand, thus winning a half a bet.

Taylor was right.

The clearest way to see why Taylor was right is to examine the so-called *even money* insurance bet.

If you've played blackjack for more than a few hours, you've experienced the following: the dealer has an ace up-card, and someone is dealt a blackjack. The other players immediately start shouting, "Even money!"

"It's the only sure bet in the game," someone will invariably say.

Here's how it works. Let's say you bet $10. The dealer has an ace up, and you have a blackjack. You take insurance, putting $5 out on the insurance line. One of two things will happen:

Dealer Has Blackjack	Dealer Does Not Have Blackjack
You push your hand	You win your hand, and are paid $15
You win 2 to 1 on your $5 insurance bet ($10)	You lose your $5 insurance bet
Net: You clear $10.	Net: You clear $10.

Note that in either event, you clear $10, which is the amount you bet in the first place. That is why you can simply say "even money" when you have a blackjack against a dealer's ace. And this is why the players call this "the only sure bet in the game."

Here's what happens if you do not take insurance:

Dealer Has Blackjack	Dealer Does Not Have Blackjack
You push your hand	You win your hand, and are paid $15
Net: You clear $0.	Net: You clear $15.

So, by foregoing the insurance bet, you will win the $15 slightly more than two times out of three, and will push the hand slightly less than one time in three. In the long run, if you do not take insurance you will make a little more than $10 per hand when the dealer has an ace up and you have a blackjack. Therefore, although it is the case that even money is a "sure thing," it will cost you money in the long run.

However, if the ratio of tens to non-tens is exactly 1 to 2 (thereby rendering the insurance bet dead even), you can see how taking even money will reduce fluctuations. Instead of either winning $15 or winning nothing, you are guaranteed to win $10. Your fluctuation on that hand has been reduced to zero.

This argument is diluted slightly for good hands (20 and, to a lesser extent, 19), but still holds.

"What have the Romans done for us?"

If you plan to become a professional player, Basic Strategy is a *sine qua non*; a foundation without which you can never become a winning player. However, if you are a casual player, why bother? To paraphrase the classic Monty Python line above, "What does Basic Strategy do for us?"

Here's what it does. By learning Basic Strategy, you will play with a minimal disadvantage against the house. You will not win in the long run, but you will lose a very small percentage of what you bet.

That may not sound like a very good deal. However, if you are already playing blackjack, you can reduce your expected loss to a minimal amount. If you are currently an average player, you are probably losing between two and three times what you will lose by learning and playing Basic Strategy.

Beyond that, think about this: most casinos offer comps. Lots of them. These can add up to a remarkable amount of goodies.

Let's say you play at one of the larger casinos on the Las Vegas Strip. You play $100 per hand, and you play at full tables. At 75 hands per hour, you will put $7,500 per hour into play.

That may sound like you are risking a lot. However, if you are playing Basic Strategy at a standard six-deck game, your expectation is to lose 0.63 percent of that, or $47.25 per hour. If you play for three hours, you could easily get a damn nice room and a great meal with an expectation of losing less than $150.

If you bet your $100 whenever a pit boss is hanging around your table, and $50 at other times, you may be able to drop your expected loss to about $30 per hour, while still looking to the pit like a $100 per hand bettor. Your room and meal will cost you ninety bucks in expectation.

Bear in mind that you will experience large fluctuations around your small negative expectation, just as card counters experience large fluctuations around their small positive expectation. (The big difference: the card counters will win in the long run. You will lose, even if you learn to play Basic Strategy perfectly.) Due to these fluctuations, you will occasionally win thousands. You must resist the impulse to go out and spend those winnings. Don't do it. You must view this as a fluctuation which you will, in all likelihood, pay for someday if you keep playing.

Off-the-top Disadvantage

Here is how to figure out how much a given game will cost you to play, assuming you play perfect Basic Strategy:

1. Start out with the number of decks.

Table 1: Off-the-top Deck Advantage (player)

# of Decks	Your Advantage
1 deck	0.0%
2 decks	−0.35%
4 decks	−0.48%
6 decks	−0.63%
8 decks	−0.67%

2. Now add or subtract the following:

Table 2: Rule Advantage (player)

Rule	Effect on You*
No double on 9	0.1%
No double on 8,7,6	−0.0%
No soft double	−0.1%
Dealer hits soft 17	−0.2%
No hole card (dealer takes both)	−0.1%
Double After Splits	+0.1%
Double any number of cards	+0.2%
Resplit aces (single deck)	+0.0%
Resplit aces (multiple deck)	+0.1%
No resplit non-aces	0.0%
Draw to split aces	+0.1%
Surrender (single deck)	+0.0%
Surrender (multiple deck)	+0.1%
Early Surrender	+0.6%
2-to-1 blackjack payout	+2.3%

*these are rounded off to the nearest 0.1%.

Let's look at an example. Let's say you are playing a four-deck game in England. Start with the four-deck advantage of −0.48 percent. Now, here are the rules, the applicable rule from above, and the impact these have on you:

British Rules	Applicable Rule From Above	Impact
Dealer stands on all soft 17s (A-6)	Implicit in Vegas Strip Rules	None
Doubling is allowed on hard totals of 9, 10, or 11 only	No double on 8,7,6; and No soft double	0.0% −0.1%

Players may split any pair except 4s, 5s, or tens	Basic Strategy players never split 4s, 5s, or 10s, therefore no impact	None
Players may not resplit	No resplit non-aces	0.0%
Players may double down after splitting	Double After Splits	+0.1%
If the dealer makes a blackjack, players lose both bets if they have doubled or split	No Hole Card (dealer takes both)	–0.1%
Insurance is offered only when the player has a blackjack	Basic Strategy players never take insurance, therefore no impact	None

Adding these impacts gives you –0.1 percent. Added to the four-deck advantage of –0.48 percent gives you a Basic Strategy disadvantage of 0.58 percent, rounded to 0.6 percent. Therefore, you can expect to lose about 60p for every £100 bet when playing a four-deck game in Great Britain.

Note that playing the exact same game but increasing the number of decks to six increases your disadvantage by 0.15 percent.

APPENDIX III:

CARD COUNTING

This appendix is not meant to teach you how to count cards. There are literally dozens of good books available that teach card counting, a number of which can be found in the Bibliography. However, there are some time-tested practice strategies offered, as well as some explanations—truing, Kelly betting, the concept of an edge, etc.—that you may find helpful.

Card counting begins with Basic Strategy. When you look at the dealer's up-card, and then the cards in your hand, a play should pop into your head immediately. If you have to think about a hand for a second or so, you are not ready to begin counting cards.

When you count cards, you will assign positive, negative, and neutral values to the various cards. There are literally dozens of counts from which to choose, but they all basically do the same thing: keep track of big cards versus small cards.

There are three aspects of the game for which you will use the count as an indicator:

1. When and how much to bet;
2. How to play your hands; and
3. Whether or not to take insurance.

If you are going to play single-deck games, a complex count might be worth learning, because a complex count can help with the play of the hands. However, as the vast majority of games in the world are multiple-deck games, it is strongly recommended that you learn a simple count that focuses largely on #1, above: betting. Because of the diluted *effects of removal* in multiple-deck games (see pp. 97–98), using complex counts that assign different values to twos, threes, fours, and fives is a waste of time and effort.

The simplest counts are known as *one-level counts*. This means that you will not be dealing with card value assignments larger than one. There are basically two kinds of counts: ace-neutral counts and ace-incorporated counts. Do yourself a favor: choose a count for which the ace is incorporated in the count. This will be explained later; for now, you should know that there are ace-neutral counts that count the ace as zero, and require the player to keep a separate count of the number of aces remaining to be dealt. This is arguably worthwhile for single-deck play, but is a huge waste of time and energy when playing multiple-deck games.

The simplest count for which aces are incorporated is known as the "Hi-Lo" or "High-Low" count. It assigns cards the following values:

Table 1: Card Values

CARD	POINT VALUE
2, 3, 4, 5, 6	+1
7, 8, 9	0
All ten-value cards	−1
Aces	−1

One thing you should know about card counting: it does not take intelligence in the traditional sense of the word. There is really not a hell of a lot to figure out. Card counting does, however, take practice. A lot of practice.

It is quite easy to predict which players will ultimately learn how to count cards properly. Here is the instruction set:

Table 2: Predictor of Card Counting Success

INDICATOR	PREDICTIVE VALUE (%)
Grade point average in high school	0
Years of education	0
Number of scholastic degrees	0
IQ	0
Height	0
Weight	0
Sex	0
# of decks of cards worn out while practicing	100

PRACTICE

1. Counting Down Decks

Take a deck of cards and deal the cards out one at a time face up in front of you. Announce the value of each card as you see it, and do so *out loud*. For example, when an ace comes out, say "minus one." When a 2 comes out, say "plus one." When a 7 comes out, say "zero." After only a few decks, you should start to see some improvement in speed.

Once the card values are coming to you reasonably automatically, it is time to start counting.

Shuffle the cards and flip the top card face up. Announce its value. Now flip the second card. Instead of announcing the value, add its value to the value you have in your head. For example, if the first card out is a 2, you would say "plus one." If the next card out is a 4, you would now have to add +1 to the count in your head, which is "plus one," giving you a *running count* of "plus two." If the next card out is a ten (value of −1), your running count would now drop to "plus one."

Continue through the entire deck. If you've counted correctly, you will have a count of zero when you count the last card.

Focus on accuracy, not speed. Speed comes with practice. For most people, it takes quite a few decks before they can do this in less than a minute.

To make this more interesting, remove a card from the deck without looking at it. Then count the remaining 51 cards. You should be able to predict the last card, as follows:

- If your count at the end was −1, the last card should be a +1-value card (2, 3, 4, 5, or 6)

- If your count at the end was +1, the last card should be a −1-value card (ten or ace)

- If your count at the end was 0, the last card should be a 0-value card (7, 8, or 9)

Before you move on to the next step, you should have your single-deck time down to less than 25 seconds.

Once you can count down a deck in less than 25 seconds and predict the last card 49 times out of 50, you can move on to the next step: flipping two cards at a time face up and counting those in "chunks." In some ways, you will find that this is actually easier than counting one card at a time, because many two-card chunks cancel out. For example, if you have a thirteen that consists of a ten and a 3, your running count doesn't change— the +1 for the 3 cancels the −1 for the ten. Boom. Move on to the next chunk.

This two-card "chunking" will come in very handy when you begin to count actual hands. This is because blackjack hands do in fact consist of two cards each—at least to start.

2. Counting and Playing Hands

Once you can chunk two-card hands quickly and accurately, have someone deal to you. Remember to look at the dealer's up-card first, just as you did when you were learning Basic Strategy. However, this time you will be looking at the up-card not as a card but as a *value* (+1, −1, or 0). (This takes a little getting used to.) Count the dealer's up-card, and then add to it the count of the cards that constitute your hand.

Once you have the count embedded in your brain ("plus three, plus three, plus three…"), look at the dealer's up-card and your hand not as values, but as a *hand to be played*, just as you did when you were learning Basic Strategy. (This is why you need to have Basic Strategy down *cold* before you start to learn to count. If at this point you have to think about what to do with your hand, you are going to lose the count.)

For everyone who has ever learned to count cards, this is where the proverbial rubber meets the road. To a man, all of the players written about in this book had some version of the same initial meltdown. They had learned Basic Strategy, they had learned to count down decks, and they were looking at an actual hand for the first time. And that's when all hell broke loose.

For Taylor, it was a simple play—eleven against a three. Steve had a 3 up-card ("plus one"), and Taylor's hand consisted of a 7 and a 4 ("plus two, plus two…"). He had the count nailed. Now he stared at his cards, and could not for the life of him figure out what the hell he had in his hand.

Just remember: this confusion will pass. Relax. Take your time. Stare at the cards. Before long, you'll be able to figure out that you have an 11 against a 3, and the correct play (double!) will pop into your head.

You will spend a considerable amount of time on this step. Don't rush. It will take a while for your brain to separate the two tasks you are demanding of it—viewing a hand consisting of a 7 and a 4 as a count of +1, and viewing the same hand as an 11. This separation will happen if you practice. But *only* if you practice. There is no substitute. According to Reed, drinking does *not* help.

Because of your Basic Strategy practice, you will begin to recognize two-card hands relatively quickly. Then you will have to deal with three-, four-, five-, and even six-card hands. Just keep practicing.

Once you can play your hand while keeping track of the count, you should have your friend deal out multiple hands the way they are dealt out in real casinos; that is, the dealer deals one card face up to each spot on the layout, starting with the spot to her left ("first base") and finishing with the spot to her right ("third base"). She then deals herself her up-card. (In most of Europe, this card is dealt face up. However, in much of North America, the Caribbean, and certain other lands, this soon-to-be dealer up-card is initially dealt face down.) The dealer then proceeds clockwise around the table, from first base to third, providing each spot with a second card face up. (In most of Europe, the dealer stops dealing when she reaches third base. However, in certain other lands, the dealer deals herself a "hole card"—a face down card onto which her until now face down up-card is turned face up.) The players then play their hands, beginning with the player at first base.

You may already know all this. The reason for this belaboring of the obvious is that, once you begin to count cards as they are dealt out at a real blackjack table, you are going to make a decision that will affect the way you count for the rest of your life. You must decide the order in which you are going to count the cards that are dealt out on the table.

There are a number of ways you can do this.

- You can count each card as it is exposed; that is, you count the first baseman's first card first, and follow the dealer around the table as each card is dealt out, counting the dealer's up-card in midstream (in casinos where the dealer's up-card is exposed immediately), and follow the dealer around the layout again as the players each receive their second card.

- You can count each card as it is exposed; that is, you count the first baseman's first card first, and follow the dealer around the table as each card is dealt out, skipping the dealer's not-yet-exposed up-card (in casinos where the dealer's up-card is *not* exposed immediately), and follow the dealer around the layout again as the players each receive their second card.

- You can wait until each player has two cards, count the dealer's up-card first, and then count the cards in pairs ("chunks") as they lay upon the table, working your way from first base to third, and then counting the various hit cards as they are dealt out. (This is how most pros count.)

- You can count the dealer's up-card first, and then count the players' hands one at a time as they play them, and count the dealer's hit cards last.

- You can count the first baseman's hand first, count the other players' hands one at a time as they play them, and then count the dealer's hand last when she plays it.

And there are other methods you can develop yourself. It doesn't matter which method you choose.[36] They all work. The point is, you should find a method of card counting you're comfortable with and *stick with it*. If you decide to count the dealer's up-card first, *always* count the dealer's up-card first. If you decide to count the first baseman's cards first, *always* count the first baseman's cards first. Once you decide to use one method exclusively, your eyes will automatically go to the right place on the layout, and your brain will begin to count the round. Always using the same order when counting cards means you will always know which cards you have already counted and which cards you haven't.

Once you begin to practice, the above paragraph will make a lot more sense. Before you begin serious practice with multiple hands, you should have decided upon your count methodology.

3. Whence Your Advantage: A Digression

Once you can accurately count six or seven hands at a time, and play one or two of those hands quickly and correctly, you are ready to make use of that count you have worked so hard to maintain.

By now you probably know that a positive count is good for you. This is because a preponderance of small cards must be removed for the count to go up. When small cards have been removed, that means a preponderance of big cards (tens and aces) remain.

Table 3 and the explanation that follows show exactly why a preponderance of tens and aces is good for the player:

---

36 Strictly speaking, the more cards you count before you decide how to play your hand(s)—to be dealt with later—the more accurate your playing decision will be. However, counting a couple of extra cards before playing your hand(s) will gain you perhaps a few hundredths of a percent in the long run. Counting cards in the way most comfortable for you will enable you to count those cards rapidly and accurately, and will gain you far more in winnings than those few extra cards ever will. Do what is most comfortable for you.

Table 3: Dealer-Player Comparison

HAND TYPE	DEALER	PLAYER
1. Blackjack	Wins even money (the amount bet) when she gets a blackjack	Wins 150% of amount bet for blackjack
2. Double Down	May not double down	Option to double down
3. Pair	May not split pairs	Option to split pairs
4. Stiff	May not stand short (must hit 16 or fewer; must stand with 17 or higher)	Option to stand with (or hit) anything
5. Ace Up-Card	May not take insurance	Option to take insurance

Given what you now know about the game, you can figure out the following:

1. Blackjack: Blackjack consists of a ten and an ace. Blackjacks are much better for the player than for the dealer; therefore, the more tens and aces left, the better it is for the player. (In the long run, you and the dealer will receive the same number of blackjacks. You will get time and a half for yours; she'll only get even money for hers.)

2. Double Down: If you think about when you double down, you'll see that you often hope to get a ten (when you double with 8, 9, 10, or 11), or an ace (when you double with 8, 9, or 10), and you almost always hope the dealer has a ten in the hole, and hits with a ten. Therefore, tens, and to a lesser extent aces, are good for doubling down. However, since the dealer does not have the option to double down, tens and aces are good for the player, but not for the dealer. (In the long run, you and the dealer will receive the same number of double-down hands. You will double when it is profitable; she cannot.)

3. Split Pairs: If you think about when you split, there are basically two kinds of splits: offensive splits and defensive splits.

Offensive splits are those splits you make when the dealer is likely to bust, and you want to get as much money out as possible; or, when you have two good cards (like a pair of nines) and hope to make two good hands (two of 19) instead of one pretty good hand (one 18). All splits against dealer stiff cards are offensive splits.

Defensive splits are those splits you make to reduce your loss. Splitting eights against a nine or ten is not a good play, but the alternative (playing your hand as 16) is worse.

For all offensive splits, an abundance of tens remaining to be dealt is a good thing. In virtually all cases, you are hoping the dealer has a ten in the hole and hits with another ten. (The 7 up-card is an exception to this.) Defensive splits are a little more complicated; however, for the most part, extra tens are good for splitting. Since splitting is not an option for the dealer, extra tens are good for the player and not for the dealer.

4. Stiff: This one is easy. Whenever you stand short (that is, stand with a total of less than 17), there is one and only one way you can win your hand—if the dealer busts. Note that you stand short against dealer up-cards of 2, 3, 4, 5, and 6, meaning if the dealer has a ten in the hole and hits with a ten, you win. Since the dealer cannot stand short, tens benefit the player and not the dealer.

Bear in mind that, as always, we are talking about the *long run*. In the long run, the dealer will beat your nineteen with a twenty as often as your twenty will beat her nineteen. In the long run, you will have a stiff against the dealer's pat hand as often as you have a pat against the dealer's stiff hand. In these cases, the preponderance of tens does not give you an edge.

However, it is when you and the dealer are both stiff that this edge manifests itself. You have the option to stand with your stiff; the dealer does not. (Is this rare? Relatively. That is why a card counter's edge is only around 1 percent.)

5. Ace Up-Card: This is similarly easy. When you take insurance, you are betting the dealer has a ten in the hole. The dealer cannot take insurance. Therefore, tens are beneficial to you and not to her.

So, we know that "an abundance" or "a preponderance" of tens and aces is good for us. But how many extra tens and aces constitutes "a preponderance"?

The answer to that is: it depends. A more specific answer is: it depends on how many decks are being used.

4. Truing

If there is an aspect of card counting that could be considered difficult, it would be truing. However, if you can divide, you can true.

Truing is necessary because of the dilution of effects of removal as the number of decks increase, as explained in chapter 6. When you remove one 5 from a single deck, you have removed one-quarter (25 percent) of the fives in the deck. When you remove one 5 from a six-deck shoe, you have removed only one twenty-fourth (4.167 percent) of the fives in the deck. What truing does is correct for this dilution of the effects of removal. In short, the +1 count you have at the top of a six-deck shoe is only one-sixth as powerful as the same +1 count at the top of a single deck.

The Hi-Lo count indicates a 0.5 percent advantage for every *true count*, or *count-per-deck* of 1. This means that if you have a true count of three, you have an advantage of 1.5 percent on the upcoming hand. But what is a *true count?*

> Your true count is your running count, adjusted for
> the number of decks remaining to be dealt.

Another way of saying this is:

> Your true count is your running count *divided by* the
> number of decks remaining to be dealt.

Let's say you are playing a four-deck game in which one deck has been dealt out, meaning there are three decks left. If you have a running count of +3, you have a true count of 1 (your running count divided by the number of decks remaining to be dealt).

You already know how to figure out your *off-the-top disadvantage*, using the rules of the game and the number of decks (see appendix 2). Let's say you are playing a four-deck game on the Vegas Strip. You have an off-the-top disadvantage of 0.48 percent. Make it 0.5 percent. This off-the-top disadvantage must be subtracted from your indicated count advantage to figure out your actual advantage. In the above example, a true of three indicates an advantage of 1.5 percent. From this we must subtract the off-the-top disadvantage of 0.5 percent, leaving you with an actual advantage of 1 percent.

This may sound daunting, and it is—at first. However, there are a number of shortcuts you can take.

1. You don't have to true when the count is hovering around zero, or is negative.

2. You will learn to figure out how much to bet *in chips* with any given true count before you go out to play. You won't be making the above calculation at the table for every hand.

This is big. Betting is explained in the next section. Suffice it to say here that you will not be saying, "Uh, running count of twelve, two decks left, divide by two, true of six, three percent edge, subtract the off-the-top disadvantage of half a percent, leaves two and a half percent, two and a half percent of ten grand is two hundred and fifty dollars."

Instead, you will be saying, "Running count of twelve, two decks left, true of six, subtract one, and bet half of that in black chips."

Like everything else about learning to count, truing takes practice. You first have to be able to estimate the number of decks remaining to be dealt. You will do this by learning to estimate the number of cards in the discard rack.

Make up packets of cards consisting of ½ deck, 1 deck, 1½ decks, 2 decks, 2½ decks, 3 decks, 3½ decks, 4 decks, 4½ decks, and 5 decks. Rubber-band them, and label the bottom card so you'll know which packet is which (you can either write "1½" on the bottom card of the 1½ deck packet, or write it on a piece of paper and slip it under the rubber band holding the packet together).

Now put all of the packets in a shoe box. Grab one at random, put it on the table in front of you, and guess how many decks are sitting in front of you. Check your work.

Once you can recognize a stack of cards to within a half deck, you can begin working on what to do with this information. First, you should focus on one game—four decks or six decks. Let's assume you are going to practice for a six-deck game.

Your job is to translate the number of decks in the discard rack into the number of decks left to be played. If you see a half deck in the discard rack, it means there are five and a half decks to be dealt. If you see one deck in the discard rack, it means there are five decks left to be dealt. And so on.

This is important. There have been players who learn to estimate the number of cards in the discard rack, but use that number (instead of using that number as an indicator of the number of decks left to be dealt). As a result, their truing was far from true.

> Remember: you are going to divide your running count by the number of decks *remaining to be dealt*.

Now comes the final practice. Write the numbers 1 through 30 on index cards, one number on each card. Shuffle the index cards and place them face down on the table. Take the top card and turn it face up. This will represent your running count. Then grab a packet from the shoe box and place it on the table near the index card. True the running count displayed on the index cards based upon the packet you are looking at.

Example #1: You turn up a 20, and pull 1 deck out of the shoe box. You say, "running count of twenty, one deck in the discard rack, five left, divide by five, true of four."

Example #2: You turn up a 15, and pull 3 decks out of the shoe box. You say, "running count of fifteen, three decks in the discard rack, three left, divide by three, true of five."

Example #3: You turn up a 13, and pull 4 decks out of the shoe box. You say, "running count of thirteen, four decks in the discard rack, two left, divide by two, true of more than six (but less than seven)."

The last example is instructive. When truing, you should always be conservative. That means *round down*. Round down when using your true count to determine how much to bet, and round down when estimating the number of cards in the discard rack.

If the cards in the discard rack are between one deck and one and a half decks, use one deck. This will help prevent overbetting, and will help ensure that you change Basic Strategy correctly.

Note that the deeper into the shoe you get, the more powerful any given running count will be.

When truing, it is critical that you keep your running count in your head. This is the aspect of truing that gives players the most trouble, especially at first. You have a running count of 12, you glance at the discard rack, you estimate that there are two decks there, you divide by four, you have a true count of 3, giving you an advantage of 1.5 percent, you subtract the off-the-top disadvantage of 0.5 percent, leaving you with an edge of 1 percent, meaning you bet $100. The dealer begins to deal. Now, what was your running count again?

5. BETTING

In the long run, the size of your bets and the size of your bet spread will determine how much money you will make counting cards. The size of your bets will be a function of two things: your edge on the upcoming hand and the size of your bankroll. Your bet spread will similarly be a function of two things: the size of your *cojones*.

Before we get to that, however, we must deal with something that the overwhelming majority of gamblers either do not understand, or understand only poorly. It is the concept of an edge.

What Is an Edge?

One of the most difficult concepts to get across to aspiring professionals is that of an edge. However, without a thorough knowledge of exactly what an edge is and what it means to you, you will not win money playing blackjack.

As you know, to play blackjack professionally you must play with an edge; in fact, without an edge, you cannot hope to win in the long run. The entire *raison d'être* of card counting is to provide you with that edge. But what does an edge mean? Does it mean you will win all of the time? Most of the time? Some of the time?

An edge means you have a positive expectation on a bet. But knowing how best to exploit that positive expectation is an art. It separates the men from the boys; the professionals from the wannabees; the winners from the schmucks.

Let's take a look at a huge edge. Is 100 percent big enough for you? All right, we are going to offer you the opportunity to make a bet with a 100 percent edge. How much are you willing to bet?

Most people think a 100 percent edge is a sure thing; if you bet a hundred dollars, you'll win a hundred dollars. Given the opportunity, most people would bet as much as they could with a 100 percent edge. But they would be wrong to do so.

It is the case that, in the long run, a 100 percent edge means that you will win one hundred dollars for every hundred dollars bet. But in the short run, some bad things can happen.

Let's take a concrete example. You go to the racetrack. There is a horse running today that is going off at 50 to 1; that is, if you bet a hundred dollars on that clunker and he wins the race, you'll get paid $5,000. However, you know that this horse is not that bad—you know for a fact that he will win this race once in every twenty-five races. This translates into a 100 percent edge—in the long run, for every hundred dollars you bet on this horse, you will win a hundred. (Every twenty-five races you will bet a total of $2,500 and win once, coming away with $5,000, thus profiting $2,500, or 100 percent of your money.)

Question: Are you willing to sell your house and car and shirt and put everything you own on this horse *in one race?*

Of course not. You see, the bet you make on this horse has a positive expectation. You have a huge edge. But it doesn't mean you are going to win. As a matter of fact, in this instance, you are going to lose twenty-four out of twenty-five bets you make on this horse. When the horse does win you will realize a nice profit, but in the meantime, you are going to lose a lot of bets, even playing with a huge edge.

Blackjack is a little different. Since blackjack is largely an even-money proposition, we don't have to deal with the confusion of multiple payoffs. So let's look at another example of an edge—this time in an even-money game.

You meet a guy in a bar who has had too much to drink and has too much money in his pocket. He offers you a proposition: he will flip a coin (a fair coin), and you will bet. If heads comes up, you will lose your bet. If tails comes up, you will win twice your bet.

This translates into a 50 percent edge—much larger than any edge you'll ever get counting cards, and an edge that will manifest itself more quickly than the horse-racing edge. Should you sell your house and car and shirt and put it all down on one flip of the coin?

No, you should not. Even though you are playing with an enormous edge, you could easily lose several flips in a row. What you have to do is structure your betting so that your edge has a chance to manifest itself. The key is to stay in the game long enough so that your chances of busting out are minimized. (After all, the guy could easily flip three or four heads in a row, but his chances of flipping twenty heads in a row are pretty remote.) Structuring your betting so that your blackjack edge has a chance to manifest itself is what the next section is all about.

Proportional Betting (The Kelly Betting Criterion)

The optimal way to place your bets when you are playing blackjack with an edge is to *bet that percentage of your bankroll that represents your edge on the hand you are about to play.* This is called Kelly Betting, after the mathematician who first formulated it. If you have a 1 percent edge on the upcoming hand, you can bet 1 percent of your total bankroll on the hand. Similarly, if you have a 2 percent edge on the upcoming hand, you can bet 2 percent of your total bankroll on the hand. If you do this for the rest of your life (or even for two years playing forty hours per week), you will become a millionaire, and you will do so optimally; that is, there is no way you could bet differently and become a millionaire more quickly. (By the way, if you learn to count cards properly and bet according to Kelly, you can become a millionaire, and there is no doubt about this whatsoever. The math doesn't lie.[37])

There are three problems with Kelly betting, however. First, Kelly betting dictates that you bet your edge on every hand. That means that when you have a count-per-deck of 3 you bet 1.5 percent of your bankroll. No problem. But what if you have a count-per-deck of –4? That means the casino has an edge of 2 percent—so the proper play, according to Kelly betting, is to bet 2 percent of your bankroll on the casino! In general, casinos tend to frown upon this behavior. Since you have to bet something when the casino has the advantage, you are forced to make small bets on negative-expectation hands, which means you are *overbetting* your bankroll.

Second, your count is an estimate of your edge at any given time. However, it isn't an exact reflection of that edge. For example, if four 2s come out, you will have a count of +4, indicating an edge of 2 percent. If your playing partner sees four 5s come out at his table, he will also have a count of +4, indicating a 2 percent edge. However, in reality he will have an edge of about 2.75 percent, while your edge will be only 1.5 percent.

The best way to deal with these issues is to bet less than optimally when you do have an edge. This means you will win slightly more slowly than you would if you were betting optimally, but you won't be exposed to the risk of busting out because of all those negative-expectation hands you are going to have to play. (Whenever the house has an edge, you have a negative expectation on the money you put out on the layout—regardless of what happens on the hand.) One suggestion is that you bet between half and three-quarters Kelly. In other words, if you have a count-per-deck of 2 (meaning you have a 1 percent edge on the upcoming hand), you can safely bet between 0.5 percent and 0.75 percent of your bankroll.

The third problem with Kelly betting is logistical. Let's say you have a bankroll of $1,235. With a count-per-deck of 2, you should bet 1 percent of your bankroll, according to Kelly. One percent of $1,235 is $12.35. Dealers and pit bosses are not the least bit amused by players who regularly attempt

---

37 The huge, unspoken caveat, of course, is that you not only have to count, bet, and play properly, but you also *have to get away with it.*

to bet $12.35 a hand. You are going to have to round off somewhat because of the chips available to you, so you may as well round down so that you are betting between half and three-quarters Kelly, as suggested above.

The beauty of Kelly betting is that, if you bet according to your edge and according to your bankroll, you will never go broke. Your bets will track your bankroll up and down, and you will win optimally; that is, you will win as much as you can as fast as you can.

By the way, Kelly betting only works if you are playing with an edge. If you are not playing with an edge, no betting system in the world can ever help you. Martingales, reverse Martingales, LaBouchères, reverse LaBouchères—none of these address the central problem—the casino has an edge over the players employing these worthless betting systems. If you count cards properly you will play with an edge. Kelly betting best exploits this edge.

Bet Spread

Another difficult concept to get across to players who are learning to play with an edge is the concept of a *bet spread*. A bet spread is the multiplier you would have to assign to your small "waiting" bets to arrive at your top bet. For example, if you bet $25 per hand when the count is neutral or negative, and you spread up to $500 per hand when the count is very positive, your bet spread would be from 1 to 20 ($25 x 20 = $500). Generally speaking, the bigger your bet spread, the more money you will make.

The amount you bet is determined by two things: your edge and the size of your bankroll. It is *not* determined by how you feel, or what day of the week it is, or anything else. Even players who should know better tend to bet more after they have won a few hands, and less after they have lost a few.

The amount you bet on any given hand in the game of blackjack has *nothing* to do with whether you won or lost on the previous hand. Players who let the results of previous hands dictate how much they will bet on upcoming hands do not understand the *Law of Independent Trials*. There is a word for players who let the results of previous hands dictate how much they will bet on upcoming hands. They are called gamblers.

The whole point of learning to count cards is to stop gambling. When you play with an edge, you are not gambling. You are *investing*. (When asked what he does for a living, one well-known pro responds by saying, "I'm in short-term investments and insurance.") And investing in the game of blackjack means *spreading your bets*, and doing so in a very special fashion.

Multiple-deck games *cannot* be beaten without a bet spread. You must make large bets when you have an advantage, and small bets when the casino has an advantage. But how large is large? How much larger should your big bets be than your smaller bets?

When playing a four-deck game, your large bets should be at least six times as large as your small bets. Eight times is better, and ten is better yet. A spread much greater than one to ten, however, may result in some heat, so be careful. If you can do it, go for it! The bigger your spread, the more money you will make.

When playing a six-deck game, your minimum bet spread should be one to ten; that is, your big bet should be at least ten times your small bet. That is because you have to wait longer to get an advantage when playing against six decks, and that entire time you have to make many small negative-expectation bets. You have to make up for those bets when the edge comes.

> This is important. Re-read the previous section. You must realize that playing your hands and taking insurance properly are not enough to overcome the casino's overall advantage over the average player. You **must** raise your bets when the count goes up, and you **must** lower them when the count goes down. Otherwise, you **will not** be playing with an edge.

Imaginary Bankroll

Now that you know what an edge is and how to bet, let's take a bankroll of $10,000 and play with it. You are at a table with a minimum bet of $10. You have decided to bet one-half Kelly to avoid overbetting.

Assume you are playing a four-deck game on the Las Vegas Strip. As per table 1 in appendix 2, your off-the-top disadvantage is 0.5 percent (actually −0.48 percent—close enough). This means you will be even with the house with a true of 1.

What follows is a table that shows a number of running counts, and what happens to that running count as it is converted first to a true count, then an edge, then a bet based upon the Kelly Betting Criterion.

Table 4: Running – True – Edge – Kelly Conversion

Running Count	Decks Remaining	True Count	Your Edge	Full Kelly	Half Kelly
1	3	1/3	< 0%	min	Min
2	3	2/3	< 0%	min	Min
3	3	1	0	min	Min
4	3	1 1/3	.16%	min	Min
5	3	1 2/3	.3%	min	Min
6	**3**	**2**	**.5%**	**$50**	**$25**
7	3	2 1/3	.66%	$66	$33
8	3	2 2/3	.8%	$80	$40
9	**3**	**3**	**1%**	**$100**	**$50**
10	3	3 1/3	1.16%	$116	$58
11	3	3 2/3	1.3%	$130	$65
12	**3**	**4**	**1.5%**	**$150**	**$75**
13	3	4 1/3	1.66%	$166	$83
14	3	4 2/3	1.8%	$180	$90
15	**3**	**5**	**2%**	**$200**	**$100**

Note the bolded rows, which indicate those true counts which are whole numbers. You can see that with a true of 2, one-half Kelly dictates a bet of $25. A true of 3 indicates a bet of $50, a true of 4, $75. So, your betting rule for a $10,000 bankroll betting one-half Kelly is:

Bet the true count minus one in green.

In other words, if you have a true of 11, you will bet ten green chips (or the equivalent). This will serve to greatly simplify your betting calculations at the table.

With this in mind, let's go to work. The dealer shuffles, you cut, and you begin by betting the table minimum—$10.

You continue to play the shoe, betting the $10 minimum, for several hands. You maintain the count, truing at the end of each round. Finally the count goes positive, and you have a true count of 2.

You already know the rule: subtract one, and bet that much in green. So you bet one green chip.

Why? Well, you have a 0.5 percent advantage over the casino. Because you are betting one-half Kelly, you can bet 0.25 percent of your bankroll on this hand, and 0.25 percent of 10,000 is $25.

The count soars. You have a true of 4. Now you can bet three greens, or $75 on the hand.

You continue to play for several hours, betting one-half Kelly. You experience a losing streak and lose $1,000. Now your bankroll is $9,000. You should adjust your betting accordingly. Reworking the above chart, you will find that you will end up rounding off to a nickel less than you were betting before. The rule will be: bet true minus one minus five bucks in green (or four reds) per true.

You now experience a winning streak. Your bankroll is up to $11,500. With a true of 2, you can now bet $28.75. Make it $30. With a true of 4, you can bet $86.25. Make it $90.[38] The rule now is bet true minus one in green, with a nickel on top.

---

38 Because you are betting only one-half Kelly, you can easily round up a little without overbetting.

After a couple of weeks, your bankroll may be up to $17,000. Now you can bet $40 with a true of 2, $125 with a true of 4, and so on. As a professional, your bets should always reflect both your edge and the size of your bankroll.

Multiple Hands

One of the problems with spreading your bets is that it may arouse suspicion. Some casinos know that good players must spread their bets to win, so they may take countermeasures if your bet spread is too obvious. Playing multiple hands (that is, playing two or three hands per round) can help you disguise the fact that you are spreading your bets.

In and of itself, playing multiple hands should not arouse suspicion. Many regular gamblers like to play multiple hands when playing blackjack. Playing multiple hands gives the average gambler more action (instead of playing fifty hands per hour, he can play a hundred), and if the gambler is betting the limit, playing multiple hands will enable him to get more action out on the table.

You should try to play two hands when you have an advantage. Playing two hands will not only help you to disguise the size of your bet spread, it will also serve to reduce fluctuations in your bankroll.

The way to figure your bets when spreading to two hands is that you can bet approximately three-quarters of your normal bet on each of two hands. So, if you have a $10,000 bankroll and you have a 2 percent edge on the upcoming hand, and you are betting one-half Kelly, you can bet one hand of $100, or two hands of $75 each. Your risk of ruin will remain the same, but the fluctuations in your bankroll will decrease because the risk is spread out over two hands. (You cannot, however, bet two hands of $100 because the hands are not independent—they both must play against the same dealer's up-card. If you were playing at two separate tables, and you had a 1 percent edge at each, you could bet $100 at each of the tables. This may sound a bit strange, but it really works this way.)

6. CHANGING BASIC STRATEGY

It is with a certain reluctance that this section is being written. As you will see, changing Basic Strategy is an important weapon in the professional's arsenal, but many players use the weapon inappropriately. It is a common belief among beginners that changing Basic Strategy is somehow a sign that you are a pro.

Here is the problem: changing Basic Strategy when you should not is approximately three times worse than not changing Basic Strategy when you should. So bear that in mind when reading this section.

If you've read the Insurance section of appendix 2, you already should understand the reasoning behind changing Basic Strategy. Basic Strategy dictates that you never take insurance. However, when the ratio of tens to non-tens is greater than 1 to 2, insurance is a profitable bet. Therefore, you change Basic Strategy, and take insurance.

The same holds true with a number of hands. Basic Strategy dictates that you hit a 12 vs. 3. However, when there are a lot of tens left, this increases the chances of busting—both your chances, and the dealer's. Why not stand and let the dealer take that hit?

For different plays, there is a point at which changing Basic Strategy becomes the correct play. You will use what are called *index numbers* to determine if the true count is sufficiently high to warrant changing Basic Strategy.

There are perhaps a hundred index numbers for the Hi-Lo count. However, you can get a large fraction of all of the possible gain by learning the most important fifteen numbers.[39] These numbers represent the strategy variations (for positive counts) that are worth at least 10/1,000 (that's ten one-thousandths!) of a percent.

---

39 It turns out that, in theory, knowing when to hit a stiff against a stiff is very valuable. However, because almost all of the games in the world are multiple-deck games, and because all of the stiff against a stiff numbers are negative, and because you should have a small bet out with a negative count, these numbers are not quite as valuable in reality as they are in theory.

COUNT STRATEGY – MULTIPLE DECK

DEALER'S UP-CARD

♣	2	3	4	5	6	7	8	9	10	A
< 9	H	H	H	H	H	H	H	H	H	H
9	H	D	D	D	D	+3	H	H	H	H
10	D	D	D	D	D	D	D	D	+2	H
11	D	D	D	D	D	D	D	D	D	0
12	+3	+1	0	S	S	H	H	H	H	H
13	S	S	S	S	S	H	H	H	H	H
14	S	S	S	S	S	H	H	H	+10	H
15	S	S	S	S	S	H	H	+7	+4	H
16	S	S	S	S	S	+5	+4	+3	0	H
> 16	S	S	S	S	S	S	S	S	S	S
10-10	S	S	S	+5	+4	+4	S	S	S	S

Take insurance with a true count of +2 or higher.

A couple of things you should know:

1. If your true count is at least the number shown, you will stand, split, or double down, whichever is appropriate.

    Example #1: 9 vs. 7 is normally a hit. However, if the true count is +3 or higher, you will _double down_ instead of hit.

    Example #2: 12 vs. 2 is normally a hit. However, if the true count is +3 or higher, you will _stand_ instead of hit.

2. To determine whether you are past your index number, you do _not_ remove the off-the-top disadvantage of the game you are playing. If you have a 16 vs. 9 with a true of 4, you stand. The off-the-top disadvantage affects your true count for betting, not for playing.

3. You may be wondering about a 16 vs. ten. How is it that Basic Strategy says to hit with a 16 vs. ten, but the number is zero? That seems to indicate that Basic Strategy should indicate a stand.

If Basic Strategy did not take into consideration the cards that constitute your hand, 16 vs. ten would be a stand. The dealer's up-card gives you a count of –1, and your hand (either ten-6 or 9-7) provides a count of zero, leaving you with a running count of –1, which is less than zero, meaning you should hit.

Aces

Earlier it was mentioned that there are certain counts (called "ace-neutral counts") that do not incorporate aces in the main count. These counts require the player to keep a separate count of aces. Why is this? Because of all the cards in the deck, aces are the strangest.

As you know, when a preponderance of tens remains to be dealt, you have an advantage on the upcoming hand. You have that advantage when deciding how much to bet, and when deciding how to play your hand.

When a preponderance of small cards (2, 3, 4, 5, and 6) remains to be dealt, you have a disadvantage on the upcoming hand. You have a disadvantage when deciding how much to bet, and when deciding how to play your hand.

And when a preponderance of neutral cards (7, 8, and 9) remains to be dealt, neither you nor the casino have an advantage for betting or playing.

Aces, however, are the only card in the deck that exhibit major schizophrenia. Aces exhibit different aspects of their personalities depending on what you are about to do.

When you are about to make your bet, you want many aces remaining to be dealt. In other words, for betting purposes, aces act like tens. Many aces means your chances of getting a blackjack are increased, which means you are more likely to get paid that nice 50 percent bonus on your hand.

However, once the cards are dealt out and you do not have a blackjack, aces change. First, if the dealer has one of these fickle cards up, she will ask you if you want insurance. In terms of the insurance decision, aces most certainly do not act like tens. If the dealer has an ace beneath her ace you lose your insurance bet, so in that regard, aces act like all of the other non-tens in the deck.

Also, when it is time to play your hand, aces largely act like small cards. They do not bust the dealer's stiffs the way tens do. In fact, they are positively helpful to the dealer when she has a six up. She could have an ace lurking beneath that six or hit her six with an ace, giving her a pat hand, or she could hit her dreadful sixteen with one of those damned aces, giving her a total of seventeen.

However, they aren't *all* bad when it comes to playing your hand. They help when doubling with totals of 9 or 10 (but stink on ice when doubling 11), and help some split hands. In short, a lot of aces remaining to be dealt:

- Are the best card in the deck when betting

- Are bad for you when taking insurance

- Are sometimes good but mostly bad for you once the hand is dealt and must be played

It is because of this pronounced case of multiple personalities that ace-neutral counts were developed. When betting, the count is adjusted for the density of aces remaining. If there are extra aces remaining to be dealt (that is, if the remaining cards are "ace-rich"), the count is increased. If aces have been depleted (that is, if the remaining cards are "ace-poor), the count is decreased.

As mentioned, this may be worthwhile if:

- You are going to play single decks exclusively;

- You can count aces perfectly accurately;

- You can adjust your count perfectly; and

- You can do all of this quickly.

If you are going to play multiple decks, this is not worth the effort. If you have found a great single-deck game, it may be worth the effort (but probably not).

Casino Cheating

No book on blackjack would be complete without a mention of casino cheating. How much of this goes on in the world? After years of play, Taylor thinks he can put the issue to rest.

1. Casino cheating is extremely rare. If only one dealer in twenty cheated, Taylor and his teammates could not have made any money playing blackjack. More direct proof: cheating in a handheld game involves "peeking" at the top card and then "dealing seconds" if the dealer wants to preserve that top card, either to bust the player or to help herself. Because the Slicers and Dicers knew how many cards they had cut, they would have known if the dealer wasn't dealing the first eight or so cards.

2. Casino cheating does occur.

Exhibit I: The "short shoe" encounter in Antigua mentioned in chapter 13.

Exhibit II: Taylor saw a dealer "peek" at the top card in the Cal Neva on Tahoe's north shore. The guy scratched his nose, and Taylor could see the top card bubble out as the dealer looked down.

"I can't believe it!" Taylor said. "I can do it better than that!" The dealer turned bright red as Taylor dropped his bets down to two hands of a nickel.

"What's the problem?" a pit boss asked.

"No problem," Taylor said. I'm not playing against this guy, that's all."

"Did he make a mistake or something?" the pit boss asked disingenuously. "It's understandable. Pete's normally a craps dealer."

"That so?" said Reed. "Pete, what's the payoff on a hard twelve?"

Pete turned redder. No answer was forthcoming. Two hands later, Pete was pulled.[40]

---

40 Reed then had the balls to tell the pit boss, "You know, I used to play slot machines here, but I could never win." The other dealers in the pit cracked up as the pit boss burned. The Cal Neva had recently been fined by the Nevada Gaming Commission for rigging some of their slot machines.

Exhibit III: A dealer at the Opera House in North Las Vegas occasionally had trouble dealing face up hit cards. He would deal the card, and another card (the actual top card) would flip straight up into the air and land in the chip rack. Taylor was more amused than mad at this—he never expected to see anything quite that obvious. (Try it at home. Holding the deck loosely, pull the second card from the top out about halfway, then begin to flip it face up. The tail end of the "second" card will catch the actual top card and propel it into the air.)

Exhibit IV: During one of Taylor's early trips to Vegas, he and Steve played at the Silver City—a small joint across the street from the Stardust. For some reason, Steve saw a large number of ten up-cards. He quickly figured out what was going on: sometimes the dealer would turn the first card face up, and other times turn the second card up. This is clearly cheating; the casino should consistently turn one card or the other face up. (Not yet knowing any better, Taylor called the Gaming Commission to report the incident. The agent wanted Taylor's name, address, phone number, and an explanation of how Taylor knew so much about the game of blackjack. He didn't seem too interested in the details of Taylor's story.)

Exhibit V: Slicing and Dicing at the Union Plaza, Taylor had two hands of a thousand on the layout against the dealer's deuce. Taylor had two stiffs, so he stood. Guppy, playing the two spots at third, grabbed the two cards that made up his first hand to look at them. In doing so, he dragged the cards across the felt. This move looked like he was scratching for a hit, so the dealer did her job. She hit him. With a nine.

"No, no," said Guppy, valiantly protecting that massive $5 bet he had out. "I didn't ask for a hit." Guppy showed the dealer his hand—a fourteen.

The dealer turned to the pit boss. Sizing up the situation immediately, the pit boss said, "He didn't want a hit? Fine."

In Las Vegas, cards that are exposed inadvertently are burned. That's the rule. End of story.

However, this nine wasn't getting burned. It was clear that the pit boss noticed how nicely that nine would go with the deuce up-card the dealer was showing. So he pushed the card over to Guppy's second $5 hand. It was clear that if Guppy didn't take that card, it would become the dealer's hit card. It was equally clear to Taylor that, had the card been a ten, it would have been as dead as can be in the discard rack where it belonged.

This was a tough situation. Taylor was supposed to be a gambler, and the average gambler probably wouldn't know that an exposed card was supposed to be burned. However, he had two grand on the table, and he wasn't about to face a dealer's eleven instead of a two.

After some gentle coaxing from Taylor ("You're gonna hit that hand, even if you have a goddamn blackjack"), Guppy hit his fifteen with that nine, busting purposely. The dealer flipped up her hole card—a ten—and busted. The pit boss looked at Taylor and shrugged. What the hell. He had tried.

APPENDIX IV:
SHUFFLE TRACKING

What follows is a brief overview that is meant to describe what the shuffle trackers worked so hard to accomplish.

As a shuffle tracker with buttons in your shoes and a computer on your leg, the first thing you would have to do is enter the cards into the computer in the order in which they enter the discard rack. This may sound straightforward, but is not. There are a number of ways dealers can scoop the cards when a hand is finished. We'll assume the simplest version: the face up game, lay and pay.[41]

Once a round is dealt, the first cards to enter the discard rack are cards that constitute blackjack. In some casinos, blackjacks are paid first; in others they are paid as the dealer arrives at the hand; in still others they are paid whenever the dealer feels like it. And in games in which there is no hole card (or, as in Atlantic City, where they didn't peek), blackjack hands are paid in turn after the dealer has completed her hand.

A blackjack can take two forms:

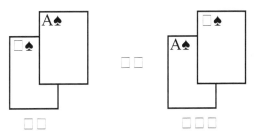

---

41 Face up means what it says. Lay and Pay means the cards stay on the table until the dealer has finished paying winning bets, taking losing bets, and pushing pushes, as explained in appendix 1.

In hand (a), the ace will enter the discard rack first, then the jack (the dealer turns the cards face down before putting them in the rack; hence, the ace will end up beneath the jack). In hand (b), the jack will go in first, then the ace. Simple enough, no?

How about this hand: you start with an A-2, hit with a 3, then a 6, then a 2, then you bust your 14 with a big, fat ten. The hand adorns the layout as follows:

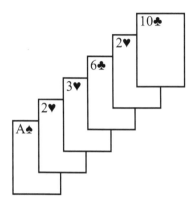

These cards will go in the rack in the following order: 10, 2, 6, 3, 2, ace. There are two problems with this:

1. The last card you see (the 10) will be the first card into the rack. That means the instant you bust, you have to bang those 6 cards in from top to bottom. This brings us to:

2. Dealers "zip" those cards up very quickly—especially on a hand like this, where the dealer can anticipate a bust. Unless you have a photographic memory, you are very likely to make mistakes trying to remember that sequence of cards.

Therefore, Brian decided that the cards would go into Butch's internal array in the *opposite order* in which they were entered. So, you would enter ace, 2, 3, 6, 2, 10, and the program would reverse their order automatically upon the input command (LRR). This would allow you to enter the cards on a hand like this as they were coming out. Enter the ace and deuce, enter the 3, enter the 6, enter the deuce. If the ten comes, enter it and then press LRR to enter. If you don't bust (for example, a six comes instead of that ten), simply erase (RLL), and move on to the next hand. (You will have to enter those cards again at the end of the round. However, you'll have plenty of time to do that while the dealer is resolving the hands on the layout.)

What happens at the end of the round, when the dealer either makes a hand or busts, and then must pay, take, and/or push? Well, there are a number of permutations. The good news is that all dealers in a given casino are supposed to pay and scoop the same way. This allows them to reconstitute a hand if and when some irate gambler claims he won a hand that the dealer either pushed or took. You would have noticed and memorized the routine in this particular casino before playing your first shoe.

Now for the shuffle.

For the sake of this example, imagine that just over three decks out of four have been dealt out. The dealer has placed each dealt card in the discard rack, and you have managed to enter each card into the computer's virtual discard rack in the proper order. The cut card emerges, meaning it is time for the dealer to shuffle. You inform Butch that it's shuffle time with an LRL.

Photo 1: Remains

First the dealer removes the unused slug of cards from the dealing shoe. These cards—referred to as the "remains"—can go a number of places relative to the cards in the discard rack: on top, on the bottom, or one or more places in the middle. Key presses tell Butch where this slug went.

Assume the remains went to the top, as pictured above. Click L. (An R would indicate remains to the bottom; both toes down would indicate remains inserted somewhere in the middle. Butch would then have to be told *where* in the middle the slug went.)

Bear in mind that Butch doesn't know the exact order of the cards in the remains. However, he does know the exact number of cards in the remains, and he also knows the overall count. If the shoe ended with a count of –4, well, the slug must have an overall count of +4 (remember the "balanced count" discussion near the end of chapter 5—any number of decks will comprise a total count of zero). Butch will "smear" this final overall count over those 40 or so cards, adjusting for errors as the various clumps are played.

Now comes the good part: the shuffle.

The simplest shuffle played by the team was referred to as The Hilton Shuffle. Four decks were used, with about one cut off, meaning the shuffle took place with on average about 40 unseen cards (remember: in the States, the round is completed when the cut card emerges, meaning cards will continue to be dealt after the dealer arrives at the cut card). The unseen "remains" went on the top or bottom, and the four decks were dragged out of the discard rack and placed in the middle of the table. The four decks were then split roughly in half, as follows:

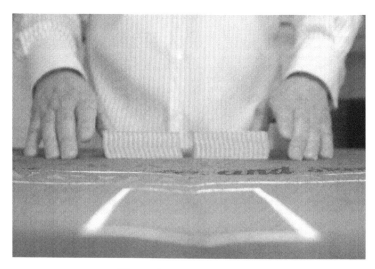

Photo 2: Major Split Left

This was referred to as the *Major Split* (to distinguish it from *Minor Splits* that were part of some of the more complex shuffles the players encountered). You first tell Butch that the split went to your left (left toe down; both down to enter the direction), then the side that is higher, then by how much (right toe down indicates that the right side is higher; then left toe down once enters 5, indicating that the right side is in fact five cards higher, then both for enter).

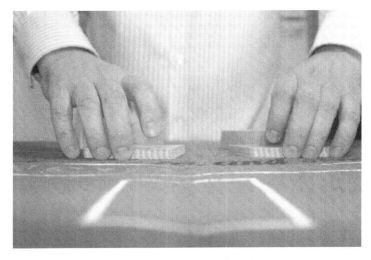

Photo 3: First pair of grabs

Now the dealer "grabs" some cards from the left stack, some from the right, and shuffles them together. You must estimate the number of cards in the grab that came from the left and enter it (right for 5 cards, left for 25 cards, both down to enter), then estimate and enter the grab that came from the right. Let's assume 30 cards are grabbed from the right side, and 30 are grabbed from the left, as in the photo above. From left to right, the number of cards in each packet is entered into the computer. (Left, then right, then both to enter 30 for the packet on the left; left, then right, then both to enter 30 for the packet on the right.)

This 60-card clump is shuffled and placed on the felt in front of the dealer.

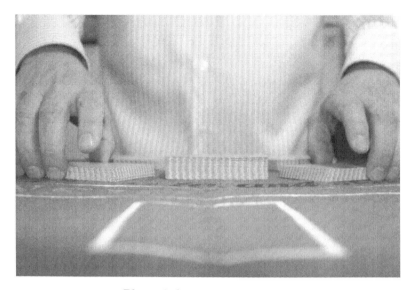

Photo 4: Second pair of grabs

Assume the second pair of "grabs" was 35 cards and 35 cards, as pictured above. Enter left-right-right-both to indicate 35 cards for the left packet; then left-right-right-both to indicate 35 cards for the right packet. These 70 cards will be thoroughly shuffled, and placed on top of the previously shuffled 60-card packet.

For the sake of this demo, let's assume that the above 70-card packet contains a count of 14; that is, there are 14 more tens and aces than there should be in a normal packet of this size. This will give us a true count (or count-per-deck) of about 10 for this clump.

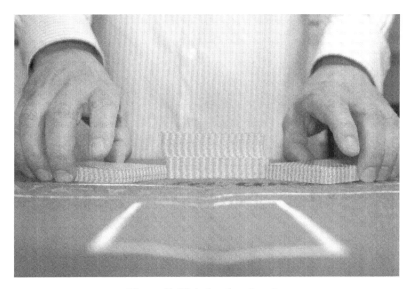

Photo 5: Third pair of grabs

Assume the dealer makes a final grab, shown above. These grabs are 40 and 35, and will be entered as left-right-right-right-both, then left-right-right-both.

You then enter a command to tell Butch that the shuffle was completed. Butch will output a suggested cut point, and then wait for the actual point at which the cards were cut. When the cards are cut, Butch will have to reconstruct his internal array to match what happened at the table.

Photo 6: The cut is offered

The dealer now puts the multiple decks down on the table and offers the cut. As we can see, if we place the cut card between the first and second packet (note the exaggerated "seam" in the photo demarcating the separation), that 75-card packet will be moved to the back of the pack, leaving the 70-card packet containing approximately 14 extra tens in the front of the pack.

You bet big, the pit boss turns away (everybody knows card counters don't bet big off the top of a freshly shuffled shoe), and life is good.

Bear in mind the above was the simplest shuffle the players ever encountered. However, betting two hands of the limit off the top of a shoe and watching the dealer cover the table with tens and aces made all of the practice and all of the expense and all of the dead ends worth it.

GLOSSARY OF TERMS

Ace-Adjustment   Adjusting for the proportion of aces remaining in a depleted deck to determine bet size, whether to take insurance, or how to play a hand. For example, if the count suggests you double down with an 11 against a 10, but the deck is "ace-rich," the correct play may be to hit.

Ace-Poor   A depleted deck or decks containing proportionally fewer aces than normal; e.g., 104 cards containing 6 aces (two *fewer* than would be "normal") would be ace-poor. Bad for the player.

Ace-Rich   A depleted deck or decks containing proportionally more aces than normal; e.g., 104 cards containing 10 aces (two *more* than would be "normal") would be ace-rich. Good for the player.

Action   The total amount being bet in a casino at any given time; or the relative amount being bet by an individual. Big action at Foxy's Firehouse would be small action at Caesars Palace.

Back Counter   One who stands behind a table and keeps track of the count as the cards are dealt. If the count goes up, the counter will jump into the game with a large bet. If the count goes down, the back counter will wander off and find another table to ogle. This activity is referred to as "Back Counting" or "Wonging."

Back Room   A small office (usually the security office) into which suspected counters or cheats are brought where they can be detained, illegally questioned, or beaten without ordinary casino patrons around to witness the carnage; or, the act of dragging a suspect into said room (e.g., "Bob was *back-roomed* at Harrah's last night").

Bad Fluctuation or Bad Flux   A large negative fluctuation; a large loss due to mathematical deviation, not poor play.

Balanced Count   A count for which all of the positively valued cards cancel out the negatively-valued cards so that every complete deck—or combination of decks—counted properly will result in a count of zero; cf. Unbalanced Count.

Bank, or Bankroll   The total playing stake for a player or a team of players.

Bar   The act of forbidding a player to return to a particular casino; cf. 86ed.

Basic Strategy   A strategy that indicates the mathematically correct play given any dealer up-card and any player hand. The basic strategy play assumes no other information about the deck, such as the count or the value of the dealer's hole card.

Bet Spread   The distance, or "spread" between your lowest bet and your highest, reduced down so the low number is one (1). If your low bet is $5 and your high bet is $100, your bet spread is "one to twenty." Note that if your low bet is $100 and your high bet is $2,000, your bet spread is still "one to twenty."

Black $100 chips. "He was betting stacks of *black*."

BP   The Big Player. The team member who bets significant amounts; cf. Small Player.

BP-Spotter Routine   A play during which a player betting small amounts (the "Spotter") counts and signals betting (and sometimes playing) strategy to a player betting significant amounts (the "BP").

Bunco Steering An archaic word for cheating, still common in Nevada (both the word *and* the activity).

Burn Card or Burned Card The card on the top of the deck that is discarded before the dealer begins to deal. In single-deck games the card is often put on the bottom of the deck; in multiple-deck games the card is normally placed face down in the discard rack. Atlantic City casinos show the players the burn card; most Nevada casinos do not. Some casinos burn more than one card.

Burn Out To play a game until it is no longer offered; until the conditions that made the game profitable are changed. "Shuffle tracking in Vegas was *burned out* by Vince and his teammates."

Burned Out A player who is readily recognized upon entering a casino and therefore can no longer play; or, a game that was once profitable but no longer is due to a change of some sort.

Bust A hand totaling more than hard twenty-one; or, an attribute shared by most cocktail waitresses.

Busted Out A hand totaling more than twenty-one; or, to lose all one's money; cf. Tapped Out.

Butterfly Effect See Sensitive Dependence on Initial Conditions.

Cage The cashier's window, where chips are exchanged for money.

Center Field The spot or spots toward the center of a blackjack table; the third or fourth spot from the end; cf. First Base and Third Base.

Checks Casino chips.

Comp Short for complimentary. Anything given to a desirable player by a casino; may include food, drinks, rooms, and/or airfare. Used as a noun and a verb. "Did you get a *comp*?" "Yeah, the pit boss *comped* me."

Correct As in, "Did you make the correct play?" There are two possible meanings: (1) Did you win the hand? (2) Did you make the mathematically correct play? Professional players are interested in meaning (2) only.

Complete the Cut	The act of reconstituting the deck after the cut has been made. This positions the clump of cards that were cut off the top underneath the cards that originally were on the bottom.
Count Down	A common practice technique used by card counters that entails removing one or more cards from a full deck and then flipping through the remaining cards. If the counter has counted properly, the counter will know the value of the card or cards that were removed.
Cover	Any measures used by professional players to disguise what they are doing.
Cross Roader	A synonym for "cheater," used often in Nevada.
Cut Card	A plastic card used in most multiple-deck games. It is inserted in the pack of cards by the dealer, usually toward the back. When this card is reached, the round is completed and the shuffle commences. Often this card is offered to a player at the table to make the cut when the shuffle has been completed. (In France and some other European casinos, the round is halted immediately upon the emergence of the cut card and commences after the completion of the shuffle.) Also called a Stop Card.
Cutting	See Slicing and Dicing.
David	The name of a computer invented by Keith Taft that allows the player to input the value of every card dealt out. The computer then calculates the proper betting and playing strategies based upon the exact subset of cards remaining to be dealt.
Dealer	A casino employee who physically deals the game, takes losing bets, pays winning bets, and puts up with an ungodly amount of crap from both players and pit bosses. In the game of casino blackjack, the dealer makes no decisions. He or she follows rules strictly laid out by the casino.

Dealer Weaknesses — Anything a dealer does that allows a player to glean more information than is supposed to be available. A dealer who shows her hole card when thrusting it beneath her up-card is said to have a "weakness." Also known as a "leak."

Dealing Seconds — A cheating move in which the dealer deals the second card from the top of a deck instead of the top card; useless without a peek or a mark. See Peek.

Double Down — An option available to players to double their original bet and receive one and only one more card. This option can be limited to certain totals (such as in Northern Nevada, where doubling is often restricted to totals of 10 or 11), and may be limited to your first two cards only (as is the case in most Nevada casinos). The option to double down is favorable to knowledgeable players.

Double After Splits — An expansion to the double down rule that allows players to double down after splitting a pair. This option is favorable to knowledgeable players.

Drop — The total amount players have bought in for; i.e., the total amount of money that makes its way to the drop box dangling beneath the gaming tables; cf. Hold.

Early Surrender — A valuable rule offered by some casinos that grants the player the option to give up his hand and lose half his bet before the dealer has determined whether or not she has a blackjack. This rule is *very* favorable to the knowledgeable player; cf. Late Surrender.

86ed — Throwing a player out for good; if a player is eighty-sixed from an establishment, he can be arrested for trespassing if he returns.

Einbinder and Dalton v. Sheriff — Case decided by the Nevada Supreme court that clearly states the casino's responsibility to hide the hole card. It is not the player's responsibility to look the other way.

Even Money   To insure a blackjack. If you do, you win your bet no matter what. In some casinos, you can say "even money," and the dealer simply pays you—what else?—even money.

Expectation or Expected Value   The amount, expressed in dollars, units, or top bets, that a given play or game is worth mathematically. Often referred to as "E.V."; cf. Fluctuations.

Fill   The act of bringing additional chips from the casino cage to a table to replenish, or "fill" the dealer's chip rack; or, the security guard carrying said chips. See Phil.

First Base   The seat at a blackjack table immediately to the dealer's left; the first person to whom cards are dealt.

First-Baser   A dealer who inadvertently shows the hole card to the person sitting (or standing) at first base while peeking beneath a ten up-card.

First-Basing   The act of seeing the dealer's hole card from first base during the peek.

Flat Bet   To bet the same amount on each successive hand. "Everybody knows you can't beat the game of blackjack flat-betting."

Fluctuations   Swings (monetary or otherwise) that are a result of normal mathematical deviation. Fluctuations occur outside of expectation and may continue over the course of days, weeks, months, and perhaps years of play; cf. Expectation.

French Stop-Card   A casino policy—first encountered in France—wherein the cards are shuffled the instant the stop card appears. This means that players must wait for the shuffle to be completed to finish their hand(s).

Front-Load   The act of exposing the hole card as it is placed beneath the up-card; or, the act of seeing said card.

Front-Loader   A dealer who inadvertently shows the hole card as it is placed beneath the up-card; or, the individual who sees said card.

Front-Loading	The act of seeing the dealer's hole card as it is placed beneath the up-card.
Gaming Control Commission	An organization charged with enforcing gaming laws. Theoretically, the Gaming Control Commission protects players from casino predations as well as the other way around. In reality, gaming agents for the most part tend to work at the behest of the casinos.
Gorilla BP	A BP who doesn't know basic strategy, meaning the "small player" has to signal all playing decisions as well as betting decisions.
Green	$25 chips. "Green bettors can get comped in North Las Vegas."
Griffin Detective Agency	An agency hired by a number of casinos worldwide to track cheaters, card counters, and other "undesirables." Protestations to the contrary notwithstanding, the "Griffin Book," which contained literally thousands of photographs of card counters (1) existed; and (2) was almost certainly illegal.
Griffin, Peter	Author of *The Theory of Blackjack*, the single most authoritative book on the mathematics underlying the game of blackjack.
Handheld	A blackjack game in which the dealer holds the deck in her hand. Virtually all single- and double-deck games are handheld; cf. Shoe.
Hard Hand	Any hand for which there is only one total; if the hand contains an ace, the ace must be counted as one because counting it as eleven will bust the hand; cf. Soft Hand.
Head Up or Heads Up	A player playing alone against the dealer.
Heat	Any potential detrimental attention given by casino personnel or their agents to players.

Heisenberg, Werner A physicist instrumental in the development of quantum mechanics. Best known for the Heisenberg Uncertainty Principle, which states that the very act of attempting to measure something impacts the measurement. Relates to professional blackjack because the act of spooking or front-loading often changes the very dealer behavior the players are attempting to exploit.

Hi-Lo Stack A situation in which the cards in the deck are in order so that high-value cards and low-value cards alternate.

Hi-Lo Stacking The act of scooping played cards from the table so that high-value cards and low-value cards alternate.

Hit To request another card from the dealer.

Hold The total percentage of buy-ins that the casino ultimately keeps. For example, if a player buys in for $100 and cashes out for $75, the casino has held $25, or 25 percent of the amount he bought in for; cf. Drop.

Hole Card The dealer's down card, located face down beneath her up-card; cf. Up-Card.

Hole Carding Any one of a variety of ways of obtaining the value of the dealer's hole card and playing accordingly.

Index The number or letter that appears in the upper left-hand and lower right-hand corner of playing cards.

Infinite Loop See Loop.

Insurance A side bet offered to the player when the dealer has an ace up-card. The player is permitted to bet up to half the amount of his original bet. If the dealer has a ten beneath her ace the player loses his original bet, but gets paid two to one on the insurance bet; hence, breaking even (and whence the name). If the dealer does not have a ten beneath her ace, the player loses the insurance bet and the hand continues.

Insurance Count A count that perfectly correlates to insurance. The count starts at −4 for each deck in play, and counts −2 for each 10 and +1 for each non-ten. Whenever the count is positive, the insurance bet has an edge.

Kefauver Commission A Senate investigatory committee convened in the early 1950s and chaired by Tennessee Senator Estes Kefauver which, among other things, found mob influence in the legal Nevada casinos. Who woulda thunk it?

Late Surrender A rule offered by some casinos that grants the player the option to give up his hand and lose half his bet after the dealer has determined that she does not have a blackjack. This rule is mildly favorable to the knowledgeable player; cf. Early Surrender.

Lay and Pay A method dealers use to resolve hands. The cards remain on the layout until the dealer has paid, taken, or pushed all of the hands; cf. Pick and Pay.

Long Run The length of time, or number of hands, required before a player can expect to be on his expectation curve. If a player is above or below expectation, he is by definition not yet in the long run. For those of you who recognize the tautology, congratulations; cf. Expectation and Fluctuation.

Loop See Infinite Loop.

Loose An adjective used to describe a dealer who inadvertently provides some information to the players. Dealers who expose their hole card or show the bottom card before offering the cut are said to be "loose"; cf. Tight.

Misdirection Any activity designed to lead an observer's eyes and/or mind away from what is really happening and toward what the misdirector wants the observer to see or think.

Mistake An incorrect decision *vis-à-vis* the mathematically correct play. A mistake may result in a win on any given hand, but in the long run the player will win more (or lose less) by making the mathematically correct play.

Natural Another term for a blackjack, or Robert Redford.

Nickels $5 chips.

On-The-Square
A player who is not counting or making any effort to play with an edge; often a counter will begin to play "on-the-square" when there is heat in an attempt to throw the pit off the trail.

Overbetting
Betting a greater percentage of one's bankroll than conditions indicate. Overbetting is ultimately devastating to a player's bankroll.

Paint
Slang term for all ten-value cards. Derived from the fact that picture cards (jacks, queens and kings) are covered with ink, or "paint."

Pat
In blackjack, a hand totaling seventeen or higher.

Peek
The act of looking beneath a ten or an ace to check for a dealer blackjack; or, the act of a cheating dealer who surreptitiously glances at the top card of a deck. The top card may or may not be dealt depending on its value to the player or the dealer. See Dealing Seconds.

Phil
The appellation used by Taylor for any security guard carrying a "fill" to his table, regardless of the name displayed on his name tag. See Fill.

Pick and Pay
A method dealers use to resolve hands. The cards constituting each hand are removed from the layout as the bet is paid, taken, or pushed; cf. Lay and Pay.

Piñata
A hollow papier-mâché form filled with candy. At children's parties, piñatas are hit with sticks or bats until they break open and the candy spills out. Card counters are often beaten in this fashion by casino security guards, although not candy but more often money spills forth.

Pips
The clubs, diamonds, hearts, and spades arranged on the face of all playing cards except picture cards; cf. Index.

Playing Blackjack as a Business
A book written by an author who called himself Lawrence Revere. It started the careers of all of the main characters in this book.

Preferential Shuffle   A method by which a dealer shuffles the cards if a subset of cards favorable to the player remains, and deals the cards if a subset of cards favorable to the casino remains. This is a devastating countermeasure to card counters who do not recognize it.

Prisoner's Dilemma   In its most famous incarnation, a hypothetical situation in which two accomplices are apprehended for a crime. The prosecutor offers each the following deal (and informs each that the other has been offered the same deal): If both perpetrators claim innocence, they will both be convicted and each will get two years. But if one admits guilt to help convict his accomplice, the one who admits guilt will go free and the accomplice will get five years. However, if both admit guilt, they'll both get four years. Logic unfortunately drives each perpetrator to rat out the other, even though they would both be better off claiming innocence.

Pull Up   A play or player detected and stopped by casino personnel. Taylor was "pulled up" at Harrah's for spooking.

Push   A tie hand; no money changes hands.

Quarters $25 chips.

Rain Main   A movie in which Dustin Hoffman portrays an autistic savant who is taught to count cards by his younger brother, portrayed by Tom Cruise. The movie leads viewers to conclude that card counters must memorize large numbers of cards and therefore need almost superhuman talents to succeed.

Reader   The player who makes minimal bets and gathers hole card or other information to be signaled to a player betting significant amounts. See Spotter.

Red $5 chips. See Nickels.

Relay   In spooking, the individual who receives a signal from the spook and in turn signals or "relays" the information to the Big Player.

Return Joint A casino in which the dealers return to the same table after each break for the duration of their shift; cf. Rubber-Band Joint.

Revere, Lawrence The pseudonym of the author of *Playing Blackjack as a Business*.

Rubber-Band Joint A casino in which the dealers returning from their breaks are sent to different tables by a pit boss who consults a clipboard and rolls a rubber band, cinching its width along the names of the dealers.

Seconds See Dealing Seconds.

Sensitive Dependence on Initial Conditions A hallmark of non-linear systems in the new science of Chaos. Large effects can be caused by extremely small, seemingly insignificant differences in starting conditions. The lay explanation is called the Butterfly Effect, and states that a butterfly flapping its wings in Brazil may cause a hurricane in Texas a month later.

Shoe A plastic box from which multiple-deck games are dealt; or, a game in which the cards are dealt from a shoe (e.g., "They have all shoes at Caesars now"); cf. Handheld.

Shuffle Tracking The act of following clumps of high cards and low cards through the shuffle and then playing those clumps accordingly.

Silver $1 chips. These are usually made of metal; hence, "silver."

Sky The area from which the gaming tables are surreptitiously observed. Originally, this was located above the casino where "walkers" could observe play through one-way mirrors on the ceiling. Now this surveillance takes place via video cameras dotting the ceiling of the casino. The surveillance office containing the video monitors is referred to as part of the "sky," even though this office could conceivably be located in the basement.

Slicing and Dicing The act of seeing the bottom card, and cutting in such a way that the bottom card goes to the dealer (if it is a small card) or to the Big Player (if it is a 10 or an ace). Also known as Steering and Cutting.

Small Player See Reader.

Snap Another term for a blackjack.

Snapper Another term for a blackjack.

Soft Hand Any hand that contains an ace for which the ace can be counted as one or eleven; cf. Hard Hand.

Spook An individual who can see the hole card from across the pit when the dealer peeks beneath a ten up-card; or, a dealer who lifts the hole card high enough to be seen from across the pit.

Spooking The act of determining the dealer's hole card from across the pit and signaling the information to a BP or a relay.

Spotter An individual who makes minimal bets while counting, and signals this information to a player betting significant amounts.

Stanley, Robert Pseudonym of a pseudonym of a much frowned-upon blackjack author.

Steering See Slicing and Dicing

Stiff In blackjack, a hand that totals hard twelve through sixteen.

Stop Card See Cut Card.

Tapped Out To have lost all one's money; to have busted out.

Tell An inadvertent idiosyncratic movement or response by an individual that announces something about his/her hand.

Ten In blackjack, any ten-value card; i.e., jacks, queens, and kings as well as tens.

Third Base The seat at a blackjack table immediately to the dealer's right; the last person to whom cards are dealt. It is because the player at third base makes the last playing decision before the dealer plays her hand that many gamblers believe the "third baseman" is responsible for their miserable luck.

Tight	A dealer from whom the players get no additional information. A dealer who hides her hole card properly is said to be "tight"; cf. Loose.
Toke	A tip for a dealer; in blackjack, often bet along with the player's bet.
Tragedy of the Commons	Specifically, an occurrence during the Middle Ages when townsfolk grazed their cattle in a "common" area. Once one farmer started grazing more than his fair share, everybody tried to catch up, and the resultant overgrazing destroyed the commons entirely; hence, the "tragedy." In more general terms, whenever there is a resource that can be shared, and someone takes more than his fair share, it is likely that the resource will be destroyed, and everyone is ultimately worse off than they would have been had everyone cooperated.
Unbalanced Count	A count for which the positively valued cards do *not* cancel out the negatively-valued cards. This means the count at the end of one or more decks will not equal zero. An example of an unbalanced count is the insurance count, for which 10-value cards are assigned a value of +2, and all other cards are valued as –1. If you start at 0, you will have a count of +4 at the end of the deck; cf. Balanced Count.
Up-Card	The dealer's card that is face up in front of her; cf. Hole Card.
Wonging	A method by which counters count while standing behind a table, and jump in to play only if the count goes up. Called Wonging because the author who first published this method called himself Stanford Wong. See Back Counter.

ACKNOWLEDGEMENTS

Any work of this nature is a collaborative process. Each of the main characters participating in the escapades explicated herein were interviewed extensively, and I thank them for their candor and openness. Although some of the techniques discussed here have been written about by other authors, many were pioneered by the players who are the stars of this work. And the Ultimate Edge is revealed in all its glory for the first time.

Even though many of their exploits took place two decades ago, it is simply not in the nature of these players to reveal what they have revealed here. The same instincts that helped make them the players they were cautioned them to remain in the shadows. It was only a combination of factors that convinced these individuals that the time had come to tell their story. I can only hope that I've done their story justice.

What follows would not have been possible without the amazing talents and unique personalities of the players who made this work possible. These players attempted to communicate to me as best they could what was involved in their various endeavors. I am in many respects a messenger only. Any mistakes or problems with the transmission of this message are, of course, entirely my responsibility.

A number of people perused, reviewed, and otherwise struggled through numerous early versions of the manuscript, and I would like to thank them for their efforts. These include D. L., J. M., B. W. M., D. P., R. W. R, T. R., Laurance Scott, Eric Scott, A. T. and J. W. Those of you who insisted upon remaining anonymous know who you are. I will therefore respect your wishes, and not thank you here.

I would like to express my deep appreciation for my editor, who reviewed the manuscript with an eye toward detail that I found remarkable.

I'd also like to thank Wolfgang Taylor for the excellent photos that appear in Chapter 17 and in Appendix 4.

BIBLIOGRAPHY

Beat the Dealer, Edward Thorp

This is the book that started it all. The system and playing conditions are terribly outdated; good for historical interest only. No blackjack library is complete without it, however.

Blackbelt in Blackjack, Arnold Snyder

Terrific how-to book for the would-be card-counter. Contains a number of counts. Importantly, Snyder addresses the importance of disguising what you are doing, which some authors seem to avoid.

Blackjack Forum, Arnold Snyder (editor)

Starting as a modest, 8 page pamphlet, the Forum grew to a glossy publication containing information indispensable to pros, containing articles written by a wide array of blackjack experts and playing conditions for games all over the globe.

Chaos, James Gleick

Excellent explication of Chaos theory for the layman. Beautifully written.

Counting without Winning (manuscript), Reed Richards

Self-explanatory

Day of the Jackal, The, Frederick Forsyth

Fictional account of a relentless, meticulous assassin as he plans for his next kill—Charles de Gaulle. Indispensable if you are planning to roam the French countryside by car.

Drifters, The, James Mitchener

Fictional account of a number of young people from various locales who end up on the beaches of Torremolinos. Indispensable if you are planning to roam southern Spain.

Fear and Loathing in Las Vegas, Hunter Thompson

Utterly unique description of a wild week-end in Vegas. This is the pinnacle of Gonzo journalism. Chapter 9 is an homage to Thompson's work. Indispensible if you are planning to roam Las Vegas.

Million Dollar Blackjack, Ken Uston

Largely a how-to book, with a number of counting systems and tips on training and practice. However, Uston also regales us with personal stories about his involvement in the game in the mid to late '70s, interleaving his exploits with the how-to parts of the book. Don't bother learning his complex count system (even he didn't!), but the book itself is a very good read.

Playing Blackjack as a Business, Lawrence Revere

This is the book that launched the professional careers of all of the main characters in this book. Although the betting strategy proposed by Revere is woefully inadequate, it is the perfect book for the novice player. If you aren't particularly inspired when you start reading, you almost certainly will be by the time you're finished.

Professional Blackjack, Stanford Wong

Very solid how-to for beginning and intermediate-level professional card counters.

Roughing It, Mark Twain

Great for a flavor of Virginia City, Reno and Tahoe in the years during the Civil War. An early work; displays the promise but lacks the brilliance Clemens would later show in his writing.

BIBLIOGRAPHY

Scarne's New Complete Guide to Gambling, John Scarne

Good source for the history of the game of blackjack; however, his perusal of card counting is worse than worthless. Ignore it.

Theory of Blackjack, The, Peter Griffin

The mathematical Bible of the game. Not of much use for actual play (although you never know; see chapter 16), because Griffin focuses almost exclusively on single decks, which are very rare in the world today. However, this is an unparalleled look at the mathematics that underlie the game of blackjack.

Turning the Tables on Las Vegas, Ian Andersen

One of the first (if not the first) blackjack book that focuses almost exclusively on the act. Andersen's creed was, learn the simplest count out there, learn it well, and put your energy toward disguising what you are doing at the table. Excellent advice.

We Only Kill Each Other: The true story of mobster Bugsy Siegal, Dan Jennings

Many of the details of Bugsy's early life and how he ultimately ended up in Vegas were sourced here.

INDEX

INDEX